THE THAI ECONOMY

Since the mid-1980s, Thailand has experienced a period of remarkable economic growth and structural change. But is Thailand's pattern of development sustainable, especially in view of the 1997–8 financial crisis? This volume looks at the origins and consequences of this period of accelerated growth, with particular emphasis on the historical development and contemporary economic structure that tend to set Thailand apart from other Asian, African and Latin American countries, such as the non-colonial mode of incorporation into the global economy. Beginning with an overview of Thailand's economic growth since the eighteenth century, Chris Dixon goes on to look at such key factors as:

- the role of the state since the late 1950s
- the neglect and underdevelopment of the agricultural sector
- the uneven pattern of development and regional disparities in income
- the continuing gap between Bangkok and the rest of the Kingdom

Also discussed is the apparent failure by successive Thai governments to invest in the necessary infrastructure and training that enabled the old Asian Newly Industrialising Economies to move to higher technology production as they lost their comparative advantage in labour intensive manufacturing. This has resulted in an apparent slowing of foreign investment, owing to an increasingly overcrowded infrastructure, shortages of skilled labour, rising costs and the opening of such lower cost locations as the PRC and Vietnam.

Providing an extremely thorough analysis of Thailand's economic development, this volume will be an excellent resource for students, researchers and policy makers interested in this region and in economic development generally.

Chris Dixon is Professor in the Department of Politics and Modern History at London Guildhall University. He first visited Thailand in 1971, subsequently researching a wide range of developmental issues in the South East Asian region. His recent books include *South East Asia in the World Economy* (1991) and *Uneven Development in South East Asia* (1997).

GROWTH ECONOMIES OF ASIA
Series editors:
Chris Dixon, *London Guildhall University*
and David Smith, *University of Liverpool*

Each book in this series provides a concise and up-to-date overview of one of the countries in the region. It examines its place in the world economy, its historical development and its resource endowment. The analysis of its growth to date is balanced by an account of its prospects for future development. The relationship between the different sectors of the economy are discussed, as is the role of multinational enterprises, the government and the financial markets.

The interaction of political and social forces and economic growth is given special consideration, and any special features of individual countries are highlighted.

PAPUA NEW GUINEA
The struggle for development
John Connell

THE THAI ECONOMY

Uneven development and internationalisation

Chris Dixon

London and New York

First published 1999
by Routledge
11 New Fetter Lane, London EC4P 4EE

Simultaneously published in the USA and Canada
by Routledge
29 West 35th Street, New York, NY 10001

© 1999 Chris Dixon

Typeset in Times by
The Florence Group, Stoodleigh, Devon
Printed and bound in Great Britain by
Clays Ltd, St Ives PLC

British Library Cataloguing in Publication Data
A catalogue record for this book is available
from the British Library

Library of Congress Cataloging in Publication Data
Dixon, Chris, 1944–
The Thai economy: uneven development and internationalisation /
Chris Dixon.
Includes bibliographical references and index.
1. Thailand – Economic conditions. I. Title.
HC445.D59 1998

330.9593′ 044–dc21   98–4882

ISBN 0–415–02442–0

CONTENTS

FIGURES

TABLES

PREFACE

Since this book was originally planned, during the mid-1980s, Thailand has undergone remarkable changes. The original intention was to explain the Kingdom's remarkable uneven pattern of development, unusual non-colonial mode of incorporation into the global economy and generally limited appeal to TNCs (Transnational Corporations) and foreign investors. These latter issues are compounded by the economic and political uncertainty that characterised Thailand during the early 1980s – the imposition, and apparently limited success, of formal structural adjustment under the auspices of the IMF and World Bank. Against this had to be set signs of economic recovery and indications that Thailand might prove the 'dark horse' of Pacific Asia. This view appeared to be vindicated when, during the late 1980s, the Kingdom began to experience a period of growth and structural change, and became a regional investment 'hot spot', particularly for labour-intensive manufacturing activities decanting from Japan and the Asian NIEs (Newly Industrialising Economies) in search of lower cost locations. These changed internal and external situations necessitated a substantial change in both the structure and emphasis of the book. However, during the early 1990s signs began to emerge that behind Thailand's remarkable growth a series of long-term problems were emerging. Rising costs, lack of skilled labour, overloaded infrastructure, congestion and pollution, combined with the opening of such lower cost locations as Vietnam and the PRC to undermine Thailand's comparative advantage in labour-intensive manufacturing, while inhibiting the transition to more skill- and capital-intensive activities. In the absence of rapid and perhaps radical policy changes it seems likely that there would be a slowing of growth. The timing and degree, however, remained unclear. During 1996 there was a sharp slowing of the rate of growth of exports, though the impact of this on economic growth was masked by rapid expansion of the property and financial sectors. As the manuscript was being finalised for publication, a major financial crisis erupted. This has necessitated some late additions to Chapter 8. The critical question is whether the 1997 crisis heralds a major slow-down of the Thai economy and, perhaps, of Pacific Asia as a whole, or, as some commentators maintain, it is merely a short-term financial problem. While at the time of writing (October 1997), the outcome of the crisis remains far from clear, it is important to stress that Thailand has over the last 30 years experienced high and consistent rates of growth. Despite the various political and economic issues that remain the Kingdom has shown great resilience to both internal and external disruption. In examining these issues I have continually to remind myself of the profound changes that Thailand has undergone since my first visit in 1971.

The intention of this book is to provide both a general overview of Thailand's development that would be accessible to the non-specialist, while also seeking to throw some new light on Thailand's unusual form of development. To achieve both these aims some compromise on sources, coverage and detail has been inevitable. In the final draft the references in Thai have been minimised, as have some of the more obscure English-language sources.

ACKNOWLEDGEMENTS

Given the long period that this book has been in preparation and the wide range of material covered, thanks are due to a very large number of people for advice and help with source material. In producing the final version particular thanks are due to David Smith for commenting in detail on an earlier draft, Don Shewen, and Garath Owen from City Cartographic for their production of such excellent figures, and Chrissy for endless patience, support, and comments on content and style.

Inevitably in a book of this sort particular debts are owed to other writers on the subject. Particular acknowledgement is due to Ingram (1971), Suehiro (1989), Muscat (1994), Sompop Manarungsan (1989) and Pasuk Phongpaichit and Baker (1995). The latter excellent account has been cited in a number of cases in place of a variety of less accessible Thai and English language sources. In Chapter 8, in the discussion of civil society and political stability, particular use was made of Hewison's (1993b) incisive account.

MEASUREMENT AND NAMES

Wherever possible values have been given in US$ and amounts in metric units. Some land areas have also been given in Thai measure: 1 rai = 0.16 hectare.

The name Thailand is used throughout the book except in direct quotations. However, the official name was Siam until 1939 and again from 1945 to 1949. Similarly, the modern place name is used unless the particular context or source dictate otherwise. The European Union is referred to as EU throughout.

THE CHAKRI DYNASTY

Rama 1	Phra Phutthayotfa	1782–1809
Rama 2	Phra Phutthaloetla	1809–1824
Rama 3	Phra Nangklao	1824–1851
Rama 4	Mongkut	1851–1868
Rama 5	Chulalongkorn	1868–1910
Rama 6	Vajiraveudh	1910–1925
Rama 7	Prajadhipok	1925–1935 (abdicated)
Rama 8	Ananda Mahidol	1935–1946
Rama 9	Bhumipol Adulyadet	1946–

GOVERNMENTS AND RELATED
EVENTS SINCE 1932

June 1932	End of the absolute monarchy, government of Manopakorn Nitithada
June 1933	Government of Phahol Phonphayuhasena
October 1933	*Coup d'état* attempt
March 1938	Elected government of Pibul Songkram
December 1941	Japanese invasion
August 1944	Government of Khuang Aphaiwongse
August 1945	Government of Thawee Bunyaket
September 1945	Government of Seni Pramoj
January 1946	Election, second government of Khuang Aphaiwongse
March 1946	Government of Pridi Banomyong
August 1946	Government of Thamrong Nawasawat
January–April 1948	Election, *coup d'état* and second Pibul Songkram government
October 1948	*Coup d'état* attempt
February 1949	*Coup d'état* attempt
June 1951	*Coup d'état* attempt
September 1957	*Coup d'état* by Sarit Thanart and the government of Pote Sarasin
December 1957	Election, government of Thanom Kittikachorn
October 1958	*Coup d'état* by Sarit Thanart
December 1963	Second government of Thanom Kittikachorn
February 1969	Election, third government of Thanom Kittikachorn
November 1971	Thanom Kittikachorn *coup d'état* and fourth government
October 1973	Student uprising, government of Sanya Dharmasakati
January 1975	Election, second government of Seni Promoj
March 1975	Election, government of Kukrit Pramoj
April 1976	Election, third government of Seni Promoj
October 1976	*Coup d'état*, Thanin Kraivichien government
March 1977	*Coup d'état* attempt

October 1977	*Coup d'état*, Kriangsak Chomanan government
April 1979	Election, second Kriangsak Chomanan government
March 1980	First government of Prem Tinsulanonda
March 1981	Second government of Prem Tinsulanonda
April 1981	*Coup d'état* attempt
December 1981	Third government of Prem Tinsulanonda
April 1983	Election, fourth government of Prem Tinsulanonda
September 1985	*Coup d'état* attempt
July 1986	Fifth government of Prem Tinsulanonda
July 1988	Election, Chatichai Choonhaven government
February 1991	*Coup d'état*, interim government of Anand Panyarachum
March 1991	Election, government of Suchinda Kraprayon
May 1992	Democracy movement
June 1992	Second interim government of Anand Panyarachum
September 1992	Election, Chuan Leekpai government
July 1995	Election, government of Banhard Silpa-Archa
November 1996	Election of Chavalit Yongchaiyudh

ABBREVIATIONS

AFTA/ASEAN	Free Trade Area
AID	Agency for International Development
ALRO	Agricultural Land Reform Office
APEC	Asia Pacific Economic Cooperation
ARD	Accelerated Rural Development
ASEAN	Association of South East Asian Nations
ASEAN–3	Indonesia, Malaysia and Thailand
ASEAN–4	Indonesia, Malaysia, the Philippines and Thailand
ASEAN–5	Brunei, Indonesia, Malaysia, the Philippines and Thailand
BAAC	Bank for Agriculture and Agricultural Cooperatives
BIBF	Bangkok International Banking Facility
BMTA	Bangkok Metropolitan Transit Authority
BMA	Bangkok Metropolitan Area
BMR	Bangkok Metropolitan Region
BOI	Board of Investment
BUILD	Board of Investment Unit for Industrial Linkage Development
CDD	Community Development Department
CBR	Crude Birth Rate
CDB	Central Business District
CDR	Crude Death Rate
CPT	Communist Party of Thailand
CSC	Communist Suppression Command
DAE	Department of Agricultural Extension
DLD	Department of Land Development
EBMR	Extended Bangkok Metropolitan Region
EGAT	Electricity Generating Authority of Thailand
EIC	East India Company
ESCAP	Economic and Social Commission for Asia and the Pacific
EOI	Export Oriented Industrialisation
EPZ	Export Processing Zone
EU	European Union

FAO	Food and Agricultural Organisation of the United Nations
FDI	Foreign Direct Investment
GDP	Gross Domestic Product
GNP	Gross National Product
HEP	Hydro-electric Power
HIV	Human Immunodeficiency Virus
HYV	High Yielding Varieties
IEAT	Industrial Estates Authority of Thailand
IFCT	Industrial Finance Corporation of Thailand
IMF	International Monetary Fund
IMR	Infant Mortality Rate
IRRI	International Rice Research Institute
ISI	Import Substituting Industrialisation
ITCs	International Trading Company
JPPCC	Joint Public-Private Consultative Committee
MAC	Ministry of Agriculture and Cooperatives
NEC	National Economic Council
NEDB	National Economic Development Board
NEDCO	National Economic Development Corporation
NERPC	North East Regional Planning Centre
NESDB	National Economic and Social Development Board
NIE	Newly Industrialising Economy
NFR	National Forestry Reserve
NGO	Non-governmental Organisation
NTB	Non-tariff Barrier
NSCT	National Student Centre of Thailand
NSO	National Statistical Office
OAE	Office of Agricultural Economics
OTCP	Office of Town and Country Planning
PFT	Peasant Federation of Thailand
REGS	Rural Employment Generation Scheme
RFD	Royal Forestry Department
RID	Royal Irrigation Department
SAL	Structual Adjustment Loan
SET	Securities Exchange of Thailand
SIFO	Small Industry Finance Office
TAT	Tourist Authority of Thailand
TDRI	Thailand Development Research Institute
TNC	Transnational Corporation
UNCTAD	United Nations Conference on Trade and Development
UNDP	United Nations Development Programme
USOM	United States Overseas Mission

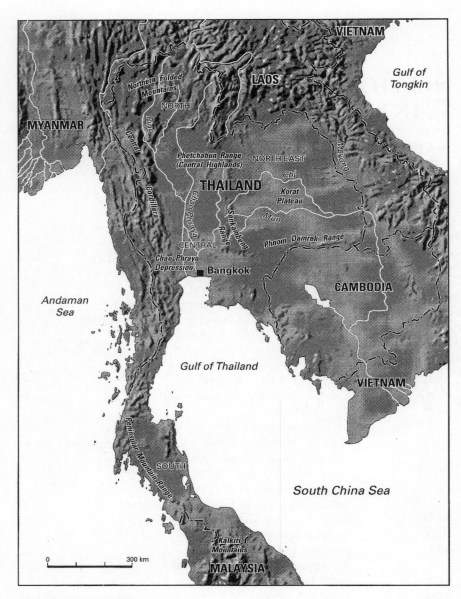

Figure 1.1 Map of Thailand

1

NATIONAL GROWTH AND THE INTERNATIONAL CONTEXT

Introduction

Between 1986 and 1991 Thailand became one of the fastest growing economies in the world. The Kingdom's economic performance during these years has been described as 'virtually unparalleled' (Narongchai Akrasanee *et al.*, 1991: xii) with the value of manufactured exports growing at 26.6 per cent a year, total exports at 18.1 per cent and GDP at 9.6 per cent. This growth was accompanied by a surge in foreign direct investment, particularly from Japan and the Asian NIEs. Overall, from 1986 Thailand experienced a period of accelerated integration into the global economy. After 1991 growth slowed, but GDP still grew at an average of 6.8 per cent between 1992 and 1996. Perhaps more significantly, since 1993 foreign investment has declined and overseas debt increased, while during 1996 the rate of growth of export earnings contracted sharply. These issues have come to the fore with the 1997 financial crisis and a dramatic slowing of growth (see pp. 239–40).

The rapid economic growth and structural change that Thailand has experienced since the mid-1980s has attracted a great deal of attention from the international and regional development agencies, transnational corporations, development planners and policy makers. The Kingdom has been widely described as a 'New NIE'; Muscat (1994) has written *The fifth tiger* and Kulick and Wilson (1992) *Thailand's turn: profile of a new dragon*. Thailand, together with Malaysia and, increasingly, Indonesia has been depicted as the 'second generation' of Asian NIEs and members of the World Bank's (1993a) Highly Performing Asian Economies group.

It has been considered that Thailand's recent pattern of development is likely to have important lessons for the rest of the Third World (Castells, 1991: iii). For at first sight, Thailand appears to have very much more in common with other countries of the Third World than was the case with four 'old' Asian NIEs – Hong Kong, Singapore, South Korea and Taiwan. For, unlike these, Thailand is not a city state or a former Japanese colony with very special circumstances attendant on their development.[1]

1

Compared to the old Asian NIEs not only has Thailand's recent rapid growth taken place in a radically different context, but it also appears to have been promoted by a very different balance of factors. The Kingdom's industrial development has been associated with a much greater involvement of foreign investors and transnational corporations than was the case in Taiwan and South Korea, and a much lower degree of state intervention and direction than was the case in Singapore, South Korea and Taiwan. Indeed, the Kingdom's rapid economic development has been associated with deregulation, liberalisation and a reduction in the economic activities of the state which have facilitated the activities of foreign investors and transnational corporations. These developments have been presented as providing a 'new model of development'. Handley has summarised this view:

> Economists, development agencies and international development specialists are already starting to forsake their hallowed Japanese, South Korean and Taiwanese models of development for a new one: the Thai model. To them, Thailand's four years of double digit growth represents the success of a decade of deregulation and the honing of investment codes to produce one of the most user-friendly investment environments among developing countries.
>
> (1991: 34–5)

Such a 'deregulation' model of economic growth is very much in line with the current 'neo-liberal' development orthodoxy.

For adherents to this view, the 'Thai economic miracle' is seen as primarily the result of the comparatively recent application of the 'correct' government policy. For such international agencies as the World Bank, Asian Development Bank and the International Monetary Fund these 'correct' policies were part of a programme of 'structural adjustment' which from the early 1980s transformed the Kingdom's development environment. Indeed, Thailand has been widely cited as an example of 'successful structural adjustment' (World Bank, 1988a, 1992). This view is part of the 'new orthodoxy' of development which views policy as *the* critical factor. This represents a fundamental reorientation, which plays down both the role of the state in promoting development and the importance of interaction with the international economy (see Dixon *et al.*, 1995).[2]

The views that Thailand's recent rapid growth is the product of changes in government policy, particularly in the direction of liberalisation, and that the background to development has sufficient in common with other less developed countries to constitute an appropriate model of development for many of them, are open to serious questioning. Such views neglect the historical development of Thailand which, particularly during

Table 1.1 Average annual rate of growth of GDP, 1963–94

	1960–69	1970–79	1980	1981	1982	1983	1984	1985	1986	1987	1988	1989	1990	1991	1992	1993	1994
ASEAN-4																	
Indonesia	3.5	7.6	9.6	7.6	5.4	3.3	5.3	1.6	2.0	2.5	5.7	6.2	7.0	7.0	6.3	6.6	7.0
Malaysia	6.5	7.6	8.0	6.5	4.9	3.8	5.9	-1.5	0.0	3.0	7.4	8.5	10.0	8.6	7.8	8.5	8.6
Philippines	5.1	6.3	5.4	3.0	3.5	-1.4	-1.4	-4.0	1.0	5.7	4.5	3.6	2.5	0.0	0.1	1.7	4.5
Thailand	8.2	7.2	4.9	7.6	6.0	5.8	5.5	3.5	4.5	8.4	11.0	10.8	10.0	7.9	7.2	7.9	8.8
Asian NIEs																	
Hong Kong	10.0	9.3	9.8	10.4	4.3	5.2	6.0	0.8	6.0	13.6	7.3	2.5	2.3	3.9	5.0	5.9	4.9
South Korea	8.5	9.5	-6.7	7.1	3.5	9.5	7.5	5.1	10.0	11.1	12.2	7.4	8.9	8.4	4.8	4.5	6.3
Singapore	8.8	8.8	10.2	9.9	3.7	7.9	8.0	-2.9	2.0	8.8	11.0	9.2	8.9	6.7	6.0	9.8	6.8
Taiwan	9.2	8.0	7.2	5.5	5.0	7.5	11.0	5.1	10.8	11.7	7.0	7.1	5.2	7.0	7.0	6.0	6.2
OECD	5.1	3.3	1.4	1.2	-0.2	2.7	4.9	3.6	2.8	3.5	4.5	3.5	2.5	3.6	1.5	1.5	0.9
Low and middle-income countries	4.8	2.1	2.1	0.5	2.3	3.7	4.5	3.7	3.3	3.9	3.7	3.0	1.9	2.2	0.3	2.4	1.3
Sub-Saharan Africa	4.6[a]	3.0	3.2	0.7	2.7	0.0	0.2	3.4	3.6	0.9	4.4	3.1	1.1	2.5	0.6	0.3	0.8

Source: World Bank, *World Tables*, various issues.
Note
a 1965–73.

Table 1.2 The growth of export earnings (annual average percentage change)

	1972–75	*1976–80*	*1981–85*	*1986–90*	*1991–94*
The ASEAN–4					
Indonesia	28.4	3.4	0.7	6.8	13.7
Malaysia	–0.4	8.8	9.2	11.3	18.1
Philippines	6.5	10.2	0.8	8.0	7.7
Thailand	7.8	13.6	11.2	18.4	15.0
The Asian NIEs					
Hong Kong	8.3	21.9	11.6	23.2	12.0
Singapore	32.9	32.1	3.7	15.2	11.4
South Korea	33.1	17.1	13.3	11.6	8.5
Taiwan	30.1	22.9	11.3	8.7	13.2

Source: World Bank, *World Tables*, various issues.

the period 1950 to 1980, laid the basis for the rapid expansion of export-orientated manufacturing and the international conditions, which from the mid-1980s were conducive to such development. Similarly, the unusual features of Thailand's development are ignored, notably, the low level of urbanisation, the markedly uneven spatial pattern of economic activity, the comparative abundance of agricultural land and the Kingdom's highly distinctive non-colonial mode of incorporation into the global economy from the mid-nineteenth century.

The euphoria which has surrounded the recent rapid growth of the Thai economy has also tended to obscure the impact of the rapid change in the Kingdom's society and environment, and the degree to which internal and external developments are raising question marks over the long-term sustainability of the Kingdom's growth. It is the intention of this book to put the recent growth in perspective through an examination of the Kingdom's historical and contemporary patterns of development, and the changing nature of the interaction with the wider Asian and international economies. Quite simply it is intended to get behind the 'hype and myth' and to place Thailand's recent rapid economic growth in perspective.

Economic growth and structural change

The labelling of Thailand as a new NIE and a successful case of development rests principally on the achievement of rapid growth of GDP since the early 1980s (Table 1.1), a spectacular expansion of overseas trade (Table 1.2) and a dramatic change in the composition of exports in favour of manufactured goods (Table 1.3). There is no doubt that the achievements in these areas have been spectacular by any standards, with growth

Table 1.3 Export earnings: percentage composition

	1970	1975	1980	1985	1986	1987	1988	1989	1990	1991	1992	1993	1994
Agriculture	77.1	75.1		38.0	34.0	27.8	26.4	23.0	18.0	15.1	15.0	12.2	11.4
Fishing			68.3	5.5	6.4	6.1	5.2	5.5	5.3	6.0	5.9	5.7	6.0
Forestry				0.2	0.3	0.3	0.2	0.1	0.2	0.1	0.1	–	–
Mining	0.1	0.1	2.1	5.2	2.7	1.6	1.9	1.6	1.4	1.2	0.8	0.5	0.6
Total primary	77.2	75.1	70.4	48.9	42.4	35.8	33.7	30.2	24.9	22.4	21.8	18.4	18.0
Manufacturing	15.4	15.4	26.8	49.5	55.4	62.7	65.4	68.6	73.8	76.2	76.9	80.0	81.1
Others	3.2	2.2	1.5	0.8	0.8	1.0	0.7	1.0	1.1	1.1	1.2	1.3	0.7
Re-exports	3.6	1.9	1.3	0.9	0.6	0.3	0.3	0.2	0.2	0.3	0.2	0.3	0.2
Total exports	100.0	100.0	100.0	100.0	100.0	100.0	100.0	100.0	100.0	100.0	100.0	100.0	100.0

Source: Bank of Thailand, *Monthly Bulletin*, various issues.
Note
– = less than 0.1.

Table 1.4 Composition of imports (percentage of value)

	1960	1965	1970	1975	1980	1985	1990	1992	1993	1994
Consumer goods	35.0	26.7	19.4	12.6	10.2	9.5	8.5	10.0	9.8	10.6
Intermediate products[a]	18.1	20.8	24.9	24.1	24.0	30.1	33.8	32.1	30.0	23.8
Fuels and lubricants	10.6	8.7	8.6	21.3	31.1	22.6[b]	9.2	8.1	7.9	7.6
Capital goods	24.6	30.1	34.7	33.3	24.4	30.0	38.8	41.2	43.0	44.3
Other	11.7	13.7	12.4	8.7	10.3	7.8	9.7	8.6	9.3	13.7
Total	100.0	100.0	100.0	100.0	100.0	100.0	100.0	100.0	100.0	100.0

Source: Bank of Thailand.
Notes
a Includes components and raw materials, but excludes fuels and lubricants.
b The sharp drop in oil prices during 1986 reduced the import bills share to 13.4 per cent.

Table 1.5 Geographical pattern of imports (by value)

	1960	1965	1970	1975	1980	1985	1990	1992	1994
USA	16.7	16.0	15.0	14.0	14.4	8.6	10.9	11.7	11.8
EU	24.8	22.0	18.0	13.0	19.3	13.6	13.7	14.4	10.2
Japan	25.6	33.0	37.0	32.0	21.2	20.0	30.1	29.2	30.2
Asian NIEs	14.6	6.2	4.0	4.8	11.5	9.5	17.1	19.0	16.3
Hong Kong	6.5	3.0	1.0	1.0	0.9	0.9	1.3	1.9	1.3
South Korea	–	–	–	0.8	2.1	1.5	3.2	4.4	3.6
Singapore	7.3	1.0	1.0	2.0	6.5	5.6	7.5	7.4	6.3
Taiwan	0.8	2.2	2.0	2.0	2.0	2.3	5.2	5.5	5.1
ASEAN–5	5.0	3.0	2.0	2.0	5.5	8.0	4.8	5.4	5.3
Brunei	–	–	–	1.4	2.3	2.7	0.5	0.5	0.1
Indonesia	2.9	2.0	1.0	–	0.5	0.5	0.6	0.7	0.2
Malaysia	2.1	1.0	1.0	0.2	1.8	4.3	3.4	3.9	4.8
Philippines	–	–	–	0.4	0.9	0.5	0.3	0.3	0.2
Asian Socialist	1.1	0.5	2.4	0.4	4.6	2.2	4.1	3.8	3.2
Cambodia	–	–	–	–	–	–	–	0.2	0.2
China	1.1	–	2.4	0.4	4.5	1.8	3.3	3.0	2.5
Laos	–	0.5	–	–	–	–	0.1	0.1	0.1
Myanmar	–	–	–	–	0.1	0.4	0.4	0.3	0.3
Vietnam	–	–	–	–	–	–	0.3	0.3	0.1
Other	12.2	18.5	21.6	33.8	18.0	38.5	19.3	16.5	23.0
Pacific Asia	46.3	42.7	45.4	39.2	42.8	39.3	56.8	57.4	55.0
Total	100.0	100.0	100.0	100.0	100.0	100.0	100.0	100.0	100.0

Source: Bank of Thailand.
Note: – = less than 0.1 per cent.

rates comparable to those of South Korea during the 1970s. However, Thailand's successful economic growth and the expansion and restructuring of the Kingdom's export economy need to be placed in context and qualified in a number of respects.

In terms of value, the expansion of exports has been driven by the manufacturing sector. However, the rapid change in the composition of exports has to be set against the dramatic decline in the relative level of primary export prices since the early 1980s. This tends to obscure the very substantial increases in the volume and variety of primary exports, which between 1986 and 1994 more than doubled their value. Thus Thailand remains a substantial exporter of primary products. In the mid-1990s the Kingdom was one of the only two net food exporters in Pacific Asia (the

Table 1.6 Geographical pattern of exports (by value)

	1960	1965	1970	1975	1980	1985	1990	1992	1994
USA	13.9	7.0	13.0	11.0	12.6	19.7	26.2	22.4	21.0
EC	14.6	13.0	17.0	14.0	22.2	17.9	21.5	19.2	9.3
Japan	17.8	18.0	26.0	28.0	15.1	13.4	17.2	17.5	17.1
Asian NIEs	20.9	13.6	18.0	18.0	14.9	15.3	15.1	16.8	33.7
Hong Kong	8.7	7.0	8.0	6.0	5.1	4.0	4.5	4.6	5.3
South Korea	0.2	0.2	–	1.0	0.8	1.8	1.7	1.6	12.6
Singapore	11.2	6.0	7.0	9.0	7.7	7.9	7.3	8.7	3.6
Taiwan	0.8	0.6	5.0	2.0	1.3	1.6	1.6	1.9	2.2
ASEAN–5	21.2	17.6	8.0	7.9	8.6	6.5	4.3	3.7	3.1
Brunei	–	–	–	–	0.1	0.2	0.1	0.1	0.1
Indonesia	4.1	2.0	2.0	2.0	3.6	0.6	0.7	0.7	1.0
Malaysia	17.1	15.0	6.0	5.0	4.5	5.0	2.8	2.6	2.4
Philippines	–	0.6	–	0.9	0.4	0.7	0.7	0.3	0.5
Asian Socialist	0.2	4.0	8.8	3.4	3.3	2.4	1.8	2.2	4.4
Cambodia	–	–	–	0.8	0.5	–	–	0.2	0.6
China	–	–	4.6	2.0	1.9	1.8	1.3	1.2	2.1
Laos	0.2	1.6	2.8	0.6	0.7	0.5	0.3	0.4	0.6
Myanmar	–	–	–	–	–	0.1	0.2	0.2	0.5
Vietnam	–	2.4	1.4	–	0.2	–	–	0.2	0.6
Other	11.4	27.8	9.2	17.7	23.3	24.8	13.9	18.2	11.4
Pacific Asia	60.1	53.2	60.8	55.3	41.9	37.6	38.4	40.2	58.3

Source: Bank of Thailand.
Note
– = less than 0.1 per cent.

Table 1.7 Integration into the international economy: the value of foreign trade as a percentage of GDP (openness ratio)

	1970	1975	1980	1985	1990	1994
ASEAN–4						
Indonesia	33.0	44.2	53.1	42.3	55.6	53.2
Malaysia	71.4	86.9	113.2	105.2	155.8	156.3
Philippines	39.1	48.2	52.0	45.9	62.7	71.8
Thailand	37.1	41.3	54.7	51.1	76.7	79.3
Asian NIEs						
Hong Kong	176.7	161.1	198.5	216.7	285.7	249.9
Singapore	231.7	290.2	424.0	307.7	340.8	367.4
South Korea	44.6	61.7	75.4	67.9	61.4	50.1

Source: World Bank, *World Tables,* various issues; *Industry of Free China,* various issues.

other is Vietnam); in world terms the Kingdom was the largest exporter of rice, rubber and cassava, and the second largest exporter of sugar. In addition to these established bulk products, since the late 1970s there has been substantial growth in the export of fruit, vegetables, flowers, chickens and marine products. As well as the continued importance of the primary sectors, a proportion of the exports *classed* as manufactured are produced by the rapidly expanding agri-business sector. Most rapidly expanding have been tinned fruit (particularly pineapples), frozen boned chickens, and frozen and tinned seafood.[3] In 1994 Thailand was the world's largest exporter of tinned tuna fish, providing 80 per cent of world exports. The continued importance of the agricultural and marine products to Thailand's export economy has led some observers to label the Kingdom a Newly Agro-Industrialising Economy rather than an NIE (Ammar Siamwalla, 1993).

Within the manufacturing export sector there have, since the early 1980s, been substantial changes in composition (see pp.134–7). The initial accelerated expansion of manufactured exports was heavily concentrated in the textile, garment and footwear sectors. Subsequently, exports have become much more diverse, with particular growth in the electronics and electrical sectors.

Since 1980 there have also been dramatic changes in the composition of imports (Table 1.4). First, the decline in oil prices after 1985 and the exploitation of the oil and gas reserves of the Gulf of Thailand (see p.15) have drastically reduced the expenditure on energy imports. Second, and closely related to the rapid expansion of manufactured exports, is the growth in the importation of machinery, non-consumer manufactured goods, components and raw materials. In these respects the Thai manufacturing sector has become heavily dependent on imports, particularly from Japan and the NIEs.

Table 1.8 GDP at constant 1972 prices: percentage sectoral distribution, 1951–94

	1951	1955	1960	1965	1970	1975	1980	1985	1987	1988	1989	1990	1991	1992	1993	1994
Agricultural	50.1	42.0	39.7	34.8	30.0	30.4	23.2	16.8	16.4	16.6	15.2	14.4	12.8	12.0	10.0	11.4
Mining & quarrying	1.9	1.6	1.1	2.1	1.5	1.2	3.4	4.0	3.0	3.1	3.5	2.7	1.6	1.5	1.5	1.6
Manufacturing	10.3	11.8	12.6	14.2	17.1	17.2	21.3	22.1	23.1	24.8	25.4	24.7	28.1	28.0	28.5	31.3
Construction	2.9	4.0	4.6	5.6	5.8	4.6	5.3	5.6	5.3	5.6	6.6	5.2	6.8	6.7	6.9	6.1
Electricity & water supply	0.1	0.2	0.4	0.8	1.5	1.6	1.0	2.3	2.5	2.3	2.3	3.0	2.1	2.3	2.4	2.6
Transportation & communication	3.1	5.1	7.5	7.1	6.8	6.1	5.8	7.7	7.4	7.1	6.9	7.1	7.0	7.2	7.5	7.7
Wholesale & retail trade	18.0	19.6	15.2	16.5	17.4	17.5	16.7	15.1	15.6	15.9	15.5	17.6	17.0	16.6	16.6	16.2
Banking, insurance & real estate	0.4	1.4	1.9	2.6	3.9	4.5	3.1	3.6	4.0	4.3	4.6	5.3	5.4	6.5	7.3	7.6
Ownership of dwelling	3.7	3.0	2.8	2.5	1.9	1.7	3.5	4.1	3.9	3.5	3.2	3.6	2.9	2.7	2.6	2.6
Public administration and defence	2.8	4.8	4.6	4.3	4.3	4.1	4.7	4.8	4.2	3.7	3.6	3.8	3.4	3.5	3.8	2.6
Services	6.7	6.5	9.6	9.5	9.3	10.6	12.3	14.1	13.7	13.0	13.2	12.3	12.9	12.8	13.0	10.3
Gross Domestic Product	100.0	100.0	100.0	100.0	100.0	100.0	100.0	100.0	100.0	100.0	100.0	100.0	100.0	100.0	100.0	100.0

Source: National Economic and Social Development Board.

The rapid growth of trade since the mid-1980s has been accompanied by an acceleration of the longer-term trend towards a reorientation of imports away from the USA and EU and towards Japan and the Asian NIEs (Table 1.5). Thus while there has been no increased dependence on the other members of the ASEAN–4 Group, Thailand has become much more dependent on the wider Pacific Asian region. In contrast, during the period 1985 to 1990 the Kingdom increased its dependence on the USA and EU markets (Table 1.6). While there has been a subsequent decline in the importance of these markets, particularly the EU, Thailand's pattern of trade remains distinctive within Pacific Asia – only Taiwan exhibiting a similar pattern of dependence on the USA and EU (Dixon and Drakakis-Smith, 1995). The US market remains particularly important for Thai textiles and electrical/electronic appliances. This situation leaves the Kingdom particularly vulnerable to increased protectionism (for a fuller discussion of Thailand's long-term export prospects see pp. 252–5).

The changing composition of imports and the contrast between the geographical distribution of imports and exports reflects the position that Thailand has developed within the global economy since the early 1980s. Increasingly the Kingdom has become an importer of components and materials from Japan and the Asian NIEs and an exporter of part or fully assembled products, principally to the USA and the EU but increasingly back to Japan and the Asian NIEs. The latter trend is particularly well illustrated by the trade in integrated circuits and computer parts (see pp. 131–4).

As may be seen from Table 1.7 during the 1970s Thailand was the most closed of the pro-capitalism Pacific Asian economies. To a degree this shielded the Kingdom from the international economic vicissitudes that characterised the decade. Since the early 1980s the rapid growth of Thailand's overseas trade has made the economy much more dependent on the international economy. Thailand is now significantly more trade dependent than Indonesia and the Philippines. However, unlike the other ASEAN–4 economies the expansion of trade during the 1980s was not accompanied by any reduction in the level of tariff protection. Not until after 1988 was there effective liberalisation of the Thai trade regime (see Chapter 4 for a fuller discussion). By the mid-1990s the increased importance of international trade to the Thai economy has combined with liberalisation of the Kingdom's trade regime to make it much more vulnerable to the vagaries of the international economy and protectionism on the part of major trading partners.

The striking changes in Thailand's export economy which have led to the country becoming labelled an NIE have been far less apparent in the domestic economy. As may be seen from Table 1.8, while there has been a long-term decline in the contribution of the primary sector to GDP, since the mid-1980s this has been slight compared to the decline in the

Table 1.9 The structure of employment, 1960–94

	Millions					Percentage share				
	1960	1970	1980	1990	1994	1960	1970	1980	1990	1994
Agriculture	11.42	13.29	18.32	19.25	19.70	82.3	79.3	71.9	63.5	60.8
Industry	0.58	0.97	2.01	4.31	5.10	4.2	5.8	7.9	14.2	15.8
Service	1.87	2.50	5.15	6.78	7.58	13.5	14.9	20.2	22.3	23.4
Total	13.87	16.76	25.48	30.34	32.38	100.0	100.0	100.0	100.0	100.0

Source: National Statistical Office.

sector's share of export earnings (Table 1.3). However, by the early 1990s the primary sector's share of GDP and export earnings had become broadly similar. As with export earnings, the primary sector's contribution to GDP has been substantially depressed by the level of commodity prices, which serve to hide the continued expansion of output, in particular of agriculture and fisheries. For example between 1980 and 1991 rice production increased by 15.23 per cent (from 17,385.000 tons to 20,040,000 tons), while the crop's share of GDP fell from 8.6 per cent to 4 per cent.

More striking than the contrast between the composition of export earnings and GDP is that with the structure of employment (Table 1.9). In this respect Thailand remains very firmly an agricultural economy. There has been a long-term decline in the proportion of the work force directly employed in agriculture, and, particularly since the early 1980s, a marked rise in the proportion engaged in manufacturing. However, the number of people directly employed in agriculture continues to increase.

The resource base and development

As has been outlined, until the early 1980s both Thailand's domestic and export economies were heavily dependent on the primary sector. In this respect Thailand has much in common with the other so-called new Asian NIEs – Indonesia and Malaysia – and little with the old Asian NIEs (Castells, 1991). Thailand however, has by far the narrowest and most exploited resource base of the three economies. Most strikingly, Thailand lacks the substantial oil, gas and timber reserves which continue to play major roles in the Indonesian and Malaysian economies. While Thailand possesses a comparatively wide range of minerals, they are generally only present in small commercial quantities. Similarly, the Kingdom's offshore oil and gas resources which have been developed since the early 1980s have principally served the domestic market. In terms of the growth of the economy and exports, the key resource has been the comparative abundance and ease of access to agricultural land.

Until the early 1980s the utilisation of resources was the key element in the Kingdom's development. Resources, particularly land, were regarded as something to exploit, with little effective control. The lack of controls over land clearance reinforced the comparative abundance of agricultural land, enabling the cultivation of an exceptionally large proportion of the Kingdom's surface area. As is examined more fully in Chapters 2 and 5, long-term expansion of agricultural production was able to take place with little regard for land shortage or need for capital investment or intensification. Thailand thus had a massive comparative advantage in agricultural production and until c. 1980 the low-cost expansion of the agricultural sector was a major, and highly unusual, factor in the Kingdom's economic growth.

13

The corollary of the expansion of the cultivated area has been the loss of forest area. Widespread clearance for agriculture has been reinforced by the demand for fuel wood and timber for local use and heavy commercial cutting with few effective controls, little conservation or replanting. Much cutting has been illegal and organised on a very large scale. By the late 1970s saw mills were producing 6.5 million m^3 from an annual legal cut of only 2.5 million m^3 (Hurst, 1990: 228–9).

Timber production has been falling since the late 1970s and Thailand has been a net importer since 1978. In 1989 a complete logging ban was imposed. This resulted from large-scale flooding in the south[4] which was attributed to the affects of uncontrolled timber cutting and a series of 'logging scandals' (Hurst, 1990: 208, 226–30). The ban has inevitably proved difficult to enforce and small-scale cutting continued to take place in many areas. However, regardless of any ban the reserves of commercially viable timber are now extremely small and increasingly unattractive to large-scale operations, legal or otherwise.

Since the 1960s forestry has ceased to make a significant contribution to the national economy or exports. The domestic wood-working industry has become heavily dependent on imports. In rural areas timber is becoming in short supply for construction and fuel, resulting in the clearance of increasingly unsuitable areas, particularly for charcoal production. Despite the timber shortage official production of charcoal (almost certainly a substantial under-estimate) increased from 234,000 tons in 1980 to 588,500 tons in 1994. In rural areas in particular households remain heavily dependent on fuel wood and charcoal.

In terms of production Thailand has the third largest marine fishing sector in Asia: production is only exceeded by China and Japan. The marine fishing industry expanded rapidly from the 1950s onwards with the rapid introduction of motorised vessels and trawling, and the replacement of bamboo stakes by purseseine nets (Ammar Siamwalla et al., 1993: 87; Anat Arbhabhirama et al., 1988). These technical changes resulted in substantial increases in the size of catches. From the early 1970s there were signs of serious depletion of inshore fish stocks[5] and catches began to decline during the late 1970s. This combined with the introduction of 200-mile exclusion zones and the rapid rise in fuel prices after 1973 to slow the growth of the industry until the early 1980s.

Since 1980 there has been a second major phase in the development of marine fishery technology. This was associated with access to new, and generally much more distant, fishing grounds and the development of prawn and shrimp 'farming'. Thus annual production expanded from 1.6 million tons in 1980 to 2.6 million tons in 1994. Of critical importance were agreements with Bangladesh, India and Oman which have given access to distant waters, and agreements with Indonesia and Myanmar have permitted joint exploitation of their territorial waters. However, increasing competition for marine resources is placing all of these arrangements in jeopardy. Indeed, the fisheries have become a major source of friction between the South East Asian nations.

Other than fisheries, and cultivable land, until the 1980s Thailand's principle resource was tin. Until the collapse of the international tin trade in 1985 Thailand supplied 12–15 per cent of world exports (see Chapter 2 for an account of this sector). Despite the continued depression of the demand for tin it remains Thailand's most important metallic mineral product. A wide range of other minerals are present in commercial quantities, but most are produced in small and declining quantities.[6] In the 1990s expansion of production has been largely confined to gypsum, iron ore, lignite and zinc. However, Thailand remains a rich source of precious stones, including sapphires, rubies, zircon, garnet, quartz and jadite. The expansion of the jewellery industry which had, by the early 1990s made Thailand the world's principal exporter, has outrun the capacity of the domestic mining industry and has become dependent on imports. Increasing amounts of gems are being obtained from Laos and Cambodia; much of the traffic with the latter country is illegal.

The production of lignite has increased steadily since the early 1970s when its potential as a substitute for imported oil in the generation of electricity was realised. Production increased from 333,710 tons in 1972, to 6.3 million in 1988 and 16.5 million in 1994. By the later year some 27.2 per cent of national electricity output was generated by lignite. Most Thai lignite is of low quality, however the deposits are extensive. There are some 75 recognised deposits mainly in the North and South; of these only 26 have been explored and are estimated to contain reserves of 2,600 million tons. Further exploration and evaluation may be expected to raise this estimate considerably. However, the pollution resulting from the increased use of lignite for electricity generation is giving rise to increasing concern.

During the late 1970s offshore oil and gas exploration established that there were substantial reserves in the Gulf of Thailand. By 1994 it had been established that there were 12 offshore fields, with estimated reserves of 173,400 million m^3 of gas and 119.5 million barrels of condensate. The first gas came ashore in 1981, by 1994 daily production had risen to 20 million m^3 of gas, 23,600 barrels of condensate and 24,700 barrels of crude petroleum, and supplied 30 per cent of domestic demand. Exploration is continuing, both on and offshore, though to date the former has met with only limited success, with only the Shell concession at Kamphaenphet proving viable and producing 17,000 barrels/day of crude petroleum. While the exploitation of the gas and oil reserves since the early 1980s has not given rise to the expected heavy industrial complex along the Eastern Seaboard (see pp. 200–03) it has made a major contribution to the Kingdom's economic growth, through the reduction of imports and the generation of employment and investment.

Table 1.10a Thailand in perspective, 1970, 1980 and 1993

	Per capita GDP (US$)			Rank from bottom		Percentage change in per capita GDP	
	1970	1980	1993	1980	1993	1970–80	1980–93
The ASEAN–4							
Indonesia	180	430	670	38	37	94.4	91.4
Malaysia	970	1620	2790	76	94	79.4	60.3
Philippines	520	690	770	52	46	26.9	16.7
Thailand	510	670	1840	51	76	37.3	162.9
The Asian NIES							
Hong Kong	1230	4240	15360	92	114	324.4	194.2
South Korea	1080	1520	6790	75	106	58.3	297.1
Singapore	1410	4380	15360	95	115	241.8	218.7

Source: World Bank, *World Tables*, various issues.

In terms of renewable energy Thailand has considerable potential for HEP. It is estimated that the utilisation of all the recognised sites would generate some 10,051 MW. Utilisation of HEP dates from the construction of the Bhumipol dam in Tak province in 1964. By 1990 some 30 per cent of the estimated capacity had been achieved. Further expansion is limited by the majority of the undeveloped sites being only suitable for comparatively small-scale projects, and an increasing number of conflicts over water use and concern over environmental damage. In 1987 the Nam Choan project (Hurst, 1990: 235–9) was postponed following vigorous campaigning by environmental and farming interests. The most significant potential lies in the development of projects in border areas in conjunction with neighbouring countries, notably on the Salween, with Myanmar and the Mekong with Laos.

The declining importance of and increasing problems associated with the primary sector can be read as indicative of the closing of the intensive resource exploitation phase of Thailand's economic development. However, as has already been stressed, the primary sector continues to make a major contribution to the domestic and export economies. More significantly, the majority of the population remains directly involved in primary activities.

The Thai economy in comparative perspective

In terms of most measures of living conditions Thailand appears to be close to the position expected for the level of per capita GNP. While the Kingdom remains very firmly a member of the World Bank's lower middle income group, its relative position has changed very rapidly since the early 1980s (Table 1.10a). In terms of per capita GDP, while Thailand has increased its lead over Indonesia and the Philippines, the gap between the old Asian NIEs and, more importantly, Malaysia, has widened significantly. This should be borne in mind and used to temper the euphoria that has surrounded Thailand's rapid economic growth since the mid-1980s and the labelling of the Kingdom as a new NIE.

The changes in the relative level of per capita GNP have been closely paralleled by improvements in most key indicators of living conditions – with the provision of electricity in rural areas, housing, health facilities, piped water and sanitation, particularly in rural areas. In some respects, notably the provision of piped water in rural areas[7] and health facilities, Thailand may well be ahead of many developing economies with similar levels of per capita income. In other respects – most strikingly with respect to the nutritional levels of pre-school children, Thailand appears to have lagged, certainly until the early 1980s (Chalogphob Sussangkarn et al., 1988: 168).[8]

While Thailand may be regarded as a representative of the more fortunate of the lower middle income group of economies and more typical of less developed countries in general than the Asian NIEs, the Kingdom has a number of highly distinctive features which are both contributory factors to, and reflections of, the Kingdom's long-term pattern of development. These include the rate of population growth, the levels of secondary education, agricultural employment and urbanisation, the degree to which the capital dominates the national economy and the markedly uneven spatial pattern of development.

In 1993 Thailand had not only the lowest rate of population growth in the ASEAN–4 group but one of the lowest in the lower middle income band (Table 1.10b). However, during the 1970s the Kingdom had the fastest rate of population growth of the ASEAN–4 group and was well above the average for the lower middle income group (Table 1.10b). Indeed, during this period considerable concern was expressed over the rate of population growth and the likely impact on development, land supply and the maintenance of agricultural exports, particularly rice (NESDB, 1974). Subsequently there was a rapid fall in the crude birth rate from 39 per thousand in 1968 to 17 per thousand in 1990. This dramatic change reflects the receptiveness of the population to a remarkably effective national birth control programme (see Chapter 3 for a fuller discussion). The sharp fall in the rate of population growth has made a significant contribution to the rate of growth of per capita GDP. In this respect Thailand could not contrast more strongly with such economies as the Philippines. However, in terms of those demographic indicators that more closely reflect living conditions – life expectancy, death rate and infant mortality rate – Thailand remains

Table 1.10b Thailand in demographic perspective, 1972, 1980 and 1993

	Life expectancy			CDR			CBR			IMR			Annual average rates of growth		
	1972	1980	1993	1972	1980	1993	1972	1980	1993	1972	1980	1993	1970–80	1980–93	1993–2000[a]
The ASEAN-4															
Indonesia	49	55	60	18	13	10	45	35	25	118	99	66	2.3	1.8	1.4
Malaysia	63	67	71	10	7	5	36	31	28	45	30	14	2.4	2.5	2.0
Philippines	58	61	65	11	7	7	38	35	32	66	52	40	2.5	2.4	2.3
Thailand	60	62	69	9	8	6	39	30	20	73	44	26	2.7	1.8	1.3
The Asian NIES															
Hong Kong	54	61	78	5	5	6	21	19	12	19	11	6	2.5	1.2	0.6
South Korea	61	67	71	9	7	6	30	24	12	51	32	13	1.6	1.8	1.4
Singapore	69	72	75	5	5	6	23	18	16	20	12	5	2.9	1.8	1.4
Low income	50	58	62	14	12	10	39	31	28	n.a.	99	73	2.2	2.0	1.7
Lower middle	60	59	67	12	11	9	36	38	24	n.a.	57	45	2.6	1.8	1.4
Upper middle	65	65	69	10	9	7	33	31	24	n.a.	65	40	2.5	1.8	1.5

Source: World Bank, *World tables*, various issues.
Note: a Projection.

Table 1.11 Agricultural employment and GDP: Thailand and selected Asian countries

	(a) Labour (1980) %	(b) GDP (1982) %	Ratio (b/a)	(a) Labour (1993) %	(b) GDP (1993) %	Ratio (b/a)
Bangladesh	75	47	0.63	64	29	0.45
China	74	37	0.50	60	35	0.58
India	70	33	0.47	63	29	0.46
Indonesia	57	26	0.46	55	22	0.40
Malaysia	23	23	1.00	26	19	0.73
Myanmar	53	48	0.90	69	57	0.89
Pakistan	55	31	0.56	50	24	0.48
Philippines	52	22	0.42	41	22	0.54
Sri Lanka	53	27	0.51	42	23	0.52
South Korea	36	16	0.44	18	9	0.50
Thailand	71	22	0.28	67	12	0.18

Source: World Bank, *World Tables*, ILO *World Labour Report*, Geneva, various issues.

very close to the averages for the ASEAN–4 and lower middle income groups (Table 1.10b).

In terms of formal adult literacy rates, the expansion of rural primary education facilities, in particular since the 1960s, had by the mid-1980s made the Thai population the most literate in the ASEAN–4 group. The formal rate rising from 68 per cent in 1960 to 92 per cent in 1987. However, Thailand's participation rate in secondary education remains well below that of the other ASEAN–4 group and generally low for the countries' level of per capita GDP. This is a cause of considerable concern in view of the government's avowed aim to move the economy towards more skill-intensive activities and the increasing reports of skilled labour shortages (see Chapters 4 and 8 for a fuller discussion).

The level of agricultural employment remains exceptionally high for the level of per capita GDP and high compared to other Asian countries. The rapid rate of industrial growth that Thailand has experienced since the early 1980s has not been accompanied by any acceleration in the decline in the proportion of the work force employed in agriculture. In consequence the ratio of agricultural employment to agricultural GDP has become by far the lowest of any major less developed Asian economy (Table 1.11).

This does, however, need some qualification because the level of full-time employment in the agricultural sector is undoubtedly exaggerated by official statistics. The wording of the census question on primary employment is thought to bias agricultural employment upward (Ammar Siamwalla, 1993: 89). Studies of rural income suggest that while many people record their primary activity as agriculture they derive a substantial proportion of their income from other activities (Narongchai Aransanee, 1983). In addition, a number of studies have stressed the seasonal, partial and irregular nature of much agricultural employment. In 1990 the Office of Agricultural Economics' (OAE) survey of agricultural labour indicated that only 46.4 per cent were employed all the year and another 27.6 per cent during the dry season months. Similarly, the National Statistical Office's (NSO) 1990 Labour Force Survey suggests that 57.3 per cent of the labour force was engaged in agriculture during the period January to March and 66.4 per cent during the period July to September. The volume of seasonal migration is believed to be expanding very rapidly. It has been estimated that dry season migrants into the BMR exceed 2 million (Paritta Chalermpow Koanantakool, 1993: 28). Thus the slow rate of decline in the proportion of the labour force classed as agriculturalist may mask a much more substantial decline in the sector's importance as a source of livelihood. From various evidence of this type, Ammar Siamwalla *et al.* (1993: 92) have concluded that the official figures certainly over-estimate the agricultural labour force. It may well be that in the early 1990s the proportion of the labour force that may be regarded as agriculturalists is nearer 55 per cent than 66 per cent. However, whatever qualification is made the employment in the agricultural sector does remain exceptionally high.

The corollary of the high level of employment in the agricultural sector is a remarkably low level of urbanisation for the Kingdom's level of economic development. In 1995 according to the World Bank only 20 per cent of the population was recorded as living in urban areas. Only 9 countries had a lower level of urbanisation and those were amongst the poorest in the world (World Bank, 1997). There are a number of explanations for this situation.

The urban population is probably under-estimated. It is believed that a large number of urban inhabitants, particularly in Bangkok, regard themselves as 'rural' and continued to be registered in their 'home village'. In addition, it is highly likely that an increasing number of the poorest urban dwellers are not enumerated at all. There is every indication that there has been a very substantial influx of rural migrants into Bangkok and its immediate vicinity since the mid-1980s (see Chapter 6). An increasing proportion are almost certainly not registered as Bangkok residents. In consequence it is highly probable that the size of Bangkok and its recent growth are seriously under-estimated.

Similarly, the definition of 'urban places' is, as in so many countries, profoundly unsatisfactory. The definition used in the international statistics includes only municipal areas (*tessa ban*). This under-estimates the number of urban places as many 'sanitary districts' (*sukapi ban* – a lower order of administrative unit) could equally well be classed as 'urban places'.

Table 1.12 Comparative rates of urban growth

	1960–5	1956–70	1970–5	1975–80	1980–5	1985–90	1990–5[a]	1995–2000[a]
Indonesia	1.58	1.56	9.51	2.74	3.31	3.07	2.74	2.40
Malaysia	0.68	0.67	2.56	2.44	2.27	2.07	1.85	1.62
Philippines	0.85	0.85	1.51	1.00	1.34	1.28	1.34	1.35
Thailand	0.55	0.66	2.68	2.61	2.67	2.69	2.66	2.59

Source: United Nations *Demographic Yearbook*, Geneva, various issues.
Notes: [a] Projections.

Tirasawat Penporn (1990) has proposed that the definition of urban places should include all municipal areas and sanitary districts when they have a population of 5,000 or more and a minimum density of 1,000 per square kilometre. However, sanitary districts adjacent to municipal areas are included even when they do not meet the density criteria.

The use of Tirasawat Penporn's (1990) definition of urban places raises Thailand's level of urbanisation to 28.4 per cent for 1990, still extremely low. Making allowance for the under-registration may raise the level of urbanisation into the 30 to 35 per cent range – still remarkably low for the level of per capita GDP.

As is discussed in Chapters 5 and 6 the key to Thailand's low level of urbanisation lies in the availability of land and ease of access to it. This enables a much higher proportion of the population to remain in the agricultural sector than would be expected from the rising level of per capita GDP. This situation was reinforced until comparatively recently by the limited development of urban-industrial employment opportunities. This situation is changing rapidly, however, with the elimination of the 'land frontier' (see Chapter 5) and the acceleration of industrial development since the mid-1980s. Thailand is now experiencing an extremely rapid rate of urbanisation (Table 1.12).

In addition to the low level of urbanisation, the urban population is disproportionately located in the capital. Indeed, as is discussed in Chapter 6, Bangkok is perhaps the most primate city in the world. As well as a disproportionate share of the urban population the capital and its immediate environs contain an unusually large share of the Kingdom's service provision, manufacturing output, infrastructure and foreign investment. This imbalance between the capital and the rest of the Kingdom is a long-standing one and has increased over time (see pp. 193–9). Since the early 1980s the situation has been exacerbated by the concentration of accelerated growth and structural change. Thus the Kingdom has come to exhibit a strikingly high level of regional income inequality (see pp. 214–6).

Comparative studies of poverty and income distribution are fraught with difficulties (Booth, 1997). However, there are indications that while the incidence of poverty has declined in Thailand, until the 1990s income inequality continued to widen (pp. 216–23). Indeed, it has been suggested that the Kingdom has developed one of the most unequal income distributions in Pacific Asia (Pasuk Phongpaichit and Baker, 1996: 213; Thailand Development Research Institute, 1995).

In total these distinctive features comprise a series of interlocking imbalances which give the character to an extremely unevenly developed national economy. It is not that any of the elements in Thailand's unevenly developed economy are not common to a large number of countries, but that their intensity and combination produce an extremely unusual situation.

2

INCORPORATION AND INTERNATIONALISATION

1850–1957

Introduction

Thailand represents a situation unique in South East Asia: a state that avoided the process of formal colonisation and retained in consequence many pre-capitalist and non-Western forms of economic, social and political organisation. Thus the Kingdom presents a complex pattern of inter-penetrating Western and non-Western, capitalist and pre-capitalist structures which, despite the extensive socio-economic literature devoted to Thailand, has perhaps not received the attention it deserves.

The present pattern of Thai development cannot be understood in isolation from the way the Kingdom was incorporated into the world economy from the middle of the nineteenth century. Unlike the other pre-colonial states of South East Asia, Thailand survived the colonial period with territory and political sovereignty largely intact. The Kingdom was, however, called upon to make considerable sacrifices to the colonial powers, particularly the French and British. Between 1867 and 1909 large areas of the Kingdom were lost to France and Britain (see Figure 2.1). Serious as the losses were to Thailand, more significant for the long-term development of the Kingdom was the loss, after 1855, of jurisdiction over fiscal and financial affairs to Britain.

Thailand before 1855

Thai speaking peoples migrated slowly from southern China (where there are still Thai speaking groups) absorbing, both culturally and linguistically, such groups as the Mons. The first Thai state was Sukothai, established in 1238, initially subject to the Khmer empire centred in Angkor. During the reign of Ramkamheng (1283–1317) Sukothai established its independence, extending its power south into the lower Chao Phraya valley. It is during the Sukothai period that the Thai script and Theravada Buddhism were adopted. The southerly movement continued and in the mid-fourteenth century a new Thai centre was established at Ayutthaya.

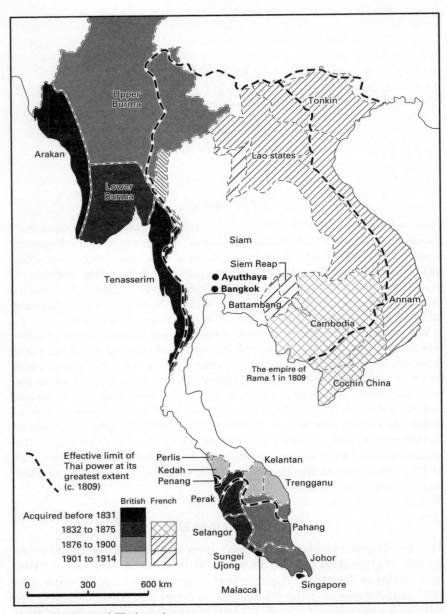

Figure 2.1 Loss of Thai territory.

Source: Fisher, 1964: 150; Wyatt, 1984b: 159.

Ayutthaya's location on the lower Chao Phraya at a point accessible to seagoing shipping enabled it to participate extensively in international trade, including that between Europe and Asia. In addition, the new capital had very direct access to the much more productive alluvial lands of the lower part of the Chao Phraya valley.[1] In 1767 the Thais, weakened by internal rivalries, were unable to defeat a major Burmese invasion and Ayutthaya was sacked and completely destroyed. The subsequent disruption and turmoil lasted until 1767 when the Kingdom was reunified under Taksin who had established his base at Thonburi near the mouth of the Chao Phraya in 1768 (see Hall, 1968: 457–64; Wyatt 1984b: 140). In 1782 the capital was moved to Bangkok on the opposite bank. The second king of this new state, Phra Phutthayotfa (or Ramathabidi, 1782–1809), was the first of the Chakri dynasty (see pp. xv).

Following the recovery from the Burmese invasion, Thailand underwent a remarkable period of economic growth and territorial expansion. These developments were closely related to the expansion of international trade (Hong Lysa, 1984: 38–72; Evers, 1987: 762–3; Sarasin Viraphol, 1977: 177). Bangkok was better suited to development as a trading centre than Ayutthaya. In addition, the serious disruption of the Kingdom following the Burmese invasion appears to have reduced the ability of the new rulers to extract the necessary surplus from domestic production; in consequence trade became the main source of revenue (Hong Lysa, 1984: 48). The significance of trade during the early Bangkok period has led to it being labelled the 'port polity' (Kathirithamby-Wells, 1990; Hong Lysa, 1984: 39–74). These developments have also to be seen in the context of the expansion of trade in the region as a whole from the late eighteenth century onwards.

Production for the international market appears to have expanded rapidly from the late eighteenth century (Hong Lysa, 1984; Nidhi Aeusrivongse, 1982: 75; Evers, 1987: 762–3; Sarasin Viraphol, 1977: 177). Indeed, Nidhi Aeusrivongse (1982: 75) goes as far as to suggest that 'the production of agricultural goods for export can be regarded as the basis of the economy. As such the Thai economy can be defined as an exchange economy long before the Bowring Treaty [1855]'. A very similar argument has been put forward by Evers (1987).

From the late eighteenth century there were sharp increases in the production of a wide range of primary products, as well as refined sugar, metal goods and textiles (Hong Lysa, 1984: 38–74). The comparative technical sophistication of the textile sector has been commented on by a number of writers (see e.g. Lefferts, 1992). However, perhaps the most striking developments took place in the shipbuilding industry. From the latter years of the eighteenth century Western shipbuilding techniques and designs were being incorporated into the indigenous industry. Hybrid junk-brig designs that rivalled the largest ships used by the EIC were emerging from the Bangkok yards which were, by the 1820s the most sophisticated in the region (Sarasin Viraphol, 1977: 180).

In the expansion of production and trade, Chinese immigrants, who had been encouraged almost from the beginning of the Bangkok period (in marked contrast to the Ayutthayan policy), played a major role (see discussion on pp. 65–8). While Chinese merchants and factors came to dominate international trade, until 1851 this took place under the auspices of the royal trade monopolies. This was a far from static system which evolved to accommodate expansion and was not necessarily a barrier to wider participation (Hong Lysa, 1984: 38–74; Evers, 1987: 765). Thus, as well as the Crown, a variety of nobles and officials came to have substantial financial interests in international trade. However, the trading operated to the disadvantage of Western merchants. These were subject to a variety of additional charges, restrictions, delays and import and export duties (which generally ranged from 8 to 15 per cent of value; Hong Lysa, 1984: 57–9). These limitations on Western traders become sources of considerable friction between Thailand and, in particular, Britain.

Details of the scale, regularity, composition and direction of trade before the 1860s are scant. It is probably dangerous to infer too much from the snap-shot provided by Malloch (1852) summarised in Table 2.1. However, the trade in certain items was both long established and regular – notably timber, hides and rice. Trade with China was certainly established by the thirteenth century and included rice from the sixteenth century (Sarasin Viraphol, 1977: 1–2, 72–3; Reid, 1988: 31). Thai textiles were widely traded in the South East Asian region prior to the European incursions (Gittinger and Lefferts, 1992). Cane sugar production developed rapidly during the early nineteenth century and refined sugar became a major export. By the 1850s annual exports exceeded 12,000 tons (Ministry of Commerce, 1922: 6–16). The presence of manufactured goods, textiles, tin and other metal goods, pottery and refined sugar do give credence to the view that Thailand was far from merely a primary producer in this period.

As well as the expansion of the export of domestically produced goods Bangkok developed a substantial regional entrepôt function. A wide range of South East Asian products: rattan, pepper and other spices, tin, birds' nests, betel-nut, coral amber, sandalwood and rice had long been traded with China. Most of this trade was in Chinese hands and by the early 1800s Bangkok had become the principal entrepôt for this trade (Sar Desai, 1977: 26). However, this position was rapidly eroded following the founding of Singapore in 1819. Given the advantages of location, harbour, lack of tariffs and security, by 1834 Singapore had supplanted Bangkok as the collection centre for South East Asian produce destined for China (Wong Lin Ken, 1978).

By the 1830s Bangkok was the centre of one of the largest and most powerful states in South East Asia, exercising sovereignty over an area

Table 2.1 Thai exports, *c.* 1850

Commodity	Value (baht)
Bark	110,000
Bird's nests	172,800
Cardamom	124,000
Cotton (raw)	450,000
Cotton goods	211,500
Fish	213,500
Iron and iron goods	180,000
Oil	101,100
Hides and horns	503,000
Ivory	80,000
Gamboge	31,000
Rice	150,000
Pepper[a]	99,000
Tin and tin goods	253,500
Sticklac	254,000
Sugar	708,000
Lard and fat	146,000
Sapanwood	350,000
Agilawood	100,000
Other items	1,127,200
Total	5,585,000

Source: Ingram (1971: 22), based on Malloch (1852).

Note
a On the basis of the volume of pepper exports and the average price reported by Malloch (1852) the value of pepper exports should have been at least 700,000 baht and the total value of exports at least 6,285,000 baht.

that included much of present-day Cambodia and Laos as well as the northern parts of Malaysia (see Figure 2.1). Overall, Wyatt concluded that the 'Siamese Empire ... was more powerful and extensive than at any previous time. It dwarfed all its mainland neighbours and set an example for them by its ability to act constructively and forcefully in a dangerous world' (1984b: 180).

Thailand's incorporation into the world economy

The 1850s are rightly seen as a watershed in Thai development. It is from this period that the Thai economy became incorporated into the Western dominated world economy and the Kingdom's role as a supplier of raw materials, recipient of cheap manufactured goods and field of activity for foreign, particularly British, capital began to develop.

It is important to appreciate that Thailand was by no means an isolated state in the pre-1850 period. As well as the varied and long-established trading pattern there had been trading and diplomatic contacts with the West since the early sixteenth century. The Portuguese established trading posts soon after their initial contact in 1512; the Dutch from 1602; the East India Company from 1661;[2] and from 1664 French missionary trade and diplomatic links were established. Despite these contacts Thailand remained very much on the periphery of the Western trading rivalries of the sixteenth and seventeenth centuries, and relations with the Western nations were by no means cordial. By the 1650s the Dutch hegemony was impinging on Thailand and demands for a virtual monopoly over parts of the country's overseas trade and various extra-territorial rights could not be resisted. The encouragement of the EIC and the French between 1661 and 1688 was very much an attempt to counteract the influence of the Dutch (Tate, 1971: 501). This intention badly misfired and during the late 1680s France made a serious attempt to establish a major foothold in Thailand. Tate very well summarised the lessons of the first brush with the West:

> Today it seems unlikely that the French of Louis XIV would have been able to maintain their foothold in Thailand during the seventeenth century, even if their plans had been successful, when the difficulty and slowness of communications, the resources and the political circumstances of the time are borne in mind. But the narrowness of their escape was burned into Thai consciousness. Phraya Phet Raja ... [King 1688–1703] ... continued the policy of keeping his relations with European states to an absolute minimum, and the policy was strictly adhered to by those who followed him for another one and a half centuries.
>
> (1971: 503)

The success of the Thai rulers in keeping the Western powers at a distance has to be seen also in terms of Thailand's continued position peripheral to the main interests and rivalries of the Dutch and the British. However, Thailand, particularly in the late eighteenth and early nineteenth centuries, remained open to the import of Western ideas and technology.

From the early 1800s the onset of a period of rapid colonial annexation brought Thailand into close contact with Britain (see Figure 2.1). From the foothold established at Penang in 1786 British influence spread in the Malay Peninsular; Singapore was occupied in 1819 and Malacca acquired in 1824. Following the First Burma War (1824–6) Britain obtained control of Assam, Arakan and Tenasserim, which has a long frontier with Thailand. In the 1850s Britain annexed the whole of 'Lower Burma' and in 1885 'Upper Burma'. During the 1870s the major Malay states were acquired. Meanwhile the French had, in the 1860s, established control over Cambodia and Cochin China, the mainland. As may be seen from

Figure 2.1 Thailand was being rapidly hemmed in by the colonial powers.

During the early nineteenth century agents of the Western powers made a number of largely unsuccessful attempts to establish closer commercial links with Thailand. British interests were reinforced by the desire either to control or to divert Bangkok's entrepôt trade to Singapore (Sar Desai, 1977: 20), the need to secure the border with British Burmese territory (seized in 1826), and clarify the extent of Thai control over the Malay peninsula.

Between 1818 and 1822 Britain made a number of approaches to Thailand but they appear to have been received coolly, if not with some suspicion. The Thais appeared to feel no need for trade with the West and were unwilling to sign treaties because of the possible dangers involved (Dixon and Parnwell, 1991: 213). There was also a reluctance to open their markets to competition from Western traders (Likhit Dhiravegin, 1977: 84).

In 1825 a mission headed by Henry Burney[3] was rather better received. The British acquisition of Malacca, but more especially their aggression in Burma, made the Thais anxious to arrive at an agreement over the Malay states that would not provoke Britain on the Tenasserim border (Tate, 1971: 505). The Burney Treaty of 1826 confirmed Thai control of Kedah and the independence of Perak and Selangor. The treaty's commercial content was limited, taxation of British trade was reduced and simplified, and some of the restrictions on trade relaxed (Dixon and Parnwell, 1991: 213).

Following the signing of the Burney Treaty there was a marked increase in trade, particularly with Singapore and numbers of traders and missionaries appeared, particularly British and Americans. However, from the late 1830s restrictions and taxation on Western trade were increased (Hong Lysa, 1984: 64; Sar Desai, 1977: 84). The motivation for this is unclear, but the loss of trade to Singapore, increased competition from Western goods and traders (all of which reduced state revenue), events in neighbouring countries and China's humiliating defeat in 1839–42 (which also seriously reduced Thai trade), must all be seen as increasing the Thai rulers' distrust of the West. However, a position was emerging where either major concessions or confrontation with the Western powers was unavoidable.

In 1851 the Crown passed to the scholarly Rama 4 (Mongkut) who had educated himself in much that was Western. He appears to have been convinced of the need for reform, both of Buddhism and of the state, and of the danger that Thailand faced from the Western powers. King Mongkut and his supporters seemed to have been convinced that Thailand would benefit from closer relations with the West and set out to foster them (Ingram, 1971: 33). It is important to note that amongst Mongkut's principal supports there were families deeply involved in international trade (Pasuk Phongpaichit and Baker, 1995: 98). Trade restrictions were eased

– most significantly through the abolition of most of the royal monopolies, the reduction of the privileges of the licensed Chinese merchants, the lowering of certain port duties and the legalising of the opium trade[4] (Pasuk Phongpaichit and Baker, 1995: 98). In addition, moves were made to introduce Western ideas, methods and institutions (Dixon and Parnwell, 1991: 214).

In 1855 Sir John Bowring (the Governor of Hong Kong) headed a mission to Bangkok which under the changed conditions and attitude of King Mongkut rapidly achieved all its objectives. While the mission came by invitation, a naval presence and at least veiled threats formed an important background to the negotiations, as did events in Burma (see Cady, 1958: 143, 148).

The treaty contained four major elements (see Ingram, 1971: 34 for a summary and for the complete text Sompop Manarungsan, 1989: 234–44). First, it gave the British rights of residence, trade and extra-territoriality, free trade and import and export duties. Second, it removed all the remaining privileges granted to Chinese merchants and the monopolies over trade and commodities with the exception of opium. Third, a flat 3 per cent duty was agreed on all imports and fixed export duties (averaging 5 per cent) agreed on some 51 items which covered virtually all the major and minor exports of the country. These measures effectively took the control over customs out of Thai hands and thereby a large proportion of the state's finance. Given the state revenue had already been reduced by the abolition of the royal trade monopolies, in respect of finance the treaty represented a major loss of sovereignty for Thailand. Fourth, it was agreed that opium would be exempt from all duties and sold only through the government monopoly, to the mutual benefit of the Thai and British interests. By the end of the nineteenth century sale of opium was the largest source of state income.

Between 1855 and 1870 treaties of a similar form were concluded with most of the major powers. Despite this it was the Bowring Treaty and the British which were to have by far the most serious impact. However, the rate of change remained slow until the 1870s, with a gradual influx of Western interests and control over trade. As Pasuk Phongpaichit and Baker (1985: 99) have argued, the treaties tended to codify and promote transitions in trade policies and organisation already in progress before 1855. Thus in these respects it is perhaps important not to exaggerate the sharpness of the break resulting from the Bowring Treaty.

The provisions of the Bowring Treaty appear to have been steadily implemented, giving the British few grounds for complaint. However, the concessions that Thailand was forced to make to the Western powers did not end with the Bowring and similar treaties.

The first major concession was the loss in 1867, after protracted manoeuvring and negotiations, of the Thai suzerainty over Cambodia. Thailand did manage to reaffirm its control over the east bank Mekong provinces of Battambang, Siem Reap and Sisophon. However, the loss of all these and all the other Thai territory east of the Mekong followed in 1893, 1902 and 1907 (see Figure 2.1). Thailand was incapable of resisting French demands, and the British, wishing to avoid any conflict with the French, advised the Thais to give way. The 1893 treaty was a particularly humiliating one. Thailand not only ceded all the east bank Lao territories but had to pay a 3 million franc indemnity for damage to French ships fired on by the forts at the mouth of the Chao Phraya when they forced their way through to Bangkok to 'lend weight' to the French demands (Wyatt, 1984b: 203).

The period 1893–96 was characterised by mounting Anglo–French tension over their respective South East Asian territories (see Chandran Jeshurun, 1977 for a detailed account). This was resolved in 1896 with Thailand becoming in effect a 'buffer zone' between British and French interests. While the 1896 Anglo–French treaty can be read as guaranteeing the continued independence of the Thai state, it also established Thailand as a field of interest for British capital (Harrison, 1963: 211).

The loss of territory to the French and British was accompanied by pressure to establish clear linear boundaries with neighbouring states. This was to a degree resisted by Thailand, particularly in the North, because of the difficulty and cost of such control and the resulting loss of access to resources. However, against this has to be set the need for the Thai state to establish clear boundaries in order to facilitate control over the outer regions. In the event, the boundaries remained in many areas remarkably open, particularly with respect to the in-migration of people from Burma, China and French territory. However, the colonial annexations and related boundaries have, as elsewhere in the region, created long-term problems of separating previously closely related groups of peoples and isolated minority communities in many border areas.

The response of the Thai rulers to the economic and political pressures of the colonial powers appears to have been a remarkably passive one. After 1855 Thai policy was characterised by deference to the demands made by the British and the French. However, as Tate has stressed, this:

> was also a policy of accommodation to the ineluctable conditions of the times and did not represent a sell out to foreign interests. Thai policy above all was conditioned by the overriding fear of precipitating colonial intervention and control through failure to meet Western commercial needs or to protect Western financial interests already staked in the country.

(1979: 499)

31

It is in this context that the economic, social, judicial and administrative reforms that took place from the late 1880s onwards must be seen (see pp. 37–40). While these reforms were essentially aimed at the creation of an effective and efficient administration of the whole Kingdom, this in turn 'was regarded as essential if Siam were to maintain her political independence' (Brown, 1978: 193).

To survive these losses and a series of diplomatic crises which, to varying degrees, threatened the state's continued independence was, as many writers both Thai and Western have asserted, no mean achievement. However able and, in some ways, lucky the rulers of Thailand were in the nineteenth century, it would be dangerous to adopt a 'great man' explanation for Thailand's survival. The rulers of the Chakri dynasty, notably Chulalongkorn (Rama 5, 1868–1910), were, to a degree, able to play one colonial power against another. However, by the last years of the nineteenth century when annexation by the British was politically feasible, the strength of Imperial economic control over Thailand was such that it was probably unnecessary.

Reform and modernisation

Between 1892 and the 1920s the pace of change was remarkably rapid. Tej Bunnag summarised the changes:

Siam in 1925 was vastly different from the Siam of 1868. From a loose conglomeration of states and provinces without clear boundaries, she became a smaller and more compact state with clearly defined frontiers. During the same period, her people were emancipated from semi-vassalage and slavery and her central government was modernised.

(1977: 1)

A major feature of the reforms was the employment of a large number of foreign technical specialists and advisers. A wide range of nationalities was employed, but in general most government departments drew their foreign employees from only one nation. Thus, the Ministry of Justice employed French lawyers, the Railway Department German engineers, Danes advised the Navy, Americans the Ministry of Foreign Affairs and the British dominated the Ministry of Finance. To a degree, as Brown (1978: 194) has noted, this policy provided for continuity within ministries and departments, but also limited the possibility of any one nation exerting a dominant influence on the national administration.

While the contribution of the foreign experts to the development of infrastructure and administration is unquestionably great, the degree to which advisers in the key ministries influenced major policies and the course of economic development is much less clear. Reeve (1951: 33–5) noted that many of the advisers became *de facto* heads of their respective departments or ministries.

Financial advisers, usually British, were present from 1902 onwards and although their role was reduced after 1926 they were retained until 1950. Most commentators on the part played by the advisers have adhered to Ingram's view that the financial adviser:

> was one of the most powerful figures in the government until about 1930. Without his approval a foreign loan could probably not have been marketed successfully, and the government could scarcely have carried out any financial measures to which he had strong objections.

> (1971: 196)

However, Brown (1975, 1978) concluded from detailed reviews of the material that the role of the financial advisers has been exaggerated. He concluded 'that the British Financial Advisors had relatively little effective influence in Siam in the late nineteenth and early twentieth centuries' (1978: 210). The financial advisers reinforced the very conservative monetary and fiscal policies that Thailand had followed for most of the period since the 1850.[5] It appears that the central aim of monetary policy was to establish very large, highly liquid reserves in order to safeguard the international value and stability of the Thai currency:

> The principle reason for the desire of the government to place the Baht in a sound international position has doubtless been the very real fear of foreign intervention. The experience of other nations in this respect was not lost on Thailand, and ever since 1850 there is ample evidence that the government has deliberately pursued an ultra conservative policy in order to make certain that no nation would ever have an excuse to intervene in Thailand on these grounds. Because it tied up national reserves of liquid funds and necessitated the postponement of productive investments, this policy entailed a certain cost to the nation. On the other hand it may have been the means of preserving the independence of the nation.

> (Ingram, 1971: 170)

In the period 1902 to 1941 the reserves averaged nearly 100 per cent of the currency in circulation and on occasions touched 130 per cent (Ingram, 1971: 172). The apparent contradiction of borrowing £13.6 million between 1905 and 1924 while holding foreign exchange reserves of between £8.6 million and £17.2 million in addition to treasury and other reserves and postponing major developmental projects has been highlighted by Ingram (1971: 173). Indeed, £5.9 million of the loans were used to bolster further reserves, the rest was almost entirely devoted to railway construction (Ingram, 1971: 181). Brown (1978: 211), while agreeing the level of reserves was in retrospect excessive, stressed that if they had been too low foreign intervention might have been precipitated. The degree to which these financial policies delayed or distorted Thai economic development has attracted considerable discussion. Particular attention has focused on the extent to which they were influential in the failure to construct major irrigation works during the early 1900s.

The need for irrigation and flood control in the Central Plain was demonstrated during the early 1900s by material collected by the Dutch engineer van der Heide and the Ministry of Agriculture. Between 1902 and 1909 van der Heide drew up a series of proposals for the development of irrigation (see p. 45 for details) – all were rejected by the Thai government. The role of the financial adviser in these decisions has been much debated, for he was very clearly opposed to expenditure on irrigation:

> It is, in my opinion, impossible to think of embarking ... upon the gigantic irrigation project lately submitted by the Ministry of Agriculture: I do not think that project can be thought of for many years to come. ... Before we can think of a great Irrigation scheme we must provide funds for the strategic railways which are essential if the outlying Provinces are to be properly governed. These railways must be constructed out of borrowed capital and I am altogether adverse to borrowing money for irrigation at present in addition to money for Railway Construction. Such a course would be rash in the extreme.[6]

Further:

> To my mind it has not yet been satisfactorily shown that new irrigation works are required in Siam, except as feeders to the existing system, owing to the wants of sufficiently dense population, and I have consequently always been opposed to the government committing itself to any of Mr. van der Heide's ambitious projects.[7]

However, Brown (1978: 204) stressed that 'the Siamese ministers in the 1900s were essentially united in their decision to reject all proposals for large scale irrigation works' (see also Brown, 1988: 40–51). Pelzer (1945: 60) also suggested that the landlords in the privately constructed Rangsit irrigation scheme exerted political pressure to prevent the development of large-scale public schemes because of a fear of a loss of tenants (see also Feeny, 1982).

In terms of public policy towards irrigation and agricultural development in general before the 1930s, it is worth noting that it was not necessarily favoured by the Crown. In particular King Vajiraveudh (1910–1925) was opposed to investment in agriculture not merely in terms of cost but also of ideology. His view was that the Thai peasantry were free, happy and strangers to poverty (cited in Vella, 1978: 170).

In essence, Brown explains policy in the early 1900s in terms of how far it would contribute to the maintenance of the Kingdom's political independence. Thus priority was given to the maintenance of large currency reserves and:

> to the construction of railways linking Bangkok with the more distant regions of Siam in order to secure the more effective government of the whole Kingdom from the capital. The railways promised a clear strategical and administrative benefit. In comparison, though large-scale irrigation schemes would have undoubtably encouraged the general economic development of the Kingdom, it could not be said that they would have contributed directly to the maintenance of Siamese independence.
>
> (Brown, 1978: 211)

Indeed, Hirsch (1990: 460) has stressed that the railways were seen by the elite as necessary for national security purposes, specifically in establishing control over the outer areas, given fears of European expansion (Feeny, 1982: 80–4) and provincial rebellions (Johnston, 1975: 93). There is some agreement that there is a direct connection between the failure to build irrigation facilities and the construction of railways (see Feeny, 1982; Johnston, 1975: 93; Takaya, 1987: 225).

It is clear that by and large the recommendations of the financial advisers, the recorded views of the Cabinet Ministers and British interests coincided. Clearly the inter-relationships are more complex than the Thai government 'dancing to the financial advisors tune'.

In the final analysis the decision not to build large-scale irrigation schemes during the early 1900s contributed significantly to the development of the extensive, low yielding systems of rice cultivation which came to dominate Thai agriculture (see pp. 43 and 46 and Chapter 5). At the same time the development of railways enabled rapid expansion of rice cultivation to take place in the less productive areas of the North and North East. However, their main role was to enable the full incorporation of the outer regions of the North, North East and South into the Thai state, and facilitate the implementation of the centralised programme of reforms.

The development of communications

As has been noted, one important element in the integration of the outer regions of the Thai state was the development of communications. Only with the establishment of effective transport could capitalist relations of production be established and local autonomy broken down. Only in the Central Plain – where there was a dense network of canals and water-ways – was travel reasonably easy and the transportation of goods economic. Ingram (1971: 116–17) suggested that in the nineteenth century it was probably cheaper to ship a ton of cloth from England than to send it from Chiang Mai to Bangkok. In the 1860s the journey from Bangkok to Chiang Mai took as long as 49 days (Tej Bunnag, 1977: 6). The comple-tion of the rail link to Nakhon Ratchasima in 1901 reduced a journey of some three weeks, by boat and ox-cart, to less than a day (see Warrington-Smyth, 1898, vol. 1: 114–69 for an account of pre-railway communications in the North East).

Railway construction represented the main state expenditure on infra-structure until the 1940s. Between 1900 and 1930 cumulative expenditure on railway construction was £17.63 million compared to £2.85 million on irrigation (Ingram, 1971: 86). Despite the strategic nature of the railway network it proved highly profitable and of major importance in the devel-opment of the economy (Holm, 1977). By 1939 the outer regions were all linked to Bangkok. Some 3,330 kilometres of line had been constructed at a cost of £21.33 million. In terms of the relative length of lines and the connecting of the main areas of the Kingdom to the capital, by the late 1930s Thailand had one of the better railway systems in South East Asia (Table 2.2).

In contrast to the development of railways, road construction received little attention until the 1930s (Sompop Manarungsan, 1989: 181). In 1936 the Kingdom had only 75 miles of first class highway (Tate, 1979: 503). In that year a major road building programme was announced. However, little was achieved by the involvement of Thailand in World War II.

Table 2.2 Per capita provision of communications during the late 1930s

| | *Kilometres per 10,000 people* | | |
	Railways	*Roads*	*Telegraph*
Malaya and North Borneo	3.37	20.74	n.a.
Burma	1.96	16.25	7.98
Indo-China	1.26	15.50	8.69
Netherlands East Indies	1.18	15.50	2.31
Philippines	0.85	15.39	8.55
Thailand	2.36	2.47	5.79

Source: Calculated from Tate (1979: 27).

Road construction in Thailand is very much a story of the post-1950 period. Thus by the late 1930s Thailand had one of the worst road provisions in South East Asia (Table 2.2). This was a major factor in the limited development of centres not directly connected by the railway. Falkus has noted the Kingdom's lack of roads before the 1950s and 'hence the embedded isolation of much of provincial Thailand cannot be emphasised too strongly' (1991: 57).

Other than the poor and highly seasonal road links the most serious communication weakness was the port of Bangkok. A beginning was made on new facilities between 1937 and 1941 but the port was seriously damaged during the war. Despite reconstruction and expansion after the war, major problems remained (World Bank, 1978).

In all the developments of communications prior to the 1950s the emphasis was on linking the outer regions to Bangkok. This radial pattern of communications with little development on inter-provincial connections underpinned the centralisation of administrative controls and decision making that took place from the late nineteenth century onwards. In addition, communications were primarily established to consolidate control and administration rather than to exploit particular resources. Thus in this respect the development of infrastructure in Thailand differed significantly from the South East Asian colonial regimes.

Reform and the incorporation of the outer regions

Prior to the radical reform of the late nineteenth century the provinces generally enjoyed considerable autonomy (Riggs, 1966: 95; Tej Bunnag, 1977; Vella, 1955; Vickery, 1970; Wyatt, 1984a). Governors received no salary from Bangkok, deriving their income from the collection of fees and taxes (London, 1980: 49). In addition, provisional governorships were hereditary, power was derived locally and owed nothing to Bangkok. This situation was reinforced by the very poor and often seasonal nature of communications alluded to earlier. Thus in many ways the outer regions could be regarded as tributary states.

The princes of Chiang Mai, although nominally under Thai control since 1775, maintained almost complete autonomy until the appointment of the first resident commissioner in 1874. This move to increase Bangkok's control over the North resulted at least in part from Western pressure. The teak cutting interests wished to see greater control and security over the North and an end to the clashes between the forces of Chiang Mai and the Shan states (Calavan, 1977: 61). In addition, as has already been noted, the Thai rulers wished to consolidate their control over all the outlying regions because of the threat of losing territory to the British and French.

For similar reasons resident commissioners were established during the late 1870s and 1880s to control the South (Phuket), East (Battambang) and North East (Nongkai, Bassac, Nakhon Ratchasima and Ubon Ratchasima). As Tej Bunnag has noted, the main responsibility for some of the commissioners 'was the military defence of the Kingdom' (1977: 101–4). In 1875 the establishment of a Revenues Office laid the basis for the subsequent reduction of the financial independence of the provinces. Between 1874 and 1890 the resident commissioners gradually reduced the autonomy of their areas and paved the way for the reforms of the 1890s (London, 1980: 70–2).

One of the main goals of the Ministry of the Interior, established in 1892, was the integration of the outer regions and the imposition of a uniform system of administration centring on Bangkok. The reforms progressed gradually for fear of antagonising the provincial nobility into allying themselves with the foreign powers (London, 1980: 74). Additionally, while the British favoured Bangkok increasing control over the North, similar moves in the North East might have offended the French and in the South the British (Riggs, 1966: 247–50). While a skeleton national administration was in place by 1899, it was not effective until 1915 (London, 1980: 73) and the North East was not fully integrated until the 1930s (Keyes, 1967: 17).

The incorporation of the outer regions was greatly complicated by their ethnic, cultural and linguistic distinctiveness as well as by the desire of their ruling elites to maintain power and political autonomy. The formation of a unified Thai state involved the subordination of these regions to the centre. Between 1899 and 1902 new regulations were imposed on the provinces which would increase the Ministry of the Interior's 'control over every level and sphere of administration' (Tej Bunnag, 1977: 263). In 1901–2 Bangkok faced large-scale opposition to increased control and financial demands. The main focus of resistance was in the North East – the 'revolt of the Holy Men' – and in the North the 'Shan Revolt'. In 1895 the imposition of a poll tax had resulted in a small-scale revolt in the North Eastern province of Khon Kaen (Chatthip Nartsupha and Suthy Prasartset, 1981: 115–16). Bangkok responded to the Northern and North Eastern risings with rapid military action, killing many hundreds and imprisoning and executing others (Tej Bunnag, 1977: 276). Much attention has been focused on the violence of the events in the North and North East but considerable passive resistance to the demands of the state took place in all regions (Chatthip Nartsupha and Suthy Prasartset, 1981: 117; Tej Bunnag, 1977: 275). Limited concessions were made after 1902 and the Ministry of the Interior appears to have moved more gently after the revolts but there was no change in the central aim of fully integrating the Kingdom (London, 1980: 85–6, citing various authors). Indeed, increasing resistance to the centre was a significant factor in the rapid increase in military expenditure and, from 1905, the creation of a standing army (Pasuk Phongpaichit and Baker, 1995: 230).

The North East was the most remote and poorly integrated of the outer regions and was regarded long after 1900 as a 'fringe area almost beyond the pale' (Cripps, 1965: 1–4). Cultural, ethnic and linguistic separateness was reinforced by the poor environment. In 1912 Grahame provided a description of the North East which reflected the view from Bangkok:

A population of some million and a quarter Laos, Siamese and Kambodians, that is about 20 people to the square mile, inhabits this inhospitable land, wresting from the reluctant soil, crops barely sufficient to maintain an existence which, passed amidst damp and mud for one half of the year and in dry, hot dust-laden atmosphere for the other, is one of the most miserable imaginable, more especially since the whole neighbourhood is peculiarly liable to the visitations of epidemics of diseases affecting both men and cattle.

(1924, vol. 2: 9)

From the later part of the nineteenth century the North East began to experience a subordination of regional interests, culture and language to Bangkok (Keyes, 1967: 29–30). A clear antipathy developed between the North Eastern and Central Thais. The North East was made to feel inferior and the region became a focus for opposition to Bangkok (Keyes, 1967: 30–1).

While most attention has focused on the 'internal-colonisation' of Bangkok over the North East – a reflection perhaps of the process's greater intensity in the region – all the outer regions had a similar experience (see Grabowsky, 1995; London, 1980: 95–112).

The establishment of control over the outer regions was complicated by the gathering pace of forest clearance (see Chapter 5) and settlement formation. Attempts to establish the rule of Bangkok over both new and established settlements centred on three main areas. First, the establishment of a system of village headmen (*pu yai ban*) and land registers to facilitate administrative control and tax collection. Second, the provision of a mass education system designed to impose the Thai language, identity and culture on the complex of cultures, languages and loyalties that characterised so much of the North, North East and South. Third, the government established control over the Buddhist Sanha in order to minimise the possibilities of monks serving as foci of opposition (Pasuk Pongpaichit and Baker, 1995: 71).[8]

The imposition of uniform village-based administration did not always closely correspond with the realities of the settlement structure. For many parts of the Kingdom it seems possible that villages and related communal organisations are not the long-established features that has been generally assumed. Rather, in many instances villages as an organisational unit were a creation of the 1890s (see Kemp, 1991; Rigg, 1994).

The incorporation of the outer regions from the 1890s onwards has left a legacy of 'negative attitudes to the Thai state' (London, 1980: 96; Moerman, 1968: 405; Parnwell and Rigg, 1996; Van Roy, 1971: 29). A widely held view is that the centre subjected the outer regions, exploited them and constrained their economic development. They were, in summary, forcibly integrated into the Thai state on markedly disadvantageous terms. The legacy of the process remains as the Thai 'regional problem' (see Chapters 3 and 7), the political and economic domination of Bangkok (see Chapter 6), and the role of regional and ethnic identity as foci of opposition – key elements in the establishment of the Kingdom's remarkable uneven pattern of development. However, it could be argued that the process was perhaps a necessary one if the Thai state w as to survive the colonial period with territory and sovereignty largely intact.

Economic change and the establishment of the export economy

From the 1850s there was a slow spreading of capitalist relations of production in Thailand as the Kingdom emerged as a supplier of a limited range of primary products for the world market. By the third quarter of the nineteenth century the diverse, if irregular, export economy described previously (Table 2.1) was replaced by a rapidly expanding trade in rice, tin and teak. The importance of manufacturing – particularly sugar refining, textiles and metals – declined sharply. To some extent domestic production of manufactured goods was displaced by cheaper, principally British supplied imports (Brown, 1988: 2–3; Chatthip Nartsupha and Suthy Prasartset, 1981: 2–5; Resnik, 1970; Suehiro, 1989: 33–8). There was in particular an expansion in the import of textiles (Ingram, 1971: 25–6). However, it should be stressed that the domestic manufacturing sector, particularly textiles, was not eliminated from the domestic market, particularly in provincial areas (Ingram, 1971: 113–19; Pasuk Phongpaichit and Baker, 1995: 102). Shipbuilding, the most highly developed industry in terms of technology, finance and organisation, contracted sharply after 1855 (Sarasin Viraphol, 1977: 190). More surprising was the contraction of the sugar industry, particularly in the light of Bowring's prediction (1857, vol. 1: 203–4) that it would become the principal export (see pp. 54–5).

As may be seen from Table 2.3 primary exports came to dominate the export trade in a way they had not done before 1855. By the end of the nineteenth century 85–90 per cent of export earnings consisted of tin, teak and rice. From the early 1900s rubber also became a significant export. While the share of rice fell as the other commodities expanded,

Table 2.3 The major exports, 1867–1969

	Rice	*Tin*	*Teak*	*Rubber*	*Total*
	Percentage of the total value of exports				
1867	41.1	15.6	–	–	56.7
1890	69.7	11.1	5.5	–	86.4
1903	71.3	6.4	10.4	–	88.2
1906	69.1	11.0	11.2	–	91.3
1909–10	77.6	7.8	6.4	–	91.9
1915–16	70.1	15.9	3.9	–	89.9
1920–24	68.2	8.6	4.5	0.8	82.1
1925–29	68.9	9.0	3.7	2.3	83.9
1930–34	65.4	13.8	3.9	2.0	85.1
1935–39	53.5	18.6	4.2	12.9	89.2
1940–45	60.5	11.6	1.6	12.1	85.9
1947–49	49.5	7.7	4.1	9.6	70.9
1950–54	54.2	5.6	4.4	21.0	85.2
1955–59	44.6	6.1	3.7	23.2	77.6
1960–64	34.2	7.0	2.2	22.0	65.4
1965–69	28.6	9.9	0.9	14.2	53.6

Source: Ingram (1971: 94, 313).

it generally accounted for over 50 per cent of the value of exports until the early 1950s. The four commodities of rice, tin, teak and rubber accounted for between 80 and 90 per cent of the export earnings in the period 1890–1953 (Table 2.3).

The growth of rice production and exports

The production of rice was stimulated by the opening of Thailand to international trade and the rapidly expanding global and regional demand for the crop. In addition, there was official encouragement for the Thai population to engage in, and produce for, the export market (Johnston, 1975: 21–2). The introduction of the tax concessions for newly cleared lands encouraged the expansion of the cultivated area, initially in the Central Plain, but later in the 'outer regions' of the North and North East (Ingram, 1971: 76). These developments have to be seen against the background of the continuing reforms, outlined previously, which laid the groundwork for the establishment of capitalist relations of production. The abolition of corvée labour, debt-bondage and slavery was accompanied by the development of wage labour and the emergence of what was effectively private property rights. These changes opened the way for farmers to produce for a growing overseas market and to purchase cheap imported goods, notably textiles. In the process a new agrarian society was created, dominated by the individual peasant cultivator. The expansion of the rice sector was

41

further supported by state expenditure: initially by the construction of canals in the Chao Phraya Delta during the nineteenth century, and after 1900 the construction of railways and, to a limited extent, the development of small-scale irrigation and drainage works. In addition, the expansion of the rice sector was both driven and supported by the growth of the population.

Evidence for the size and distribution of the population before the first census in 1911 is sparse and far from reliable. Estimates for the 1800–20 period vary from 1 to 3 million (Skinner, 1957: 79; Sternstein, 1993: 18). A detailed examination of the evidence by Sternstein (1965: 1984) suggests very gradual growth from the 1780s to reach a population a little short of 5 million by the middle of the nineteenth century. Growth began to accelerate from the 1870s and, more significantly, from the 1880s to reach the 1911 census figure of 8.27 million. However, as Sternstein (1984) has stressed, evidence in the shape of contemporary estimates and data are of very uncertain accuracy (see also Caldwell, 1967; Sompop Manarungsan, 1989: 31–9; Sternstein, 1965).

While it is tempting to argue that peace and stability encouraged population growth (Reid, 1988: 18; Wyatt, 1984b: 99, 136–7) and the opening of new opportunities may have encouraged earlier marriages and house-hold formation, there is little hard evidence.[9] Indeed, Sternstein (1984: 54) concluded that there is no evidence for a divergence in the CBR and CDR that would account for an acceleration of population much before 1900. Thus he explains the earlier expansion very largely in terms of in-migration, particularly of Chinese. During the nineteenth century some half million Chinese entered the Kingdom (see pp. 65–8). Given the very sharp expansion of this immigration during the 1880s and its volume in relation to the total population it is tempting to accept migration as the principal factor behind the population growth of the late nineteenth and early twentieth centuries. Indeed, it has been suggested that during the late nineteenth and early twentieth centuries Chinese immigration accounted for as much as half of Thailand's net population increase (Falkus, 1991: 62). In the early part of the nineteenth century the Chinese inflow was supplemented by migration from adjacent areas. Some of the recorded spontaneous movements were large, for example in 1815 c. 30,000 Mons (from present-day Myanmar) requested permission to settle (cited Pasuk Phongpaichit and Baker, 1995: 13). Perhaps more significant were the large number of captives resulting from the military campaigns that took place in the period from the 1770s to the 1840s. During these campaigns, large numbers of Laos, Malays, Khymers and Vietnamese were captured and used as labour for construction projects and/or settled in newly opened up agricultural areas. In 1830, for example, some 30,000 Laos were forcibly resettled in the North East (Keyes, 1967: 11). Movement of peoples on this scale must have played a significant role in the growth of population and the expansion of the settlement frontier.

Whatever the estimates for the total population for early nineteenth-century Thailand, the Kingdom was, like most of mainland South East Asia, very sparsely peopled. During this period policies towards the control of labour suggest concern over shortages in the face of comparatively abundant land and ease of access to it (Hong Lysa, 1984: 9). The population was, however, heavily concentrated in a small number of areas. The most significant of these were in the Chao Phraya Delta, the valleys and basins of the North, the coastal fringes of the Gulf of Thailand and in the North East along the lines of the Mekong and Mun-Chi rivers. By far the most important core was in the Chao Phraya Delta where settlement was concentrated around Bangkok and Ayutthaya. Sternstein (1993: 22–3) suggests that in the early nineteenth century a narrow corridor extending from Chai Nat to the coast contained three-quarters of the population of the Delta and half of that of the Kingdom. It was from these cores, particularly that of the Central Plain, that the population gradually spread out seeking new economic horizons.

In response to increased domestic and foreign demand, rice production grew rapidly after 1855. The area planted almost doubled the estimated 0.93 million hectares of 1850 (estimate by Ingram, 1971: 44), to 1.53 million in the early 1900s. However, expansion was much faster during the next 50 years, reaching 3.35 million hectares by 1930 and 5.77 million by 1950 (Figure 2.2 and see Chapter 5 further discussion).

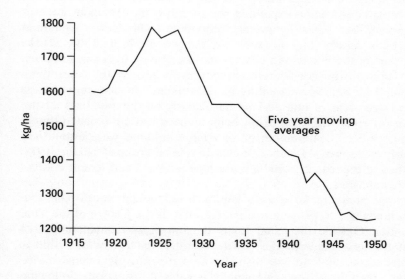

Figure 2.2 Rice yields, 1917–50.
Source: MAC.

Between 1850 and 1900 the principal expansion in rice area took place in the Central Plain. In 1905–6 van der Heide (1906: 90) calculated that the Central Plain accounted for 98 per cent of exports. As well as its proximity to Bangkok, the Central Plain possessed a network of watercourses and canals which provided a cheap means of transport for bulk commodities. A variety of observers (Grahame, 1912; van der Heide, 1906; Warrington-Smyth, 1898) commented on the commercial cultivation of the Central Plain and the contrasting subsistence agriculture of the North and North East. Until the construction of the railways only small quantities of rice reached Bangkok from the North and the more accessible parts of the North East by oxcart and river.

The lands of the Chao Phraya delta were in general far from an easy environment for rice cultivation. Over large areas deep seasonal flooding made cultivation and settlement virtually impossible, while elsewhere the conditions largely precluded all but the most extensive methods of cultivation. During the dry season months there were serious shortages of water over wide areas which further discouraged settlement. Thus the progress and intensification of cultivation necessitated the development of water control. Some element of this was provided by the construction of canals from the early part of the Bangkok period (Small, 1973; Tanabe, 1977). These canals played a significant role in the spread of cultivation of rice and, until the 1870s, sugar, by providing transport, elements of drainage during the wet season, water during the dry season and settlement sites along their embankments. In the second half of the nineteenth century canal construction expanded considerably, mostly under government auspices but some by private individuals who were given land concessions in return (Ingram, 1971: 80; Tanabe, 1977: 30, 1994: 52). In the later part of the nineteenth century the investment in canals in return for land grants was considered an extremely profitable undertaking (Johnston, 1975: 82). Some wealthy individuals and groups were able to purchase large areas of unused land particularly on the east bank of the Chao Phraya river, the cultivation being carried out by tenant farmers (Johnston, 1975: 82). A number of very large holdings were established particularly by the royal family and closely related groups (Tanabe, 1978: 75–8). Thus in the 'canal tracts' a pattern of landlord and tenant cultivation was established.

The initial phase of large-scale landlord and tenant development in the delta lands was to prove a major exception in the history of the Thai land frontier. Outside the canal tracts the only major development of large estates took place in the North. Here in the basins and valleys there were areas of long established and comparatively intensive rice cultivation often involving communally organised irrigation. Following the construction of the railway links with the North (the line reached Uttaradit in 1909 and Chiang Mai in 1921) and the spread of commercial rice cultivation, members of the Northern aristocracy and merchants began to grab rice land, often forcibly evicting established farmers and establishing ownership titles (Pasuk Phongpaichit and Baker, 1995: 26). These activities appear to have been very largely ignored by Bangkok in the light of the need to establish full control over the North. On a very much smaller scale some estates were also established in the coastal basins of the South (Pasuk Phongpaichit and Baker, 1995: 26). Elsewhere the occasional limited estate was established by merchants and there were instances of land grabbing in many frontier areas (see Chapter 5). However, with these exceptions, as cultivation expanded through the delta lands and beyond, land colonisation became almost exclusively the province of the small-scale cultivator.

In general the canal development of the nineteenth century was not primarily aimed at water distribution; however, in 1889 a scheme was initiated that was more clearly focused on irrigation. The Siam Canals Land and Irrigation Company was given a concession to develop 150,000 hectares of flat swampy land at Rangsit, north east of Bangkok.[10] Some 100,000 people had acquired land titles by 1910 but the scheme was by no means an unqualified success. There was no provision to store or control the flow of water – merely to distribute what was there. Thus the annual water supply for much of the land remained uncertain and canals were subject to heavy silting and flood damage. In the event only 60,000 hectares was ever successfully cropped.

The problems associated with the Rangsit scheme led directly to the establishment in 1899 of the Canals Department of the Ministry of Agriculture (later the Department of Irrigation) and the appointment of J. M. van der Heide as adviser to the government. He conducted a detailed survey of the existing canal system, water supply, economy and benefits of irrigation, published in 1903. It represented what Ingram (1971: 82) has described as 'a brilliant statement of the irrigation needs of Thailand and the solutions to them'. The proposal centred on a barrage across the Chao Phraya at Chai Nat; the cost was estimated at £2.5 million over 12 years. As has already been discussed this scheme was rejected as was a reduced scheme costed at £1.5 million. Van der Heide, Director of the Department until 1909, proposed a series of small-scale projects all of which were rejected. In 1909 van der Heide resigned and in 1912 the Department of Irrigation was abolished.

The series of poor harvests resulting from flood and drought in the 1905–1912 period reinforced the argument for large-scale water control in the Central Plain. In 1913 Sir Thomas Ward, a British irrigation expert, was brought in to draw up a plan and in 1916 the Department of Irrigation was recreated. Starting with the South Prasak Canal in the Rangsit area, completed in 1925, a number of projects were developed during the 1920s and 1930s, almost all located in the Central Plain. However, important as these schemes were locally, overall by 1950 there had been very limited development of water control facilities (see Chapter 5 for a discussion of the development of irrigation).

From the early 1900s onwards the development of rail links to the North and North East and the relative shortage of suitable land in the Central Plain shifted growth to these outer areas. The extension of the railway network into these outer regions was marked by the rapid development of commercial cultivation and the establishment of rice milling and storage facilities at key centres. For example in the North East at Nakhon Ratchasima from 1900, Khon Kaen from 1933 and Ubon Ratchathani from 1928. As a result of these developments the Central Plain's share of the total area planted to rice fell from some 75 per cent in 1905 to 50 per cent in 1950. During this period the average annual rate of growth of rice area was 3.4 per cent in the Central Plain and 15.2 per cent in the rest of the Kingdom. By 1935 Northern and North Eastern regions were supplying nearly 25 per cent of exports (calculated from Ingram, 1971: 47).

The expansion of rice production, particularly in the North Eastern region, brought increasingly less fertile and less reliable land into cultivation. As a result there was a fall in average yields (Figure 2.2; see also Chapter 5), and even in the Central Plain yields fell by 17.8 per cent in the period 1920–1941 (Feeny, 1982: 45). In the absence of the development of effective large-scale water control in the most favoured areas of the Central Plain the region continued to have a high level of crop loss. Large areas remained under sown rice because the risk of crop damage was too great to warrant transplanting.[11] Thus growth of rice production was achieved by expansion of the cultivated area with methods, particularly in the North East, becoming more extensive. Intensification of production was not a viable option for Thai farmers in this period (see Chapter 5 for a detailed discussion).

Despite the fall in average yields and the increase in the population, the growth in production, through the expansion of the area cultivated, was sufficient to support the continued increase in the volume of exports (Figures 2.3 and 2.4). On the basis of Sompop Manarungsan's data (1989: 209–11) it appears that per capita rice production increased from 291kg in 1860 to 342kg in 1900 and 389kg in 1950. In addition, the per capita export of rice increased from 66kg in 1900 to 97kg in 1950. While the accuracy of the 1860 data on population and rice production may be questioned, the later figures indicate the long-term strength of the Thai rice sector, which enabled substantial and sustained expansion with little investment or technical change.

While rice production remained the preserve of small-scale Thai farmers, the marketing, finance, milling and export of the crop was dominated by the Chinese. The first steam rice mill, an American enterprise, was opened in Bangkok in 1858 and this was followed by the construction of five

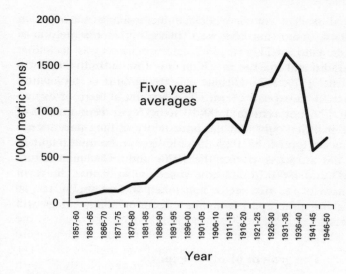

Figure 2.3 Rice exports, 1857–1950.
Source: Sompop Manarungsan 1989:49.

further foreign owned mills and a number of Western concerns entered
the rice trade. Thus by 1888 an estimated 68 per cent of exports was controlled by foreign firms (Pasuk Phongpaichit and Baker, 1995: 99). However, provincial milling and the entire domestic trade remained very firmly
under Chinese control. The low cost of rice mills resulted in little of the
advantage that European concerns enjoyed over Chinese undertakings in
more capital-intensive activities, such as tin dredging and teak logging (see
pp. 49–51). This, in conjunction with the Chinese control of the domestic supply of rice to the mills resulted in a steady erosion of the Western position. By 1898 Chinese concerns controlled 38 out of Bangkok's
42 major mills and handled 90 per cent of exports.[12] By 1920 there was
only one Western company left in the rice trade (Suehiro, 1989: 51).

The expansion of rice exports was at its most rapid in the period 1880 to
1900 when they increased fourfold (Figure 2.3). Between 1905 and 1912 a
series of poor harvests, increased levels of tax, falling yields and possibly
labour shortages adversely affected the most commercialised areas.[13] It was
reported that many tenant farmers abandoned land particularly in the newly
colonised areas of the east bank of the Chao Phraya river (Johnston, 1975:
312). After 1912 growth of exports was very much slower and in 1919 a major
crop failure reduced the level of exports in 1920 and 1921. The poor harvests
of 1905–12 and 1919 emphasised the unreliability of production under
predominantly rain-fed conditions, and reflected the way in which the rapid
expansion of production had brought less reliable land into cultivation.

The international market for rice became increasingly uncertain in the 1920s and 1930s. Asian markets were becoming increasingly self-sufficient and the demand for Thai rice in Western markets was declining. In addition, the traditional market in China was lost to Indo-China by the early 1930s (Tate, 1979: 513). Despite this the volume of production and exports continued to expand (Figure 2.3) but rice's share of export earnings fell from 77.6 per cent in 1909–10 to 53.5 per cent in 1935–9 (Table 2.3). There is little doubt that the uncertainty of the international rice market coming on top of the 1905–12 recession made investment in the sector much less attractive during the 1920s and 1930s than it had been between 1880 and 1900. In addition, it seems likely that the form that the development of the rice sector had taken was beginning to put pressure on the sector quite apart from the effects of falling prices and contracting markets.

The growth of other exports

The other staple exports during the hundred years following the signing of the Bowring Treaty, tin, teak and rubber, contributed between 14 and 38 per cent of export earnings (Table 2.3). Unlike rice the production of these commodities was localised – tin and rubber in the South and teak in the North. More significantly, their production involved the creation of a regular non-agricultural based labour force. For tin and teak, and to a lesser extent rubber, production was dependent on foreign labour, capital and enterprise (Ingram, 1971: 93). The development of these commodities represented a very direct response to the international market, for tin and rubber there was little domestic demand.

The forests of Northern Thailand had long been a source of teak for domestic consumption. Rapid expansion of production took place from the 1880s in response to international demand (Figure 2.5). Until this period international demand and Western timber interests focused attention on Burma. Rising demand, exhaustion of accessible reserves, increases in the levels of royalties payable to the government of India on teak cut in Upper Burma, the disruption accompanying the Third Burmese War of 1885, and treaty revisions in 1884 which increased the freedom of British subjects to operate in Northern Thailand resulted in Western firms becoming interested in Thai teak (Suehiro, 1989: 57–8). Overall, the consolidation of Thai control over the North facilitated the penetration of the Western firms. Indeed, as was noted previously, the full incorporation of the North was needed to oversee the relations between the Western forestry interests and the local communities and aristocracy.

Until the entrance of Western firms the exploitation of the teak reserves was largely in the hands of Chinese and Burmese (Ingram, 1971: 105). During the 1860s and 1870s considerable quantities of teak were cut by

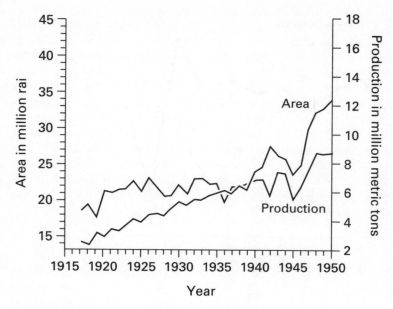

Figure 2.4 Rice area and production, 1917–50
Source: MAC

Burmese foresters and rafted down the Salween to Moulmein (Falkus, 1989: 133). However, between 1888 and the early 1900s Western timber firms effectively took over the industry (Suehiro, 1989: 57–63). By 1902 80 per cent of the capital was British (Tate, 1979: 519) and four or five British firms were cutting 60–70 per cent of the teak (Falkus, 1989: 143; Suehiro, 1989: 57–63). This situation persisted until the Second World War. In 1938 88 per cent of the teak forest was worked by Western firms, six of which dominated production (Ingram, 1971: 107; Sompop Manarungsan 1989: 127). The Western firms' advantage lay in their ability to raise the large amounts of capital needed for large-scale logging operations. Thus from the late nineteenth century the organisation and ownership of the teak industry was remarkably similar to that in colonial Burma (Lindblad, 1995: 5).

While European firms displaced the Chinese and Burmese cutting operations and dominated the export trade, Chinese interests remained important in the saw milling sector. In 1940 two of the seven large modern saw mills were Chinese owned and virtually all the labour in the sector was Chinese (Ingram, 1971: 107).

The rapid expansion of teak production from the 1880s took place without any controls over the size of trees to be cut or provision for

49

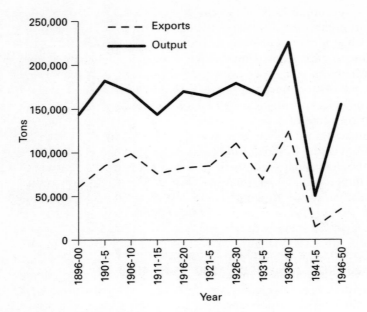

Figure 2.5 Teak production and export.
Source: Tate, 1979: 576–7.

replanting. Western teak firms appealed to the Thai government to regulate the industry (Tate, 1979: 520). In 1895 the Royal Forestry Department (RFD) was established. The RFD came to control the granting of concessions, introduced conservation measures and a stricter system of royalty collection. These measures necessitated a large capital outlay by firms, thus eliminating the small cutter and paving the way for dominance of the industry by a small number of Western firms (see Suehiro, 1989: 61), whose interests were probably furthered by the RFD being run by British officials from 1901 until 1930 (Pasuk Phongpaichit and Baker, 1995: 100).

The RFD conservation and replanting schemes had overall only a limited impact. National reserves were steadily depleted. Increasingly large areas were earmarked as timber reserves and felling regulations were made more stringent. These measures were in practice largely ineffective. The RFD was under-staffed and under-financed. Lack of control and limited replanting in the 1930s already heralded a decline in the quality of teak[14] and its eventual elimination as an export commodity.

The main export market for teak until the early 1900s was Europe. This market subsequently declined sharply, a reflection of the shortage of high quality teak, higher freight charges for Thai as against Burmese timber, and, from the 1920s, the imposition of increased import tariffs by the UK[15] (Sompop Manarungsan 1989: 137). In 1919 20 per cent still went to Europe and the USA while 60 per cent went to India and Ceylon – most of the remainder going to Japan and China. Like rice, the Thai teak market became increasingly an Asian one with increasing trade with Japan and China. By the mid-1930s almost half the teak exports were to the Far East.

Tin production and exporting was well established by the 1850s, although information on the scale of activity is scant. Chinese miners using simple hydraulic techniques were widely established in the Malay Peninsular by the late eighteenth century (Wong Lin Ken, 1965: 3; Yip Yat Hoong, 1969: 56). Tin from the Peninsular features in Thai records from the fourteenth century and Phuket Island had emerged as a major production centre several centuries before the Bowring Treaty (Harrison, 1963: 10; Ingram, 1971: 98; Reid, 1988: 115).

Production expanded steadily during the late nineteenth century, accelerating markedly after 1900 (Figure 2.6). Until the early 1900s Thai tin production remained almost entirely in Chinese hands (Carter, 1904: 242; Dixon, 1991a: 98). Operations remained small in scale, utilising simple hydraulic techniques; ore was crudely smelted using charcoal. Despite the importance of tin to Thai export earnings (see Table 2.3), the industry remained very backward compared to the operations in the neighbouring

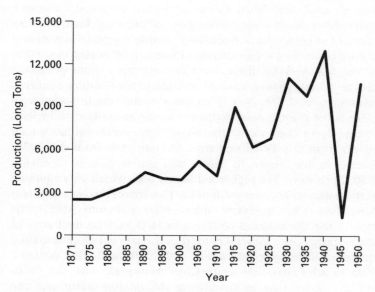

Figure 2.6 Production of tin metal, 1871–1950.
Source: Tate, 1979: 576–7.

Malay states. Unlike the Malayan industry where the British closely regulated the industry, the Thai mining operations took place in a region remote from close state control and subject to a far from rigorous system of licensing and levying of royalties. By the early 1900s increasing amounts of Thai tin ore were being exported to Malaya for smelting (Ingram, 1971: 99). From 1907, under the stimulus of high tin prices and the exhaustion of the richest and most easily worked Malayan reserves, Western mining interests began to take a major interest in Thai tin. The Western share of production rose from 10 per cent in 1907, to 50 per cent in 1929 and 65 per cent in 1936 (Tate, 1979: 217). As in Malaya the large-scale Western dredging operations broke the Chinese tin monopoly. The dredged proportion of production increased from 7 per cent in 1906–10, to 35.6 per cent in 1916–20, and 65.0 per cent in 1936–40 (Sompop Manarungsan, 1989: 152). Similarly the local Chinese smelting was almost completely eliminated by the early 1920s. By 1930 all tin exports were of ore – 90 per cent of which went to the Straits Settlements for smelting (Tate, 1979: 517). Thus the Thai mining sector became in effect an extension of British activity in the Malay states.

The European advantage, as in teak logging, lay in the ability to raise the large amounts of capital necessary for dredging operation. However, the Chinese were far from eliminated from the tin industry for the labour force remained almost entirely Chinese and small-scale hydraulic operations continued. The Chinese were able to recruit large amounts of labour much more easily than Western concerns and operate at lower cost levels.[16] In part this reflected their operation of ancillary businesses to meet the needs of the labour force (including gambling, opium and money lending) and the existence of secret societies (Sompop Manarungsan, 1989: 145). Unlike the Malay states these were not attempts to suppress the secret societies in the interests of labour recruitment for Western concerns (Sompop Manarungsan, 1989: 146). The lower costs, simple technology and limited capital of the Chinese hydraulic sector enabled it to expand and contract rapidly in the face of the volatile price movements which characterised tin from the 1920s onwards. Despite this, from the 1920s onwards Chinese capital began to move into the large-scale dredging sector. In 1950 there were 324 registered mines – of which 25 employed dredges. Of the latter three were Chinese–Thai concerns and the rest British or Australian (Department of Mines, *Mining Statistics*, 1951: 17).

The creation of the Department of Mines in 1891 had the dual aims of increasing state control over mineral resources as well as accommodating Western enterprises. Mining legislation in 1892, 1901 and 1919 set up a modern system of administrating concessions. However, until the 1930s the state took no active part in developing the mining sector and the development of the industry was seriously hampered by the lack of communications (Sompop Manarungsan, 1989: 147). This contrasted strongly with the Malay states where the colonial administration constructed a network of railways and small port facilities which played a major role in the development of the West Coast mining (and later plantation) complex. The extension of the railway down the east of the peninsular during the 1920s provided some improvement, but the main deposits and the centres of the industry were on the west coast, where even roads were scarce (Brown, 1988: 95).

In contrast to tin and teak, Western capital and enterprise played a very limited role in the later development of rubber production. This reflected restrictions on foreign ownership of land (Sompop Manarungsan, 1989: 115) and the more attractive conditions for production in the Malay states. Thus, only three Western owned estates were ever established in Thailand (Suehiro, 1989: 102). Unlike Malayan rubber production, in Thailand it was almost entirely in the hands of small holders.[17] While these were Thai and Malay as well as Chinese growers the control of the sector was very firmly in Chinese hands. The Chinese growers tended to have larger holdings[18] and the collection, processing and export sectors were almost exclusively Chinese spheres of activity.

Rubber was introduced into Southern Thailand by Chinese immigrants from the Malay States immediately before and during the 1914–18 War, a decade after developments in the Malay States and Dutch East Indies. As may be seen from Table 2.4, the sector only began to expand rapidly from the mid-1920s. This expansion was stimulated by high prices and the opening of the southern railway link with its branches to Nakhon Sri Thammasat, Pattani and Padang Besar. Like tin, the rubber sector was closely linked to the economy of Malaysia. Until 1940 almost the entire crop was exported to Malaya for further processing and/or re-export. Compared to the Malayan industry the Thai rubber sector was backward with lower yields and poorer quality latex. Indeed, much of the rubber

Table 2.4 Rubber production and area

	Planted area (ha)	Production (tons)
1910	0.4	13
1915–16	4.0	85
1920–1	11.2	44
1925–6	20.0	3218
1930–1	60.0	4749
1935–6	146.4	31199
1940	273.0	44551
1945	294.4	2000
1950	315.8	109144

Source: Sompop Manarungsan (1989: 109, 113).

production was a cash adjunct to wet rice cultivation rather than a highly specialised cash crop (see Chapter 5 for a discussion of the post-war expansion of rubber). However, by the late 1930s rubber was rivalling tin as an export earner. Unlike tin, the rubber sector was considerably stimulated by the construction of the southern railway line.

From the late nineteenth century until the mid-1950s the four staple products had no serious rivals as earners of export income. The penetration of the international market displaced the wide range of goods for which Thailand was known (Table 2.1). They continued either as minor export items or became confined to the domestic trade. In the long run, an exception to this was sugar.

Cane sugar, as against the long established palmyra and coconut product, was probably introduced into Thailand by Chinese immigrants during the early 1800s. The crop spread rapidly in provinces within easy reach of Bangkok, notably Chon Buri, Chachoengso and Nakhon Phathom. By the 1850s the crop probably accounted for 10 to 15 per cent of export earnings (Malloch, 1852).[19] As was to be the case subsequently with teak and tin, this area of Chinese enterprise attracted Western interest. European and American sugar mills began to appear in the 1860s. The largest foreign operation was the British Indochinese Sugar Company which obtained a lease on 1260 hectares of land and opened a large steam mill in 1870 (Ingram, 1971: 124).

The rapid fall of world sugar prices during the 1870s and 1880s brought an equally rapid decline in the Thai industry, exports ceasing in 1889.[20] Under the conditions of the Bowring Treaty import duties were limited to 3 per cent and thus Thailand was unable to protect its sugar industry from the influx of cheap sugar, particularly from Java. Thus the domestic as well as the export market collapsed and most sugar land was replanted to rice. Sugar as a domestic product recovered slowly from the 1920s, particularly after the treaty revisions of 1927 which allowed increases in tariff protection. The re-establishment of sugar in the domestic market during the 1940s and 1950s took place behind tariffs as high as 45 per cent, and, for a period after 1952, a ban on imports (see Chapter 5).

The sugar industry illustrates the very exposed position that the Thai economy occupied between 1855 and 1927. In the absence of the ability to increase tariffs or significantly raise government revenue to subsidise domestic activities, an economy outside the measure of protection that imperial economic structures afforded was vulnerable to the full force of both short- and long-term fluctuations in the international economy.

It is apparent that in both the exploitation and marketing of staple commodities Thailand operated at the margin. In effect the Thai economy acted as an overspill for Western, particularly British, South East Asian economic activity. The tin and rubber producing areas of the South were extensions of the British dominated primary producing economies of the Malay States. Teak production in the North similarly developed as an extension, and to a degree, a replacement for British exploitation of the Burmese forests. The dominant export, rice, occupied a frequently uncomfortable position in the region, with markets predominantly in British and Dutch controlled areas. During the 1920s and 1930s Thai exporters looked increasingly to markets outside the imperial structures, most significantly to Japan and the traditional China markets.

The extent of Western control

In terms of trade, modern business and finance, the Thai economy during the late nineteenth and early twentieth centuries came to exhibit some of the characteristics of a British colony (Dixon and Parnwell, 1991). The Kingdom had become a significant exporter of a narrow range of primary products (Tables 2.3 and 2.5). Trade became closely tied to the British Empire which in 1938 took 68 per cent of exports and supplied 42 per cent of imports. As may be seen from Table 2.6 these shares fit into the pattern of trade found in the South East Asian colonial territories.

International trade and shipping became dominated by Western firms. By 1890 70 per cent of foreign trade was in the hands of foreign companies (Holm, 1977: 124) and 90 per cent of exports were carried in British and German shipping, and Thai–Chinese shipping (which had carried 40 per cent of exports in 1871) had become almost non-existent (Suehiro, 1989: 52–7).

The Western agency houses established during the late nineteenth century controlled a wide range of trading and service activities. These included banking, insurance, warehousing, lightering, importing and the management of port facilities (Falkus 1989: 120–6). It was these agencies that supplied the gradually rising demand for such imported goods as sacks, textiles, beer, mineral water and soap. One of the largest, the

Table 2.5 Thai commodity production, 1938–40

Commodity	Percentage share of production	
	South East Asia	*World*
Rice	10.3	10.2
Rubber	36.5	31.1
Sugar	1.1	0.2
Tin	10.0	9.5
Teak	17.8	19.7

Source: Tate (1979: 25).

Table 2.6 Share of trade with the metropolitan power, 1938–40

	Percentage of value	
	Imports	*Exports*
Burma	58.7	68.8
Indo-China	56.3	53.4
Malaya	58.5	33.0
Netherlands East Indies	22.0	20.0
Philippines	68.8	78.4

Source: Tate (1979: 26).

Borneo Company, owned rice and saw mills, operated shipping, lightering and port facilities, and was the local agent for 120 companies (Suehiro, 1989: 44).

While Thailand may have become from the 1890s a primary sphere of activity for British capital, the scale of investment was significantly less than in the colonial territories (Table 2.7). Estimates of the composition of investment in 1930 suggest that unlike the rest of the region Chinese investment greatly exceeded that of Western interests, perhaps by as much as four times. Tate (1979: 28) using a variety of sources for the late 1930s also concluded that Chinese investment was more significant in Thailand than elsewhere in the region.

Outside the fiscal, financial and trading spheres Thailand retained a degree of political independence. However, this independence was to a considerable extent preserved by the Kingdom refraining from exercising it to more than a very limited extent. While from the 1850s until the 1930s Thailand may be viewed as subservient to Britain, British policy towards the Kingdom appears to have been far from clear cut. Some six or seven ministries, including the India Office, and from 1936 the Burma Office, claimed an interest in Thailand's affairs. As Aldrich (1995) discusses, during the 1920s and 1930s these interests were frequently in conflict. British interests were furthered through the complex and far from co-ordinated operation of commercial strength, the presence of advisers, treaty obligations and the direct support of London. However, while in many areas of activity the Thai rulers obliged Western interests, it was also possible to limit them, as in the teak and rubber areas, or to fail to support them, as in the tin sector. The intensity of Western assimilation of Thailand was limited by the lack of colonial style controls over land and labour, and support through the development of appropriate infrastructure. In the absence of such support Western enterprise found it difficult to compete with Chinese concerns and was perhaps unable to maintain the level of control over the economy that they did in the colonial territories.

Table 2.7 Estimated investment in South East Asia in 1930 (million US$)

	Western			
	Portfolio	Direct	Total	Chinese
Burma	10	210	220	a
Indo-China	25	255	280	236
Malaya	113	447	560	491
Netherlands East Indies	397	1600	1997	620
Philippines	85	300	385	189
Thailand	57	75	132	468
Total	687	2887	3574	2004

Sources: The estimates for Western investment are based on Callis (1941: 23, 36, 56, 70, 85 and 108). They have been judged 'very rough estimates and probably on the low side' (Allen and Donnithorne, 1954: 288). The figures for Chinese investment are from Fukuda 1942: 100–2 – cited by (Brown, 1993b: 87). They are calculated on a basis different from that used by Callis and are almost certainly far less reliable (Brown, 1993b: 85–6).

Note
a Chinese investment was very limited in Burma. However, by the 1930s some 50 per cent of investment in Burma was Indian (Tate, 1979: 28).

Jacoby (1961: 55) suggests that Thailand's position of partial political independence and economic subservience gave the worst of both worlds. Thailand did not benefit from the limited welfare development that colonial rule might have brought, nor was the Kingdom given the benefit of the British Imperial economy's protection from the worst of the fluctuations in the world economy. This is a matter of considerable debate. The Thai economy was far less integrated into the world economy than the other Asian colonial territories. It may well be that for the majority of the population the much lower degree of incorporation and the limited development of non-rice export crops more than compensated for the lack of imperial economic protection during the deep inter-war recession (Brown, 1993a; Dixon, 1991a: 133–4).

The preservation of a degree of Thai political independence and the consequent less intensive mode of assimilation that resulted almost certainly ensured a slower pace of change compared to neighbouring colonial economies. The rapid disruption and disintegration of the traditional social structures that marked French rule in Indo-China and British rule in Burma was largely avoided. To a degree the Thai state could control the rate and path towards the establishment of capitalist production. In the long term the much more gradual development of production and internationalisation of the economy probably served the mass of the population well.

Rice production remained based on small-scale owner occupied farms without development of large-scale production or foreign landlords as was the case in Burma. The comparative abundance of land suitable for cultivation, combined with continued ease of access, produced living conditions in rural areas that were by the 1930s probably significantly better than those generally prevailing in the neighbouring colonial areas. However, it should be stressed that data on comparative living conditions are sparse. Zimmerman's rural survey suggests that compared to other Asian countries, Thailand had larger average farm holdings, significantly lower incidence of tenancy and debt, higher average incomes, and lower work intensity (Zimmerman, 1931: 318). Similarly, Falkus (1991: 59) notes that many accounts stress the comparatively good conditions and light work loads that prevailed in the Thai agricultural sector. In addition, although the issue is a complex one, the burden of taxation and the rigour with which it was collected may well have been very much lower for the rural Thai population than for their neighbours in Burma and French Indo-China (Ingram, 1971: 76–9; Sompop Manarungsan, 1989: 63). Perhaps more significantly, unlike the neighbouring colonial regimes, there were few effective controls over access to land or forest products. In the long term this maintained the living standards in the rural sector, retained a large proportion of the population in the agricultural sector and enabled the long-term expansion of production with little input of capital (see the fuller discussions in Chapter 5).

While much attention has focused on the similarities between Thailand and the South East Asian colonial regimes (see Dixon and Parnwell, 1991), perhaps the differences, particularly in degree, merit more attention. With the reduction in the level of Western, particularly British, influence during the late 1920s (see p. 60) Thailand was able to begin to reassert control over the pattern of national development. The limited degree to which Western enterprises controlled the economy gave considerable scope for the expansion of the indigenous sector once it became possible to raise revenue and tariffs and steer exports away from the British Empire (see p.65). Thailand was fortunate in its resources, the survival of elements of a domestic manufacturing sector, the development of a national railway network and administrative system, and the large and dynamic Chinese business sector. All of these gave an important basis for the development of the economy under the changed domestic and international conditions that prevailed during the 1930s.

The inter-war crisis, the end of the absolute monarchy and the rise of nationalism

Thailand like all primary producers suffered severely during the deep world recession of the late 1920s and early 1930s. The collapse of commodity prices from 1929 brought serious hardship to many elements in the population. The Bangkok export price of rice fell from a peak in

1926–7 of 7.58 baht per picul (60kg) to below 4.10 during the 1930s (Elliott, 1978: 95). As has already been noted, Thailand was experiencing difficulties in rice marketing throughout the 1920s. These were compounded during the 1930s by the price fall and the growth of economic nationalism which resulted in increased tariff barriers, imposition of quotas and outright import bans. China imposed a tariff on Thai rice imports in 1933 and India followed suit in 1935; in the Netherlands East Indies controls introduced in 1933 reduced Thai imports by 20 per cent; and Japan banned Thai imports in 1934. Despite these difficulties Thailand managed after 1929–31 to restore and even expand the volume of rice exports. Malaya remained a steady source of demand and new markets were opened up in the Philippines, Peru and Tunisia (Tate, 1979: 514). However, while the volume of rice exported between 1930 and 1939 was 25.2 per cent more than that exported between 1920 and 1929, the earnings were 25.5 per cent less.

Sharp falls in the prices of tin, teak and rubber during the early 1930s, while seriously disrupting these sectors, had much less impact on the economy and the Thai population as a whole than the contraction of rice prices. The tin and rubber interests were reluctant to participate in the attempts to restrict production during the recession. However, both the 1933 Rubber Restriction Scheme and the 1931 Anglo–Dutch agreement over tin production gave Thailand very favourable quotas (Caldwell, 1978: 10).

The impact of the recession on the Thai economy has been a matter of some debate (see Brown, 1986, 1993b). It appears that it was the rice growers in the most commercialised areas of the Central Plain that suffered most (see however, earlier comments on the increasing difficulties faced by the rice sector before the recession pp. 47–8). Sitiporn Kridakara (1969: 56) comments on the fate of farmers who had extended and improved holdings, in some cases obtaining petrol-driven water pumps. Many of these were faced with debt, loss of land and poverty. However, many Thai farmers appear to have been able to revert to the subsistence production of a variety of goods (Hirsch, 1990: 40–1; Johnston, 1975: 411–12). It may well be that Thailand's less intensive assimilation into the market economy and, for the majority of the population, a much lower level of direct dependence on the export of commodities generally, mitigated the impact of the recession. These factors may well have more than offset any loss of protection resulting in Thailand not being fully incorporated into the British Imperial structure.

During the inter-war period such 'informal' structures as Britain's in Thailand came under increasing pressure from other countries anxious to expand their export markets. In the case of the British market in Thailand this pressure came first from the USA and then from Japan. Indeed during the 1930s Thailand was at times central to Japanese–American rivalry over South East Asia (Caldwell, 1978: 10). While the British viewed increased American involvement and interest in Thailand with grave suspicion there were times during the 1930s when the two powers cooperated in the face of the perceived threat of increased Japanese involvement (Aldrich, 1993: 4).

In 1920 the USA signed a treaty which recognised the complete fiscal autonomy of Thailand, and in 1925–6 new treaties were negotiated with all the major powers (Ingram, 1971: 180). The treaty negotiated with the UK was a compromise which left the UK in a very favoured position with the import duty on the main exports to Thailand – cotton goods, iron and steel products – restricted to 5 per cent for the next ten years. In addition, assurances were given that there was no intention of raising the export duties on teak and rice (Ingram, 1971: 181). Despite these limitations Thailand effectively regained control over its financial affairs for the first time since the signing of the Bowring Treaty in 1855. The remaining unequal elements in the treaties were removed during 1937–8 following their repudiation and subsequent renegotiation.

In 1927 a new tariff structure was established; this was subject to frequent revisions and the level of tariffs generally rose. The increases were principally driven by the need to raise government revenue (Ingram, 1971: 183; Muscat, 1994: 105). Import tariffs' share of government revenue rose from 7 per cent in 1926–7 to 21 per cent in 1941 and 27 per cent in 1950 (Ingram, 1971: 183). While the increased tariffs may have provided some protection for domestic industry it was not until the late 1930s that a beginning was made in manipulating them for this purpose.

Important as the treaty revisions were they did little to stem the demands for reform and reduced foreign domination of the economy that developed during the 1920s. The emergent Thai–Chinese interests were becoming increasingly frustrated with a situation which was depicted as holding back the country's development (Elliott, 1978: 55).

By the late 1920s some very clear – principally Chinese – business groups had developed (Suehiro, 1989: 43–105). In the rice sector five families were coming to control exporting and milling (Suehiro, 1989: 79–87, 110–16). These were descended from nineteenth-century immigrants who had started operations in a variety of trading and shipping operations. Their emergence was, as in the South East Asian colonial regimes, far from simple. In general the government was unhelpful and at times hostile (see pp. 67 and 70 later in this chapter), and they had to compete and deal with Western companies who had come to dominate such areas as shipping and insurance. The Chinese concerns tended to build integrated businesses in which the rice operations were linked to other operations, such as shipping, general importing, insurance, banking, warehousing and lightering; thus they were in general well placed to weather the inter-war recession (Pasuk Phongpaichit and Baker, 1995: 111–12).

A second major group of entrepreneurs, again principally Chinese, had also emerged in the manufacturing sector. These had set up plants to supply the products and services offered to the expanding, mainly urban, markets by the Western agency houses. From the early 1900s domestic manufacturing began partially to replace and supplement imports of such items as mineral water, soap, cooking oil and a variety of foodstuffs (Pasuk Phongpaichit and Baker, 1995: 112–13; Suehiro, 1989: 37–9). As with the rice-based entrepreneurs there was considerable diversification of activities. However, the structure of the economy tended to favour Western enterprises and, particularly after the 1926 treaty revisions, business interests began to appeal to the government to assist them in competing against the strength of colonial capital (Pasuk Phongpaichit and Baker, 1995: 114–15). From 1910 business associations were formed and these lobbied for support of domestic manufacturing and control over imports (Nakarin Mektrairat, 1992: 97).

There was a general upsurge of feeling against the privileged position of Western enterprises in Thailand:

> The businessmen and their journalist advocates blamed the privileged position of western merchants on the monarchy, which had negotiated the original treaties, had welcomed the foreign merchants, had liberally used foreign advisers to help administer the economy, had invested in foreign enterprises including agency houses, had popularized foreign goods, and not responded to the petitions of the new businessmen.
>
> (Pasuk Phongpaichit and Baker, 1995: 246)

Indeed, during the 1920s the absolute monarchy was increasingly criticised and depicted as a major barrier to Thailand's development (see e.g. Stowe, 1991: 2–3).

The economic difficulties and recession that characterised the period 1928–32 gave additional impetus to the movement against the absolute monarchy. For the King was cast in the role of an economic manager and the person ultimately responsible for the imposition of retrenchment policies. More damagingly, during 1932 King Prajadhipok in a speech to senior military stated that the management of the economic cisis was beyond him (cited in Stowe, 1991: 2).

In 1912 and in 1917 small groups of military officers made unsuccessful attempts to overthrow the monarchy. In contrast the membership of the group that conducted the successful 1932 *coup d'état* were drawn from a much wider base. It started with a small group of young, foreign-educated bureaucrats and military, spreading to encompass minor aristocracy, more senior members of the bureaucracy and military, intellectuals, business interests and organised labour. In 1927 the first meeting of the *Khana*

Ratsadorn (People's Party) was held in Paris.[21] The critical element in the success of the conspiracy was the recruitment during 1931 of senior members of the military. These were mostly foreign educated and frustrated by the controls of the monarchy – a situation that was exacerbated by budgetary cuts in the wake of the recession (Wilson, 1962: 173).

On 24 June 1932 in a bloodless *coup d'état* power was seized in the space of three hours. On 26 June 1932 a constitution was promulgated. It reduced royal power to the absolute minimum without actually abolishing the monarchy (Stowe, 1991: 26).[22] The Kingdom would be ruled by a People's Committee and People's Assembly with 70 members, initially nominated by the senior military commanders involved in the *coup d'état*. There was provision to move to the election of half the assembly as soon as conditions permitted. In the event none of the provisions in the constitution put a brake on the consolidation of power by the military.

The leaders of the *coup d'état* have been described as representative of those varied groups that were merging into the Thai bourgeois class (Elliott, 1978: 78–80). However, it is going too far to label 1932 as 'Thailand's bourgeois revolution' but it does form an important watershed. The break was by no means complete – as most members of the immediate post *coup d'état* cabinet were officials who had served the absolute monarchy (Ray, 1972: 62).

The period 1932 to 1938 was, in political terms, far from stable. A second *coup d'état* in 1933 shifted power within the military; and three elections were held – in 1933, 1937 and 1938. In 1938 Pibul Songkram emerged as Prime Minister. This, while heralding in a period of comparative stability, also marked the consolidation of the ruling position of the military (Elliott, 1978: 88–90; Stowe 1991: 83–111).

Between 1932 and Thailand's involvement in the Second World War governments appear to have been generally more preoccupied with power struggles than with economic policy. However, a wide range of economic measures were proposed and, particularly from 1938, some significant developments took place.

In 1933 a national economic plan was produced; in many ways it was more of a wide-ranging economic manifesto (Stowe, 1991: 251). The main emphasis was on land and the welfare of the rural population.[23] While the need to promote industry through import substitution and protection was mentioned they received little emphasis. The most striking aspect of the economic plan was its stress on the central role of the state in controlling land and the development of infrastructure and industry. It is perhaps not surprising that the plan was depicted by its detractors as a 'communist document' and a replacement was commissioned (Stowe, 1990: 37–8). This showed much more influence from business interests, but it also placed even more emphasis on the rural sector (see Makoto Nambara,

1993 for a review of the plan and its author Pra Sarasana). It proposed the further development of railways and canals, provision of storage facilities, improved irrigation, rural credit and land colonisation. However, there were also comments on the need for the state ownership of major industries (Landon, 1939: 62–3). From both the economic plans suggestions emerged for the elimination of middlemen and the suppression of the Chinese who exploited the peasantry. As is discussed more fully below (see also p.67), many of the economic measures proposed, and to a degree implemented, during the 1930s contained strong nationalistic elements and stressed the reduction of the influence of Chinese businesses. Indeed, the slogan 'a Thai economy for a Thai people' came increasingly to the fore.

From the mid-1930s until the mid-1940s successive administrations established a wide variety of wholly or partly state-owned industrial enterprises. During this period state activities included the extension of rail, power and water supplies, the establishment of abattoirs and the manufacture of, amongst other items, cigarettes, paper, textiles, soap, glass, silk and gunny sacks. In addition, there was state involvement in distilling and the processing of cassava, rubber and sugar (Ingram, 1971: 139–40). From 1942 many of these state activities were financed through the Thai Industrial Development Company and by 1945 some 30 state concerns had been established (Suehiro, 1989: 139).

As well as establishing new enterprises the state took over all or part of concerns established by Europeans and Chinese. During 1939 the government attempted to remove the control of the rice trade from Chinese hands (Suehiro, 1989: 123–6). Traders were ordered to sell rice to the newly established Thai Rice Company which as a result handled some 30–80 per cent of exports during 1939 (Suehiro, 1989: 125). Between 1939 and 1942 the Thai Rice Corporation leased 17 of the 45 major rice mills in Bangkok and its immediate environs. The government also entered rice shipping through establishing a half share in the Siam Steam Navigation Company, the establishment of the Providence Bank and the Setgakit Insurance Company. Attempts were also made to set up provincial trading firms to purchase rice and other products. In the event these measures aimed at state control of the rice sector were doomed to failure because of the lack of non-Chinese expertise in the industry. The state rice mills and trading concerns had to retain their former Chinese managers and many of their operators. Overall, the cooperation of the major Chinese business interests was vital to the government. In the longer run, many of the Chinese was able dexterously to turn state control into an instrument for expanding their own business activities (Suehiro, 1989: 132).

Increased tariff protection for a wide range of products had been made possible by the 1926 treaty revision. The possibilities inherent in the new situation are well illustrated by tobacco.[24] Until the 1930s the Thai cigarette market was dominated by Western, particularly British, brands. In 1927, in an attempt to encourage local tobacco growing and manufacture, a 25 per cent tariff on manufactured tobacco was imposed; this was raised to 59 per cent in 1934. The result was initially a growth in the imports of raw tobacco and subsequently an expansion of domestic tobacco growing. In response to these measures the largest importer of tobacco, BAT (British American Tobacco Company), began to encourage Thai production, setting up tobacco stations particularly in the North and supplying seeds and advice to growers. The activities of BAT were reinforced by Department of Agriculture promotion – an active government campaign to encourage consumption of the domestic product, further increases in tariffs, reduction of local taxation and in the late 1930s a general increase in world tobacco prices. By 1940 two-thirds of the tobacco consumed in Thailand was domestically produced, and foreign cigarette brands had been largely eliminated. In 1941 the BAT activities were nationalised and a state tobacco monopoly established (Suehiro, 1989: 129).

The development of tobacco production was by far the most successful example of the involvement of the state in the economy during the 1930s. Attempts to promote cotton production in the absence of a modern textile industry met with only limited success. However, during 1936 measures were introduced aimed at developing the textile sector (Suehiro, 1989: 123) and during the late 1930s the imports of yarn for the domestic industry began to increase faster than the imports of textiles.

The moves towards protection, economic recovery and the changed conditions of the 1930s resulted in a general expansion and diversification of the indigenous industrial and service sectors. The expansion of domestic manufacturing was reflected in the increased share of raw materials and capital goods in the composition of imports (Ingram, 1971: 129). Overall, these developments paved the way for expansion of ISI during the war and, more especially, the 1950s (see Chapter 3).

The nationalist and interventionist complexion of the 1930s government was reinforced by the need to negotiate quotas for rubber and tin. This led the government to seek greater information and control over the national economy. The *laissez faire* approach to the economy – with the priority of smoothing the path for Western enterprise – came to an end. State participation in production as a way of promoting economic development and Thai participation in the economy had begun to emerge by the late 1930s. In the teak industry the government expressed interest in the direct working of the forests. In 1940 the renewal of Western concessions took place on a new basis: one-third to be worked by the concessions, one-third to be opened up to local exploitation and one-third as government reserve (Tate, 1979: 522).[25] Limited government participation in tin mining and rubber processing was also initiated in 1940 (Thompson, 1941:

479–83). Attempts were made to develop the fishing industry: Japanese advisers were brought in, experiments with fish canning were financed and in 1939 the industry was restricted to Thai nationals (see Thompson, 1941: 477–79).

By the late 1930s Britain's pre-eminent position was being challenged by the USA and Japan. The attraction of Thailand as an uncolonised state in South East Asia was reinforced by the comparatively low level of development of both the country's considerable potential for raw material production and market for manufactured goods. To a degree Thailand was able to exploit the rivalry between Britain, Japan and the USA (see Aldrich, 1995). Trade was beginning to diversify away from the British Imperial structure and Thailand was able to exercise increasing independence in international relations and economic policy.

The role of the Chinese in the economy

The Chinese community[26] in Thailand was well established in the early nineteenth century and exercised a considerable measure of control over trade and non-agricultural production. After 1855 the Chinese lost control of the Kingdom's export trade to the Europeans and in the early twentieth century their position in tin and teak production was similarly eroded. However, by the late 1930s it is estimated that 70 per cent of the ethnic Chinese in Thailand were engaged in business or trade, and they controlled 80 per cent of the domestic trade, including complete control of the rice sector – from which 75 per cent of the national reserve was derived (Skinner, 1958: 216–17).

The influx of Chinese and their entry into trading, teak cutting, processing, rubber production and tin mining produced a clear ethnic division of labour between them and the Thais. This pattern has been variously attributed to labour shortages, the official encouragement of immigration, the exemption of the Chinese from corvée and similar obligations, the strength of Chinese secret societies and the Thai preference for agriculture. It seems probable that the controls over Thai labour which persisted until 1905 discouraged its use in the non-agricultural sector and maintained the attractiveness of the agricultural frontier areas (Pasuk Phongpaichit and Baker, 1995: 174). However, Wilson (1989) in a study of Bangkok in the 1880s has questioned the intensity of the ethnic division of labour, concluding that there were large numbers of Thais active in the trading and commercial sectors. She suggests that subsequently there was a relative decline in Thai activity in these areas. If this was the case the details and mechanisms remain unclear. It might be that the decline in Thai activity was part of the late nineteenth century shift in economic power away from groups who had emerged from the ranks of tax farmers and traders sponsored by the Crown towards a principally new generation of Chinese immigrants (see Suehiro, 1989: 71–90).

Thai involvement in the modern economy was thus even by the late 1930s extremely limited. The classes that were linked to the world economy – the comprador capitalist and petty bourgeoisie – were almost entirely Chinese and were coming less and less under the control of the Thai state (Elliott, 1978: 78–9). The 1932 *coup d'état* which placed an alliance of the bureaucracy and the military in control gave rise to an antagonistic relationship between the Chinese who controlled the domestic economy and those who had political power. Discrimination against the Chinese after 1932 foreshadowed much more serious clashes elsewhere in South East Asia during the 1950s and 1960s. These reflected the manner in which the Chinese had come on the coat tails of colonialism to occupy an intermediate position between the indigenous population and Western powers.

The Thai rulers until the 1920s not only looked favourably on Chinese immigration but also actively promoted it. King Mongkut saw the Chinese as one of the principle elements in the modernisation of the Kingdom (Tate, 1979: 545). In 1907 King Chulalongkorn stated:

> It has always been my policy that the Chinese in Siam should have the same opportunities for labour and profit as are possessed by my own countrymen. I regard them not as foreigners but as component parts of the Kingdom and as sharing in its prosperity and advancement.
>
> (cited in Skinner, 1957: 159–60)

Statistics on the influx of Chinese are far from reliable (see the discussion in Sternstein, 1984). Net immigration perhaps rose from *c.* 3,000 in the 1820s, to *c.* 7,000 in the 1870s, and to 15,000 *c.* 1900 (Skinner, 1957: 57–61). The partial census of 1904 suggests 400,000 Chinese, 200,000 in Bangkok. Skinner (1957: 74) considered this an under-estimate and suggested that the actual number was *c.* 600,000 – 10 per cent of the population. The net average annual inflow rose to a peak of almost 40,000 during the 1920s, falling to some 10,000 during the 1930s (Sompop Manarungsan, 1989: 207–8) – the latter being a reflection of the recession and increasing restrictions on Chinese activity (see below). During the late 1940s, Thailand, like other parts of South East Asia, received a further brief period of Chinese immigration, averaging some 30,000 a year during the period 1946–50 (Sompop Manarungsan, 1989: 208). Overall, between 1820 and 1950 perhaps 4 million Chinese entered Thailand, at least 1.5 million of whom did not leave (Skinner, 1957: 61, 72–3).

By the late 1930s Chinese dominated the labour force in the railways, ports, saw mills, rice mills, trading, retailing and manufacturing. The

Chinese probably supplied 60–75 per cent of the non-agricultural labour force (Pasuk Phongpaichit and Baker, 1995: 178) since this was heavily concentrated in Bangkok – in many ways the city could be considered a Chinese city (see Chapter 5).

The Chinese revolution of 1911 resulted in a general change in the attitude towards the Chinese throughout South East Asia. In Thailand, as in French Indo-China, the Philippines, Malaya and the NIE, reference began to be made to the 'Chinese problem'. While Thai–Chinese relations deteriorated after 1911 there was no clear anti-Chinese policy until the 1930s. Between 1938 and 1941 a series of measures were implemented to reduce the hold of non-Thai nationals on the economy:

> All restrictions were on the basis of nationality, not race, and so did not directly affect the great majority of local born Chinese. ... It should be made clear that the legislation ... scrupulously avoided singling out the Chinese; restrictions applied to all aliens of whatever nationality and were generally enforced without favouritism.
>
> (Skinner, 1957: 264)

However, it was the Chinese at whom the restrictions were aimed. While life was made difficult for the Chinese and their privileged position in the Kingdom finished, there was little real reduction in their economic role. Between 1941 and 1944 there was much more overt discrimination against the Chinese but it was principally the petty bourgeoisie who suffered rather than the Chinese capitalists who remained vital to the economy (Elliott, 1978: 89; Suehiro, 1989: 134). From the late 1930s the Chinese became, at least superficially, more fully integrated into Thai society and their role in the economy became steadily less overt. Many Chinese changed their nationality and took Thai names. In consequence for the government 'they were no longer "alien" people to be regulated, but "Thai" people to be economically promoted with the new policy' (Suehiro, 1989: 134). Despite further discrimination during the late 1940s, in the longer term the Chinese of Thailand became the most highly and effectively assimilated in South East Asia. However, in 1950 some 3 million people – 15 per cent of the population – could be regarded as Chinese either ethnically or by ancestry (Caldwell, 1967: 32–3; Ingram, 1971: 4).

The Second World War and its aftermath

The increasingly nationalist and militaristic government of Pibul Songkram – while enjoying cordial relations with Japan – was not willing to join the Axis powers. However, the landing of Japanese troops in Thailand at the same time as the attack on Pearl Harbour was not resisted. The rapid passage of Japanese troops through Thailand to attack Malaya and Burma and the subsequent declaring of war on the Allied Powers[27] was seriously to damage Anglo–Thai relations in the post-war period. The Japanese occupation pandered to the territorial ambitions of the Pibul government 'returning' to rule former Thai territory annexed by the Western powers.

The collaboration with the Japanese split the Thai cabinet. Disaffection with the Japanese occupation and with the Pibul regime gave rise to a Free Thai Movement under the leadership of Pridi Banomyong (one of the leaders of the 1932 *coup d'état*). As any likelihood of a Japanese victory waned, support for Pibul and the military waned, and from 1944 until 1947 a variety of civilian governments were in power (Ray, 1972: 100).

The Thai economy was seriously damaged by the Second World War in general and the 1941–43 period of Japanese occupation in particular. Foreign trade was cut off with only limited exports within the sphere of Japanese control. The port facilities of Bangkok were destroyed by bombing, and railways and power generation facilities seriously damaged (Silcock, 1967a: 5). The disruption of infrastructure was reinforced by the limited investment and maintenance that took place during the war years. In many rural areas commercial production ceased and the breakdown of law and order resulted in a retreat of the settlement frontier in parts of the North and North East. There is evidence of abandonment of land and settlements and an increased incidence of disease, including malaria (Mounge, 1982: 131). It is highly likely that overall, but particularly in the outer regions of the country, death rates rose and living standards fell during the war. The damage suffered by the Thai economy was, however, nothing like that experienced by neighbouring Burma, and post-war reconstruction and recovery took place rapidly.

The war reduced the inflow of Western manufactured goods, and Western firms were closed down by the Japanese occupying forces. While after the war some of these either failed to reopen or sold out to local interests the majority re-established their operations (Suehiro, 1989: 172–7). During the war period many domestic concerns grew and expanded their range of activities to accommodate the restriction of imports and the removal of Western competition. A number of the major business groups were either founded or first began to show appreciable growth during the war (Pasuk Phongpaichit and Baker, 1995: 122). Of particular importance was the development of the banking sector, which until the suspension of their activities by the Japanese occupation had been dominated by European concerns (Naris Chaiyaasot, 1994: 227–30). Five of the major banks were established between 1941 and 1945. These developments heralded the further development of domestically controlled banks during the late 1940s and early 1950s.[28] The Thai–Chinese banking groups were to play a major role in the subsequent development of the economy.

The war effectively brought an end to British influence in Thailand. Anglo–Thai relations were slow to recover from the war and the reparation payments demanded by the Allies.[29] The ending of British involvement opened the way for the incursion of the USA into Thai and wider South East Asian affairs – developments already heralded during the 1930s.

The period 1944 to 1947 was one of great political and economic instability with five governments and ten cabinets. Inflation reached 100 per cent during 1944–46 and overt official corruption increased public unrest (Stowe, 1991: 364). The civilian government was further destabilised by the mysterious death of the young King Ananda who was found shot in bed.[30] Attempts to implicate the Prime Minister, Pridi, in the death resulted in his resignation – and the lack of any resolution as to who was responsible for the King's death was used as an excuse for a military *coup d'état* in 1947 (Stowe, 1991: 364). The *coup d'état* heralded the way for the establishment of a military government under Pibul in 1948 and the beginning of 25 years of almost uninterrupted military rule.

Economic development under military rule: 1947–57

The Pibul government attempted to establish a political power base which rested on the 1932 constitution and a parliamentary system which, although heavily manipulated and the opposition suppressed, provided a facade of democracy. Pibul's regime essentially belonged to the '1932 promoters' (Saneh Chamarik, 1983: 4) who had the educational and political aspirations of 'Western democracy'. However, the power of the 1947–57 Pibul government rested on the bureaucracy. The cabinet and National Assembly were dominated by civilians and military personnel drawn almost exclusively from the bureaucracy (Saneh Chamarik, 1985: 5). In the last years of the Pibul regime the lack of popular support greatly weakened the government, and in a remarkable *volte face*, attempts were made to build support outside the bureaucracy with, in particular, the labour movement (Ray, 1972: 14). These attempts largely failed, leaving the government increasingly isolated and vulnerable in the face of deteriorating economic and security conditions. Overall, the period 1948 to 1957 was one of political instability, continuing power struggles within the military, rivalry within the military, plots and attempted *coups d'état* (in 1948, 1949 and 1951).

As with the earlier Pibul regime, much was initially made of 'economic nationalism' and high priority was given to changing the structure of ownership in the non-agricultural sectors. During the late 1940s legislation and decrees further restricted the activities of 'aliens' – effectively first-generation immigrant Chinese (Coughlin, 1960: 132). As well as the restrictions, officials probably discriminated against the Chinese in a variety of ways. Despite this, Coughlin (1960: 136–7) concluded that the regulations were generally ineffectively implemented – they were full of 'loopholes', officials could be bribed. As with the earlier phase of discrimination the Chinese were generally able to respond by adopting Thai citizenship and the main occupations of the Chinese were not affected. Overall, as with the discrimination implemented during the late 1930s, the nationalist climate of the late 1940s and early 1950s accelerated the assimilation of the Chinese community. By the late 1950s the nationalistic policies were being gradually abandoned as a spent political force.

While the majority of the Chinese may well have avoided the effects of the legislation and general discrimination it is apparent that the relationship between major Chinese business groups and the Thai elite changed dramatically. Accommodations had to be reached between a business community that was treated as 'alien' and an elite that needed access to its wealth-creating ability.[31] As a result senior politicians and members of the bureaucracy and military joined the boards of major Chinese companies. In return Thai officials supplied government contracts, tax exemption and protection against discrimination (Skinner, 1957: 191–2). This symbiotic relationship developed rapidly during the early 1950s, becoming a key element in Thai development by the early 1960s (see Chapter 3). By the mid-1950s all the major Thai–Chinese banking, rice trading and manufacturing groups that had emerged during the 1930s and 1940s had formed alliances with government figures (Suehiro, 1989: 170).

The strong anti-communist flavour of the Pibul military regime made it particularly acceptable to the USA under the developing conditions of the Cold War and the emergence of the hegemony of the USA in Asia. From 1950 strong economic, military, and security relationships developed between Thailand and the USA (Muscat, 1990: 20). During 1950 the USA sent two 'fact-finding missions' to Thailand. The leader of the second of these stated that his objective was to formulate 'a constructive programme of aid to help prevent in Southeast Asia a repetition of the circumstances leading to the fall of China' (cited in Caldwell, 1974: 39). Thus during the 1950s American advisers and aid programmes began to make significant contributions to Thai economic policy and development programmes, particularly after 1954. American aid under the auspices of USOM (United States Operations Mission) was particularly significant in such areas as training (including military), education, health, transport, power generation, public administration, telecommunications and agriculture.

Initially, considerable emphasis was placed on the agricultural sector, which between 1952 and 1960 received some 30 per cent of the aid budget (Muscat, 1990: 69). Of particular significance was the funding of the first national soil and land capability survey and attempts to raise the productivity, in particular, of maize and rice. For the latter crop, efforts centred on the 1951–8 Rice Improvement Programme and the establishment of the Bangkhen Research Station at Kasetsart University. Some slightly improved fertiliser responsive rice varieties were developed and gradually adopted by farmers. By the late 1950s it was estimated that one-sixth of farmers were using improved varieties (Muscat, 1990: 76). However, as is discussed more fully in Chapter 5 there was no significant long-term development, and Thailand remained one of the least productive rice growers in Asia. The promotion of higher yielding maize was significantly more successful, with some 60 to 85 per cent of the planted area comprising the more productive Guatemalan variety by the early 1960s (Behrman, 1968: 47).

By lending money for the Chai Nat Dam in 1950 the World Bank recognised the importance of irrigation for the development of rice production. The 1957 World Bank mission stressed the importance of irrigation in order to expand rice production, thus ensuring the continuation of an exportable surplus (World Bank, 1959: 272). Between 1951 and 1958 the USA funded the vast majority of the irrigation and water conservation projects (Muscat, 1990: 78) and an important beginning was made in the development of irrigated agriculture with the area served increasing from 0.97 million hectares in 1947 to 1.59 million hectares in 1960 (see Chapter 5 for a fuller discussion of irrigation).

Between 1954 and 1960 some 50 per cent of the American aid was devoted to road construction. Most notably the Friendship Highway linking the North East to the Central Plain. The American contribution was instrumental in increasing the length of paved roads from 760 km in 1949 to 2,972 km in 1960. From 1955 the transport sector was recognised by the USA as strategic, and aid spread into virtually every mode (Muscat, 1990: 103–4). Particular significance was attached to the development of air transport. In 1955 a major ten-year USOM programme was implemented, aimed at developing the facilities at Bangkok's Don Muang International Airport and 13 provincial airports (see p. 84).

With respect to health, the largest and most significant American aid project was the suppression of malaria (Muscat, 1990: 87). In 1950 with a death rate of 250/100,000, malaria was the Kingdom's leading killer. Following an initial mass spraying scheme carried out in 1950 with the assistance of WHO (World Health Organisation) and UNICEF (United Nations International Children's Fund) a national malaria suppression programme was established during 1951. While health statistics during the 1950s have to be treated with caution, the reduction in the malaria death rate was spectacular, falling to 30/100,000 by 1960.

The period 1949 to 1950 saw a rapid 'internationalisation' of development in Thailand with American activity being reinforced by that of such UN agencies as the FAO. In 1949 Thailand became a member of the IMF and the World Bank, and in 1950 received a loan from the latter for the development of the railway system, the Bangkok port facilities and the construction of the Chai Nat Dam.[32]

The combination of American and international agency activity in Thailand resulted in aid-related activity spreading through most parts of the Thai bureaucracy, most aspects of which were subjected to detailed studies by the aid agencies concerned. These reported a consistent picture of inadequate planning and coordinating capability, lack of trained personnel, overlapping responsibilities, inadequate statistical information and mechanisms for collecting it (Muscat, 1990: 77–8, 1994: 50–4). Many of the criticisms made in these studies – for example of the agricultural sector – could equally be made during the 1990s (see Chapter 5 and Chapter 8). In 1956 an overall survey of development planning by an American economic adviser to the Ministry of Finance concluded that decision making was totally centralised in Bangkok, was based on superficial analysis of inadequate information, lacked any systematic judgemental mechanism and resulted in random and uncoordinated projects (cited Muscat, 1994: 52). In 1957 a World Bank mission reiterated these points and proposed a major programme of institutional development in order to facilitate decision making and the coordination of development activity (World Bank, 1959). (These findings and the Thai response are discussed in Chapter 3.) Despite these criticisms the period 1950 to 1957 should be seen as one which saw the beginnings of significant long-term change in the bureaucracy and in its ability to operationalise development programmes.

A major feature of the second Pibul period was the rapid expansion of the programme of state enterprise formation initiated during the 1930s. By the mid-1950s there were well over 100 of these state concerns. These took a variety of forms, including fully owned state concerns, joint government–private sector enterprises – involving both domestic and foreign capital – and a variety of enterprises started by members of the government or the bureaucracy.[33] A wide range of manufacturing was involved, including textiles, glass, salt, gunny sacks, paper, ceramics, chemicals, cement, distilling and iron and steel, and extended into the processing of such products as sugar, rubber, vegetable oil and cassava, and such activities as shipping and a national lottery (Ingram, 1971: 287; Silcock, 1967b: 263; Suehiro, 1989: 138–50). The largest single concern was NEDCO (National Economic Development Corporation) set up in 1954 as a holding company with five subsidiaries processing sugar, kenaf (upland jute), marble and paper.

During the early 1950s:

As the original nationalist impetus and justification for state intervention in private economic activity receded, the process actually expanded in scope and permutations and forms employed, driven now ... by the exigencies of political competition and the corrupting effects once the method for rapid and easy access to economic rents had been demonstrated, and indeed sanctioned as being in the purported public interest. Perhaps the most striking generalization one can make, in retrospective, is that the government of Thailand during this period, at the highest levels and extending across and down the bureaucracy, plunged into the extensive practice of intervention from the political and military realms into the economic activities of society.

(Muscat, 1994: 58)

Examples of broader intervention include the awarding of monopoly positions to companies operating in such areas as kenaf purchase and export and animal slaughter and export (Sungsidh Piriyarangsan, 1983: 169–79, 180–3). Most striking (and lasting) was the intervention in the rice trade. As was noted earlier the removal of the rice trade from Chinese control was given high priority during the late 1930s, although in practice little was achieved. However (as is more fully discussed in Chapter 5), during the 1940s and 1950s, first through the operation of the Rice Office (1947–55), then through a range of controls and export taxes, the export and domestic prices of rice were effectively controlled. Given the impact that this had in depressing farm incomes and reducing the cost of living of the urban, principally Bangkok, population, this must be regarded as the most significant single intervention by the government (see Chapter 5). Muscat has concluded that taken as a whole the various interventions that had developed by the late 1950s covered a 'considerable fraction of the country's monetised economic activity' (1994: 60).

Most of the state enterprises proved to be far from efficient in the short run, failing to meet targets, unable to compete effectively with imports and becoming a net drain on government finance (Armanoff, 1965; Ingram, 1971: 287–8). Many became bywords for inefficacy and wholesale corruption. In these respects much attention has focused on the bankruptcy of the heavily indebted NEDCO in 1957 which placed a heavy financial burden on the government until 1962 (Muscat, 1994: 61). The 1957 World Bank mission (World Bank, 1959) was extremely critical of the state sector as a whole, and strongly recommended that efforts should concentrate on the strengthening of the private sector.

Despite the criticisms, the promotion of state enterprises reinforced by increased levels of protection during the 1950s marked a decisive move towards ISI and the establishment of the Thai industrial sector. As was noted earlier (pp. 60) the increase in tariffs following the 1926 treaty revision was largely driven by the need to raise government revenue. Thus by the early 1950s there were widely differing rates that 'lacked any economic rationale' (Muscat, 1994: 105). However, while the main motive was not to protect domestic industry, the tariffs on a range of consumer goods did give a measure of support for domestic industry. During the 1950s there was a general rise in the level of tariffs and further attempts to protect, in particular, domestic consumer goods production (Ingram, 1971: 281–2; see also Chapter 3).

While data on the sectoral composition of national income are far from reliable during this period, the industrial share (including construction, manufacturing, power generation, transport and mining) of GDP appears to have increased from 18.3 per cent in 1951 to 26.2 per cent in 1960 – an annual rate of growth of 12.1 per cent. The growth of the manufacturing sector alone was, however, much more modest, increasing from 10.3 per cent of GNP in 1951 to 12.5 per cent in 1960. The growth of the manufacturing sector is also reflected in the composition of imports which showed a decline in the share of consumer goods from 59 per cent in 1950 to 35 per cent in 1960 and an increase in that of capital and intermediate goods from 25 per cent to 41 per cent. Overall, the increase in the level of imports began to exceed the growth of exports, and from the early 1950s the balance of payments surplus which had been a constant feature of the Thai economy at least from the 1850s (with the exception of the period 1943–6) was rapidly eroded. After 1953 there was a deficit in every year except 1955, 1956 and 1986.

The period 1950 to 1957, despite the political instability and uncertain policy directions, was of major significance to the development of the Thai economy. Many developments initiated during the 1930s came to fruition during the 1950s, notably the development of infrastructure, state-sponsored manufacturing, import substitution and health schemes. In all these areas a significant beginning was made in the modernisation of the economy.

Conclusion: Thai development 1855–1957

Between 1855 and 1957 Thailand underwent considerable economic, social and political change. As a result of major reforms a uniform pattern of national administration was established with control and decision making highly concentrated in Bangkok. The reforms also removed barriers to modernisation and put in place the framework for the establishment and extension of the exchange economy. Until the 1930s the lack of fiscal and financial autonomy limited the development of infrastructure and the role of the state in economic development. Some progress in the establishment of a national primary educational system had been made, but even by the late 1940s for the majority of the rural population there had been remarkably little development and change, particularly compared to neighbouring colonial territories. In general the limited spread of education, health facilities and communications had resulted in very little social change in rural areas. While elements of the market economy had spread widely by the late 1940s, there were many areas of the North and more especially the North East where many communities remained highly subsistent in character. This, taken in conjunction with the concentration of administration, trade and manufacturing in Bangkok, had produced an already remarkably uneven pattern of development.

Ingram concluded that in 1950 there had been:

> many changes in the economy of Thailand in the last hundred years, but not much 'progress' in the sense of an increase in per capita income, and not much 'development' in the sense of utilisation of more capital, relative to labour, and of new techniques. The principle changes have been the spread of the use of money, increased specialisation and exchange based chiefly on world markets, and the growth of racial division of labour. The rapidly growing population has been chiefly absorbed in the cultivation of more land in rice.
>
> (1971: 216–17)

In terms of the growth of GDP and per capita income evidence is however far from clear. Sompop Manarungsun (1989: 32, 251) suggests very slow growth between 1870 and 1950. He calculated that the average annual growth of GDP was 0.4 per cent between 1870 and 1913 and zero between 1913 and 1950. It should be stressed that the statistical basis for these growth rates is extremely flimsy (see discussion in Falkus, 1991).

From c. 1950 there appears to be a marked acceleration in the rates of growth, which averaged 4.5 per cent between 1950 and 1960. The sharpness of this break is almost certainly an exaggeration. However, as has been outlined, by c. 1950 there is a very marked increase in development related activity – including expenditure on infrastructure, influx of foreign (particularly American) funds, the expansion of manufacturing, the growth of primary exports under the impetus of the Korean war boom – all in a period of comparative political stability. The growth of GDP during the 1950s was extremely uneven, falling to 2 per cent in 1954 and 2.5 per cent in 1957, largely as a result of serious droughts. This reflected the degree to which the economy remained heavily dependent on the production of a narrow range of crops, produced under extensive, unreliable, rain-fed conditions.

From the middle part of the nineteenth century the state had taken a lead in reforming and modernising the economy and the development of railways and telegraph facilities. However, until the 1920s there seems to have been little consideration or discussion of national economic development and policy. Under the changed conditions of the 1930s the governments began to a take a very direct hand in the development and control of the economy. By the late 1950s these policies, under the prevailing regional and international conditions, were beginning to establish a substantial industrial and infrastructural base. However, Thailand's growth, despite some diversification of agriculture during the 1950s, remained dependent on a narrow range of primary products.

3

THE ESTABLISHMENT OF A DEVELOPMENT FRAMEWORK

1958–79

Introduction

Most studies of Thailand's development consider the *coup d'état* of October 1958 and the establishment of the regime of Marshal Sarit Thanart as marking the beginning of the modern economic growth of the Kingdom. However, it is important not to overlook the foundations that were laid during the 1950s by the Pibul government (see Chapter 2) or to exaggerate the differences between the policies of the two regimes. During 1957 and 1958 there were clear signs that the Pibul government was beginning to shift economic policy in the directions advocated by the 1957 World Bank mission and towards those subsequently followed under Sarit (see comments on policy in Ingram, 1971: 231).

The government of Marshal Sarit in many ways represented a more radical change in form than in content.[1] It is all to easy to over-stress the actual level of democracy during the Pibul period and underplay the level of repression. Democratic gestures ended, and once assured of the backing of the USA, the constitution was abolished and rule by marshal law and decree implemented. Absolute power was vested in the Prime Minister (Sarit) in order 'to forestall or suppress any acts subverting, disturbing or threatening public order' (Constitution of the Kingdom, 1957, Article 17). Very similar provisions were to be made after subsequent *coups d'état* in 1971, 1976 and 1977 with all opposition groups being banned or seriously restricted.

Sarit imposed political stability and was prepared to use harsh measures in order to maintain it and his own position. However, this was underpinned by economic development and modernisation (Thak Chaloemtiarana, 1979: 278–85). Here the Sarit regime did differ sharply from the governments of the 1932–57 period in terms of the role of the state in promoting development. Muscat describes this as:

> Probably the most important development policy choice by any
> Thai government in the past forty years was the decision of the

Sarit regime around 1958–59 to repudiate the Thai ethnocentric state *dirigisme* – economic intervention and the creation of state commercial and industrial enterprises to preempt economic development from non-Thai control – that had marked socioeconomic policy since the coup that marked the end of the absolute monarchy in 1932. This decision allowed the private business sector (largely Chinese or Sino-Thai at the time) to come forth as the engine of growth of Thai development and set the stage for the later emergence of a new political force.

(1990: 276)

While this perhaps over-stresses the sharpness of the change there is no doubt that the Sarit period heralded a lasting change in both views of development and the means of achieving it. However, while a clear halt was called to the expansion of direct state involvement with production there was no major disposal of state concerns. Nor was there any dismantling of the controls over the rice sector (see Chapter 5) or attempts to reduce other distortions to the market.

The regime of Marshal Sarit (1958–63) was able to build on the broad foundations laid during the Pibul period. This included investment in transport, power, irrigation, research into maize and rubber production, education and malaria suppression.[2] Thus to a degree Sarit was able to reap the benefits of these programmes and in consequence receive the credit. However, his regime had initially also to face the problems of deteriorating economic and security conditions.

The end of the Korean War boom resulted in lower primary export prices and slower economic growth. This general slow-down emphasised the need for diversification of the economy away from primary production and at the same time exposed the weakness of the state manufacturing concerns (Ingram, 1971: 287). In addition, increasing international tension over the role of China in South East Asia and events in Indo-China acted as a back-drop to increasing rural insurgency in Thailand, particularly in the North East, and increased American involvement in the Kingdom.

The establishment of formal development planning

Despite the overt role of the state in development since the 1850s Thailand came comparatively late to formal national and regional planning (Phisit Pakkasem, 1973: 23–4; Prayod Buranasiri and Snoh Unakol, 1965: 339). In 1946 the Thai government obtained foreign loans from India and the USA, and from 1950 the World Bank began to lend money tied specifically to the infrastructure, particularly roads, railways, irrigation and electric power (Ingram, 1971: 187). Foreign loans, grants and overseas investment became regular features of the economy from the early 1950s.

These developments were closely related to the USA's increasing involvement in the Pacific Asia region.

During the 1950s a variety of government organisations grew up to handle 'aid'. In 1950 the NEC (National Economic Council) was established, its main function was to become the collection of national income statistics. In the same year the Thai Technical and Economic Cooperation Committee was established to generate requests for aid. Neither of these bodies had any power to coordinate the needs of the various government departments however – their role was merely an advisery one.

Until the late 1950s 'major decisions regarding resource allocation and related economic policy formulation centred in the Ministry of Finance' (Phisit Pakkasem, 1973: 6) and were largely uncoordinated. At this time the Ministry lacked the necessary personnel to carry out proper evaluation of the projects. In practice expenditure was decided by arbitrary negotiations with those with the strongest influence obtaining funding (Puey Ungphakorn, 1965: 159). American agencies which were becoming increasingly active in the country during the 1950s largely bypassed the Ministry of Finance and the central government planning funds and personnel directly.

The 1957–8 World Bank visiting mission strongly recommended the setting up of a new coordinating agency for national planning (World Bank, 1959). This view was reinforced after the *coup d'état* of 1957 when large-scale misuse and mismanagement of funds came to light (Ingram, 1971: 88–94). In 1959 the NEDB (National Economic Development Board) was set up to provide tight centralised national planning and from 1960 planning became an established feature of Thai development. During the early 1960s planning machinery was developed to accommodate both national and regional dimensions.

The establishment of the NEDB was accompanied during 1959–60 by the setting up of a series of other developmental institutions. Notably the Board of Investment, the Budget Bureau and the Office of Fiscal Policy. These were headed by a small number of Western trained 'technocrats' who came to play major roles in the Kingdom's developmental policy (Muscat, 1994: 65–73, 88–94). In addition, a series of new agencies and councils were established to facilitate policy formulation and coordination in such areas as education and power generation.

None of these new agencies and institutions were without their individual problems and serious conflicts of interest and policy occurred. In addition, the established individual ministries, while subject to closer budgetary control, continued to operate with a remarkable degree of independence – with little cooperation or even acknowledgment of the policies of their fellows.[3] However, from 1959 it is possible to discern the emergence of an increasingly coordinated developmental programme which contrasts markedly with the haphazard state-led development of the 1947–57 Pibul regime described in Chapter 2.

While the early 1960s saw the establishment of formal and coordinated development planning, the period was also characterised by clear ideological changes. The elements of state-led development that had characterised the Pibul period gave way under Sarit to a fostering and guaranteeing of domestic and foreign private enterprise. While the state continued to provide a lead in major investment programmes, particularly for infrastructure, it was no longer to be a significant provider of enterprise. Planning was to create the environment for economic development and provide a secure and attractive environment for private enterprise. In this change one can discern both the interests of Sarit and his principle backers as well as that of the USA and the recommendations of the 1957–8 World Bank mission.

Under Sarit a 'triple alliance' of the military, bureaucracy and business interests emerged. While the emergence of this can be traced to the 1950s and, to a degree, the 1930s (see Chapter 2), under Pibul the power base remained very firmly within the bureaucracy. With a brief interlude between 1973 and 1976, the alliance (although at times an uneasy one), dominated the political and economic development of Thailand until the 1980s and remains a significant feature even in the mid-1990s. As Ingram has noted:

> an ingenious *modus vivendi* emerged and helped to achieve two important objectives – namely to reduce the fears of the Chinese (and foreign) domination of industry and to provide a way for certain government officials to share in the profits of new firms.
>
> (1971: 231)

Large numbers of influential members of government and the military were appointed to the boards of major private enterprises. Riggs (1966: 258–64) cites 148 large concerns which had more than three cabinet level ministers as directors.

In sectoral terms policy formulation during the 1960s and subsequently was weak, far from clearly stated, and at times contradictory[4] emphasis was laid on industry, trade, banking and services. Agriculture, despite its dominance in the economy, received comparatively low priority. Indeed, as is discussed in Chapter 5, for most of the post-war period the rice sector was heavily taxed and comprised a major source of government revenue.

The First and Second National Economic Development Plans: 1961–6 and 1967–71

In 1960 the newly established NEDB began to formulate the First National Economic Development Plan (1961–6). The recommendation of the 1957–8 World Bank mission that coordinated national planning should be developed was reinforced by fears that American grants and 'soft loans' would be withdrawn (Caldwell, 1974: 49), concern over the long-term prospects for economic growth, and the perceived need to direct development to impoverished areas of the Kingdom where insurgency was increasing. The development of the Plan was seriously hindered by the embryonic nature of the planning machinery, the lack of experienced planners, and inadequate statistical information. To a degree some of these weaknesses were recognised during the formation of the Plan, and in an attempt to allow for them implementation took place in two phases, 1961–3 and 1964–6. The intention was that the experience gained in the first phase could be used to improve both planning and implementation in the second.

In sum, the 1961–6 Plan set a variety of vague and generally unrealistic national targets which 'were, at best projections of likely and desirable trends which seemed to correspond with the intentions of the planners' (Phisit Pakkasem, 1975: 8). The Plan was essentially geared to the national economy with the clearly stated aim of maximising economic growth. The fostering of the manufacturing sector was central to the Plan. To this end there was heavy investment in infrastructure, particularly transport and power generation. The main element in the expenditure on agriculture was irrigation for wet rice cultivation. It could be argued that the expenditure on agriculture was both low, given the sector's importance, and myopic, given the low productivity of rice cultivation and the possibilities for crop diversification (see Chapter 5).

While there was little coincidence between targets and actual achievements, GDP grew overall by an impressive annual average of 7.2 per cent. Despite the questions that can be raised about the accuracy of national income estimates during the 1950s and early 1960s it seems that a considerable acceleration of growth took place during the First Plan period. Ingram (1971: 223) suggested that GNP grew by an annual average of 4.7 per cent between 1951 and 1958 and 8.6 per cent between 1959 and 1969. The period 1960 to 1963 may be seen as one of transition from the lower to the higher rate, and as such represents a critical period in the Kingdom's development.

The degree to which the implementation of the 1961–6 Plan was responsible for the acceleration of growth rates is highly debatable. Comparatively buoyant international trading conditions also combined with a stable domestic political environment – which gave encouragement to investment and business interests, whether Thai, Chinese or foreign. Total investment accelerated sharply, rising from an annual average increase of 8.8 per cent between 1952 and 1960 to 28.7 per cent between 1960 and 1969 (34.7 per cent between 1966–69). However, during the whole period 1952 to 1969 there was little change in either the government or foreign investors' contributions.[5]

Despite the low priority given to agriculture the diversification and expansion of commercial agriculture during the 1960s was of considerable importance to the growth of the economy. There is little doubt that the infrastructural investment during the First Plan contributed significantly to this process (Hirsch, 1990: 50). Road construction brought increasing areas of the Kingdom into the market economy for rice and new export crops, most notably maize and kenaf. A ready international market and a dynamic and widespread network of merchants interacted with a growing need for cash income amongst Thai farmers (Dixon, 1974: 232–4; Rigg, 1986). In addition, large areas of tree crops, particularly rubber, planted during the Korean War 'boom' were coming into production. Indeed, as was noted earlier, much of the accelerated growth during the early 1960s can be attributed to foundations laid during the 1950s.

During the second phase of the First Plan, despite the general neglect of the spatial implications of national and sectoral targets, a beginning was made in regional policy. Regional planning boards were set up for the 'backward regions' of the North, North East and South. During the period of the First Plan these boards developed little that could be construed as 'regional planning'. In effect, where they acted at all, it was to implement nationally oriented policies. The only major exception to this was the North East, where rural insurgency and general political unrest were giving increasing concern to the Thai government, the USA and the international and regional development agencies. In consequence the North East received a large number of specific projects aimed at promoting development and loyalty to the government. Under the First Plan the North East received 28 per cent of total development expenditure – rather less than the region's share of population (Phisit Pakkasem, 1973: 15–16). However, these were largely security and strategically oriented projects which in no way constituted a regional plan, and the North East Regional Planning Board remained largely ineffective.

In response to the statistical weaknesses exposed during the formulation and implementation of the First Plan the NSO (National Statistical Office) was established in 1963 and in the same year an agricultural census was organised. Neither of these developments solved the problem of statistical availability and reliability but the problems were no longer neglected. Doubts over such basic questions as rice area and production continued long after the end of the First Plan, with the Ministry of Agriculture, the NSO and NEDB often producing substantially different figures.

The Second Plan (1967–71) was a considerable technical improvement over the First (Bangkok Bank, *Monthly Review*, 1981, 25: 435). The NEDB and its various sub-committees learnt from the experience of the earlier plan (NEDB, 1967a). Regional development plans and the goal of balanced as well as national economic growth were spelled out. There was no longer the implicit assumption that rapid national economic development would unaided solve the problems of poverty and insurgency. Greater attention was paid to spatial and personal inequality as well as to agriculture.

During the Second Plan period economic growth began to slow down in response to world conditions. Thailand remained dependent on a narrow range of primary exports with uncertain price levels and, for agricultural commodities, very variable production levels. The recognition by NEDB of the inevitability of a very uneven pattern of growth under these conditions resulted, from 1968, in the institution of Annual Operations Plans, which revised targets and budget allocations.

To a degree the slow-down in growth was compensated by increased 'aid' from the USA because of Thailand's strategic importance as a base for operations in Vietnam and as a 'buffer' against the 'domino' spread of communism. American military presence grew rapidly during the 1960s and major military bases were established.[6]

American aid, security and rural development

Between 1950 and 1970 Thailand received American economic and military 'aid' to the value of $US1.13 billion (Caldwell, 1974: 63; Elliott 1978: 131). In addition, the presence of American personnel generated a high level of expenditure and the expansion of the service sector, and the growth of urban centres adjacent to major military bases, particularly in the North East (Elliott, 1978: 129–33).[7] The bases gave rise to considerable, if localised, transport, manufacturing and service industry development. In addition, the American presence and the use of Thailand as a major 'R and R' destination resulted in the expansion of hotel and related leisure and service activities which laid the basis for subsequent expansion of the tourist industry. At the peak in 1968, 43,750 Thais were directly employed by the US military, over half in the North East (Elliott, 1978: 131). Overall, the scale of American aid was far short of that received by South Korea and Taiwan[8] during the key periods of their growth. However, Caldwell (1974: 31, 63–9) concluded that American aid to Thailand had an impact out of proportion to its volume because of the 'targeting' of 'bottlenecks' in the economy. Similarly, Muscat stresses that American development assistance made:

> salient contributions to the removal of development bottlenecks and laying the basis for one of the more successful growth performances in the third world.
>
> (1990: 255)

The USA promoted, and largely paid for, a number of major highway projects. While these were primarily strategic they opened up new agricultural areas, increased access to markets (particularly in the North East) and gave an important boost to the domestic construction industry. In 1965, as a direct result of the escalation of the Vietnam war, a major American-funded expansion of Bangkok's airport facilities was implemented:

> When the project was finally phased out in 1974, Bangkok had become one of the hubs of the world. . . . Only eleven other airports in the world had more scheduled carriers operating. Tourism was already the fifth largest earner of foreign exchange, and 80 percent of all visitors to Thailand were coming by air. Cargo traffic was also growing rapidly (over 25 percent a year due to the Vietnam conflict). . . . It is not an exaggeration to conclude that two decades of US assistance . . . [was] fundamental for the growth of this transport subsector into one of major importance for the country's economic development, quite apart from the importance for the role of the Royal Thai Airforce and the defence of the country.
>
> (Muscat, 1990: 104)

In general the involvement of the USA, as in South Korea and Taiwan, both supplemented foreign investment and boosted the confidence of investors. In consequence, despite the concerns over security, a number of TNCs established operations in Thailand during the 1950s and 1960s (Hewison, 1985: 273).

The Second Plan drew particular attention to the need 'to preserve national security which depends in the final analysis on the country's economic strength and social unity' (NEDB, 1967b: 23). From 1965 the government was beginning to lose control of parts of the North East to 'insurgents' (Nakahara and Witton, 1971: 31). Insurgent activity was reported in 12 of the 16 North Eastern provinces during the late 1960s: a number were officially labelled as 'particularly sensitive' and military deputy governors responsible for 'terrorist suppression' were appointed (Nakahara and Witton, 1971: 31). In consequence rural development in combination with counter-insurgency and expenditure on the police and administration received considerable attention, particularly in the North East (Bell, 1969).

During the late 1960s the national network of primary schools and village administration first proposed during the 1890s was finally completed. Considerable effort went into the firm establishment of the system of village headmen (*pu yai ban*) in the North and North East. While the headmen were nominally elected, increasing amounts of authority and patronage were channelled through them in order to incorporate them as fully as possible into the state bureaucracy (Pasuk Phongpaichit and Baker, 1995: 74). As part of the extension of firm central control over the outer regions, villages were – in many cases for the first time – visited regularly by district officers (*nai amphur*) and local representatives of the various ministries.

Rural development was seen as of major importance in maintaining and increasing loyalty to the government. As a Thai Deputy Prime Minister put it: 'If stomachs are full people do not turn to communism' (Air Chief Marshal Dawee Chulasupp, quoted in the *Bangkok World*, 17 November 1966). A series of Thai–American 'rural development' schemes were initiated from the mid-1960s. These combined rural development with propaganda stressing the evils of communism and the benefits that would stem from the government (Caldwell, 1974: 135). A number of research projects were initiated which aimed to gauge the 'loyalty' of North Easterners and their degree of resistance to 'communist subversion'. This type of work was focused in the Department of Community Development and organised under the auspices of USOM and AID. In addition, these American agencies either conducted or commissioned a large number of reports and investigations on a very wide range of developmental topics. In retrospect one is struck by the sheer volume of material that appeared, particularly between 1966 and 1970. Other activities included the widespread use of American Peace Corp volunteers in projects at all levels. American military personnel were involved in a number of schemes as well as with the wide-ranging CSC (Communist Suppression Command) (Caldwell, 1974: 135). The main vehicle for rural development during the Second Plan was the ARD (Accelerated Rural Development) programme. This scheme – aimed at the most backward and politically sensitive areas – was initiated in 1964 but was only fully implemented during the Second Plan. The programme was initially only applied to the North East, but with deteriorating security problems in some Northern and Southern provinces these regions were also included. Between 1964 and 1971 over 70 per cent of the ARD budget was spent on road building (Berger, 1972: iv–17). The benefit to the rural population of the development of roads, water supply, electricity, irrigation as well as educational and health facilities were undoubted. However, it is clear that the location of much of the expenditure was dictated by strategic and security considerations. In many instances projects were located in the so-called 'pink areas' adjacent to the 'red areas' considered to be under communist control (*Bangkok Post*, 29 April 1975). A number of major road building projects had little immediate economic benefit. This was most notable in the case of routes constructed to facilitate the movement of American military supplies.

Overall during the 1960s substantial progress was made in road construction, electricity generation and irrigation. However, major technical, organisational and budgetary problems were apparent in the road building and irrigation sectors. The maintenance of roads as well as their durability was limiting the impact of the impressive lengths constructed and/or surfaced (Berger, 1972: 129). In the case of irrigation major shortcomings were apparent before the end of the Second Plan. The area classified as irrigated was a considerable over-estimate; much of the land could not be watered by the prevalent gravity methods. Weaknesses in design, original surveys and sub-standard construction materials curtailed the utilisation of many schemes. Additionally, the lack of an effective implementation and maintenance programme limited the actual adoption of irrigation by farmers (see Chapter 5).

An important element in the planned expansion of irrigation and power generation programmes from 1957 until the early 1970s was the grandiose multi-lateral Mekong Scheme and the related tributary projects (see Jacobs, 1995; Muscat, 1992: 137–41). A number of the major North Eastern schemes were seen in part as pilot schemes for the mainstream Mekong projects. Well before the end of the Second Plan it was clear to the Mekong Committee itself that under prevailing political conditions the programme had no prospect of even partial implementation. The effective abandonment of the scheme, shortage of funds and deteriorating security left a number of irrigation projects in the North Eastern region only partly completed or uninitiated after substantial expenditure on planning design and survey work. The completion and full implementation of most of these schemes was to take place gradually during the 1970s and 1980s (see Chapter 5).

Despite the importance attached to the expansion of agricultural production in order to supply domestic needs and increase exports under the First and, more significantly, the Second Plan, in practice, probably the most important contribution to the growth of agricultural production was the construction and upgrading of roads. Alongside this comparative neglect of agriculture has to be set the continued high level of taxation of, in particular, the rice sector (see Chapter 5).

Industrial promotion

In contrast to the limited effective promotion of agriculture during the 1960s there was significant support for the manufacturing sector. Under both the First and Second Plans considerable emphasis was placed on the development of ISI. This built on the developments initiated under the Pibul regime during the 1950s (see Chapter 2). The emphasis on ISI is understandable in the light of the experience of the Second World War when:

> The bitter lesson learnt from the wartime shortage of goods and services was that Thailand must be industrialised, at least to the point of self-sufficiency, in a number of essential items in order to avoid a repetition of such economic hardships.
>
> (Board of Investment, n.d.: 127)

This view was reinforced by the World Bank's advocacy of ISI and the closely inter-linked government, bureaucracy, manufacturers and investors were understandably enthusiastic (Bangkok Bank, 1963 *Monthly Review*, 4(3): 61–3). A key element in the development of ISI from the early 1960s onwards was the promotional programme operated by the BOI (Board of Investment).

The BOI was given wide powers to grant benefits to promoted enterprises. Amongst the most significant of these were: guaranteeing that the government would not nationalise promoted firms or establish competing activities; provision for the employment of foreign staff that would otherwise be restricted by immigration and employment legislation; tax 'holidays' of up to 8 years; and the ability to impose protective tariffs of up to 50 per cent *ad valorum*.

The imposition of tariffs continued to be influenced by the need to raise government revenue (see Chapter 2). During the 1960s 35 per cent came from this source, and they were subject to frequent revisions in the light of the state of the budget and the balance of payments (Ingram, 1971: 284–8, 300). However, despite this a system of differential tariffs was established which generally supported the development of the import substituting sector through the imposition of high levels of tariffs on imported consumer goods and intermediate goods that could be produced locally, and low levels on other intermediate goods and capital equipment (Narongchai Akrasanee, 1973; Somsak Tambunlertchai, 1993: 140). However, it should be stressed that the rate system was complex and policies appear to have been far from consistent (Muscat, 1994: 105). Overall, there was a general rise in the level of protection during the late 1960s (Warr, 1993: 142). Despite this Thailand remained amongst the less highly protected Third World economies until the end of the 1970s (World Bank, 1983a: 186; see pp. 104–05).

From 1960 there was a rapid expansion in the number of enterprises granted promotional status by the Board of Investment. Between 1959 and 1969 607 certificates were issued and some 350 projects eventually came into operation. In terms of approved capital[9] 66.7 per cent was Thai and of the foreign component 31.7 per cent was Japanese, 16.1 per cent from the USA and 14.5 per cent Taiwanese. Some 43 per cent of the approved investment was in consumer non-durables and 22 per cent in intermediate goods (Ingram, 1971: 290–2).

In addition to protection and tax concession, the industrial sector was supported by the concentration of infrastructural investment in the Bangkok area where the vast majority of manufacturing was located. Overall, the sector also benefited from the tax on rice exports which depressed the domestic price of rice and hence the level of urban industrial labour costs. This in general has been regarded as a long-term subsidising of the urban sector as a whole by agriculture (see Chapter 5).

In 1960 the manufacturing sector accounted for 12.6 per cent of GDP. However, consumer goods accounted for 77 per cent of value-added: this included food, beverages and tobacco, which accounted for 57 per cent – a substantial proportion of which comprised such activities as rice milling. Indeed, little of the 1960 industrial production could truly be described as advanced manufacturing. By 1970 the manufacturing sector's share of GDP had risen to 17.1 per cent, but perhaps more significantly, the share of consumer goods had fallen to 61.2 per cent and that of food and related products to 36.8 per cent (Somsak Tambunlertchai, 1993: 121). However, the expansion and maturing of the manufacturing sector was little reflected in the sector's share of employment, which only expanded from 3.4 per cent in 1960 to 4.2 per cent in 1970. To a degree, the limited growth of manufacturing employment reflected the way in which the BOI incentive programme encouraged the import of capital equipment.

The growth of the manufacturing sector during the 1960s was heavily orientated towards the domestic market. In general the expansion and diversification of production resulted in the substitution of finished goods for the import of raw materials, components and machinery (Ingram, 1971: 297). However, there was a marked increase in the level of exports which increased their share of export earnings from 1 per cent in 1960 to 5 per cent in 1965 and 15.4 per cent in 1970. The principal areas of expansion and their shares of manufactured exports in 1970 were: processed foods 26.0 per cent, textiles 20.3 per cent and jewellery and precious stones 17.1 per cent. The beginnings of textile exports during the late 1960s reflected the rapid expansion of the sector and signs of the saturation of the domestic market (Somsak Tambunlertchai, 1994: 128).

The formal promotion of the manufacturing export sector dates from 1963. Under the Industrial Promotion Act there was provision for the exempting of exporters from taxes on imported machinery, raw materials and other intermediate products. In addition, from the 1960s the Bank of Thailand began to offer incentives to exporters of manufactured goods through discount concessionary export rates. However, Muscat (1994: 110) has concluded that this measure was initially largely ineffective.

By the late 1960s doubts were beginning to be raised over the desirability of continuing the emphasis on ISI (Muscat, 1994: 108). These reflected the high level of dependence on imported capital equipment, components, and in some cases raw materials, the deteriorating balance of payments situation and the limits of the domestic market. Considerable criticism of the activities of the BOI began to emerge, particularly with respect to its apparent lack of any clear priorities for the granting of promotional privileges (Ammar Siamwalla, 1975). In 1970 the World Bank heavily criticised Thai industrial policy, advocating lower levels of protection and the promotion of export-orientated activities. These criticisms and concerns, reinforced by deterioration in the balance of payments, appear to have been instrumental in moves from 1970 onwards to promote export-oriented manufacturing. The Third Plan (1971-6) emphasised the development of an export-orientated sector and in 1972 the industrial promotion scheme was revised to give support to exports. However, these measures were not accompanied by any dismantling of the protection and privileges afforded to the ISI sector. Indeed, as is discussed later in this chapter (pp. 101-06), considerable conflict of policy between ISI and EOI developed, to the detriment of the latter, which only began to be resolved through policy reforms initiated during the late 1980s. In addition, a number of studies have concluded that the measures aimed at promoting the export sector through tax concessions were either ineffective (Narongchai Akrasanee, 1975: 276), or rendered so by the import protection system built up during the 1960s (Muscat, 1994: 109; World Bank, 1983a: 186). It should be stressed that the protected ISI sector enjoyed considerable political influence through the 'triple alliance' outlined earlier, and governments became heavily dependent on the revenue derived from import tariffs.

While in terms of employment and exports Thailand in 1970 remained very firmly an agricultural economy, during the 1950s and more especially the 1960s the basis of a broad, domestically orientated industrial structure had emerged. While the majority of manufacturing concerns remained small in scale, a number of major Thai–Chinese groups had emerged, most with close links to the military and the bureaucracy (Elliott, 1978: 118–23; Riggs, 1966: 258–64). The emergence of such groups owed much to the promotional programmes which gave little incentive to either small concerns or technical innovation and tended to encourage the growth of large, often inefficient undertakings, with considerable over-capacity (World Bank, 1980a). Thus, while family control and finance remained the norm during the 1960s there is a rapid development of corporate structures and finance (Suehiro, 1989: 219–44). In addition, while the level of foreign investment remained low, a number of TNCs established branch plants and partnerships with Thai firms (see Suehiro, 1989: 178–218; also pp. 106–07).

Population policy

In terms of the broader long-term development one of the most critical achievements of the 1960s was the establishment of an effective national birth-control programme. This represented a major reversal of policy, for despite the acceleration of population growth from c. 1950, the Pibul regime considered that the Kingdom was under-populated and in 1956 legislation was enacted that gave incentives to larger families (Muscat, 1994: 121).[10] As late as 1966 the government emphasised that 'Thailand is still a wide country and the population is not yet sufficient' (*Bangkok Post*, 13 April 1966). In the same year the then Prime Minister Thanom

Kittikachorn stressed that birth control was not yet necessary; however this view had a very clear racial motive behind it: 'If we cut down Thai births, and the aliens keep on producing babies, we will one day become a minority race' (*Bangkok Post*, 19 July 1966).

The CDR fell from an estimated 27/1000 in 1948 to 18/1000 in 1955, 12/1000 in 1960 and 9.4/100 in 1970 (Ministry of Health, 1984: 178). The most important single cause of this sharp fall was the success of the malaria suppression programme (see Chapter 2). This was closely linked to a series of major aid schemes – indeed it has been suggested that this was by far the most significant contribution of international aid to Thai development (Muscat 1990: 87–90). As is discussed in Chapter 5 the suppression of malaria enabled the clearance and settlement of large areas of forest which in turn reinforced the elimination of the disease. The death rate was further reduced by the implementation of other public health measures and the reduction in the incidence of infectious diseases which came to replace malaria as the principal causes of death.

The acceleration in the rate of population growth resulting from the fall in the CDR had by the late 1950s prompted the World Bank to comment on the adverse effect this was having on the growth of the Thai economy (Mounge, 1982: 62). This was based on the assumption that the rate of population growth had risen only very slightly from 1.9 per cent in 1947 to 2 per cent in 1956[11] (Committee for International Coordination of National Research in Demography, 1974: 75). However, the 1960 census indicated a much greater acceleration to an annual rate of 3.1 per cent. This revelation appears to have focused the attention of technocrats and public health officials on the need to change policy in favour of population limitation and the need rapidly to implement a national birth-control programme (Mounge, 1982: 63–5).

In 1964 the Ministry of Health established a pilot project to gauge the reaction to birth control; the first family-planning clinic was opened in 1965 at Chulalongkorn University. The success of the pilot project led to the establishment of a national anti-natal policy in 1970 and the implementation by the Ministry of Health of a national family-planning programme. There is evidence to suggest that there was a decline in the CBR in urban areas, most significantly Bangkok, before the implementation of the national programmes (United Nations, 1991: 16). However, with the establishment of the national programmes the fall in the rate of growth was remarkably rapid (see pp. 18–19). The widespread adoption of birth control, accompanied by a steady rise in the average age of marriage reduced the rate of population growth from the highest in the ASEAN group in 1970, to the lowest outside Singapore by 1990. There is no doubt that this rapid transformation has played a major, and much neglected, role in the comparatively high and consistent rates of economic growth that Thailand has experienced since the 1960s (see Campbell *et al.*, 1993).

The reasons for the rapid success of the Thai birth-control programme have been much debated (see e.g. Dixon, 1990: 131–2; Knodel *et al.*, 1987). Clearly the establishment of an effective national network of clinics, combined with propaganda and advice were of fundamental importance.[12] However, it is perhaps equally important to stress the receptiveness of the majority of the Thai population to the adoption of birth control.[13] Knodel *et al.* (1987: 35–51) stressed the importance of the spread of communications, the associated establishment of the market economy, the implementation of a compulsory primary education system and the lack of any cultural factors that inhibited the adoption of birth control.[14] They also concluded that the decline, while far from uniform in magnitude or timing, cannot be easily explained in term of education, income or urban residence. Mounge (1982: 229–37) found that the differential adoption of birth control in the rural North was related to access to land and the degree to which the household was dependent on income from labouring activities. However, in general differential fertility amongst urban, rural and social and economic groups appears to have reflected only comparatively short-term lags in the adoption rates of birth control (Knodel *et al.*, 1987: 194). Certainly urbanisation has played a very limited role, for despite some acceleration during the 1960s and 1970s Thailand remained one of the world's least urbanised societies.

Education

Allied to the implementation of a national birth-control programme was the expansion of the primary education provision during the 1960s to provide a comparatively even and effective national system. As was noted in Chapter 2 this was also part of the policy of imposing uniform national education in the Thai language and during the 1960s was closely related to the building of loyalty to the central government and the suppression of 'communism' in the outer regions (see pp. 83–6). By 1970 the primary enrolment rate was 83 per cent and there was a literacy rate of 69 per cent. These figures were high by regional and general Third World standards.

As well as expanding provision during the 1960s there was significant reform of the school curriculum in an attempt to make it more flexible, less narrowly academic and more attuned to the needs of communities and employers (Sirilaksana Khoman, 1993: 325–6). Despite these developments the Thai educational system continued to be criticised for its limited emphasis on science, technology or vocationals skill, and its consequent poor match with the needs of the labour market (see e.g. Apichai Puntasen, 1987). (The long-term developmental problems resulting from this are discussed in Chapters 4 and 8.) Perhaps more significantly, during the 1960s an educational policy emerged under which emphasis was given to the primary, and in the later years of the decade, the tertiary sectors, to the disadvantage of the secondary level (Warr, 1993: 5). Thus by 1970 Thailand had a secondary school enrolment ratio of 17 per cent, compared to 34 per cent in Malaysia and 46 per cent in the Philippines. This discrepancy was to become more marked during the 1970s and early 1980s resulting, as was noted in Chapter 1, in Thailand having by far the lowest level of secondary school enrolment in ASEAN. Similarly, the emphasis on the tertiary sector initiated during the late 1960s was by the early 1980s to give Thailand an exceptionally high level of tertiary sector enrolment – 25 per cent in 1982 – more than double that of Singapore. Between 1970 and 1983 the enrolment in tertiary education increased by 28 per cent; this was dramatically faster than the rate experienced by the other members of ASEAN in this period.[15] This rapid expansion principally reflected the creation of two 'open universities', Ramkamhaeng founded in 1971 and Sukhothai in 1978. These two institutions accounted for 56 per cent of enrolments in 1978 and 88 per cent in 1989. The rapid expansion of the tertiary sector during the late 1970s took place through the proliferation of 'low cost' courses in the social sciences and humanities (Sirilaksana Khoman, 1994: 322). This resulted in a serious mismatch between the provision of tertiary courses and the demands of the labour market, one consequence of which was the emergence of significant graduate unemployment from the mid-1970s onwards (Sirilaksana Khoman, 1994: 322).

In terms of national provision the rural areas have been poorly served by secondary and tertiary provision, thus increasing the cost and difficulty for students from rural areas progressing beyond primary level. This combines with the overall comparatively high cost of post-primary education to filter out students from poorer backgrounds at each level (Sirilaksana Khoman, 1994: 326–35). In addition, secondary and tertiary facilities are disproportionately concentrated in Bangkok (see Chapter 6).

The importance attached to the development of education in all the national plans from 1961 onwards was generally reflected in the allocation of expenditure. The proportion of government expenditure devoted to education rose from 17.3 per cent to 21.1 per cent in 1975, since when it has received the largest share of any of the ASEAN economies.[16] However, when expressed as a proportion of GNP Thai educational expenditure has trailed increasingly behind that of Malaysia.[17] Overall, in development terms, the achievements of the educational programmes implemented from the 1960s onwards, while significant, are far less satisfactory than for health and population control (Muscat, 1994: 239). This is principally a reflection of the allocation of funds within the educational sector and the nature of the curriculum and courses offered. In the long term, these weaknesses posed serious problems for the sustainability of Thailand's development (see Chapter 8).

Development achievements and perspectives, 1957–71

By the end of the 1960s a very clear pattern of development had become established based on the expansion of agricultural production and exports and ISI. These were to be the dominant elements in Thailand's development until the mid-1980s. While the Kingdom's development during the 1960s was remarkably 'low key' – the average annual rate of growth of GDP was 8.3 per cent – this compared very favourably with Taiwan (9.2 per cent), Singapore (8.8 per cent) and South Korea (8.6 per cent). However, unlike those economies Thailand remained an exporter of a comparatively limited range of primary products. In 1970, 85 per cent of export earnings were primary – principally rice, rubber, tin, maize and kenaf.

By the late 1960s a perspective on economic growth was becoming established under which the role of government was increasingly restricted to the provision of infrastructure and the creation of a secure and attractive environment for investment. This relied heavily on conservative monetary and fiscal policies in order to maintain economic stability.[18] It is this view of development that has, with limited modifications, dominated Thai development policy through into the 1990s.

The period 1957 to 1971 was then one of substantial achievements. It saw the development of a domestic and foreign-owned modern industrial sector and the beginning of an export trade in manufactured goods. National systems of statistical reporting and planning structures were established. While question marks remained over the reliability of the former and the effectiveness of the latter, the achievements in both areas were substantial. A national birth-control programme was established that was to prove particularly effective in reducing the rate of population growth during the 1970s. A national system of primary education had been established and a uniform system of administration had been extended to cover virtually all of even the most remote areas. In addition, there had been a substantial development of infrastructure. Indeed, despite the shortcomings previously commented on, by 1971 Thailand appears to have been quite well provided with infrastructure compared to other Pacific Asian and the Third World economies. This together with the progress made in health provision, education and family planning gave Thailand the appearance of a country with very considerable development potential.

The substantial developmental achievements of the period 1957 to 1971 took place under conditions of comparative political stability. Following the death of Marshal Sarit in 1963, his deputy, General Thanom Kittikachorn, assumed the premiership, continuing the pattern of autocratic rule broken only by a brief flirtation with democracy during 1969–71. This sustained period of military rule and enforced stability contrasted with the political uncertainty that had characterised the majority of the period from 1932 until 1957, and indeed was even more to characterise the period 1971 to 1981. However, behind the sustained growth and successes of the 1960s there were serious economic, social and political problems emerging which only came to the fore under the changed international and regional conditions that prevailed during the 1970s.

Economic and political instability 1971–80

In contrast to the previous period the years from 1971 to 1980 were ones of increasing economic uncertainty and political instability. To a considerable extent these changed internal conditions reflected events in the broader regional and international economic and geopolitical arenas.

From the late 1960s Thailand was adversely affected by the general slow-down of the world economy and the instability of the US dollar to which the baht was tied. However, in 1971 the US dollar – gold link was broken and the US dollar was subsequently devalued twice. The devaluations gave a boost to the already extremely buoyant Thai export sector. Between 1972 and 1974 Thailand experienced an export boom led by the rice sector. The rate of growth of exports increased from 10.7 per cent in 1971 to an average of 34.9 per cent between 1972 and 1974. The growth of GDP similarly accelerated from 5.4 per cent to 9.1 per cent in 1973.

The 1973–4 fourfold increase in the international oil price had serious consequences for the Thai economy. Energy demand increased at 16 per cent a year during the late 1960s and early 1970s, and almost 90 per cent of commercial energy was produced from imported oil. During this period the cost of oil imports averaged some 10 per cent of the total import bill. Between 1973 and 1974 the cost of oil imports almost trebled, and the share of the cost of imports rose from 11.1 per cent to 19.6 per cent.

The immediate effect of the sharp rise in oil prices was substantially to reduce the rate of growth of GDP to 4.1 per cent in 1974 and 5.0 per cent in 1985. However, the overall impact on the economy was far slighter than it was on many other oil import dependent economies. As Warr (1993: 51) has pointed out, while in the similarly energy import dependent Philippines the oil price rise had a catastrophic impact, in Thailand there was merely a 'growth recession'. To a very considerable extent the high prices and ready markets for Thai exports tended to offset the increase in the cost of oil imports. In addition, while Thailand did increase its overseas borrowings in order to pay for the increased cost of oil imports, initially the growth of GDP and exports ensured that there was no increase in either the debt service ratio or the level of current account deficit expressed as a percentage of GDP. However, both of these indicators deteriorated sharply in 1975 with the sharp fall in non-oil commodity prices.

In terms of the direct impact of the oil price rise on domestic economic activity, the government was able to provide a substantial 'cushion' through the adjustment of the level of taxation on fuels, the imposition of controls over fuel prices and the introduction of the oil fund.[19] In combination these enabled the government effectively to subsidise the prices of fuel oil, and thereby electricity, kerosene and LNG. In the longer term this 'failure to adjust' fully to the new oil trade conditions has been seen as creating major problems for the Thai economy which had then to be addressed through structural adjustment in the 1980s (see Chapter 4). However, in the context of the mid-1970s government intervention in the domestic fuel market undoubtedly played a significant role in the comparative ease with which Thailand weathered the first oil 'shock'. Indeed, given the unstable political conditions described below it is perhaps difficult to envisage a government engaging in a more painful programme of adjustment if it could in the short term be avoided. In addition to the measures already outlined there was a substantial reduction in the average level of tariff protection (World Bank, 1980a). This was aimed at controlling inflation and boosting the domestic economy.

The problems resulting from the oil price rise and the 1975–6 fall in non-oil commodity prices were compounded in a number of ways. Perhaps most significantly by the run-down, and eventual withdrawal in 1976 of the US military presence. The American presence, expenditure and level of aid were already declining before the oil price rise. However, the signing of the Paris Agreement on Vietnam heralded the final American withdrawal. The impact of loss of American military aid was magnified by the Khmer Rouge takeover of Cambodia in 1975, the subsequent Vietnamese invasion in 1979, and an escalation of rural insurgency within Thailand, particularly after 1976. In total these events resulted in a substantial increase in Thailand's defence budget and a reduction in funds available for development and economic management.

The American withdrawal from Vietnam had a profound effect on Thailand. Most directly the final run-down of the military bases and the related sharp fall in American expenditure had an immediate impact on the economy at both national and local levels. Particularly hard hit were the over-expanded service sectors of the North Eastern base towns. Indeed, subsequently a World Bank loan was arranged to rehabilitate these urban areas. More importantly the American withdrawal from Vietnam was seen both domestically and internationally as raising a question mark over the long-term survival of Thailand as a pro-Western capitalist state. This had a serious impact on both domestic and foreign investment which reinforced the impact of the oil price rise and the international recession on the economy.

In addition to these broader international and regional events it was apparent by the end of the Second Plan that there were considerable imbalances in the economy, particularly with respect to uneven regional development, related high levels of concentration of urban and industrial growth in Bangkok, income distribution, balance of payments, the low growth rate and productivity of agriculture and the slow growth of industrial employment. To a degree these long-standing issues which had been exacerbated by the development of the economy during the 1960s were recognised in the Third Plan (1971–6). However, the emerging imbalances also fostered the emergence of groups and individuals which increasingly questioned the authoritarian and narrow base of Thai political power. This development was fuelled by economic growth and rising educational level, exposure to the international media, and the influx of tourists and foreign products. Critical elements in the emergent opposition were the predominately Bangkok based middle class, the heavily suppressed labour organisations, farmers groups and students (Morrell and Chai-Anan Samudavanija, 1981: 6). These internal developments interacted with the previously noted regional and international events to produce a period of extreme political instability, with violent changes of government in 1973, 1976 and 1977, and, particularly after 1976, increased rural insurgency and state repression.

Political upheaval

The ending of the brief February 1969 to November 1971 period of parliamentary democracy and subsequent banning of political parties and increased general repression heralded a period of increasing opposition to the military government of Thanom Kittikachorn. This opposition centred on the increasingly politicised Bangkok based student movement organised under the National Student Centre of Thailand (NSCT)[20] and the illegal rural based Communist Party of Thailand (CPT). From the end of 1972 there was an escalation of demonstrations and clashes with the police, culminating in October 1973 in a student-led attack on government buildings. The army refused to assist the police in quelling the demonstration, revealing the divisions within the military and effectively undermining Thanom's power base. At this point, in an unprecedented act, the King intervened appealing to the demonstrators for calm and requesting that Thanom, his deputy Praphas Charusathien and son Narong leave the country. In the short term this was to prove instrumental in restoring stability, while in the long run this intervention effectively reversed 'the relationship between monarch and government that had existed since 1932. The King was no longer a mere symbol to be manipulated by the government in power, he had become a significant centre of authority in his own right' (Keyes, 1987: 84). This has proved to be a significant factor in the Kingdom's subsequent political stability with the King playing a balancing role in periods of crisis and uncertain transfer of power.

The fall of the military government ushered in a period of civilian rule; however the upheaval of October 1973 was perhaps no more a revolution than were the events of 1932 (see p. 62).[21] Nevertheless it did mark a watershed in the development of the Thai economic and political system. The civilian governments of the 1973–4 and 1974–6 periods were essentially weak and highly unstable coalitions that initially floated on a wave of liberal optimism (Bell, 1978: 51). Plans for wide-ranging social, political and economic reforms were discussed but it became clear that there was increasingly little chance of these being implemented. The interests of the civilian rulers and their backers were essentially those of the deposed military. Whatever its liberal trappings, economic policy was still geared to growth, creating the environment for foreign and domestic enterprise and transferring agricultural surplus into the industrial sector. Between 1973 and 1976 there was turbulent public participation in the political process and widespread demands for reforms were made by students, farmers and trade unions which had long been illegal. Particularly striking was the formation of the umbrella Peasant Federation of Thailand (PFT) to represent the demands of farmers.

There is no doubt that by the end of 1974 the level of protest, both urban and rural, was adversely affecting foreign and domestic investment. As Bell (1978: 68) has noted: 'significant multinational banks and businesses began to count the years before the communists took over'. It was clear that the civilian governments were unable to contain or satisfy the demands being made on it. The limited reforms enacted and the more far reaching ones discussed and promised for the Fourth Plan period (1977–81) satisfied neither the protesters nor the foreign and domestic financial and business interests.

By the end of 1974 there were clear signs that the military and business interests had regrouped and were working to undermine the civilian government (Crouch, 1984: 64). An organised right-wing offensive against the farmers, trade unions and student groups emerged. This was conducted by a broad range of groups and interests. Bell (1978: 68–9) provides a summary in which the USA was involved, as well as military and business interests. Para-military groups, notably the Red Gaurs, Village Scouts and Nawaphon, were backed and financed from various sources, including the Buddhist Church. From early 1975 there was a rapid escalation of intimidation and outright murders of student, farmer and trade union leaders and other identified radicals. In October 1976 the military returned to power in the wake of the massacre of students at Thammasat University by police and Red Gaurs.

The urban middle class appeared to have broadly supported the 1976 *coup d'état*, viewing the military as preferable to what they perceived as disorder and stagnation under the civilian government (Anderson, 1977). However, the military, deeply divided as it was, could not easily sweep away the organisations and general politicisation of large sections of the population which had developed since 1973 (Crouch, 1984: 64). A military dominated national administrative council took over with a civilian lawyer, Thanin Kraivichien, as Prime Minister. Political parties were banned, the national assembly was dissolved, trade unions, student organisations and farmers' associations were firmly suppressed, with large numbers of activists being arrested.

The repressed and rabidly 'anti-communist' stance of the Thanin government drove large numbers of activists into the rural insurgency movement, giving it a new lease of life. In general the 1976 *coup d'état* did much to enhance the rather flagging image of the Thai Communist Party.

In October 1977 the increasingly unstable Thanin government was overthrown by a military *coup d'état* and General Kriangsak Chomanan, the army Commander in Chief, became Prime Minister. He remained in power until March 1980, presiding over three cabinets and surviving by adroit manoeuvring amongst the various military factions who failed to combine and remove him. Despite the apparent fragility of the governments of the Kriangsak period, efforts were made to stabilise and expand the economy and to reduce rural insurgency. Here military measures, road building to open up isolated areas, and in the Southern border areas cooperation with Malaysia, and the offer of a general amnesty, were reinforced by international events. Following the Vietnamese invasion of Cambodia and the outbreak of the Sino–Vietnamese conflict, the CPT allied itself with China, thus losing its bases in Laos and Cambodia. This seriously weakened and divided the insurgents and by 1980 many were taking advantage of the government amnesty.

In 1980 Kriangsak was replaced by General Prem Tinsulanonda, the army Commander in Chief. Although it was far from apparent at the time, with the benefit of hindsight it is evident that with this change elements of stability began to re-emerge (see pp. 126–7). Prem's government, like that of Kriangsak, was based on a combination of civilian and military leaders with the ultimate policy lying with the military. The civilian elements, as in some earlier periods, played a major role in linking military, bureaucratic and business interests. While a facade of democracy emerged with elections in 1979 and 1981 it was apparent that the military was prepared only to accept an electoral assembly with limited powers. However, while the political parties remained weak and fragmented and only exercised marginal political power compared to the military, their influence was much greater than before the 1973 upheaval. Banking, manufacturing and agri-business interests together with younger army officers began to group around parties and these were increasingly seen as vehicles for achieving political power.

Development policy and planning 1971–80

The Third Plan (1971–6) represented an attempt to adapt to changing domestic and international conditions as well as to learn from the mistakes of the earlier Plans. This Plan was designed to solve economic problems that had appeared during the earlier Plans. The main objectives were to restructure the economy by emphasising the industrial sector, and like the earlier Plans, to promote overall economic growth. However, unlike the First and Second Plans, emphasis was placed on the reduction of income disparities and general social measures – hence the addition of the word 'social' to the Plan title and the change of the NEDB to the NESDB in 1972.

While both the earlier Plans (see Chapter 7) contained elements of regional policy and rural development there was little evidence of any convergence of personal or regional income levels. Indeed, what evidence there was pointed to further divergence. Poverty remained heavily concentrated in the rural areas, particularly those of the North and North East. As the World Bank noted:

> Despite the substantial agricultural development of the past 15 years, it is estimated that at least a third of agricultural house-holds (about 9 million people) remain today in absolute poverty with many having had little or no improvement in their income since 1960. In fact, three-quarters of all poverty households in Thailand, or nearly 8 million people, live in the rural areas of the North and North East and the vast majority of them grow rice under rain-fed conditions.
>
> (1978: 64)

This impression is further illustrated by the incidence of malnutrition. In the North Eastern provinces almost 60 per cent of the children below school age suffered from some degree of protein calorie malnutrition (NESDB, 1981: 70–1). It was against this background that the greater element of regional and provincial planning was established under the Third Plan (see Chapter 7).

The programme of ARD which concentrated development and frequently propaganda in selected settlements was extended under the Third Plan. In addition a national community development programme was drawn up.[22] This was to encourage community participation (principally by supplying labour) in low-cost schemes such as village road repair/construction and well digging/improvement. Under this programme village leaders, particularly in the backward and troubled areas of the North East and South, were to receive training. Attempts were made to develop community projects and activities involving *tambon* (sub-districts) usually comprising five to seven villages. It was clearly stated by officials involved in this scheme that the intention was to integrate groups of villages and increase their resistance to communist take-over. Various traditional labour organisations were utilised as were intra-village competitions and the boy scout movement to foster community spirit and integration.[23] These activities were generally organised under the supervision of provincial and district officials, including the police.

A significant and lasting development was the distribution of development funds directly to *tambon*. In 1975 some US$125 million was distributed to 5,023 *tambon* councils to spend on roads, water supply, irrigation, public buildings and electrical supply. The funds were intended to provide off-season employment as well as develop facilities. Individual projects were generally small with costs below US$1,000. A very typical project would involve laterite being delivered to the village and a grader made available for a short period once the villagers had spread the laterite on the road. At the local level some of these activities did provide important benefits, by providing infrastructure, strengthening local administration and giving a 'bottom up' dimension to Thai development planning. While the funding continued under the Rural Employment Generation Scheme (REGS), developments have been limited by subsequent limited funding, often ineffective coordination and a high level of corruption. In the longer term the initiative activated *tambon* councils and began to integrate them into the Kingdom's rural development structure (see Hirsch, 1990: 16–17). Overall, however, in the longer run perhaps the most important developments for the rural population was the promotion of institutional credit, particularly from 1975 (see Chapter 5).

Despite the increased attention paid to the regional element in the Third Plan, the regions' share of development expenditure fell: for example the North East's share declined from 28 per cent to 18 per cent. The introduction of the low-cost community development had, at least in part, to be seen as a consequence of the reduced regional budget. Similarly, low-cost social measures replaced higher cost infrastructure projects. The intention was to spread the reduced share more widely and develop projects that would have a direct and immediate impact. As well as the perceived need by the government to concentrate scarce development funds in areas that would contribute to the priorities of economic growth and restructuring of the economy, it was clear that much costly infrastructure development during the 1960s had produced little return. Formal recognition of shortcomings in earlier developments is illustrated by the irrigation rehabilitation loans negotiated with the World Bank. These were used to survey, complete, repair, modify and implement a number of schemes which had mostly been completed by the end of the Second Plan but had never functioned satisfactorily (see Chapter 5).

The Third Plan targets were largely unfulfilled. Given the general international economic conditions and domestic disruption this is hardly surprising. Thus virtually all the imbalances that the Plan was intended to address remained. These have been aptly summarised by Warr (1993: 31). First, the continued comparatively slow growth of the agricultural sector which averages 3.9 per cent compared to the overall growth of 6.2 per cent. Second, while industry had grown at an average annual rate of 8.2 per cent it was generating limited employment. The number of workers in factories – many of which were simple agro-processing plants – had risen from 185,000 in 1968 to 597,000 in 1975 (NSO *Industrial Census*, 1969 and 1975). Third, migration to Bangkok from rural areas was substantial and increasing. Fourth, the comparatively rapid growth that Thailand had experienced since the early 1960s had been at the expense of deteriorating land, forest, water and marine resources. In addition, concerns were expressed over income distribution, rural poverty and regional imbalance. It was against this background that the Fourth Plan was drawn up.

The Fourth Plan (1977–81), unlike its predecessors, did not emphasise economic growth. Rather the importance of promoting 'social justice' by reducing socio-economic disparities and 'improving mass welfare' (NESDB, 1977: 3). While the need for rapid economic recovery during 1977 and 1978 was stressed, there was a shift in emphasis from 'growth rate' to growth pattern. Targets were set for an extensive land reform programme, free health services and a greatly expanded provision of education. Some 68 per cent of the Fourth Plan budget was earmarked for these and other 'social measures'. These elements reflected the priorities of the governments of the 1974–6 period.

The implementation of the Fourth Plan (1977–81) was much delayed because of the political changes of the late 1970s. In the event the Plan was greatly modified – with much of the social, community and regional policy being either abandoned or scaled down. By 1981 not only were many of the Fourth Plan targets not realised but a number from the Third Plan remained uncompleted. During the course of the 1977–81 Plan, recurrent economic and political crises shifted the emphasis towards national goals of economic growth and stability. Many policies implemented on an *ad hoc* basis during this period were codified in the Fifth Plan (1982–6) discussed in Chapter 4.

Manufacturing development during the 1970s

The growth of the Thai economy during the early 1970s was accompanied by very limited structural change in the domestic economy, the composition of exports, or the labour force. In contrast, during the second half of the decade there was a sharp increase in the manufacturing sector's share of GDP (from 17.2 per cent in 1975 to 21.3 per cent in 1980) and, more especially, export earnings (from 15.4 per cent in 1975 to 26.8 per cent in 1980). To a degree this change was greatly exaggerated by the fall in the prices of primary products.[24]

Within the manufacturing sector there was a degree of diversification and structural change. The main growth areas remained agro-processing, textiles and a range of assembly areas aimed at the domestic consumer market. There was also significant expansion of glass, cement, paper, and iron and steel. The cores of the expansion were concerns established during the 1960s under the early phase of industrial promotion and protection. By far the most significant was textiles. Between 1970 and 1980 the sector increased its share of manufacturing value added from 18.2 per cent to 23.6 per cent. During the same period the share of food and related products declined from 36.8 per cent to 30.5 per cent. In addition, within the agro-processing sector, there was a shift towards high value added products and a decline in the importance of such simple processing as rice milling and cassava chipping.

During the 1970s a number of major agri-business concerns developed, principally out of rice milling, with interests in warehousing, feed production, the production of pigs and chickens, seeds, slaughtering, gunny sack manufacture and the freezing and canning of a variety of marine and agricultural products. In addition, there was considerable expansion and diversification of agro-processing, most notably with respect to sugar, maize, kenaf and cassava. Some of these developments reflected the relaxation of government controls, notably over sugar refining in 1969 and slaughtering in 1973.

The development of the agri-business sector is illustrated by the emergence of the Charoen Pokphand group.[25] This developed from a seed business established by a Chinese immigrant in 1921 to become the largest agri-business concern in Thailand by the 1980s. The company developed through diversification into the importation of fertiliser and other agricultural inputs, and during the 1960s into feed milling. During the late 1960s a beginning was made in the large-scale production of chickens, and in 1970 a joint venture was established with the American-based concern Arbor Acres. During the 1970s a major integrated chicken operation involving the supply of chicks on a contract basis and the processing of the reared birds for local and, increasingly, export markets. From this development Charoen Pokphand moved into a similar integrated pig production system and by the end of the decade had established a series of associated companies in transport, fertiliser, chemicals and seeds. From the mid-1970s Charoen Pokphand had 'gone transnational' – with businesses in Taiwan, Singapore and Malaysia (see also pp. 137–8).

The rapid expansion of the textile sector was similarly accompanied by the emergence of large corporations, notably Sukree and Saka-Union.

These both developed broad interests in the textile sector closely linked to (principally) foreign capital. These developments were the most prominent part of the general increase in the size of manufacturing concerns. By the early 1980s there were some 30 factories in Bangkok employing more than 1,000 workers (Pasuk Phongpaichit and Baker, 1995: 187). However, by 1980 63.3 per cent of manufacturing concerns employed less than 10 workers and only 6.5 per cent more than 50. Thus the manufacturing sector remained very much the province of small-scale, often family-owned concerns.

The long-term problems of the protected and promoted import substituting sector are seen at their most extreme in the development of motor vehicle production. Until 1961 Thailand was entirely dependent on imported vehicles. Subsequently, high levels of protection encouraged the development of a domestic assembly industry, which by 1984 supplied 91.6 per cent of commercial vehicles and 96.6 per cent of passenger cars. By this date there were 15 operating assembly plants, many were very small indeed and output was dominated by a small number of foreign-owned (principally Japanese) firms.[26] Since 1969 the development of the industry was coordinated by the Automobile Development Committee. High levels of protection were used to protect and stimulate production. By 1981 the duty on passenger cars of less than 3,000cc engine capacity was 150 per cent, and on 'pickup' trucks 80 per cent. In order to increase the 'local content' of assembled vehicles import duties were progressively raised on Complete Knockdown Kits (CKDs). However, by the early 1980s 55 per cent of the content of vehicles was still imported (Bangkok Bank *Monthly Review*, 1984, 25: 185).

During the 1970s there was overall a substantial rise in the level of effective tariff protection. This was interrupted by the drastic reduction in tariffs following the 1974 oil price rise (see p. 95). Subsequently the level rose rapidly, particularly after 1978. The latter rise reflected in part the authorisation in 1977 of the BOI to impose tariff surcharges on goods produced by promoted concerns. This operated independently of the tariffs imposed by the Fiscal Policy Office – the inter-ministerial Tariff Committee which dealt with individual requests for protection – the Ministry of Commerce – which administered import licences and had the power to impose quantity restrictions – and the Ministry of Industry – which could specify local content and limit new entry and the expansion of capacity (Muscat, 1994: 153). The largely uncoordinated activities of these various bodies, while in total providing high levels of protection for certain sectors and concerns, also frequently made highly conflicting decisions. It is perhaps not unfair to say that this situation was not untypical of the manner in which much of the Thai administrative and policy implementing mechanism was operating by the end of the 1970s.

The World Bank (1980a, 1983a) considered that the increase in the level of effective protection that took place from the late 1970s onwards propelled Thailand from being one of the Third World's less highly protected countries to one of the more protected. In addition, the Bank considered that this, coming on top of the long-term protection and promotion of the import substitution sector, had tended to foster inefficiency and over capacity. Muscat (1994: 149–50) considered that the limited period for which these higher levels of protection were imposed and their concentration in the consumer goods sector which had limited linkages with the wider industrial economy resulted in Thailand not being saddled with uncompetitive domestic production of inputs. However, he did concede that within the consumer sector promotion and protection had fostered the emergence of a large number of concerns that had little prospect of continued profitability in the absence of continued support (Muscat, 1994: 151).

As well as the increased protection offered to the manufacturing sector during the 1970s there were also moves to promote exports. The Bank of Thailand's policy of providing credit to exporters was extended, tax and import duty refunds were introduced, and perhaps inevitably, a number of government departments and agencies began to offer services aimed at promoting exports. However, as with earlier measures, in total they were of limited impact and insufficient to balance the general bias against exports (Muscat, 1994: 150; NESDB, 1977: 209–10; see also Chapter 4). Thus, it is not unreasonable to see the development of manufacturing exports during the 1970s as taking place in spite of official policy. Indeed, the expansion and diversification of exports has to be seen in terms of the dynamism of individual firms, and their ability to establish partnership deals with foreign capital and exploit new markets. Thus, according to the NESDB the export sector was consistently the most rapidly growing from the early 1970s onwards (see Tables 3.1a and 3.1b).

The near stagnation of the manufacturing sector's share of export earnings at 15.4 per cent during the early part of the decade was replaced by rapid expansion to 26.8 per cent by 1980. The expansion was led by the Thai-owned textile sector being reinforced as the decade proceeded by Japanese and Asian NIE-based firms. In 1973 the American-based National Semi-Conductor began to be assembled for export. By 1980 four more concerns were in operation, two from the USA, one from the UK and one tied to an Indian producer.[27]

The composition of manufactured exports changed considerably during the 1970s. There were significant increases in the share of processed foods (during the first half of the decade), garments (which began to replace textiles), wood products (as timber exports declined), leather products (as the export of hides declined) and electrical products (during the later part of the decade). This change in composition was also accompanied by a

Table 3.1a Average annual growth rates of the manufacturing sector at constant 1972 prices, 1972–91 (percentages)

Sector	1972–6	1977–81	1982–6	1987–91
Export oriented	13.0	9.2	8.4	15.1
agro-industry	12.0	6.4	12.7	7.6
other	13.4	10.2	7.8	11.6
Domestic oriented	10.5	7.6	3.6	14.4
agro-industry	9.8	8.1	4.1	5.1
other	10.7	7.5	3.6	11.2
Total	11.3	8.1	5.3	14.7

Source: NESDB.

general change in the direction of manufactured trade, with a general rise in the importance of Japan and the EU and a decline in the significance of the USA.[28]

As well as increasing its share of export earnings significantly during the 1970s, the growth of the manufacturing sector also became markedly more dependent on export markets. By the end of the decade this was particularly the case for food products (21.2 per cent of output), electrical products (33.1 per cent of output) and textiles (10.1 per cent of output). For the manufacturing sector as a whole exports as a percentage of the growth of output rose from 6.5 in 1968–72, to 8.5 in 1972–8, to 28.2 in 1975–8 and to 35.2 per cent in 1978–80 (World Bank, 1984; see also Table 3.1b). This does indicate the very marked reorientation of the manufacturing sector that was taking place in the late 1970s, led by textiles and garments, processed food and electrical products.

Table 3.1b Average percentage shares of manufacturing GDP at constant 1972 prices, 1972–91

Sector	1972–6	1977–81	1982–6	1987–91
Export oriented	31.7	32.8	36.8	40.1
agro-industry	5.5	5.3	6.4	5.9
other	26.3	27.5	30.5	34.1
Domestic oriented	68.7	67.2	63.2	59.9
agro-industry	9.7	9.8	9.72	9.9
other	59.0	57.4	53.5	50.0
Total	100.0	100.0	100.0	100.0

Source: NESDB.

The increased importance of the export markets tended, particularly after 1975, to increase the concentration of manufacturing in Bangkok and its immediate vicinity. The capital's share of manufacturing value added increased from 39.4 per cent in 1970 to 54.6 per cent in 1980 (World Bank, 1984). As well as the growth of the export market this reflected the importance of the capital's market, and the general concentration of infrastructure, administration and services in Bangkok (see Chapters 6 and 7).

Foreign investment

There was little increase in foreign direct investment during the 1970s. Given the uncertain internal conditions that prevailed, particularly prior to 1976, it is perhaps not surprising that Thailand did not become a major recipient of foreign investment during the decade, remaining a far less attractive destination than, for example, Indonesia, Malaysia, or the Philippines (see p. 129). During the 1970s Japan came to replace the USA as the largest source of foreign investment in the Thai economy. During the period 1970–5 39.9 per cent of the net investment inflow was from the USA and 26.4 per cent from Japan; in contrast between 1976 and 1980 the USA contributed 24.9 per cent and Japan 31.7 per cent. There was also, over the same period, a rise in the contribution of Hong Kong and Singapore – from 15.2 per cent to 20.9 per cent. Apart from a brief recovery of the importance of American investment during the early 1980s, these trends in foreign investment continued through into the 1990s, gathering momentum after 1987 (see pp. 124–5). As has already been noted these changes in the source of investment were also reflected in that of trade (see pp. 104–5). Indeed, the 1970s can be seen as the decade in which Thailand began to pass from an area of strong American activity to one of Japanese and increasingly Asian NIE activity.

There were changes too in the sectoral distribution of foreign investment, with the industrial sector increasing its share from 28 per cent during the first half of the decade to 34 per cent during the second. Within the industrial sector during the period 1971 to 1975 46 per cent of foreign investment was in textiles. In contrast, between 1976 and 1980 the share of textiles declined to 20.1 per cent while the electrical and electronics sectors, which had only received 12.6 per cent in the first half of the decade, rose to 37.5 per cent.

In general the Japanese investors established comparatively few wholly owned concerns in Thailand. This reflected the preferred mode of operation of Japanese companies (Somsak Tambunlertchai, 1977) and the general orientation of foreign investment towards the domestic market where local contacts and knowledge was particularly useful. Wholly owned foreign plants were heavily concentrated in the chemical, pharmaceutical, petroleum and engineering sectors. In 1979 308 of the 500 largest firms were fully or almost fully Thai owned, and of the remainder many were joint undertakings (Suehiro, 1989: 188–9). Similarly Hewison (1985: 275) has stressed that in 1979 'the largest and most profitable companies in Thailand were to a very large extent Thai owned'. However, in terms of registered capital, by the end of the 1970s a number of significant sectors had become dominated by foreign capital, notably textiles, motor vehicle production, petroleum and tin.[29] In a number of cases single TNCs dominated production, for example sheet glass, chemical fertiliser, tin plate and tin smelting (Suehiro, 1989: 204). For other products such as motor cycles, soft drinks, detergents, polyester staple, milk products and tyres, two or three TNCs accounted for 80–100 per cent of production (Suehiro, 1989: 204).

The importance of foreign control over the Thai economy was probably greater than the figures above suggest. Thai concerns frequently relied very heavily on overseas expertise and technology. Thus many foreign investors, particularly Japanese, tended to keep very tight control over operations even when they were minority shareholders (Somsak Tambunlertchai, 1994: 136). Indeed, Japanese firms appear to have tended to opt for minority holdings (Somsak Tambunlertchai, 1977). During the 1970s it seems likely that some Japanese concerns reduced their holdings to minority status, and adopted more indirect means of control, at least in part, because of the increasing hostility towards their perceived domination of the economy (see Hewison, 1989: 107).

Conclusion: economic development during the 1970s

Despite the economic and political problems that faced Thailand during the 1970s the economy grew at an annual average of 7 per cent – low compared to the Asian NIEs, but high, and consistently so, compared to global and Third World trends. The slowing of growth during 1974 and 1975 was offset by recovery during 1976–8 when the annual average growth of GDP was 9.3 per cent and of exports 20.5 per cent. Indeed, the majority of the decade was characterised by a very dynamic export sector, which despite domestic inflation, and, particularly in the second half of the decade, an over-valued currency,[30] achieved a doubling in the volume of exports. There was considerable diversification of products and markets. Notable developments included tapioca pellets for animal feed, exported principally to the EU, and light manufactured goods, particularly textiles, transistors, and canned pineapples and marine products. These developments heralded the very substantial expansion of manufactured and agri-business exports from the mid-1980s onwards.

The growth of exports was reinforced by the rapid growth of tourism and remittance income from overseas workers. These provided important 'cushions' for the Thai economy during the increasingly difficult international trading conditions that prevailed during the 1970s. Tourism began to expand during the early 1970s and was earmarked for promotion during the Third Plan 1972–6). Though uncertain economic and political conditions tended to discourage visitors and investors, annual tourist arrivals nevertheless increased from 485,366 in 1970, to 850,459 in 1975 and 1,348,919 in 1980. Similarly, the growth of organised labour exports dates from the early 1970s when a number of private recruitment agencies were established (Pasuk Phongpaichit and Samart Chiasakul, 1993: 161–2). There was rapid expansion from the mid-1970s, with labour going principally to the Middle East. In 1978 in recognition of the importance of the traffic, and the need to regulate it, the Ministry of Labour began to provide its own service to migrant labourers. Between 1975 and 1980 remittances increased from 0.1 million baht to 8.4 million and earnings from tourism from 1.7 million baht to 14.1 million. In total these sources were the equivalent of 9 per cent of the trade deficit in 1975, and 36.4 per cent in 1980. In the latter year tourism was the second largest earner of foreign exchange after rice exports.

Overall, given the international economic conditions, the loss of American expenditure and aid, and the disrupted domestic political conditions, the growth of the Thai economy during the period 1971 to 1978 was remarkable. However, behind this growth there were serious problems which reinforced the imbalances in the growth process mentioned earlier. The balance of payments current account, adverse in almost every year since 1953 (except 1955 and 1956) rose from an average of 1.6 per cent of GDP during the first half of the decade to 5.2 per cent in the second. In addition, the annual inflation rate averaged more than 10 per cent between 1973 and 1980, far more than the Kingdom's main trade partners (Narongchai Akrasanee et al., 1991: 4). Government expenditure as a percentage of GDP increased from 17.0 in 1977 to 18.9 in 1980, while government income stagnated at some 15.5 per cent of GDP. In the same period the budget deficit expanded from 4.3 per cent of GDP to 8.0 per cent.

To a degree the growth of the Thai economy during the latter part of the 1970s could be described as 'debt sustained', with the established pattern of growth and attendant policies being maintained, at least in part, by overseas borrowing. Both the widening balance of payments deficit and the government budget deficit were increasingly covered by short-term borrowing, as a result of which overseas debt grew from the equivalent of 10.1 per cent of GDP in 1977 to 17.7 per cent in 1980.

During the 1970s there were some significant shifts in government policy statements away from a narrow focus on economic growth and towards some consideration of the spatial pattern of development, income distribution, welfare, land reform and the supply of rural credit. Some of these were very direct products of the 1973–6 period of civilian rule. However, by the end of the decade there had been very limited effective implementation of any of these measures. A significant exception to this general ineffectiveness was the beginning made in the provision of rural credit from 1975 onwards (see pp. 147–8). Despite the attention devoted to regional planning and the promotion of growth outside the BMR both regional disparities and the primacy of the capital had further increased (see Chapters 6 and 7). Indeed, the effectiveness of the planning structures established since the early 1960s appeared to be extremely limited.

Despite the limited and generally ineffective nature of policies towards income distribution and the concern over the level of poverty expressed during the early and mid-1970s, there was a substantial decline in the level of poverty during the decade (see pp. 216–9). With the exception of the contribution made to the rural sector by the expansion of institutional credit it is difficult to isolate any policies that made a significant contribution to this. In general, the rise in rural incomes appears to relate to the expansion, diversification and commercialisation of agriculture during the decade (see pp. 149–52) in which the government played a limited, indirect (through road building) and for many communities, largely negative role through the taxation of rice exports (see discussion pp. 141–8).

In 1980, despite policy statements in favour of export-orientated manufacturing and the introduction of various incentive measures from 1964 onwards,[31] Thailand could be characterised as a country in which the majority of the population were rural and engaged in agriculture and in which economic growth and government policy remained centred on primary production and ISI. However, with the benefit of hindsight it is apparent that while cyclical changes in the global economy were creating major difficulties for the Thai economy, structural changes in the global economy and in the Thai economy itself were making the past pattern of growth and attendant policies outmoded. Indeed, Muscat (1994: 216) has suggested that the cumulative economic problems faced by Thailand during the 1970s reflected a failure to adjust to the changed conditions that followed the 1973 oil shock.

The political instability and weakness of the governments of the 1973–80 period combined with the severity of the economic problems to undermine the effective management of the economy. To a degree there was a retreat from the conservative financial policies which had long dominated Thai economic management. During the 1970s policy makers were increasingly faced with crisis management (Aboonyi and Bunyaraks Ninsananda, 1989: 30; Muscat, 1994: 132). Further, the weak governments were reluctant to undertake potentially unpopular measures, and in the face of increased economic difficulties after 1975 policies became expansionary rather than focused on establishing economic stability (Bhanupong Nidhiprabha, 1993: 175; Muscat, 1994: 132). At least in part these problems reflect deficiencies in the mechanisms available for managing serious long-term adjustment of the Thai economy (see World Bank, 1980a). However, during the period 1976–8 the expansionary policies were endorsed by both the Bank of Thailand (*Annual Economic Report*, 1978) and the World Bank. Indeed, in 1978 the latter had advocated an even more expansionary programme than was followed (World Bank, 1980b).

During the period 1976 to 1978 comparatively rapid growth of GDP and export earnings were accompanied by a fall in real oil prices, a generally excellent international credit rating and an influx of World Bank funds as a result of Thailand being classified as a relatively strong economy (Muscat, 1994: 155). Thus the expansionary policies of the late 1970s can be seen as supported by both domestic and international financial agencies and by evidence of economic health. However, the worsening imbalances in the economy were all too apparent to the Bank of Thailand (*Annual Economic Report*, 1978: 11–16). Despite this, the prevailing view appears to have been that Thailand could continue with expansionary policies and simply grow itself out of the structural imbalances. It was for example projected that the coming into production during the very early 1980s of major projects in natural gas, chemicals, fertiliser and cement, mainly in connection with the Eastern Seaboard developments (see pp. 200–02) would lead to an increase in productivity which would enable the government to attend to adjustments in such areas as the low productivity of agriculture and the related problem of low rural incomes, urban employment, income distribution and the establishment of a national social security system (Bank of Thailand, *Annual Economic Report*, 1978: 11–16). In the event these expectations were dashed by the 1979–80 oil price rise and the subsequent international recession, when the expansionary policies served to make the economy extremely vulnerable to the external shocks.

4

STRUCTURAL ADJUSTMENT AND ACCELERATED GROWTH

1980–96

Introduction

This chapter reviews the development of the Thai economy from *c.* 1980 through to the mid-1990s. This was a period of dramatic change and development for the Kingdom. At the close of the 1970s, as was outlined at the end of Chapter 3, Thailand was experiencing serious economic problems and signs of increasing political and economic instability. During 1979–80 these problems developed into a major crisis. However, during the early 1980s the rapid re-establishment of political and economic stability, together with changed international and regional circumstances, laid the basis for a period of unprecedented rapid growth of GDP. This was accompanied by rapid internationalisation of the economy and a sharp change in the composition of exports away from primary products and towards manufactured goods. As was noted in Chapter 1 these developments have been widely depicted as heralding the emergence of Thailand as a NIE. It is the purpose of this chapter to outline and explain the changes that Thailand has experienced during the period up to the mid-199s. The broader questions of the sustainability of the growth and structural change are touched on, but are explored more fully in Chapter 8.

The crisis of the early 1980s and structural adjustment

The serious economic problems faced by Thailand at the end of the 1970s were magnified into a major crisis by the 1979–80 oil price rise, the subsequent collapse of non-oil commodity prices and sharp rises in interest rates and the severely contractionary policies implemented by the members of the OECD. Unlike the situation which accompanied and immediately followed the 1973 oil price rise there was no complementary commodity boom. In addition, as was noted at the end of Chapter 3, the expansionary

111

economic policies and worsening imbalances in the economy had left Thailand far more vulnerable to external shocks than was the case in 1973–4.

In 1979 the Thai economy was almost as dependent on energy imports as it was in 1973, with some 90 per cent of its commercial energy coming from this source; this despite a slower growth of average annual energy demand – 12 per cent compared to 16 per cent before 1973 – the expansion of HEP, and increased lignite production. The promising offshore gas yields were not yet in production, the first supplies did not come on shore until 1981. In consequence oil and oil products' share of the cost of imports rose from 22.0 per cent in 1978 to 31.1 per cent in 1980 (see Table 1.4, p. 6).

As after the 1973 price rise, a combination of tax changes, controls over prices and the use of the oil fund (see p. 95) enabled the impact of the price rise to be softened. In effect from mid-1980 until March 1985 when international oil prices began to decline, all oil products except gasoline were subsidised (Praipol Koomsup, 1993: 313). This served to reduce the pressure on inflation and cost of living, while improving the competitiveness of manufacturing. However, it also served to increase the level of government budget deficits from 3.7 per cent of GDP in 1979 to 6.5 per cent in 1982 (see Tables 4.1a, 4.1b).

The combination of the oil price rise and the fall in the returns on Thailand's principal exports resulted in the terms of trade declining by 22 per cent during 1979–80 (Table 4.1a). The current account deficit widened from 4.8 per cent in 1978 to 7.6 per cent in 1979 and 6.4 per cent in 1980, while the debt service ratio rose from 14.8 per cent in 1979 to 20.5 per cent in 1981. In addition, inflation rose from 9.9 per cent in 1979 to 19.7 per cent in 1980. The deteriorating economic situation was exacerbated by question marks over the Kingdom's long-term political stability – there had been a substantial loss of confidence on the part of both domestic and foreign investors.

By the end of the 1970s many commentators, including some Thai officials, were making extremely pessimistic pronouncements, predicting escalating economic and political turmoil culminating in violent revolutionary change within two or three years (cited in Dixon, 1979: 1072). With the benefit of hindsight these fears can perhaps be regarded as greatly exaggerated. However, they were real and profoundly depressed both domestic and foreign investment. A survey of 65 Japanese corporations conducted during 1979 concluded that the investment situation was 'hopeless' (cited in Tasker, 1991: 49). In the longer run these pessimistic views of the Kingdom's prospects played a significant role in the policy changes during the 1980s which are discussed in this chapter.

During 1979–80 the Thai government initiated an austerity programme aimed at curtailing inflation, the balance of payments deficit and the growth

Table 4.1a Key features of Thai economy, 1970–94

Year	Growth of GDP (%)	Inflation rate (%)	Current account/ GDP (%)	Debt/ GDP (%)	Exchange rate (baht/US$)	Government expenditure/ GDP
1970	6.6	0.8	−3.5	10.3	20.9	19.8
1971	5.0	0.4	−2.4	10.7	20.9	19.9
1972	4.1	4.8	−0.6	11.0	20.9	18.5
1973	9.9	15.6	−0.4	8.4	20.6	16.0
1974	4.4	24.3	−0.6	8.5	20.4	16.2
1975	4.8	5.3	−4.1	9.1	20.4	18.4
1976	9.4	3.8	−2.6	9.5	20.4	19.0
1977	9.9	7.6	−5.5	10.1	20.4	16.9
1978	10.4	7.9	−4.8	11.5	20.3	17.8
1979	5.3	9.9	−7.6	14.8	20.4	17.9
1980	4.9	19.7	−6.4	17.7	20.5	19.1
1981	7.6	12.7	−7.4	20.5	21.7	19.0
1982	6.0	5.2	−2.8	23.3	23.0	20.4
1983	5.8	3.8	−7.3	24.1	23.0	19.9
1984	5.5	0.9	−5.1	26.0	23.5	19.6
1985	3.5	2.4	−4.1	34.1	27.1	21.1
1986	4.5	1.9	0.2	33.8	26.3	20.4
1987	8.4	2.5	−1.0	32.3	25.7	19.2
1988	11.0	3.8	−3.0	25.8	25.3	16.7
1989	10.8	5.4	−3.7	23.5	25.7	14.7
1990	10.0	6.0	−8.7	23.2	25.6	14.7
1991	7.9	5.7	−7.8	35.7	25.6	14.8
1992	7.2	4.3	−5.7	34.9	25.4	17.5
1993	7.9	3.7	−5.0	36.1	25.3	16.7
1994	8.8	5.0	−5.6	42.6	25.2	17.1

Source: Bank of Thailand.

Note:
Debt includes only long-term debt.

of overseas debt. Key measures included increasing fuel prices and government revenues. In addition, moves towards longer term structural change were incorporated into the draft Fifth National Plan. However, these measures and proposals were insufficient to change the pessimistic views of investors and the international agencies. In addition, the implementation of austerity measures – particularly the proposed increase in energy prices – sparked off considerable public protest which undermined the already weak government of Kriangsak Chomanan, contributing to its fall and increasing the fears of further political disruption. This government was already under serious pressure not only because of its apparent inability to manage the economic crisis, but also because of the Vietnamese invasion of Cambodia and the presence of Vietnamese troops along the Thai–Cambodian border.

Table 4.1b Key features of Thai economy, 1970–94

	Terms of trade 1987 = 100	Budget deficit GDP (%)	Gross domestic capital formation (US$m)	Exports (US$m)	Manufactured exports (US$m)	Primary exports (US$m)
1970	178.9	n.a.	119.0	710	76	629
1971	160.0	n.a.	119.6	827	113	706
1972	151.5	−4.8	120.6	1039	190	863
1973	176.1	−3.2	132.7	1527	343	1201
1974	168.3	+0.1	132.4	2402	422	2002
1975	141.2	−2.0	131.5	2162	397	1784
1976	132.6	−4.9	148.7	2950	572	2398
1977	131.7	−3.2	184.3	3451	683	2803
1978	141.8	−3.6	204.6	3996	1039	3042
1979	134.9	−3.7	212.7	5207	1402	3879
1980	123.1	−4.9	220.5	6369	1886	4579
1981	108.9	−3.6	230.5	6849	2019	4978
1982	94.7	−6.5	226.1	6797	2014	4914
1983	100.1	−4.0	255.1	6275	2058	4284
1984	97.3	−3.5	283.0	7279	2583	4780
1985	90.6	−5.4	268.0	7056	2800	4221
1986	104.3	−4.5	256.6	8786	3944	4820
1987	100.0	−2.3	296.4	11629	6125	5446
1988	98.2	+0.7	361.0	15902	8192	7068
1989	94.4	+2.9	483.9	19976	11453	8377
1990	91.6	+4.5	664.4	23002	14796	8014
1991	90.6	+4.7	780.9	28324	18903	9138
1992	91.3	+3.7	845.5	34473	21672	10477
1993	91.9	+2.9	929.2	37137	29863	7274
1994	92.8	+1.5	n.a.	44611	36618	7993

Source: Bank of Thailand.

The depth of the economic problems prompted approaches to the World Bank and IMF for funding. The World Bank initiated a series of studies of the Thai economy and late in 1980 produced an economic review of Thailand (World Bank, 1980b). In essence the World Bank concluded that the Kingdom's economic problems were long-term structural ones. The impact of external shocks – oil price rises, falls in commodity prices, the contraction of tourism and markets for manufactured exports – had merely exposed deep-seated contradictions of the development process and the failure of previous governments to adjust to changed economic circumstances. To correct the situation a five-year programme of structural adjustment was agreed with the World Bank, the proposals for which followed the broad outline that became the norm during the 1980s (see e.g. Dixon, 1995a). Specific recommendations included:

- raising domestic energy prices to the international level;
- ending other fuel and transport subsidies;
- reducing government expenditure;
- reviewing government organisations with a view to reducing waste;
- ending the import substitution policy for industry;
- placing emphasis on export-orientated industry;
- reducing import taxes;
- removing all export restrictions and taxes;
- substantially reducing foreign exchange controls;
- imposing strong deflationary monetary and fiscal policies;
- privatising state concerns;
- reforming the taxation system to increase efficiency of collection and yields.

Overall, these recommendations were aimed at stabilising the economy, opening it more fully to international capital, and substantially reducing the state's developmental role to matters of policy. Further, the World Bank saw structural adjustment as necessary in order:

> to shift the pattern of growth from one based on the extension of land under cultivation and on import substitution to one based on increasingly intensive use of land and industries producing for domestic and export markets under competitive conditions
>
> (World Bank, 1980b: 19)

The Thai government accepted the World Bank's analysis and proposals, incorporating them as an integral part of the Fifth National Plan (1982–6). More significantly, the implementation of the recommendations was made a condition for two Structural Adjustment Loans (SALs), the first in March 1982 for US$150 million and the second in April 1983 for US$175.5 million. The World Bank did not require Thailand to undertake a series of measures before the first SAL could become available, as was more usual. It was accepted that the policy statements contained in the Fifth Plan (see pp. 116–18), the commissioning by the government of a series of studies of key areas, the imposition of austerity measures and some limited reforms during 1980 and 1981, were indicative of a positive attitude towards structural adjustment and could be regarded as a 'down payment' (Chaipat Sahansakul, 1992: 13–15).

In addition to the SALs, which were geared to the longer term adjustment of the economy, agreement was reached with the IMF on appropriate shorter term policy responses. These were aimed in particular at the restructuring of demand, reducing the public savings–investment gap, and limiting the growth of foreign debt (Panayotou and Chalongphob Sussangkarn, 1991: 6). To support these policies the IMF agreed standby credit arrangements for the period 1981 to 1983 of SDR[1] 814.5 million.

Measures implemented during 1980 and 1981 before the first SAL became available included the liberalisation of restrictions on agricultural exports,[2] increases in the charges made by state enterprises (notably the Bangkok Mass Transit Authority), the establishment of an export draw back procedure and the 8.7 per cent devaluation of the baht in July 1981 (see Bank of Thailand, *Monthly Bulletin*, 1982, 22: 19–33). The last two measures were by far the most significant, but in so far as they boosted exports and relieved pressure on the balance of payments, they appear to have only prevented further deterioration (Tables 4.1a and b).[3]

The Fifth Plan (1982–6)

Critical to the whole question of structural adjustment was the Fifth Plan. It has been described as a 'milestone document' in Thai development planning (Muscat, 1994: 180). There is no doubt that compared to its predecessors, the Fifth Plan was extremely comprehensive, the product of wide consultation, and set out a clear view of the Kingdom's situation and the key problems that needed to be addressed.

With respect to its implementation the differences between the Fifth Plan and its predecessors are far less marked. Inevitably resources fell well short of what was necessary, thus conflicts and weaknesses within the decision making processes – in both the planning bureaucracy and the government – were rapidly exposed. The Plan's two distinct areas – growth and structural adjustment, and equity, social and rural development – proved incompatible. While considerable concern was expressed, in particular by the Prime Minister, Prem Tinsulanonda, over the inequitable distribution of wealth, rural–urban differentials and the uneven pattern of national development, little was done. The questions of growth and adjustment came to dominate the implementation of the Plan.

In addition, after 20 years of rapid and supposedly planned growth the 'side-effects of development' were making themselves felt. The high rate of growth of agricultural production with limited increases in productivity, had by the late 1970s resulted in serious deterioration of land in many areas (see pp. 178–83). Similarly, there had been widespread run-down of forest, water and marine resources; since 1978 Thailand has been a net timber *importer*. The long-term environmental consequences of the largely uncontrolled expansion of the primary sector was coming very much to the fore. The rate of population growth, although slowing rapidly since the 1960s, was – even in the more buoyant years of the 1970s – resulting in an increase in the labour force that was beyond the capacity of the primary or the rapidly expanding manufacturing and service sectors to absorb. Thus there were signs that unemployment and landlessness were already increasing rapidly before the impact of the international recession was felt. Finally, the rapid growth of the previous 20 years had been far from evenly distributed. There was evidence of increasing regional, urban, rural and personal differences in income and general conditions of life (see Chapter 7). Overall there was a realisation that agriculture was no longer the 'engine of growth'; export-orientated manufacturing industry was seen the way forward and import substitution was to be given less emphasis. The Fifth Plan was indeed envisaged as paving the way for Thailand to become an NIE.

The key elements in the Fifth Plan centred on structural adjustment along the lines suggested by the World Bank. Objectives were as follows:

- to improve the economic and financial position of the country;
- to adjust the economic structure and increase production efficiency;
- to adjust the social structure and decentralise social services;
- to reduce absolute poverty and accelerate rural development in backward areas;
- to coordinate economic development activities with national security management;
- to reform economic management and distribution of ownership.

The Fifth Plan conceded that disparities had increased under earlier plans and there was a strong urban-industrial bias:

> Therefore the urban folk gained more economic power and exploited their rural counterparts. Price bargaining power, national savings and political decision making were all concentrated in the capital.
>
> (Bangkok Bank *Monthly Review*, 1984, 25: 411)

Perhaps most significantly, the Fifth Plan acknowledged that there was a relationship between poverty, insurgency and general social unrest.

Three main thrusts were proposed for rural and regional development:

- Promotion of village facilities – effectively a series of short-term plans aimed at making remote areas attractive to private investors.
- The development of five major urban centres – Chiang Mai, Khon Kaen, Nakhon Ratchasima, Hat Yai and Songkla. However, unlike earlier proposals the municipality was expected to raise up to 50 per cent of the funds and to attract private investors.
- The increase of economic growth in areas of high potential, notably in the Eastern Seaboard and in the Southern Development Belt incorporating Phuket, Krabi and Surat Thani.

In all these proposals for decentralisation the key element was the creation of a framework conducive to private investment. The Fifth Plan shifted the emphasis very firmly away from national and regional planning as solutions to developmental problems, to the fostering of broad structural change which would reduce regulations and state involvement in the economy, and stress more than ever before the role of the private sector in generating economic growth. Progress on these general aims was slow, but they were even more firmly stated in the Sixth Plan (1987–91). Under this programme the private sector was intended to become *the* principal provider of investment funds and it was envisaged that the role of the state in the development process would be reduced to a very minor one.

All of the proposed infrastructural developments, particularly the Eastern Seaboard, would involve substantial public expenditure. Thus it rapidly became clear to the Thai government and to the World Bank (1984: xxvii) that these elements of the Fifth Plan were incompatible with the SAL conditions (see pp. 200–2 for further discussion of the Eastern Seaboard).

The implementation of structural adjustment

The implementation of the structural adjustment programme proved extremely problematic. Attempts to reduce fuel and transport subsidies coming on top of the recession and government austerity measures sparked a series of mass public protests. Similarly, the public sector unions were instrumental in organising campaigns against privatisation proposals. In addition, there were powerful domestic and foreign interest groups who would have been adversely affected by many of the measures – most significantly the raising of energy and utility prices, the reduction of tariff barriers and the removal of the tax on rice exports. Given the very close and complex inter-relations between the bureaucracy, military and domestic capital there was considerable pressure to hold back on the reforms. In addition, the removal of tariff barriers and the rice export tax would have deprived the government of much needed revenue at a time when the recession was reducing tax yields. Thus – like a number of South East Asian economies – Thailand was 'caught in a bind and could engage in only a very limited degree of restructuring' (Robison *et al.*, 1987: 11–12). In consequence, between 1981 and 1985 a variety of reforms were introduced which gave the impression of great activity in implementing structural adjustment, but few were of real significance.

However, in terms of macro-economic indicators the progress was sufficiently rapid during 1981 and 1982 for the World Bank to agree the second SAL. The fall in the level of inflation, the reduction in the current account deficit and the growth of GDP were considered satisfactory, the same could not be said of the budget deficit or the level of government expenditure (see Tables 4.1 a and b, pp. 113–14). In addition, the balance of payments current account widened to a record 7.3 per cent of GDP, principally as result of appreciation of the US dollar. The view of the World Bank appears to have been that the progress of structural adjustment had been overtaken by the continued, changing nature and intensity of the international recession. Thus a longer period of adjustment than that originally envisaged was necessary (Muscat, 1994: 188). However, the progress under the second SAL continued to be slow with respect to reforms, the budget deficit and the level of government expenditure (see Tables 4. 1 a and b, pp. 113–14). As a result the World Bank's (1984) review of the structural adjustment programme was extremely critical of the limited progress.[4] The Bank was particularly concerned over the size of the budget deficit. This had expanded to 5 per cent of GDP instead of contracting to 3.5. The growth in the budget deficit reflected both the failure to reduce government expenditure and shortfalls in government revenue – the latter a product of slower growth and associated lower tax yields.[5] Relations between the World Bank and the Thai government deteriorated. During 1985 Thailand began to turn to commercial sources of finance and plans for further SALs were abandoned. Thailand was however able to reach agreement with the IMF over a two-year funding package of US$586.6 million. In December 1986 an IMF review was also extremely critical of the lack of progress in structural adjustment, particularly with respect to the size of the budget deficit. Subsequent negotiations broke down and Thailand abandoned the IMF funding having drawn on less than half of it.[6]

By 1986 very limited progress had been made towards implementing the main World Bank and IMF recommendations. Many of the structural adjustment-related targets for the Fifth Plan (1982–6) were not achieved, notably the debt service ratio, the budget deficit and government expenditure. Indeed, these only began to show significant decline in 1988.

Chaipat Sahansakal (1992) reviewed the SALs and concluded that in general they had a beneficial impact on the economy, but the impact was a very slight one. Panayotou and Chalongphob Sussangkarn concluded that while it is extremely difficult to quantify the impact of the SAL programmes:

> Nevertheless, it can probably be said that with the serious attention of the government on the structural imbalance problems, supported by the World Bank and the IMF, and the adoption of generally prudent monetary and fiscal policies, the Thai economy avoided getting into serious difficulties during the structural adjustment period. When the world economy recovered, and beneficial changes occurred in the world economic environment, Thailand did not have a serious overhang from the structural adjustment period, and was in a position to take advantage of the changes that occurred.
>
> (1991: 9)

In an appraisal of the structural adjustment period, Muscat commented on the limited progress made in such areas as institutional development, agriculture and export promotion and concluded that:

> In some important areas, the adjustment objectives were achieved only partially, or totally frustrated, due to a combination of adverse external economic circumstances and weak government resolve. Three outstanding cases were tariff reform, industrial restructuring and state enterprise privatisation.
>
> (1994: 198)

Despite limited progress and the continuing economic problems of the early 1980s the Thai economy maintained growth rates that were by international standards extremely respectable (see Table 4.1a, p. 113). More significantly the abandonment of the formal IMF and World Bank programmes in 1985 and 1986 was accompanied by signs of economic recovery. To a degree the improved global trading situation, falling oil prices and the expansion of export earnings gave the Thai government the confidence to forgo funding from the international agencies. However, the commitment to structural adjustment was not abandoned with the programmes. The Sixth Plan (1987–91) reiterated the commitment to reforms akin to structural adjustment, though not directly by name. Since 1986, and more especially since 1988, a significant number of the original recommendations have, at least in part, been implemented.[7]

The elimination of the rice export tax had been delayed because of its importance to government revenue and the fear of reaction to increased living and labour costs. The low level of prices that prevailed during late 1985 and early 1986, together with evidence of economic recovery, provided the opportunity to remove the tax. The removal was expected to raise farm incomes and stimulate rice exports. Initially, the removal appears to have little impact on domestic prices, principally because of the very depressed state of the international rice market. However, with a partial recovery during 1987 and 1988, retail prices in Bangkok rose by 60 per cent. The removal of the tax took place with little reaction on the part of employers or consumers (for a discussion of the possible reasons for this see Ammar Siamwalla, 1989: 29). However, the impact of the removal of the tax on cost of living, farm income and labour costs has received little attention (see p. 148 and p. 221). It is, however, tempting to conclude that this, like other aspects of adjustment, was only implemented when it could be done with the minimum of disruption and protest. For the rice tax – which for decades was a highly contentious issue – to have been removed with such apparent ease suggests that its role had become an insignificant one for those with political influence or for those who were in a position to protest.

A similar cautious and gradual approach was also taken with respect to fuel and public transport subsidies. These were progressively removed between 1986 and 1988. In addition, price controls and import controls on a wide range of minor items, such as certain drugs, cosmetics and toothpaste, were removed during this period.

In the key area of industrial tariff protection progress was extremely slow. Despite some reduction and simplification of tariffs under the first SAL the average level of protection rose between 1985 and 1988, principally in order to increase government revenue.[8] Indeed, tariff levels only began to decline from October 1990 when the duty on imported machinery was reduced from 35 per cent to 5 per cent. In the following July duty on computers fell from a range of 20–40 per cent to 5 per cent, and for components from 40 per cent to 1 per cent. Other reductions still provide a considerable measure of protection, notably for motor cars – where the duty on vehicles of over 3,000cc has been reduced from 300 per cent to 112. Overall, by 1997 there had still been no substantial reduction across the board in the levels of tariff protection.[9]

There was a similar long delay in reducing the foreign exchange regulations. While some simplification of procedures took place, there was no effective relaxation until May 1990 when the Board of Trade announced a three-stage programme which effectively removed all restrictions by early 1992.

Privatisation made no progress until the late 1980s, when three small enterprises – the Bangkok Jute Mill, the Gunny Bag Factory and the Wire Diffusion Company – were liquidated and the small Thai International Shipping Company sold. Since 1990 there has been a more concerted effort towards the privatisation of the remaining 60 state enterprises. This was marked by the sale of 15 per cent of the holdings in Thai International early in 1991. However, the Thai public sector is by no means a drain on public expenditure. In 1990 state concerns employed 260,000 people, had a turnover of US$11.7 billion and returned pre-tax profits of US$1.8 billion – a return of 14.7 per cent. Only five concerns made losses – the largest of which was the Bangkok Metropolitan Transit Administration (BMTA) followed by the State Railways. The post-structural adjustment pressure for privatisation has come from the inability of the concerns (and unwillingness/inability of the government) to finance the much-needed expansion of the Kingdom's infrastructure. While by 1997 little progress had been made in privatising state concerns, a variety of measures had been implemented which increased central control over their budgets and investment programmes.

During the early 1990s a series of other adjustment-related measures were introduced, notably the deregulation of the financial markets, the floating of oil prices and the revamping of the tax structure. The level of personal income tax was reduced from 35 to 30 per cent and an across the board 7 per cent value added tax imposed. These measures were specifically aimed at simplifying the structure and increasing tax yield.

Thus a range of 'home-grown' structural adjustment measures were implemented well after the boom was under way. Indeed, only with renewed economic growth, political stability and the reduction of the political influence of the ISI sector was it possible to implement some of these policies at all. Thus the reforms may be viewed as sustaining the boom rather than initiating it. As Muscat (1994: 216–22) has suggested, the Thai pattern of adjustment was an extremely gradual one. Measures appear in general to have been effectively implemented only when they would cause limited disruption and protest. In part, this reflects the weak governments of the 1980s and their need to serve a variety of often conflicting interests. Perhaps more significantly the gradual approach reflects the cautious, light-handed and conservative approach to economic development and management that has generally characterised Thailand since the late 1950s (see pp. 241–6).

The causes of the boom

It does not appear possible to relate the rapid economic growth that Thailand experienced after 1986 to the limited progress made in structural adjustment by that date. The acceleration of growth was closely related to the expansion of manufactured exports – initially textiles and later electronic products. There are, however, two questions here: first, what caused the initial acceleration of exports, and second, what has sustained the growth? In attempting to answer these two questions it is important to consider Thailand in its broader regional and global context.

As has already been noted, Thai policy and attitude remained firmly ISI orientated in 1980. Subsequent liberalisation has not dismantled the protective structure that supports ISI. Indeed, in a review of Thai commercial policies Narongchai Akrasanee et al. concluded that:

> Thailand's recent economic success appears to have been attained *despite*, rather than because of, the evolution of trade and commercial policies. Commercial policies have been of the classical import-substitution and anti-export nature and have become increasingly so in the second half of the 1980s.
>
> (1991: 17)

The liberalisation that has taken place since 1990 has almost certainly had a positive impact on manufactured exports and foreign investment. In addition, the various simplifying and streamlining of export and investment procedures implemented since the early 1980s undoubtedly sent the right messages to both Thai and foreign export-oriented firms. As Muscat

(1994: 195–7) has noted, these measures are indicative of a fundamental change in attitude on the part of successive administrations in favour of manufacturing exports. However, even by 1997 the change in attitude was by no means fully reflected in policy.

During the early 1980s the value of manufactured exports grew extremely slowly, accelerating during 1984–6 and entering a period of spectacular growth in 1987 (see Table 4.1b, p. 114). The devaluation of the baht during 1984, reinforced in 1985 as the baht declined with the US dollar, improved the competitiveness of Thai exports. During the late 1970s and early 1980s there was little doubt that the over-valuation of the baht had operated against exports. However, while the devaluation must be considered a factor in the expansion of exports as Muscat (1994: 194) has stressed, it can not be considered to have been solely responsible.

It is apparent that some textile producers were beginning to become more export oriented during the early 1980s despite the less than conducive policy environment. Thus, as was noted in Chapter 3 (see pp. 104–5) the export-oriented sector was from the early 1970s the most rapidly growing manufacturing activity. However, because of the low base from which it started it was not until the early 1980s that the export sector began substantially to increase its share of manufacturing output (see Table 3.1a,b, p. 105).

Thai producers were able to expand markets for a variety of labour-intensive products during a period of relatively rapid growth in the global economy when the Asian NIEs were beginning to lose their comparative advantage in such activities. From the early 1980s onwards, Thai exporters were remarkably successful in expanding sales – particularly in new markets outside the increasingly restricted EU and North American areas.

The acceleration of the rate of growth of exports appears to have taken place with little increase in domestic investment (see Table 4.1b, p. 114). Thus the initial stages of the export expansion reflected the ability of the Thai manufacturing sector to expand production with little additional investment. There is indeed considerable evidence of saturation of domestic markets and over-capacity in Thai manufacturing during the early 1980s. For example, in 1984 the Thai Textile Association reported that there was serious over-capacity in the industry which neither the government nor the trade association were capable of reducing. It was also revealed that as much as 30 per cent of the capacity was illegal (Dixon, 1991b: 1035). The excess capacity had resulted from the over-expansion of heavily protected and privileged sectors, exacerbated by the recession and the contraction of the domestic market. It was this excess capacity that was utilised by a dynamic export marketing sector in the initial stages of the boom. In addition, many small companies engaged in a wide range of trading, service and manufacturing were, particularly after 1985, to reorientate their activities towards the export market with remarkable speed (Pasuk Phongpaichit and Baker, 1995: 158). Similarly, many joint ventures established to assemble goods for the Thai market were transformed into exporters. This was particularly the case for the electronics, electrical and motor vehicle components sectors.

Once the rapid growth of manufactured exports had started, a significant factor in its continuation and acceleration was that from 1987 Thailand became a major focus for Japanese and Asian NIE investment in labour-intensive manufacturing operations (see Figures 4.1 and 4.2). As the Asian NIEs lost their competitive position in these activities, they sought alternative, stable, low-cost locations within the Pacific Asian region. The flow of Taiwanese investment into Thailand and later other parts of South East Asia after 1987 is particularly striking. Overall, this relocation gave rise to a Regional Division of Labour between the Asian NIEs and the ASEAN–4 – of which Thailand became a key element (this is discussed more fully on pp. 252–5).

However, it is important to stress that while there is no doubt that foreign investment has played a major role in the rapid expansion of the Thai manufacturing sector, the onset of the period of spectacularly rapid growth of exports appears to predate the influx of foreign investment (see Table 4.1b, p.114). In the period 1985–7 foreign investment's share of net domestic capital formation showed little change, averaging 1.9 per cent.

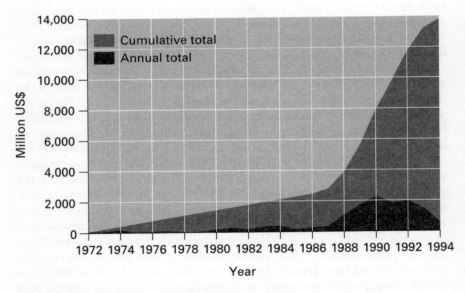

Figure 4.1 Net foreign direct investment, 1972–94.
Source: Bank of Thailand.

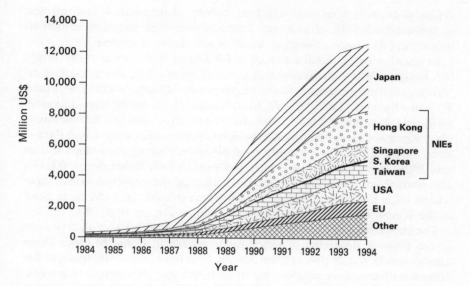

Figure 4.2 Sources of cumulative net foreign direct investment, 1984–94.
Source: Bank of Thailand.

The share rose sharply to 7.5 per cent in 1988 and peaked at 9.5 per cent in 1989, subsequently falling to 5.8 per cent in 1992. Further, as Narongchai Akrasanee *et al.* (1991: 22–3) have argued, given the normal start-up time for factories, the 1987 investment could not have been making any significant contribution to exports before 1988.[10] Thus however important foreign investment become to the Thai economy the critical early stages of Thailand's accelerated growth 'were overwhelmingly Thai supplied and financed' (Narongchai Akrasanee, 1991: 23).

The attraction of Thailand for Japanese and Asian NIE labour intensive manufacturing investment was fourfold. First, in the mid-1980s Thailand had one of the lowest levels of industrial labour costs in ASEAN[11] and the devaluation and realignment of the baht had substantially improved the competitiveness of exports. Second, the receding of the economic crisis and the appearance of relative political stability (see pp. 126–7) gave the Kingdom an advantage over the rest of the ASEAN–4. Economic and political crises in the Philippines, question marks over economic and political stability in Malaysia and the persistence of high levels of control over investment in Indonesia, all contributed to the attractiveness of Thailand for foreign investors. Third, production in Thailand, as a then marginal exporter of manufactured goods, enabled Japanese and NIE-based firms to find ways around the restrictions increasingly imposed on their exports to the EU and North America. Finally, particularly for

Japanese firms, a comparatively long history of investment had resulted in the establishment of linkages, contacts and expertise that tended to offset the attractions of slightly lower labour costs elsewhere.

In addition to Thailand's attraction for labour-intensive manufacturing, the Kingdom's lax environmental controls resulted in the relocation of highly polluting processes from, in particular, Japan, South Korea and Taiwan (Burnett, 1992: 228–9). McDowell, for example, cites Japanese textile plants which discharge 'harmful acetate dyes' and 'Asahi's mercury-discharging soda ash plants which have been relocated on the Chao Phraya river' (1990: 327). The proportion of plants producing hazardous wastes rose from 29 per cent in 1979 to 58 per cent in 1989 (Ichikawa, 1990: 17). The limited and generally ineffective nature of the enforced safety regulations were highlighted during 1992 by the explosion of a chemical plant in the Klong Toey area (International Labour Office, 1992: 78).

The importance of Thailand's political stability during the critical periods of the 1980s is deserving of much fuller attention. Prime Minister Prem Tinsulanonda was in power from March 1980 until July 1988; this was the longest parliamentary premiership in Thai history.[12] His period of government saw two attempted *coups d'état* (in 1981 and 1985), three general elections and five cabinets, but nevertheless gave an air of continuity, robustness and stability rare in the Kingdom's history. This had two important consequences. First, as was noted above, Thailand's investment rating was dramatically revised. Second, during the critical phases of recession, adjustment, recovery and accelerated growth and structural change there was considerable continuity of government policies. This is not to say that there were not considerable divisions within the cabinets over public investment and development objectives. There is little doubt that continuity contributed to the confidence of both domestic and overseas investors. The confidence that stemmed from the apparent establishment of stable and, at least quasi-democratic government, was given a substantial boost following the elections of July 1988, with the appointment of a premier (Chatichai Choonhaven) and a full cabinet who were all elected. Neher summarised the view of Thailand held by many internal and external observers:

> the capacity of the government to cope is high, the future is bright for all segments of the nation, democracy is flourishing (at least compared to other developing nations), and the remarkable stability of the Kingdom is constant. Those agreeing with this interpretation note the rapid and consistent economic growth, the manageable debt, the end of communist insurgency, the extraordinary fact that no successful military coup has taken place for ten years . . .
>
> (1988: 192)

Thus by the end of the 1980s the military was regarded by many as a spent force in Thai politics, and the age of *coups d'état* was past. An era of democratic reforming government had apparently been ushered in. As Amsden (1989) has concluded more generally for Pacific Asia, late industrialisation was being accompanied by late democratisation. However, as is discussed more fully in Chapter 8, this was not the case. The *coup d'etat* of General Suchinda Kraprayoon in February 1991 and subsequent public reaction which culminated in the May 1992 'Democracy Movement' served as a reminder of how fragile Thailand's political stability can be. However, the bloody events of May 1992 appear to have had only very short-term impacts on the confidence of foreign investors and the inflow of tourists. To a degree this reinforced the view that *coups d'état* are merely the way that Thailand changes governments, and no foreign company has ever suffered damage or loss as a result. Perhaps more significantly the limited impact of the events of 1991–2 on economic growth reflects the strength of the internal and external forces that were promoting it (see pp. 258–61).

Once the manufacturing based export boom was underway it was reinforced in three ways: first by the expansion of primary exports (see Table 4.1b, p. 114), second by the promotion of tourism and, third (to a lesser extent), the export of labour. As is noted in Chapter 3, these areas had become significant factors in Thai economic growth durin₅ the late 1970s. From the early 1980s the promotion of tourism and labour exports became major components of Thai economic policy, receiving considerable attention in the Fifth (1982–6) and, more especially, the Sixth (1987–92) National Plans (Pasuk Phongpaichit and Samart Chiasakul, 1994: 160). Muscat (1994: 197) goes as far as to suggest that tourism was the 'single most important export policy success' of the 1980–88 period. He sees the promotion of tourism that centred on the 1987 'Visit Thailand Year' as instrumental in raising receipts from US\$1 billion in 1985 to US\$3 billion in 1988. During the early 1980s the government began actively to promote the export of labour, particularly to the Middle East. By 1989 there were some 264,600 Thai workers in the Middle East and other parts of Asia. Between 1984 and 1989 official remittances averaged US\$0.79 billion. In 1988 the earnings from tourism and workers' remittances were the equivalent of 19 per cent of the income from the export of goods and services. Perhaps more significantly the combined earnings from tourism and overseas workers were the equivalent 119.5 per cent of the trade deficit during 1986 and 1987, and 56.9 per cent during 1988 and 1989. There is little doubt that together these sectors made a major contribution to the growth of the Thai economy. However, in the longer run, the initiation of a major secondary domestic-based boom by the growth of exports and the influx of investment, has played the most significant role.

The sharp rise in per capita GDP which followed the acceleration of growth was heavily concentrated in the BMR. As a result there was a rapid expansion of comparatively affluent groups who spent an increasing proportion of their income on manufactured goods, services and housing. This stimulated rapid growth in the financial services, property, construction, transport, retailing and telecommunications sectors. While foreign capital was involved in these areas the majority of the development appears to have been domestically funded (Pasuk Phongpaichit and Baker, 1995: 163). Domestic investment expanded rapidly from 1986 onwards (see Table 4.1b, p. 114). Gross domestic investment as a percentage of GDP rose from 21.8 in 1986, 33.7 in 1988 to a peak of 42.0 in 1991.

The rapid expansion of the domestic business sector resulted from the mobilisation of resources by the established major commercial groups. In addition, many of these formed partnerships with foreign investors who lacked experience of business in Thailand and who were anxious to establish operations as rapidly as possible (Pasuk Phongpaichit and Baker, 1995: 157). As was mentioned earlier, many established small firms were able to reorientate towards the export sector, diversify and expand rapidly. Behind the expansion of large, small and partnership operations lay the rapid development of the financial sector. This involved the continued expansion of the commercial banking sector discussed in Chapter 2 (p. 69), the emergence of finance and security companies and, from 1987, the rapid expansion of the Securities Exchange of Thailand (SET). None of these developments were without their problems and the financial sector has been plagued by failures, scandals and ineffective regulation (see pp. 244–5). However, it has played a major role in mobilising capital and, in consequence, in the Kingdom's rapid growth and structural change.

Overall, during the 1980s both the Thai economic and political situation changed radically and the Kingdom became regarded as politically and economically stable and an investment 'hot-spot'. However, there is in all this a clustering of favourable global, regional, and national circumstances that Thailand was able to take advantage of, rather than any particular policies or strategies that could be isolated and applied elsewhere. Certainly it is difficult to accept the World Bank's view that Thailand is one of the success stories of formal structural adjustment (see Dixon, 1995a; World Bank, 1988a, 1991).

Foreign investment, regional divisions of labour and the development of manufacturing

As has already been stressed, the rapid influx of foreign investment that Thailand experienced during the period 1986–94 (Figure 4.1, p. 124) came principally from Japan and the NIEs (Figure 4.2, p. 125). This rapid expansion of foreign investment is all the more striking because until the mid-1980s Thailand was not considered a particularly attractive location for foreign investment. A combination of its proximity to the former Indo-Chinese states, and periodic concerns over the Kingdom's long-term economic and political stability tended to discourage investment – particularly in the face of more attractive locations elsewhere in the region. This was reinforced by the general emphasis of foreign investors in the primary sectors, particularly Malaysian and Indonesian oil and gas (see Table 4.2). With the increased importance of investment in labour-intensive manufacturing and changed economic and political circumstances, a major reappraisal of the relative attractiveness of the ASEAN–4 economies took place – as a result of which Thailand became the regional investment 'hot spot' during the late 1980s.

The comparatively limited development of foreign investment in Thailand before the mid-1980s is reflected in the modest performance (until the mid-1980s) of the BOI incentive programmes. Between 1959 and 1985 only 1,037 promoted companies started operation, with a total investment of US$5,729. Of this 73.4 per cent was Thai; the leading foreign investors were Japan (7.2 per cent), Taiwan (3.1 per cent) and the USA (2.9 per cent). In contrast, between 1986 and 1994, 2,787 promoted projects started operation, with a combined investment of US$23,544 million (see Figure 4.3). Initially, there was a sharp rise in the share of foreign investors to 53 per cent in 1988; this subsequently fell rapidly to 36.7 per cent in 1990 and 16.6 per cent in 1993. Thus in the whole period 1986–93 Thai investment accounted for 66.5 per cent of projects starting operation.

The BOI promotional programme has been much criticised (Ammar Siamwalla, 1975: 38; Muscat, 1994: 159–60), particularly for its cumbersome and time-consuming procedures and general lack of any clear policy towards particular sectors or locations. Since the mid-1980s the procedures have been substantially streamlined. However, it is important to stress that prior to the mid-1980s it is difficult to see how even radical changed in the BOI programme would have resulted in a significant increase in the inflow of investment. Indeed ESCAP (1983), in a review of investment incentives in Pacific Asia as a whole, stressed their general

Table 4.2 Percentage share of net foreign investment in ASEAN, 1965–94

	1965–71	1972–6	1977–80	1981–6	1987–90	1991–4
Indonesia	21.7	17.3	12.1	11.6	9.1	13.8
Malaysia	31.2	27.5	31.6	35.7	17.2	34.5
Philippines	a	4.8	2.8	2.7	7.8	6.1
Singapore	27.6	42.5	48.2	50.0	49.1	33.6
Thailand	19.5	7.6	5.3	8.9	17.5	12.2

Source: IMF, *Balance of Payments Yearbook*, various issues.

Note
a Between 1965 and 1971 the stock of foreign investment in the Philippines fell by US$58.1m.

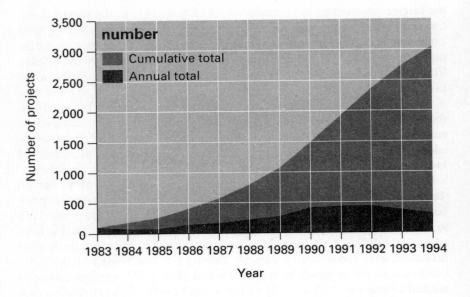

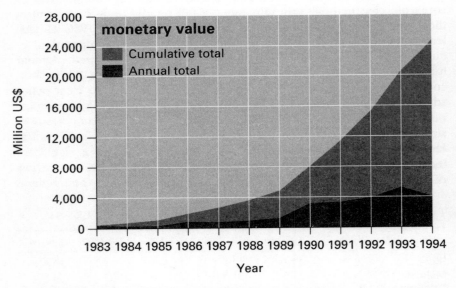

Figure 4.3 Board of Investment approved projects starting operation.

Source: Board of Investment.

Note
This is for registered capital and includes domestic as well as foreign investment.

ineffectiveness in the face of international investors' perceptions of locations; this is a question that is wider than the BOI incentives. From 1978 Thailand attempted to promote foreign investment and manufacturing exports through the establishment of ITCs (International Trading Companies) along the lines of those found in Japan and the NIEs. Thirteen ITCs were set up by 1984, but they only handled 4 per cent of the value of exports (Bangkok Bank, *Monthly Review*, 1984, 25: 253–8). Similarly, the first EPZ was established at Lad Krabang in 1978 and the development of industrial estates (which dates from 1969), was stepped up. In addition, the Bank of Thailand began to give preferential credit to exporters and the Ministry of Finance to grant refunds of taxes and tariffs levied on imports. The concessions were granted initially to the textile sector and later to traders in jewellery. These were all policies which have been linked to successful promotion of manufacturing exports elsewhere in the region. It might be said that Thailand came late to some of these policies, and that they were perhaps not as effectively and vigorously promoted as in some other countries. However, it should be stressed that it was not so much the policies that were at fault as the international and national situations.

The limited importance to foreign investors of the incentive packages is revealed by the long-term tendency for firms – particularly those from the USA – to operate outside the BOI programmes (Somsak Tambunlertchai, 1994: 136). Indeed, despite the streamlining of the BOI procedures, the foreign investment boom had been accompanied by increasing numbers of firms choosing to forgo the incentives. This had of course been encouraged by the liberalisation measures which had reduced the relative advantages of approval status.

During the late 1980s the rapid expansion of the electronics sector was closely related to the increased presence of foreign firms. In 1986 the Japanese concern Minebea started the assembly of computer parts; this lead was rapidly followed by a number of (in particular), Taiwanese and American-based firms. During 1989–90 Seagate relocated part of its disk-drive production from Singapore, and IBM established disk-drive assembly in partnership with the major Thai group Saha Union. By the early 1990s Thailand had become the world's largest single assembler of disk-drives.

The heavy concentration of post-1986 investment (principally from Japan and the NIEs), in the electrical goods and electronics sectors (Table 4.3), is reflected in the trade in integrated circuits and computers and computer parts which became increasingly tied to Japan and the NIEs (see Tables 4.4 and 4.5). Thailand became a particularly important part of the electrical assembly industry organised through Singapore. The trade in integrated circuits with Malaysia reflected Thailand's position as a lower cost, more basic skill-orientated part of the regional production system.

In contrast to the trade in integrated circuits, the markets for finished

Table 4.3 The sectoral distribution of net foreign direct investment (percentage)

Sector	1971–5	1976–80	1980–1	1985	1986	1987	1988	1989	1990	1991	1992	1993
Manufacturing	28.0	34.4	32.9	20.8	27.2	44.2	56.5	47.1	47.8	45.4	32.5	48.7
Food	13.8	7.6	5.6	30.3	16.3	9.2	6.9	8.4	5.7	7.1	7.4	4.8
Textiles	46.5	20.7	8.2	3.3	4.1	18.5	7.2	4.5	5.7	4.8	8.4	–
Metal and mineral products	6.1	3.6	11.5	7.9	5.0	15.3	12.7	13.4	9.3	9.2	9.7	11.8
Electrical and electronic	12.6	37.5	27.8	15.2	26.5	20.6	33.9	35.9	40.4	43.8	44.6	17.6
Machinery	2.0	10.4	8.6	2.4	2.5	3.1	4.4	1.5	8.0	9.6	6.2	7.7
Chemicals	11.2	14.7	13.0	29.7	21.6	18.6	12.0	11.2	13.9	16.0	9.2	24.8
Petroleum products	2.3	1.7	19.0	–	0.3	0.2	10.9	3.8	9.8	–	7.3	23.8
Construction materials	2.1	–	0.8	1.8	0.2	0.3	0.2	3.6	0.1	6.1	3.4	2.1
Other	3.4	3.8	5.5	9.4	23.5	14.2	11.8	7.7	7.1	3.4	5.2	4.2
Financial institutions	–	–	–	28.2	24.2	12.8	14.1	9.7	7.0	13.2	12.1	8.3
Trade	28.9	22.5	17.6	16.5	24.6	17.3	12.7	15.7	20.0	15.0	13.2	13.2
Construction	14.6	17.1	16.4	16.6	12.9	10.9	6.1	7.5	5.1	6.4	27.0	9.2
Mining and quarrying	23.4	10.3	21.9	5.2	2.6	2.4	1.4	1.2	1.8	4.0	5.8	7.6
Oil exploration	92.5	72.0	89.5	83.7	86.8	82.7	84.3	91.6	n.a.	n.a.	n.a.	n.a.
Other	7.5	28.0	10.5	16.3	13.2	17.3	15.7	8.4	n.a.	n.a.	n.a.	n.a.
Agriculture	0.4	2.0	0.6	0.8	1.9	2.3	1.0	1.3	1.2	1.2	–	0.8
Services	4.7	13.7	10.5	11.9	8.6	9.6	8.1	16.6	16.4	10.6	6.9	10.5
Transport and travel	42.7	57.9	34.1	25.0	35.5	19.5	16.2	6.7	n.a.	n.a.	n.a.	n.a.
Housing and real estate	29.8	13.6	14.6	26.8	5.4	28.2	34.5	45.2	n.a.	n.a.	n.a.	n.a.
Hotels and restaurants	21.1	6.3	16.8	19.8	11.3	7.8	24.4	35.5	n.a.	n.a.	n.a.	n.a.
Other	6.4	21.2	43.5	28.4	45.8	44.5	24.9	13.6	n.a.	n.a.	n.a.	n.a.
Other	–	–	–	–	–	2.9	1.5	2.1	0.7	4.2	2.5	2.5
Total	100.0	100.0	100.0	100.0	100.0	100.0	100.0	100.0	100.0	100.0	100.0	100.0

Source: Bank of Thailand.

Note
– = less than 0.1 per cent.

Table 4.4 Destination of integrated circuit exports (percentage value)

	1980	1985	1990	1991	1992	1993	1994
USA	27.7	41.2	44.9	37.1	27.8	30.6	30.4
EU	2.0	9.8	5.3	9.5	10.6	9.6	8.1
Japan	–	–	1.9	3.9	10.0	13.2	11.0
Asian NIEs	44.8	30.3	30.5	38.7	41.9	37.9	42.6
Hong Kong	6.4	2.8	9.9	7.1	5.3	3.4	3.2
South Korea	11.8	0.8	1.8	1.2	2.0	1.9	2.1
Singapore	26.6	26.7	16.7	28.1	31.8	29.0	34.0
Taiwan	–	–	2.1	2.3	2.8	3.6	3.3
ASEAN–4							
Malaysia	24.5	12.5	7.1	6.7	7.7	5.7	4.3
Pacific Asia	69.3	42.8	39.5	49.3	59.6	56.8	57.6
Other	1.0	6.2	10.0	4.1	2.0	3.0	3.9
Total	100.0	100.0	100.0	100.0	100.0	100.0	100.0

Source: Bank of Thailand.

Table 4.5 Destination of computers and parts exports (percentage value)

	1988	1989	1990	1991	1992	1993	1994
USA	40.2	36.2	31.7	27.9	28.8	27.3	25.4
EU	16.2	11.8	12.4	14.0	11.4	10.6	7.2
Japan	4.3	7.5	8.7	10.9	11.0	7.2	7.0
Asian NIEs	34.1	40.0	41.3	40.7	42.1	50.9	52.0
Hong Kong	2.4	2.0	1.3	2.0	2.7	2.5	1.3
South Korea	2.6	3.0	2.2	1.9	0.7	0.6	0.8
Singapore	26.3	29.9	35.8	35.1	36.3	47.0	48.1
Taiwan	4.8	5.1	2.0	1.7	2.4	0.8	0.9
ASEAN–4	0.6	0.7	3.6	4.2	4.7	3.2	1.9
Malaysia	–	–	0.7	2.7	2.8	2.6	1.6
Philippines	0.6	0.7	2.9	1.5	1.9	0.6	0.3
Pacific Asia	39.0	48.2	53.6	55.8	57.8	62.6	60.9
Other	5.5	3.8	2.3	2.3	2.0	0.5	6.5
Total	100.0	100.0	100.0	100.0	100.0	100.0	100.0

Source: Bank of Thailand.

appliances assembled in Thailand were, until 1992, increasingly the USA and EU, and to a much lesser extent, Japan (Table 4.6). Subsequently, the expansion of trade with the rest of Pacific Asia reduced the importance of the EU and USA. However, the patterns of trade and invest-

Table 4.6 Destination of electrical appliance exports (percentage value)

	1988	1989	1990	1991	1992	1993	1994
USA	24.1	37.9	38.1	32.6	35.8	28.3	25.7
EU	25.3	23.7	14.1	16.6	19.1	10.6	7.2
Japan	10.7	12.0	12.2	15.3	15.1	18.1	18.0
Asian NIEs	24.5	15.4	12.8	15.9	17.2	19.8	19.6
Hong Kong	10.5	4.0	2.2	4.7	5.7	5.0	6.9
South Korea	–	–	–	–	–	–	–
Singapore	6.9	7.1	9.6	11.0	9.8	12.6	15.2
Taiwan	7.1	4.3	1.0	0.2	1.7	2.2	1.5
ASEAN–4							
Malaysia	1.4	1.4	0.8	1.2	1.3	1.7	2.6
Pacific Asia	36.6	28.8	25.8	33.4	34.7	39.6	40.2
Other	14.0	9.6	22.0	17.4	10.4	21.5	16.9
Total	100.0	100.0	100.0	100.0	100.0	100.0	100.0

Source: Bank of Thailand.

ment in the electrical assembly sector as a whole continued to reflect the importance of 'third country' type arrangements. In general the Thai-owned electrical and electronic assembly sectors remained principally concerned with the still comparatively well-protected domestic market.

In terms of the pattern of exports the electronics and electrical sectors contrasted markedly with textiles and garments. For the products of these sectors there was little development of markets within Pacific Asia and they remained heavily dependent on sales to the USA and EU (Table 4.7). As well as textiles, garments and electronics a wide range of other manufactured exports expanded rapidly. Notably shoes, toys and jewellery, but also watches, watch parts, lenses, leather goods, sports goods, motor vehicle parts and artificial flowers. In all these, from 1987 onwards, investment and relocation from Japan and the NIEs played a significant role.

The most striking change in the composition of manufactured exports was the relative decline in the importance of textiles and garments, and their replacement by electrical and electronics exports (Table 4.8). Overall, there was a general diversification and increased sophistication in both the production and export of manufactured products. From the early 1990s the edging up of wage rates and the opening up of cheaper locations elsewhere in the region slowed the growth of the most labour-intensive sectors. In consequence there was a gradual shift in emphasis towards slightly high-tech production and more sophisticated products. This fits with the changes in the nature of inward investment since the mid-1980s. Much of the initial wave of Taiwanese investment, for example,

Table 4.7 Destination of textile and garment exports (percentage value)

	1980	1985	1990	1992	1994
USA	15.0	30.1	16.7	20.1	21.3
EU	33.5	27.1	36.5	21.7	19.0
Japan	3.8	1.9	6.8	7.3	6.9
Asian NIEs	10.6	7.8	6.7	5.7	8.0
Hong Kong	7.0	2.9	2.9	2.6	3.2
Singapore	3.6	4.9	3.8	2.9	5.7
ASEAN–4	3.2	1.4	1.5	–	–
Indonesia	1.4	0.2	0.4	–	–
Malaysia	1.6	0.7	0.7	–	–
Philippines	0.2	0.5	0.4	–	–
Asian Socialist	2.2	0.4	0.8	1.0	1.2
China	–	–	0.7	1.0	1.2
Laos	2.2	0.4	0.1	–	–
Total Pacific Asia	19.8	11.5	15.8	14.0	16.1
Middle East	12.1	10.8	10.9	8.4	9.4
Kuwait	1.4	1.8	–	–	–
Saudi Arabia	4.4	4.7	5.7	3.8	4.3
UAE	6.3	4.3	5.2	4.6	5.1
Other	19.7	20.5	19.7	35.8	34.6

Source: Bank of Thailand.

was in very low-tech activities indeed: plastic toys, wooden chop sticks and Christmas tree lights. This tended to move fairly rapidly into more sophisticated textile and assembly operations. However, it should be stressed that the level of technological up-grading in Thailand since the mid-1980s has been very patchy and comparatively limited overall (see pp. 248–9 for a fuller discussion).

In general the changing composition of manufacturing exports was also reflected in the structure of the manufacturing sector as a whole (Table 4.9). There was a significant decline in the importance of raw material and agricultural-based sectors. This was most striking in the case of wood-based products – a reflection of the shortage and high cost of domestic supplies (see pp. 14, 179–81). Even the production of such export items as rattan furniture – a major growth area during the early 1980s – declined in the face of a shortage of materials and the comparative high cost of imports. Despite the expansion of the agri-business sector (see pp. 9, 151–2) and the growth of food exports, the sector lost ground to such spectacularly growing sectors as electrical goods and electronics, machinery and transport equipment – the latter a reflection of the rapid expansion of motor vehicle production. From the mid-1980s the expansion of this

Table 4.8 Composition of manufactured exports (percentage value)

	1980	1985	1988	1991	1994
Textiles and garments	22.4	25.4	24.1	19.1	16.2
Footwear	0.9	3.9	3.6	4.0	4.2
Sub-total	23.3	29.3	27.7	23.1	20.4
Electrical appliances/machinery	1.2	1.5	2.4	10.4	11.3
Computers and parts	0.2	2.6	4.7	8.7	9.9
Integrated circuits	14.2	14.2	3.8	1.9	5.9
Other electrical	–	–	4.1	4.4	5.1
Sub-total	15.6	18.3	15.0	24.5	30.4
Machinery	–	–	1.5	2.3	2.8
Precious stones and jewellery	9.0	9.1	5.3	6.4	4.9
Clocks, watches and parts	–	–	–	1.4	1.1
Insulated wire	–	–	–	0.9	1.2
Vehicle parts	1.2	0.3	1.4	0.7	2.2
Optical appliance and instruments	–	–	–	0.5	2.0
Ball bearings	–	–	–	1.1	0.6
Base metals	–	–	3.0	2.3	2.7
Plastics	–	–	0.2	2.3	2.1
Furniture and parts	–	–	2.5	2.4	3.3
Canned goods	7.7	9.4	14.0	9.3	5.0
Molasses and sugar	0.9	7.4	3.8	3.0	2.0
Rubber goods	–	–	1.7	1.4	1.4
Travel goods	–	–	1.3	1.2	1.1
Ceramic products	–	–	0.8	0.8	0.8
Chemical products	–	–	–	0.7	0.6
Leather products	–	–	–	0.5	0.9
Toys and games	–	–	–	1.4	0.9
Sports goods	–	–	–	0.7	0.8
Other	42.3	26.2	25.7	12.2	11.1
Total	100.0	100.0	100.0	100.0	100.0

Source: Bank of Thailand.

sector had begun to involve the export of components, and from 1990 Mitsubishi started assembling light commercial vehicles for the American market. The only raw material based sectors to experience high rates of growth were leather products, including footwear and jewellery. These were both significant exports but were becoming increasingly dependent on imported materials.

Despite the decline in the importance of manufacturing based on domestic raw materials there were some significant developments in the sector – for example in rubber production. Until the early 1980s Thai rubber was regarded as of low quality and was almost entirely exported as unconcentrated latex. The domestic motor tyre industry, for example, imported its raw material from Malaysia. Improved quality of Thai

Table 4.9 Composition of manufacturing GDP

	1970	1975	1980	1985	1990	1994
Food	16.5	15.7	14.1	16.4	5.9	5.2
Beverages	11.7	8.9	9.8	10.6	6.0	5.6
Tobacco	8.5	7.7	6.6	4.9	2.7	1.3
Garments	9.1	9.7	9.1	10.1	10.8	8.7
Textiles	9.0	13.2	14.5	14.1	10.9	8.5
Leather, leather products and footwear	2.5	2.3	1.8	2.3	3.6	3.2
Wood and wood products	4.1	3.5	2.1	1.5	1.0	0.5
Furniture and fixtures	1.9	1.2	1.3	1.2	2.9	3.2
Paper and paper products	1.4	1.0	1.8	1.7	1.3	0.9
Printing	1.4	1.5	1.6	1.8	1.0	0.6
Chemicals and chemical products	3.6	3.4	4.2	4.7	2.6	1.8
Petroleum products	5.7	7.6	5.2	4.8	5.6	6.0
Rubber and rubber products	2.6	2.7	2.7	2.5	2.3	2.1
Non-metallic mineral products	4.0	3.8	3.6	4.1	5.8	7.5
Basic metals	2.7	1.6	1.8	1.8	1.5	1.9
Fabricated products	3.1	2.2	1.9	1.8	2.8	3.6
Machinery	3.1	3.1	3.4	3.7	5.5	6.5
Electrical machinery	1.9	2.0	2.9	3.0	9.8	12.2
Transport equipment	5.5	6.2	7.8	3.9	8.8	10.8
Others	4.8	2.7	3.8	5.1	9.2	9.9
Total	100.0	100.0	100.0	100.0	100.0	100.0

Source: NESDB.

rubber (see pp. 145–6) was from the mid-1980s accompanied by the rapid development of a latex concentrating industry, principally supplying the domestic manufacturing sector. Domestic consumption of rubber increased from 18,161 tons in 1982 to 50,000 tons in 1992. A major growth area was the production of rubber gloves, particularly for the American market.

In general there has been some increase in the size of Thai firms since the early 1980s: the proportion of workers employed in plants with more than 50 employees rose from 19.1 per cent in 1980 to 40 per cent in 1993. However, the manufacturing sector remains dominated by small-scale operations. In addition, much of the expansion in textiles, garments and other simple labour-intensive production has taken place through casual employment, outwork and sub-contracting to large numbers of very small workshops. In 1987 it was estimated that the garment industry employed 17,000 people in factories and 780,000 as sub-contracted piece-workers (cited Pasuk Phongpaichit and Baker, 1995: 201). In 1993 a survey of large textile, engineering, electrical and chemical concerns revealed that 63 per cent of the labour force was paid on a casual, piecework or daily basis (Sungsidh Piriyarangsan and Kitti Limsakai, 1994). Against these developments have to be set the emergence of a number of very large companies, some of which are beginning to operate on an international scale

(Suehiro, 1989: 219–44). Siam City Cement, for example, has a controlling interest in over 40 companies and is probably the largest export group not only in Thailand but in ASEAN as well. Other major groups that are internationalising their operations include the three major hotel groups, Imperial, Central and Dusit, and the agri-business based Charoen Pokphand which in addition to such activities as feedmills, brewing and vehicle assembly in China, has through its subsidiary Telecom Asia moved into the provision of telecommunications in Vietnam, China, Cambodia, India, Indonesia and the Philippines. There is in these types of development the beginnings of a major outflow of Thai capital to more profitable locations elsewhere in the region, particularly China, Myanmar and the former Indo-Chinese states (see Table 4.10 and Chapter 8 for a fuller discussion).

Despite the rapid expansion and changing structure that have characterised both the domestic and export-orientated manufacturing sectors since the mid-1980s, they both remain very dependent on imports of materials, components and machinery (Somsak Tambunlertchai, 1994: 125). In 1992 the Bangkok Bank (*Monthly Review*, 33: 250) estimated that the value of imports accounted for 85–90 per cent of the value of domestically produced computers, 75–80 per cent of radios and TVs, 60–70 per cent of air-conditioners, and 60 per cent of microwaves. Even in such longer established, lower-tech activities as cotton textiles, 90 per cent of material is imported. While the domestic production of synthetic fibre has

Table 4.10 Net outflows of Thai equity investment, 1988–94

| | Percentage share | | | |
	1988	1990	1992	1994
USA	7.5	59.3	23.8	16.6
EU	1.8	8.9	6.6	3.2
Japan	0.6	–	0.3	0.9
Hong Kong	1.1	28.2	7.9	16.7
Singapore	5.0	2.1	14.5	8.8
Indonesia	83.5	0.7	0.3	4.3
Malaysia	0.4	2.1	14.4	0.3
Cambodia	–	–	7.4	2.6
China	–	–	14.0	15.9
Laos	–	–	4.0	1.3
Myanmar	–	–	0.1	1.3
Vietnam	–	–	0.3	1.2
Other	–	1.5	6.6	26.9
Pacific Asia	90.7	33.1	62.9	52.1
Total (US$m)	24.1	141.4	182.0	402.9

Source: Bank of Thailand.

expanded rapidly – and by 1993 accounted for 88 per cent of demand – all the raw materials are imported. This reflects the still very limited development of basic industries other than cement. In particular there is a shortage of iron and steel products, with over 70 per cent of needs imported. This, when taken with the dominance of foreign investment and manufactured exports by the electronics sector, and the casual nature of much of the new manufacturing employment, does focus attention on the ephemeral aspects of much of the development that has occurred since the mid-1980s.

Conclusion

The period 1980–96 was a critical one for the Thai economy. It has been characterised by dramatic economic growth, restructuring of exports and general internationalisation of the economy. While the degree to which these developments can be linked to the period of formal SAPs or changed domestic policy is highly questionable, the broad aims set out by the World Bank in 1980 – of opening up the economy and reorienting it towards the export of manufactured goods – have been substantially achieved. However, as was noted in Chapter 1, the dramatic changes have yet to be transmitted into the structure of GDP, and more significantly, employment. As is explored in Chapter 5, in terms of livelihood and residency Thailand remains a strongly rural agricultural society. Additionally, as is examined more fully in Chapters 6 and 7, the developments have been heavily concentrated in and around Bangkok, thus bypassing the majority of the Kingdom and its population. Indeed, the rapid internationalisation can be depicted as exacerbating the Kingdom's already remarkably uneven pattern of national development.

While changes in government policy cannot be effectively linked to the Kingdom's recent rapid growth, it is clear that the longstanding minimalist role of the state has been further reduced. It may well be that liberalisation, particularly of trade and foreign exchange movements, has sustained the influx of investment. However, the state may also have become less capable of dealing effectively with economic crises and the consequences of rapid growth. In this respect it may well be that, as is discussed in Chapter 8, the sustainability of Thailand's growth is open to serious question.

5

THE AGRICULTURAL SECTOR

Introduction

In the euphoria generated by Thailand's recent rapid economic growth and the prospects of the country achieving NIE status during the 1990s, many observers – and indeed Thai politicians and technocrats – appear to have lost sight of the fact that the country remains essentially an agricultural one. As was outlined in Chapter 1 the agricultural sector not only remains the principal source of livelihood for some 60 per cent of the population,[1] but also continues to bolster the rapid development of industry by supplying cheap food and raw materials. In addition, processed agricultural produce still accounts for an appreciable proportion of manufactured output and exports. As Ammar Siamwalla (1993) has stressed, Thailand retains considerable comparative advantage in agricultural production and exports. Additionally, it should be stressed that while the growth of the agricultural sector has been increasingly overshadowed by the expansion of industry, by international standards it has been remarkably rapid.[2]

It is the intention of this chapter to examine the emergence of the present diverse pattern of agricultural production, the current developments and the sector's long-term prospects. Overall, the past, present and possible role of the agricultural sector in the Kingdom's economic development is reviewed.

The role of government policy

For most of the post-war period successive Thai governments have explicitly promoted industry while implicitly discouraging agriculture through heavy taxation – particularly of the rice sector – and general neglect. However, it is important to stress that the discrimination against agriculture was never clearly stated in planning documents. Further, the policies were far from consistent. Certain commodities threatened by imports received favourable treatment, notably sugar, oil seeds, cotton and dairy produce. In addition, even within the rice sector, policies were contradictory – price support and state purchasing schemes being implemented when low international prices compounded the effect of the export tax on farm incomes.

As was discussed in Chapter 2, the government began to intervene in the rice sector during the 1930s with the principal objective of increasing Thai, as against Chinese, control. From the end of the Second World War until 1949 Thailand was required to make reparation payments in the form of rice,[3] and in order to manage this all rice exports were channelled through the government Rice Office.[4] The government extracted considerable revenue from the sale of export licences and manipulation of price levels; by 1949 these activities generated 27 per cent state revenue (Ammar Siamwalla, 1975: 236–7). This was a major factor in the government's continuation of the controls over rice exports until 1955. In addition, between 1947 and 1956 exporters of rice (also rubber and tin) were required to exchange their foreign earnings through the Bank of Thailand at some two-thirds of the free market rate[5] (Silcock, 1967a: 14). In 1955–6 the multi-exchange system ended and the controls over rice export were reformed, consolidated into an export tax, the rice reserve system and, most importantly, the Rice Premium.[6] The latter was to remain in operation until 1986. In total these measures comprised a substantial tax on the rice sector.

While the taxation of rice exports comprised a major source of government revenue the Premium was also intended to even out price fluctuations, protect the domestic supply of rice and keep the cost of living – and hence wage levels – for the urban industrial sector low. To this end there was considerable variation in the amount levied. The government's control over the rice sector was reinforced by the use of government-to-government sales and export quotas. The degree to which the government's intervention in the rice sector was effective in stabilising the domestic supply and price levels has been questioned. Indeed, the whole question of the impact of these policies has been the subject of a major debate which has given rise to a voluminous literature (see e.g. reviews in Ammar Siamwalla (1975, 1989); Ammar Siamwalla and Suthad Setboosarng, 1986; Holtsberg, 1982; Silcock, 1967c; Usher, 1967).

From 1955 to 1974 the taxation of rice exports effectively depressed the domestic price of rice compared to that prevailing in the international market by 35 per cent, by 28 per cent until 1979 and by 15 per cent until 1985. The adverse impact of the Rice Premium on the incomes of rice growers was reinforced from the mid-1970s onwards by the over-valuation of the baht (Bautista, 1993: 214–20). According to Kruger et al. (1988: 262–3) the combination of the taxation and currency factors reduced the domestic price of rice by 43 per cent between 1975 and 1979, and by 34 per cent between 1979 and 1984. Ammar Siamwalla et al. (1993: 116) suggest a slightly lower figure of 40 per cent for the 1975–9 period.

The level of price reduction faced by Thai rice growers until the mid-1980s was high compared to those experienced by producers of export crops elsewhere in Asia (Table 5.1). In addition, in Thailand rice is not only an export crop but also dominates the Kingdom's land use and rural economy. Thus a review of the voluminous literature associated with the Rice Premium in particular, leads to the conclusion that it was:

> the largest single postwar government intervention affecting income distribution in Thailand, regressively falling on the rural sector and on farming households in the lowest income brackets, while increasing the real purchasing power of rice consumers (among whom, of course, were numerous urban and rural poor). In addition to the direct tax burden falling on producers, the artificial depression of the returns to rice cultivation distorted the incentive structure respecting rice, resulting in large efficiency losses from depressed output.
>
> (Muscat, 1994: 77)

Table 5.1 Impact of taxation, tariffs and exchange rates on the domestic price of agricultural products, 1975–84 (percentage)

	1975–79	*1980–84*
Republic of Korea		
Rice (F)	73	74
Malaysia		
Rice (F)	34	58
Rubber (X)	−29	−28
Philippines		
Corn (F)	−9	−2
Copra (X)	−38	−54
Thailand		
Rice (X)	−43	−34
Sri Lanka		
Rice (F)	−17	−20
Rubber (X)	−64	−62
Pakistan		
Wheat (F)	−61	−56
Cotton (X)	−60	−42

Source: Kruger *et al.* (1988: 262–3).

Notes:
F = food crop, X = export crop.

The World Bank (1983b) concluded that in 1981 the impact of these measures amounted to between 5 and 9 per cent of agricultural GDP. Overall, it is difficult to avoid the conclusion that the taxation of the rice sector depressed farm incomes and discouraged intensification and innovation. However, some commentators (e.g. Silcock, 1967c) have suggested that low rice prices were a major factor in stimulated diversification of agricultural activity and hence of farm incomes. Even accepting that this has been beneficial to the rural sector in the longer term, it is difficult not to interpret the situation as a classic case of Lipton's (1977) urban bias. This conclusion must be qualified in two respects. First, with respect to the operation of the various price support schemes, the provision of rural credit – principally through the BAAC (Bank for Agriculture and Agricultural Cooperatives) – and the impact of a whole range of rural and agricultural development programmes, including the provision of infrastructure. Second, and much more significantly, the general changes in policy which since the early 1980s have expanded and made much more effective the price support and credit provisions, suspended the Rice Premium and generally relaxed controls over rice exports.

From 1965, and more especially the early 1970s, a variety of price support schemes were operated in order to maintain farm incomes, particularly for rice growers. However, they have generally been extremely limited in their impact in the face of under-funding, the low level of the support prices, lack of an effective mechanism for direct public purchasing and the hostility of the established market system (Dixon, 1974: 480; Muscat, 1994: 76). As a result between 1974–5 and 1979–80 less than 2 per cent of annual sales were to the various government agencies[7] and the BAAC (Prakarn Virakul, 1992: 411).

The increased purchases during the period 1979–80 to 1982–3 of between 4 and 8 per cent of sales reflect the comparatively higher level at which the support price was set and the depressed nature of the international rice trade. In addition, in 1981 the BAAC instigated the Paddy Pledging Scheme, under which farmers were given loans against their unsold rice equivalent to 80 per cent of the target price. The number of farmers participating in this scheme remained limited until 1986 when the levels of interest charges were substantially reduced.[8] In addition, the BAAC rented storage space from farmers, encouraging them to keep the pledged paddy on the farms until it could be sold. These measures combined with the continued depressed international rice market to substantially increase the farmers' participation. The success of the BAAC scheme during 1986 prompted the government to increase its funding of these measures. Also in 1986 a Millers' Pledging Scheme was introduced,[9] which operated in a similar manner to the BAAC scheme. Sales through the various schemes rose to 52 per cent of sales in 1989, subsequently varying between 17 and 39 per cent.

While government intervention in the rice sector has been by far the most significant policy directed towards the agricultural sector a wide variety of measures have also been applied to other major crops. As may be seen from Table 5.2, various combinations of taxation, export quotas, import quotas, price controls and price support have resulted in the domestic prices of most major crops deviating from prevailing international levels in certain periods, sometimes to a very considerable extent. The motives for these measures are complex and have varied over time, as have the levels of intervention.

In a number of cases the domestic price reduction merely reflected the imposition of an export tax in order to raise revenue; this was particularly the case with respect to maize. The removal of the tax in 1982 was aimed at making the crop more competitive with such new low-cost producers as Vietnam and China. For rubber, the taxation of exports from 1935 until 1985 was supplemented by a levy from 1972 in order to provide funds for replanting.

Until the late 1950s the expansion of rubber production proceeded with little help or hindrance from the government.[10] Unlike Malaysia there was no substantial post-war replanting with high yielding trees, backed up by research and technical development programmes. Indeed, the expansion of the area planted since the 1920s appears to have been accompanied by little or no replanting. Thus by 1966 20 per cent of the trees were so old as to be effectively out of production and a further 31 per cent were over 30 years old (Rubber Research Centre, 1971: 46). In addition, as was noted in Chapter 2 (pp. 53–4) the Thai rubber sector was dominated by small-scale production, yields remained low and the quality poor and inconsistent (Silcock, 1967c: 252–5).

In 1959 the World Bank (1959: 5) advocated that the government should take a lead in the development of the sector. This led to the implementation of a replanting programme in 1960 under the auspices of the Rubber Replanting Aid Fund Board and the setting up of the Rubber Research Centre at Hat Yai. Progress was extremely slow until the 1970s, due principally to lack of funds. From 1972 funding was substantially through a number of FAO, World Bank and UNDP loans, and the imposition of an additional tax on exports which was returned to growers in the form of cash grants and seedlings. By 1993 some 50 per cent of the rubber area had been replanted and there had been substantial improvements in the quality and consistency of latex (Rubber Research Centre, 1994: 26). These improvements are reflected in the substitution of Thai rubber for Malaysian imports, in the manufacture of motor vehicle tyres and in the rapidly expanding rubber goods industry.

Government concern with the rubber sector since the 1970s reflects its comparative importance as an export and the buoyant state of the international rubber market. Between 1972 and 1993 Thailand's rubber production

Table 5.2 Combined effect of interventions by the government on the relative prices of agricultural products (proportional deviations from the world price)

	Rice	Maize	Sugar grower	Sugar miller	Sugar consumer	Rubber	Cotton	Soybean	Palm oil
1970	-0.3470	-0.2223	-0.0105	0.1256	0.1938	-0.3050	0.7700	—	—
1971	-0.4006	-0.2208	-0.1744	0.0344	0.1547	-0.2774	0.7225	—	—
1972	-0.3642	-0.0773	-0.3224	0.1094	-0.0052	-0.2269	0.7538	—	—
1973	-0.4619	-0.1842	-0.3613	-0.1971	-0.2363	-0.0512	0.8164	—	—
1974	-0.4994	-0.0702	-0.6396	-0.4362	-0.5806	-0.2258	0.2346	—	—
1975	-0.4266	-0.2143	-0.6284	-0.5027	-0.6936	-0.2993	0.2315	—	—
1976	-0.2835	-0.1773	-0.3262	-0.2454	-0.3617	-0.3267	0.0280	-0.1926	—
1977	-0.3907	0.2165	-0.2390	-0.2409	-0.3224	-0.3931	-0.1540	-0.0249	-0.1916
1978	-0.4517	-0.2165	0.0818	-0.1642	-0.0809	-0.3806	-0.0776	-0.0315	-0.1942
1979	-0.4148	-0.2663	0.0707	-0.1503	-0.0680	-0.4192	-0.1200	-0.0423	-0.2434
1980	-0.4045	-0.2379	-0.2168	-0.0244	0.0933	-0.4045	-0.1210	-0.0783	-0.2576
1981	-0.4171	-0.2837	-0.2950	-0.2225	-0.2197	-0.3635	-0.1820	-0.1130	-0.2067
1982	-0.2565	-0.1594	0.1440	-0.0887	0.3454	-0.2697	-0.1308	0.0923	-0.0917
1983	-0.3015	-0.2403	0.1516	0.0265	0.7902	-0.3767	-0.0802	-0.0245	-0.1436
1984	-0.2517	-0.2030	0.2202	0.1841	0.8156	-0.3223	-0.0034	-0.0245	-0.1436
1985	-0.2203	-0.1843	0.9604	0.0099	1.3517	-0.2704	0.2160	-0.0336	-0.2627
1986	-0.0999	-0.0915	0.6430	-0.0341	1.4109	-0.1920	0.4291	0.2186	0.1971

Source: Ammar Siamwalla et al. (1994: 115).

increased by an annual average rate of 6.5 per cent, faster than any other major producer. In 1985 the sector was given a boost by the removal of the longstanding export tax (but not the additional tax that funds replanting). Since the early 1980s increased rubber production has been closely related to the development of the domestic rubber goods industry and the establishment of large-scale modern processing and latex concentrating plants.

The comparative success of the rubber sector has been a significant factor in the comparatively better performance of the Southern regional agricultural economy. This has also been a consideration in the various plans to expand rubber production into parts of the Eastern and North Eastern regions. However, serious doubts have been raised over the agronomic viability of such plans (Dixon, 1994: 946).

Government intervention in the sugar sector has been particularly complex (Phitsane Jessadachatr, 1977). From the mid-1950s onwards the crop was promoted and protected as part of the import substitution programme. Protection through import controls and taxes continued long after the crop had become a major export (Ammar Siamwalla *et al.*, 1993: 85; Phitsane Jessadachatr, 1977). Maintaining prices for long periods well above the international level has played an important part in the long-term expansion of sugar production. However, a variety of price stabilisation schemes have been applied to the crop, with generally limited success.[11] Thus the sector has become locked into a 'boom–bust' cycle of expansion and contraction, which has inhibited investment and intensification. Extraction rates and sugar yields remain remarkably low for such a major producer (see Table 5.10, p. 156). As can be seen from Table 5.2, the impact of government intervention on sugar growers, millers and consumers has been remarkably different and extremely variable.

In contrast to the comparative success of long-term government promotion of the rubber sector and the rather more qualified success of intervention in the sugar sector, other initiatives have been generally shorter lived and more problematic.

Cotton and soybeans have been the subject of a variety of import restrictions aimed at stimulating domestic production. Neither have been particularly successful. The domestic production of cotton remains limited in volume and quality and of little importance to the domestic textile industry. Indeed, despite continued promotion and support production has declined steadily since the early 1980s. This reflects the inability to overcome a variety of agronomic problems and the high costs of fertiliser and pesticides. Similarly the production of soybeans has been protected by import quotas (between 1984 and 1989) and import taxes. While there has been a substantial increase in the area planted to the crop, the high domestic cost of soybeans contributes to the high price of animal feed stuffs. A number of more limited and generally shorter lived price support and promotion schemes have been applied to other crops, including some comparatively minor ones, notably garlic (1983–5), onions (1988–9), maize (1987–8) and pepper (1990).

From the mid-1970s there was a substantial increase in the government's general support for the agricultural sector, with the allocation of funds derived from the Rice Premium to the Farmers' Aid Fund administered by the BAAC. This was principally aimed at expanding the provision of farm credit. From 1975 a series of other measures was introduced to expand the provision of rural credit, notably a requirement that the commercial banks increase the proportion of their loans to the agricultural sector from 2 per cent in 1974, to 5 per cent in 1975 and 13 per cent in 1979 (Muscat, 1994: 144). In addition, the BAAC received international aid and various concessionary accommodation from the Bank of Thailand. Overall, these measures provided a substantial expansion of the availability of cheap institutional credit for the agricultural sector.

In 1990 it was estimated that institutional credit was reaching almost 60 per cent of agricultural households, compared to 15–20 per cent in 1975 – about 80 per cent of this coming from the BAAC (Ammar Siamwalla *et al.*, undated: 10; Muscat, 1994: 168). The impact of the expansion of credit on the agricultural sector is far from clear. To some extent the availability of credit compensated farmers for the income depressing effect of the Rice Premium. The encouragement by the BAAC of loan groups to whom funds could be advanced provided there were some credit-worthy members, and the provision of short-term working capital, gave some poorer farmers access to institutional credit. Inevitably, however, the majority of the institutional credit flowed to the larger farms with more secure land title deeds, leaving small farms with less secure titles dependent on higher cost, more uncertain informal sources:

> The poorest households are generally free from debt simply because no one will lend to them. The next poorest will borrow entirely from the informal sector. Those with middling income will look to the BAAC as their primary source of credit, supplemented, as the need arises, with loans from the informal sector. The richest households obtain their credit from commercial banks.
>
> (Ammar Siamwalla, 1989: 10)

The BAAC view has been that the increased availability of credit has been a major factor in agricultural development, promoting land improvement, intensification and diversification of production. Against this has to be set low repayment rates and the limited controls over (and accurate records of) the purposes to which loans are put. Some commentators have gone so far as to suggest that the BAAC's activities have been a major factor in encouraging large numbers of people to remain in scarcely viable agricultural activities (see the Conclusion to this chapter, pp. 186–9).

From the early 1980s the increased availability of rural credit and the implementation of more effective price support programmes were accompanied by the amelioration of a number of the factors which had long depressed the farm-gate price of rice. The devaluations of the baht (see p. 116) substantially reduced the adverse effects of the over-valued currency. In 1982 the ending of the compulsory rice reserve scheme began to reduce the effective tax burden on the rice sector. More significantly, from that year the level of the Rice Premium was progressively reduced, until in 1986 it was set at zero[12] (it was not, however, abolished).

The suspension of the Rice Premium in 1986 was followed by the abolition of the export tax, the lifting of export quotas and the reduction in the compulsory stocking requirements for exports. These reduced controls were accompanied by increased incentives for exporters in the form of the expansion of rediscount credit facilities. In total these reforms were aimed at increasing the competitiveness of Thai rice in the international market during a period of continued low levels of demand. They also, at least in theory, removed a major burden from the rural sector – though there is little evidence of substantial benefits accruing to the farmers.[13] This perhaps vindicates the long-held opinion that the reduction or even removal of the Premium in particular would merely benefit the rice trading system with little direct benefit being passed on to the farmers (see e.g. Amranand and Grais, 1984: 1; Silcock, 1967c).

Since the early 1980s there has overall been a general reduction in policies that reduced the income of the rice growing sector, and some increases in support for farmers through credit and public purchase schemes. Prior to these changes the generally accepted view is that agriculture was heavily discriminated against – the various, and curiously contradictory, price support and credit policies only providing limited and often short-term mitigation. Government policies succeeded in transferring resources from the agricultural sector but failed to discourage productivity or undermine the sector's international competitiveness. Ammar Siamwalla (1993: 25) has concluded that the comparative advantage in agriculture was such that government policy proved incapable of damaging it. However, some doubts have been raised over the degree to which the flow of resources was on balance entirely one way, notably by Ammar Siamwalla and Suthad Setboonsarng (1986) and Muscat (1994: 246). In the light of the sustained growth of agriculture under apparently adverse policy conditions, a comprehensive, in-depth review is perhaps needed. This would have to take account of a much wider range of data than that concerned directly with taxation, price support and credit provision, including the expenditure on rural infrastructure and agricultural development. Similarly, the impact of some of the more neglected government interventions such as controls over livestock slaughtering, oil seed processing and tobacco need much fuller consideration.

The structure of the agricultural sector

As may be seen from Table 5.3 almost 75 per cent of the value of agricultural production is contributed by the crop and livestock sectors. This position has remained more or less unchanged since the mid-1960s. However, there has been a gradual increase in the importance of the livestock sector. In contrast the share of the forestry sector has declined continuously while that of fisheries has shown a less clear general tendency to decline.

The composition of the agricultural sub-sectors has undergone considerable change since the 1950s. As may be seen from Tables 5.4, 5.5 and 5.6 there has been considerable diversification in the crop sector, particularly into vegetables and upland crops – notably cassava, sugar, maize and kenaf. There has been a similar shift in the composition of the livestock

Table 5.3 Average annual percentage structure of agricultural GDP at constant 1972 prices, 1961–91

Sector	1962–6	1967–71	1972–6	1977–81	1982–6	1987–91
Crops	76.6	73.2	73.6	74.1	75.5	73.4
Livestock	12.0	11.5	11.6	13.6	14.5	17.5
Fishing	3.6	7.7	8.2	7.2	6.5	6.9
Forestry	7.8	7.6	6.6	5.1	3.5	2.2
Total	100.0	100.0	100.0	100.0	100.0	100.0

Source: NESDB.

Table 5.4 Average percentage shares of crop GDP at constant 1972 prices, 1972–91

	1961–6	1967–71	1972–6	1977–81	1982–6	1987–91
Major crops						
Paddy	53.6	48.0	41.8	37.1	35.8	31.1
Cassava	2.8	3.4	5.3	8.6	8.0	8.0
Sugar	1.3	3.1	3.8	3.8	4.8	4.8
Maize	2.8	4.6	4.3	4.5	5.4	4.6
Rubber	4.5	5.1	5.6	5.9	6.5	9.8
Total	64.9	62.9	60.1	59.9	60.5	58.3
Other crops						
Vegetables	6.2	8.4	8.7	9.4	8.9	9.0
Fruits	9.7	8.7	7.9	8.4	9.0	10.1
Orchid	–	0.1	0.6	1.8	2.5	2.7
Coconut	2.5	2.1	2.1	1.8	1.9	2.1
Pineapple	–	0.7	2.1	1.8	1.9	2.1
Others	16.3	17.3	19.8	16.7	15.3	15.8
Total	100.0	100.0	100.0	100.0	100.0	100.0

Table 5.5 Land use, 1950–91 (percentage of the surface area)

	1950	1955	1960	1965	1970	1975	1980	1985	1991
Forest	59.3	55.6	52.7	49.1	43.5	39.1	30.1	27.4	26.7
Farm holding	15.4	17.0	18.7	23.9	28.1	33.5	35.5	39.0	41.6
Housing area	n.a.	n.a.	n.a.	n.a.	n.a.	0.8	0.7	0.9	1.1
Paddy land	10.0	10.8	11.6	12.4	17.5	21.3	22.0	22.2	21.6
Field crops	1.4	1.4	2.1	3.7	4.2	6.0	7.7	9.6	10.5
Tree crops	1.4	1.6	1.7	2.9	2.7	3.1	3.3	4.2	6.3
Vegetable and flowers	n.a.	n.a.	n.a.	n.a.	n.a.	0.1	0.1	0.2	0.3
Pasture land	n.a.	n.a.	n.a.	n.a.	n.a.	0.1	0.1	0.3	0.2
Idle land	1.6	1.6	1.6	1.5	1.2	1.4	0.9	1.1	1.1
Other	1.0	1.6	1.7	3.4	2.4	0.7	0.6	0.5	0.5
Unclassified	25.3	27.4	28.6	27.0	28.4	30.4	34.5	33.6	31.7

Source: MAC.

Note
As is discussed on p. 183, these data almost certainly over-estimate the area under forest and under-estimate the area under crops (see also Table 5.11).

Table 5.6 Expansion of major non-rice crops (thousands of ha)

	1950	1960	1970	1980	1990	1993
Sugar cane	54	158	206	457	789	1038
Cassava	14	72	225	1117	1530	1518
Cotton	40	50	82	158	77	80
Maize	36	286	829	1345	1786	1408
Mungbean	42	54	249	466	468	401
Kenaf	10	71	421	236	133	109
Soybean	23	23	58	131	443	382

Source: MAC.

sector away from draught animals (principally water buffaloes), and towards the production of poultry and eggs. The decline in the importance of draught animals, particularly water buffalo, reflects the increased use of tractors and rotavators and the increase in dry season cropping which makes it difficult to provide grazing and fodder for draught animals (see discussion of mechanisation, pp. 174–5).

While many parts of the North East are highly suited to cattle rearing there has been only limited development of production. Since the early 1980s rising incomes and related changes in diet have increased demand for beef. However, the generally small-scale cattle rearing sector has been slow to respond; in part this reflects the continuation of restrictive slaughtering practices.[14] Similar restrictions apply in the pig sector (Ammar Siamwalla *et al.*, 1994: 87). Here the growth of production has been further constrained by the very tight control exercised by the five[15] companies that largely control the marketing and supply of feed stuff, and account for roughly 50 per cent of national pork production.

A major national beef shortage has emerged with imports rising from 158 million tons in 1986 to 515 million tons in 1993. In addition, it has been estimated by the Livestock Department that some 300,000 cattle a year are smuggled into Thailand from Cambodia, Laos and Myanmar. It is probable that a number of outbreaks of cattle disease that have occurred since the late 1980s are a result of this illegal traffic.

In contrast to the other livestock sectors, poultry production has been a major growth area since the early 1980s. The growth of production has been closely related to the development of contract farming under the auspices of a small number of major agri-business concerns. There has been a substantial increase in the domestic per capita consumption of chicken, and unlike the other livestock sectors, the development of a major export trade. The export of frozen chickens, principally to Japan and the Middle East, rose from 64,800 tons in 1986 to 112,000 tons in 1993.

Despite some relaxation of controls since the mid-1980s the development of the livestock sector continues to be constrained by slaughtering regulations and the restrictive practices of major producers. However, perhaps even more significant is the limited production and high cost of domestic animal feed (Suthad Seboonsarng et al., 1989). Production is controlled by a small number of producers whose position is protected by the continuation of high levels of tariffs on imports. Thus the costs of intensive livestock production remain high, and Thai products are scarcely competitive on the international market. The advantage in frozen chicken production lies in the product being boned – the high costs of production being offset by the low labour costs. However, in the mid-1990s Thailand is losing this advantage, and the Japanese market in particular, to China.

The increased significance and long-term problems of the marine fishing industry were reviewed in Chapter 1 (pp. 14–15). In contrast to its marine counterpart the inland sector remains small in scale and largely subsistent in character. However, it has similarly experienced a depletion of stocks – a direct consequence of increased rural population. In response to the shortage of fish and the need for farmers to find additional sources of income, aquaculture developed rapidly during the late 1970s with active promotion on the part of the Department of Fisheries. Fish rearing spread initially in the Central Plain and later the North East with the production of catfish, tilapia, gourami, striped snakehead, shrimp and carp – utilising ditches, ponds, paddy fields and cages. By 1990 there were some 60,000 freshwater production units according to the Fishery Department.[16] However, total inland production was only some 200,000 tons in 1993 and this included some comparatively large-scale production in reservoirs. Thus farm-based aquaculture is generally very small in scale and near subsistent in character. Despite this the increasingly active promotion of aquaculture is seen as a means of increasing and diversifying income and nutrition for many rural households.

Marine aquaculture has also developed rapidly involving major investment, removal of mangroves and the introduction of Taiwanese techniques to raise tiger prawns. The active promotion of these developments by the Department of Fisheries and the commercial sector have made major contributions to raising and diversifying rural incomes in many coastal areas. In addition, the culture of prawns and shrimps has made a major contribution to the growth and diversification of fishery exports since the late 1970s. However, against this has to be set the environmental damage resulting from the widespread removal of mangroves and the associated adverse affects on some agricultural activities in coastal areas.[17]

The decline and comparatively limited contemporary importance of the forestry sector was commented on in Chapter 1 (p. 14). Since the early 1980s there has been some development of the cultivation of rapidly maturing trees to supply the woodchips and paper pulp industries. While, like aquaculture, this is of comparatively limited national importance it is considered to have considerable potential for the generation of additional income and sustainable production for farmers of highly marginal land, particularly in the North East (see e.g. Patanapongsa, 1990). However, small-scale growers do not appear to be obtaining significant benefits from tree cultivation (Patanapongsa, 1990: 68). Most development has involved large-scale plantations of, in particular, *eucalyptus camaldulensis* – variety which can be cut every five to six years and then left to regenerate. However, the activity generates little local employment or income and has engendered increasing conflicts between farmers and plantations over land rights and environmental damage (see Lohmann, 1991; and discussion later in this chapter, pp. 178–83).

Since the late 1970s there has been a second wave of agricultural diversification. This has centred on intensive production of high-value products – chickens, fruit, vegetables,[18] fresh flowers – for the export market, and, particularly since the mid-1980s, the burgeoning Bangkok-based middle-class market. These developments have centred on the rapid growth of agri-businesses and various forms of contract farming (see Volden, 1995). This started with the production of broiler chickens, spread to pig rearing and subsequently to fruit, vegetables and fresh flowers, and such established crops as pineapples and oil palm (see Sompop Manarungsan and Suebskun Suwanjindar, 1992). In addition, some of the major concerns, such as Charoen Pokphand, have begun to experiment with applying contract production to rice and maize (Glover and Lim, 1992: 15–17; Kulick and Wilson, 1992: 139; Volden, 1995). Overall, while the local impact of these activities can be substantial, as yet they affect a minute proportion of the rural population.

The nature of Thai crop production

Thai agriculture is dominated by extensive cultivation of rain-fed crops, most significantly wet rice, which in 1993 accounted for 50 per cent of the cropped area. Given that only some 18 per cent of the cultivated area is classed as irrigated,[19] the main constraints on agricultural production are the levels and marked seasonality of rainfall (see Norman, 1973). Indeed, the agricultural year and most aspects of rural life are determined by the timing and intensity of the wet season. Seasonal and annual variations in rainfall affect not only the timing of the agricultural year, but more significantly the area planted, the level of crop damage, yields and production levels. These variations are most serious in the North Eastern region but are of major significance to farmers in almost all parts of the country. In general, according to MAC data, only some 85 per cent of the rice area is planted in any one year, of which around 90 per cent is harvested.

Most of Thailand experiences a tropical wet and dry or 'monsoonal' climate, with the majority of rainfall in the five months from May to September. The southern parts of the Kingdom, including the eastern side of the Gulf of Thailand as well as the Peninsula, are transitional between the 'monsoonal' climate and the tropical wet climate with no marked dry season. Within these areas the shorter dry season and higher annual rainfall totals are reflected in a distinctive pattern of land use. Tree crops – particularly rubber, oil palm and fruit – replace the paddy and field crops that dominate land use of the majority of the Kingdom (see Tables 5.5 and 5.7).

While outside the southern areas land use is dominated by wet rice and field crop cultivation there are very considerable variations in land use and cropping practices, both within and between the North, North East and Central Plan (Table 5.7). For rice cultivation (at the risk of gross simplification), very clear distinctions can be made between the North, North East and Central Plain (Table 5.8). However, the variation within the regions themselves is also very great (for detailed discussions see Donner, 1978; Tanabe, 1994).

Table 5.7 Regional utilisation of farm land, 1991

	Paddy	Field crops	Tree crops	Veget-ables and flowers	Grazing land	Idle land	Other	Total
North East	65.8	23.3	3.2	0.4	0.7	3.4	3.2	100.0
North	51.7	35.6	6.0	0.9	0.5	1.5	3.8	100.0
Central	43.8	33.0	15.3	1.1	7.7	1.6	4.8	100.0
South	20.8	0.9	70.0	0.4	0.3	3.9	3.7	100.0
Country	51.9	25.2	15.1	0.6	0.5	2.7	4.5	100.0

Source: MAC.

Table 5.8 Regional rice economy, 1990–3 (averages)

	Planted area (million ha)	(%)	Production (million tons)	(%)	Yield (kg/ha)	Harvested area (%)	Second crop area (%)	Irrigated area (%)
North East	5.3	52.4	7.81	47.0	1612	93.7	1.5	16.7
North	2.2	21.8	4.3	25.9	1714	88.7	7.2	26.7
Central	2.1	20.8	3.6	21.7	2334	97.0	26.8	48.5
South	0.5	5.0	0.9	5.4	2012	87.1	5.5	2.9
Kingdom	10.1	100.0	16.6	100.0	1902	89.7	7.3	27.0

Source: MAC.

The extensive, rain-fed nature of Thai agriculture is reflected most clearly in the generally low level of crop yields (Table 5.9). Of the major crops only cassava has a level of yield that may be considered high by regional and international standards. In part this reflects the fact that in Thailand, unlike most other major producers, cassava is almost exclusively grown as a cash crop for export. Additionally, Thai cassava yields have declined steadily since the early 1970s (Table 5.8). This is a reflection of the spreading of the crop on to more marginal land, and, more significantly, the inability of the methods of cultivation (especially the generally low levels of fertiliser application) to maintain yields. However, perhaps the most surprising feature of Thai crop yields is that given the Kingdom's long-term position as a major rice exporter, the national yield is almost the lowest of any country where the crop is of major significance (Table 5.10).

Thailand has comparatively limited areas of highly fertile soils (see Donner, 1978: 20–1). For wet rice this combines with the seasonal and uncertain level of rainfall to make topography at least as important as soil type (Norman, 1973: 144). However, the combination of low soil fertility, rainfall totals and variation and topography dictate that there are few areas of the Kingdom where wet rice can be reliably cultivated in every year in the absence of effective irrigation and/or flood control. Thus in many ways Thailand can be presented as possessing a poor and unreliable environment for agriculture. Despite this, as may be seen from Table 5.11, studies of land capability conducted in 1972 and 1988 suggest that some 49 to 52 per cent of the surface area was suited to some form of permanent cultivation.

Table 5.9 Yields of non-rice crops (kg/ha)

Field crop	1960	1970	1980	1991
Cassava	16400	14100	13200	12600
Cotton	805	1047	1278	1380
Kenaf	1248	1285	1206	1242
Maize	1836	2244	1800	2310
Soybean	880	890	912	1267
Sugarcane	32566	36880	40800	49800
1991 Thai yield as a percentage of:		*Asia*		*World*
Cassava		99.2		136.2
Cotton		72.0		73.5
Kenaf		n.a.		n.a.
Maize		57.4		55.2
Soybean		94.8		66.5
Sugarcane		62.9		61.1

Source: MAC; FAO *Production Yearbook* (1995).

Table 5.10 Comparative rice yields (kg/ha)

	1949–51	1959–61	1969–71	1979–81	1991–3
Bangladesh				1952	2648
Cambodia	940	1057	1443	962	1283
China	2105	2180	3328	4240	5799
India	1071	1489	1668	1858	2646
Indonesia	1069	1749	2345	3257	4357
Japan	4209	4982	5476	5581	5571
Korea (North)	2767	4112	4358	4733	3442
Korea (South)	3821	3882	4628	5513	6053
Laos	747	798	1309	1415	2395
Malaysia	1545	1963	2395	2844	3148
Myanmar	1468	1707	1707	2689	2941
Pakistan					
Philippines	1172	1183	1585	2207	2814
Sri Lanka	1345	1857	2275	2555	3059
Thailand	1308	1444	1935	1837	2153
Vietnam	1321	2030	2056	2795	3295
South East Asia	1196	1491	1846	2251	2798
Thai as a %	109	97	105	84	77
All Asia	1609	1860	2350	2795	3235
Thai as a %	81	78	82	66	67
World	1617	1868	2331	2745	3544
Thai as a %	89	77	83	67	60

Source: FAO *Production Yearbook* (1995); FAO *World crop and livestock statistics, 1948–85* (1987).

The dynamics of agricultural expansion

The long-term growth of the agricultural sector and its related ability to support a large proportion of the population has been made possible by the existence of large areas of unused land suitable for cultivation and the general ease of access to it. Until comparatively recently Thailand remained a sparsely populated country with abundant land suited to rice cultivation (Falkus, 1991: 59). There have been few effective controls over the clearance and cultivation of land. In addition, the environmental conditions that prevailed over much of the Kingdom made for easier, small-scale land clearance than was the case in, for example, much of Malaysia and Indonesia,[20] and enabled the cultivation of an exceptionally high proportion of the national area (Table 5.12).

The long-term expansion of the cultivated area was generally supported by the Thai state, initially through land tax concessions, and later through the construction of rural infrastructure, particularly roads (see Hirsch, 1990: 49–50; also Chapters 2 and 3). In addition, from the 1940s a variety of government programmes promoted clearance and settlement. The most

Table 5.11 Land utilisation and capability

Land capability, 1972

Area (m.ha)	Percentage	Capability
9.62	18.7	Paddy
5.92	11.5	Paddy and upland crops
14.20	27.5	Upland crops
21.65	42.2	Unsuited to cultivation

Recommended land use based on the capability analysis, 1972

Area (m.ha)	Percentage	Land use
20.66	40.2	Forest
17.37	33.8	Moderately suited to upland crops
1.85	3.6	Well suited to upland crops
6.01	11.7	Well suited to paddy
5.50	10.7	Severe shortcomings for cultivation

Land capability, 1988

Area (m.ha)	Percentage	Capability
12.93	25.16	Paddy
11.28	21.95	Upland crops
2.73	5.31	Perennial crops
24.45	47.58	Unsuited to cultivation

Source: Land Development Department.

Table 5.12 Population density, 1993 (persons/km^2)

Country	Crude density	Cultivated area density	Agricultural population	Percentage of surface cultivated
Cambodia	46	245	180	22.9
Myanmar	73	370	185	15.8
Indonesia	94	800	390	23.2
Laos	18	460	340	7.4
Malaysia	54	365	128	24.9
Philippines	185	690	341	30.1
Thailand	111	270	170	42.2
Vietnam	185	767	563	22.5

Source: FAO *Production Year Book* (1995).

significant of these were organised by the Land Settlement Division of the Public Welfare Department and the Self Help Settlement Scheme of the MAC. However, in total 14 different government bodies have at various times promoted settlement programmes (Demaine, 1984). These included the Agricultural Land Reform Office (ALRO) set up in 1975 following the passing of the 1975 Land Reform Act. As Hirsch has stressed, while this Act was:

> ostensibly set up to deal with the growing problem of landless-ness, particularly in the Central Plains and parts of the Upper North, ALRO has tended to locate projects in recently settled areas in order to legitimise control over land that would other-wise be occupied by forest squatters. In other cases forest land has been cleared to make way for 'land reform'.
>
> (1990: 49)

In total since 1940 some 230,000 families have been settled on 700,000 ha of land. This included households resettled as a result of the construction of reservoirs, principally for irrigation (see pp. 170–4). However, while these publicly promoted settlement schemes are by no means insignificant, the vast majority of the clearance and settlement has been the result of individual households and communities with little specific support. This 'spontaneous' settlement was closely associated with local regional and national migration into areas of uncleared land (Dixon, 1976; Ng, 1970; Thapa and Weber, 1988). The result has been a remarkably even pattern of rural settlement (Ng, 1970, 1978).

While there was an abundance of land which was brought into cultivation comparatively easily, for much of it soil fertility was low and this combined with unreliable rainfall and limited water control to produce low yields and unreliable production levels. Indeed, the expansion of the cultivated area brought increasingly marginal land into production, thus compounding the situation. Under these conditions there was little incentive, or indeed prospect, for the intensification of production. Thus until comparatively recently the expansion of the cultivated area with little intensification of production has been the principle dynamic of Thai agricultural expansion.

In addition to the ready availability of land the attraction of the rural sector was reinforced in a number of ways. Historically, the limited growth of the urban, industrial and commercial sectors and their domination by the Chinese community limited the opportunities for the rural population to seek alternative activities. In contrast, as was discussed in Chapter 2 (p. 58), the rural sector remained attractive to labour because of the comparatively good conditions and ease of making a living.

While much has been made of the extensive nature of Thai rice cultivation, it is worth noting that until the 1950s, despite the long-term fall in average yields (see Figure 2.2, p. 43), the Kingdom's average yields compared favourably with other parts of Asia (see Table 5.10). Perhaps more significantly, production per capita appears to have been significantly higher in Thailand (Sompop Manarungsan, 1989: 168). While the data on productivity is far from satisfactory, it does serve to underline the comparative ease of making a livelihood in rural Thailand and the consequent attractiveness of the agricultural sector.

The strong comparative advantage of the agricultural sector as a source of livelihood began to break down during the 1940s (see also comments in Chapter 2 on the difficulties being faced by the rice sector during the 1920s and 1930s, pp. 47–8). This is reflected in the acceleration of the growth of the urban sector discussed in Chapter 6 (see pp. 197–8). Within the rural sector three closely inter-related factors were combining to depress the comparative level and ease of living for an appreciable proportion of the population. First, by the 1950s the expansion of rice cultivation into progressively more marginal areas, particularly in the outer regions, which had steadily reduced rice yields since the early years of the century, was beginning to falter, with the emergence of shortages of accessible land suited to cultivation in many areas (see Falkus, 1991). Second, this situation was reinforced by the dramatic decline of the death rate and consequent rapid increase in population growth (see Chapter 3, pp. 89–91). Third, the overarching effect of government rice policy on rural incomes and living standards discussed on pp. 141–3. In these respects the 1950s may be seen as a major turning point in Thailand's development (Falkus, 1991). However, the breakdown of the comparative advantage of the rural sector took place slowly and unevenly. This reflected both the strength of the advantage and the emergence of new sources of growth in parts of the rural sector (see below).

The problems that emerged during the 1950s, while heralding the eventual closure of the land frontier and changes in the relative position of the rural population – also saw the beginnings of developments that gave rise to a remarkable acceleration of the rate of expansion of the cultivated area. The first of these was a direct consequence of a major factor in the reduction in the rural death rate – the success of the malaria eradication programmes (see pp. 71–2). During the 1960s these effectively 'disarmed' the forest, opening up vast areas to clearance and settlement, particularly in the upper Central Plain, the North East, Eastern and Western regions of the Kingdom. Second, the expansion of road building programmes from the 1950s opened up large areas to settlement and production for the market (see p. 82, p. 85). Third, the construction of roads and other rural infrastructure generated dry season labouring employment, and facilitated seasonal migration in search of employment. Fourth, and most significantly, much land considered unsuitable for rice cultivation was suited to a range of upland crops – cassava, maize, kenaf and sugar cane – for which a buoyant export market began to emerge from the 1950s onwards. The expansion of these crops was assisted by the spread of tractor ploughing, particularly from the late 1960s. This facili-

tated the opening up of dry upland plots and enabled farmers to culti-
vate much larger holdings.

The expansion of upland crops from the mid-1950s onwards (see Tables
5.4, 5.5, and 5.6) resulted in substantial diversification of agriculture and
brought a large amount of land and many farmers into the cash crop
economy. However, in addition, particularly between 1965 and 1975, large
amounts of land suited to wet rice cultivation was also opened up (Table
5.5; Figure 5.1).

The rate of expansion of the cultivated area slowed from the mid-1970s,
reflecting a renewed and more general shortage of uncleared land (Table
5.13).[21] The slowing was accompanied by a sharp decline in the rate of
population growth (see pp. 89–91). This undoubtedly reduced the demographic pressure for expansion and prevented a much steeper decline in
the relative income level of many rural communities. However, as was
noted in Chapter 3 (p. 91), there is evidence to suggest a close relationship between the availability of land and the decline in the birth rate.

Since the mid-1970s the more gradual expansion of the cultivated area
has principally involved upland and tree crops (Tables 5.6 and 5.14). The
overall expansion of the area classed as rice land has ceased, and since
the mid-1980s there appears to have been a slight decline. Also since the
mid-1980s there has been a marked slowing of the expansion of the field

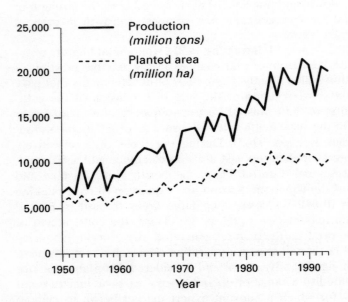

Figure 5.1 Rice area and production, 1950–93.

Source: MAC.

Table 5.13 Average annual rates of growth of the cultivated area, 1850–1991

	Farm land	Rice land	Upland crops	Tree crops
1850–1950	1.5[a]	–	–	–
1950–5	1.8	1.4	0.8	1.6
1955–60	3.2	1.5	9.2	2.4
1960–5	5.5	1.4	15.9	7.9
1965–70	3.6	8.2	2.7	–1.0
1970–5	3.9	4.1	8.4	2.9
1975–80	1.2	0.7	5.8	1.3
1980–5	1.3	0.2	4.4	5.1
1985–91	1.3	–0.6	1.8	10.0

Source: MAC.

Note
a Estimate by Marzouk (1972: 20).

Table 5.14 Comparative rates of fertiliser application (100 grams/ha)

	1979–80	1990–1
China	134	1273
India	313	743
Indonesia	440	1141
Laos	1	16
Malaysia	912	1950
Philippines	444	738
Thailand	160	471

Source: World Bank, World Development Report, 1994.

crop area. Expansion has become heavily concentrated in the tree crop sector. In part this reflected market conditions and the promotion of rubber and oil palm. However, it is difficult to avoid the conclusion that a widespread shortage of uncleared land suited to the permanent cultivation of rice and field crops has emerged.

In the 1990s we are witnessing the tail-end of over a century of rapid expansion of the cultivated area and the long-heralded closure of the land frontier. Thus the end is in sight for the expansion of the cultivated area as the principle dynamic of Thai agriculture.

The intensification of production

Since the early 1950s there has been a gradual increase in Thai rice yields (Figure 5.2). This reflects the gradual intensification of production in the most favoured irrigated areas, and, particularly since the late 1970s, the spread of improved varieties and increased fertiliser use into many rain-fed areas. However, as may be seen from Tables 5.10 and 5.14 the

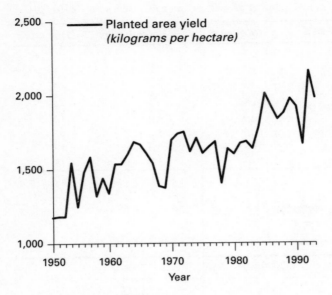

Figure 5.2 Rice yields, 1950–93.
Source: MAC.

increases in yields and fertiliser application have been insufficient to prevent Thailand's ranking amongst Asian rice producers from declining since *c*. 1970; this despite the development of the rice sector through the expansion of irrigation facilities and research being the main thrust of Thai agricultural policy (Ammar Siamwalla *et al.*, 1993: 109).

During the 1950s and 1960s the development of irrigation and the adoption in many rain-fed areas of intermediate varieties of rice that responded well to small amounts of fertiliser[22] were sufficient to maintain Thailand's admittedly low position amongst Asian and, more especially, South East Asian rice producers. From the early 1970s other South East Asian economies, particularly Indonesia, Malaysia and the Philippines, implemented major programmes aimed at substantially increasing rice production through investment in irrigation facilities and the widespread adoption of high-yielding varieties. For these economies such policies were closely related to the goal of achieving self-sufficiency in rice production. Thailand did not follow this line of development, continuing with the much more gradual establishment of irrigation facilities and the adoption of improved varieties. There were a number of reasons for this.

Thailand was under no pressure to raise yields in order to expand production. The continued expansion of the area cultivated, together with gradually increasing yields enabled production to increase sufficiently to

Table 5.15 Expansion of the irrigated area, 1947–92

	Central Plain		North		North East		South		Thailand	
	million ha	% share	million ha	% share	million ha	% share	million ha	% share	million ha	%
1947	0.62	97.4	0.17	2.6	–	–	–	–	0.79	100.0
1952	n.a.	n.a.	n.a.	n.a.	n.a.	n.a.	n.a.	n.a.	0.86	100.0
1954	0.82	89.1	0.03	3.6	0.06	7.3	–	–	0.93	100.0
1960	1.35	84.5	0.06	4.2	0.15	9.4	0.03	2.1	1.59	100.0
1965	1.43	78.2	0.18	10.0	0.17	9.1	0.05	2.7	1.83	100.0
1970	1.50	70.9	0.32	15.0	0.22	10.2	0.08	3.9	2.12	100.0
1975										
1980	1.85	59.1	0.63	20.2	0.38	12.2	0.27	8.5	3.13	100.0
1985									7.11	100.0
1990	2.17	49.4	1.15	26.0	0.68	15.5	0.45	10.1	4.45	100.0
1992	2.18	48.5	1.20	26.7	0.75	16.7	0.48	10.7	4.61	100.0

Source: MAC.

provide for rising domestic demand and exports (Figures 5.1 and 5.3). Thus, while the expansion of irrigation and rice production received the majority of agricultural development expenditure during the period 1966 to 1974, the proportion of government investment devoted to the agricultural sector was the lowest of any of the pro-capitalist Asian development economies (Douglass, 1983: 196).[23] In addition, the MAC did not favour the introduction of so-called 'high-yielding varieties' of rice. Apart from the obvious unsuitability of most of the Kingdom's rice fields – due to limited development of irrigation facilities – it was also feared that their introduction would compromise Thailand's reputation as a producer of quality rice. Given the nature of the Thai rice sector it is difficult to envisage a substantial adoption of any of the IRRI's high-yielding varieties during the 1960s and 1970s, whatever the policy adopted by the MAC. However, given the increased competition from other producers in the low-grade rice market the long-term emphasis on maintaining quality was undoubtedly a correct one. Overall, the low level of rice prices resulting from government intervention in the sector (see pp. 141–3), discouraged farmers from investing in land improvement and intensifying production. In particular the low returns from rice production discouraged the use of artificial fertiliser (see e.g. Rigg, 1985: 100–1).

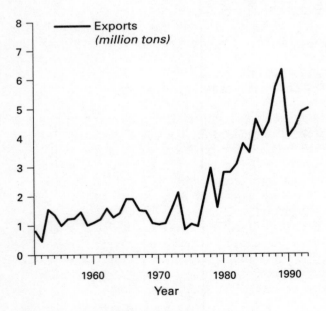

Figure 5.3 Rice exports, 1950–93.
Source: MAC.

During the 1970s while the average yields of most other South Asian countries increased substantially, in Thailand they virtually stagnated. A number of factors contributed to this. First, while the area classed as irrigated continued to expand (Table 5.15), an increasing proportion was located outside the potentially most productive areas of the Central Plan and serious problems of implementation were encountered.

Second, after the earlier success of spreading improved varieties of rice during the 1960s into both the better rain-fed and irrigated areas, something of an impasse seems to have been reached. This appears to have reflected the lack of suitable improved varieties and the very limited domestic capacity to produce improved seeds (NESDB, 1981: 44). The Mekong Committee (*Bulletin*, November, 1979: 47) concluded that in the North East during 'the wet season none of the new hybrid varieties can successfully compete (both agronomically and economically) with some of the traditional varieties'. In addition, within the irrigated areas problems of water supply (see discussion later in this chapter, pp. 170–4), low rice prices, comparatively high costs of inputs, combined with the unsatisfactory nature of some of the improved varieties to limit their adoption. Indeed, some observers saw very little prospect for the intensification of production through the adoption of higher yielding varieties in areas of rain-fed or even supplementary wet season irrigation (Dixon, 1976; Rigg, 1985a, b – see comments later in this chapter, p. 166).

Third, the very rapid expansion of the rice area during the late 1960s and early 1970s (Table 5.13; Figure 5.1) influenced the trend in yields in two ways. Much of the new land was more fertile and reliable than land that was being brought into cultivation during the 1950s and 1960s,[24] and yields tended to be higher during the first two or three years of cultivation. Thus during the late 1960s the very rapid expansion of the rice area may well have increased rather than depressed yields. Also, during the early 1970s the yield-depressing effect of the extraction of the initial store of nutrients from the land cleared during the late 1960s was reinforced by the clearance of progressively less fertile and less reliable land. Thus, during the 1970s, as in the 1950s and early 1960s, there is a general relationship at the provincial level between those provinces with limited increases in yield (and even declines), and those where there was considerable expansion of production.

During the 1970s the effect of expansion of the cultivated area was to depress yields and offset the impact of the expansion of irrigation, the adoption of improved varieties and increased fertiliser use. This was also the case with a wide range of non-rice crops. Between 1970 and 1980 the average yields of maize, cassava, sugar cane and soybean all declined (see Table 5.9, p. 156).

Since *c.* 1980 there have been renewed increases in the level of rice yields, and some rises in the yields of a number of other crops (see Figure

5.2; Table 5.9). This reflects the slowing down in the rate of expansion of the cultivated area (Table 5.13), continued expansion and improvement of irrigation facilities – including the rapid adoption of supplementary wet season pump irrigation (see Table 5.15 and discussion on pp. 170–4) – and increased fertiliser use and the spreading of improved varieties. The latter also took place comparatively widely in the more favoured rain-fed areas. This does not indicate that any major break-through in rain-fed rice cultivation took place. Rather, there was a continuation of the earlier gradual intensification with the introduction of further improved inter-mediate varieties, some of which were believed by farmers not only to be higher yielding but also hardier than the long-established varieties. Thus, by the mid-1990s the rice sector appears to have experienced a mild but widespread 'seed-fertiliser revolution' (see e.g. Rigg, 1995a on the mar-ginal areas of the North East). The extent to which these developments have been assisted by the removal of the policies which tended to depress the farm-gate price of rice is uncertain.

For rice, in particular, the improvements in yields have been extremely uneven (Figure 5.4). In consequence the variation between provinces has tended to increase,[25] as has the already considerable variation that exists within provinces and at local level. There are thus very considerable vari-ations in regional and provincial rice yields (Figure 5.5). In the period 1990–2 five provinces in the more favoured areas of the Central Plain and North averaged over 3,000 kg/ha, while in the North East four provinces averaged 1,500 kg/ha or less. In general, provinces with low average yields also tend to have high levels of variance in planted area and high levels of crop loss. Not surprisingly, the consistently higher yielding areas are closely associated with a high percentage of irrigated land and of second cropped rice.

Between 1980 and 1990 the consumption of chemical fertiliser increased from 0.79 million tons to 2.65 million tons (Table 5.16). This increased the average application rates by almost three times. However, as may be seen from Table 5.14 (p. 161), Thailand's rate of fertiliser use remained low by Asian standards. In addition, the most substantial increase was in the non-rice sector, which increased its share of use from 42.3 to 62.1 per cent. Within the rice sector the main increase was for the second crop – which increased its share of the crop's total application from 31.0 per cent in 1980 to 42.7 per cent in 1990. In the later year less than 7 per cent of the wet season planted area was second cropped, but it absorbed 30 per cent of total rice fertiliser application.

It is however important to stress that increased use of fertiliser has been forced on many farmers in the more recently cleared areas as a means of maintaining output after a few years of cultivation has depleted the stock of nutrients left after forest clearance. This appears to have been the case for both rice and cassava cultivation in the North Eastern region (Atchada

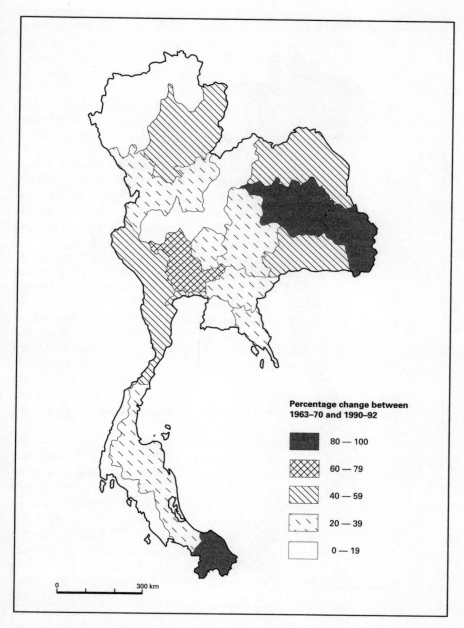

Figure 5.4 Changing rice yields of agro-economic zones between 1963–70 and
1990–92.

Source: MAC.

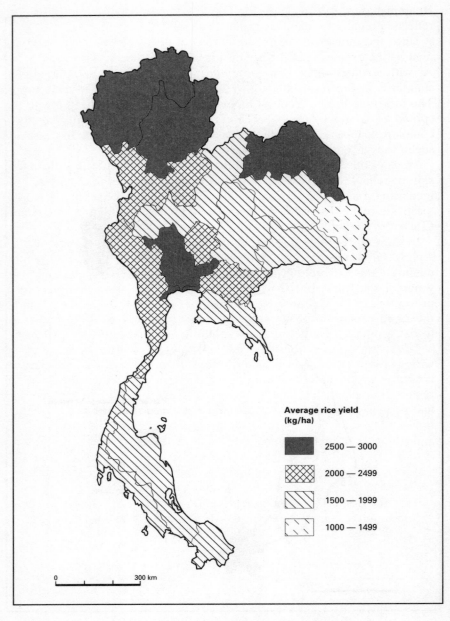

Figure 5.5 Average rice yields of agro-economic zones, 1990–3.

Source: MAC.

Ruammahasap, 1986). Thus for many farmers increased fertiliser use reflects attempts to maintain rather than raise yields.

Since the mid-1970s the increased use of fertiliser has been accompanied by the expansion in the use of fungicides and herbicides (Table 5.16). As with fertiliser the volume of application remains low by international standards and concentrated on a small number of higher value crops. The increased use of chemical inputs is in many cases connected with the spread of contract farming, where the contractors frequently supply a complete 'package' (Trebuil, 1993a: 14). This is very much the case for such crops as cotton, fruit and vegetables.

Much of this spread of chemical inputs has taken place with little extension of reliable technical advice. Thus there is considerable evidence for increasing misuse of chemical inputs and health problems; in 1985 1,400 'pesticide-related work accidents' were reported, including ten deaths (Tachai Wonaporn, 1991: 7–14).

In the Central Plain the development of intensive livestock production – pigs, chickens and ducks – has resulted in large-scale dumping of liquid manure. This is resulting in the widespread eutrophying of ponds and waterways to the point that the water hyacinth (*Eichornia crassipes*) is preventing traffic and the free flow of water (Trebuil, 1993a: 9). Similarly, the rapid expansion of intensive vegetable production in areas adjacent to the capital is resulting in heavy pollution of waterways by nitrates.

The spreading of various intensive agricultural activities (often involving various forms of contract farming) into the outer regions is bringing with it similar problems of pollution. In the North the development by the Hmong of upland intensive cabbage production for urban markets has had serious consequences for lowland rice cultivators. Cabbage production is only viable on a large scale, using heavy applications of fertiliser and pesticide. In consequence:

> Rice growers see the volume of water and the fish stocks in water courses diminish. The water is no longer drinkable, even for the domestic water buffalo and the sediments brought down accumulate behind the newly constructed concrete water diversion

Table 5.16 Application of chemicals (tons)

	Fertiliser	Insecticides	Fungicides	Herbicides
1976	664,390	6,331	1,270	2,225
1980	786,341	15,540	2,721	6,377
1985	1,250,000	14,778	3,725	14,334
1990	2,648,900	27,539	7,628	41,905

Source: MAC.

dams. The old dams consisted of tree trunks bound together and allowed most of these particles to pass through freely, but their upkeep required a commitment from villagers no longer allowed by the new agricultural work schedules, despite the fact that these are the backbone of the agricultural economy in the flooded-paddy systems of northern Thailand.

(Trebuil, 1993a: 9–10)

Thus while the intensification and 'chemicalisation' of Thai agriculture has as yet made only a limited impact, it is already creating serious if highly localised problems. However, with the virtual elimination of land suited to permanent cultivation, particularly for rice, the future expansion of Thai crop production has become dependent on widespread intensification. This in turn rests on the development of more extensive and effective water control or/and the development of suitable dry cropping systems.

The development of irrigation

As has already been noted, the agricultural strategy of successive Thai governments centred on the improvement of rice cultivation through the expansion of irrigation and water control. Indeed, until the early 1980s probably the most important positive impact of government policy on the agricultural sector was the investment in irrigation (Ammar Siamwalla *et al.*, 1993: 110). Irrigation has generally absorbed some 60 per cent of the MAC's budget. While this policy was certainly suitable for much of the Central Plain it was of much more limited application elsewhere in the Kingdom, particularly in the North East. As Ammar Siamwalla *et al.* (1993: 110) have pointed out, if the objective of irrigation investment had been merely to maximise output, investment would have been concentrated in the most favourable parts of the Central Plain. Investment in the North East reflects some concern with raising agricultural incomes and productivity in this impoverished and, during the 1960s and 1970s, politically unstable area, the availability of international loans and linkages to the ambitious multilateral schemes to develop the water resources of the Mekong River (see Chapter 3, p. 86).

As early as 1969 the World Bank questioned the Thai government's emphasis on irrigation development:

the North East is merely the most striking example of the widespread predisposition to disregard the potential for rainfed agriculture – at least at the official level.

(1969: 29)

Despite this, even under the Fifth Plan (1982–6), the development of irrigation facilities in the North East remained a major object. However, in 1973 the Rainfed Rice Improvement Pioneer Project was implemented, utilising World Bank funding. From 1979 broader research into rain-fed cultivation systems was also funded by the World Bank. While, as was noted earlier, some of the Rice Department varieties have proved suited even to marginal areas in the North East, overall the success of the rain-fed programmes has been extremely limited (Muscat, 1994: 263).

As may be seen from Table 5.15 (p. 163) there has been steady expansion of the irrigated area since the 1950s. Initially development was concentrated in the Central Plain but from the early 1960s there was a gradual diffusion, particularly into the North and North Eastern regions. However, the Central Plain has by far the largest share of facilities, the largest proportion of land which is irrigated and the largest proportion that is double cropped (Tables 5.8 (p. 154) and 5.15 (p. 163)).

It is important to stress that the development of publicly funded irrigation schemes in Thailand has taken place in far from uniform physical situations, with very different rice-growing systems and markedly different results. At the risk of extreme simplification the contrasts in these respects between the delta lands of the Central Plain, the intermontane basins of the North and the Korat Plateau of the North East are worth stressing.

The intermontane basins of the North have a long history of small-scale communal irrigation. Here the social structures and rice-growing systems were closely linked to the needs of irrigated wet rice. The highly organised and sophisticated systems enabled the supply of water to be controlled at the level of the individual plot. The development of public schemes from the late 1920s, while by no means unproblematic, at least took place in an agronomic and social environment conducive to organised control of water. The situation in the delta lands of the Central Plain is almost the polar opposite of that in the North – with almost no development of communal water control before the construction of large-scale schemes from the 1880s onwards. Particularly in the retardation basin the seasonal alternation of deep inundation with extreme dryness almost completely excluded the possibility of water control at the village level (Tanabe, 1994: 124). The completion of the Greater Chao Phraya scheme during the late 1950s and the subsequent improvement in canal systems has produced a system lacking in local control. In many areas water supply remains unreliable with little effective control; much of it could be termed 'flood irrigation'. In consequence over large areas rice cultivation remains unintensive with areas of broadcast sowing and cultivation of floating rice (Tanabe, 1994: 47–63). In addition, even in the areas where water control is comparatively effective, intensification of cultivation and the development of double cropping is increasingly hindered by a shortage of irrigation water; this in the region regarded as potentially the most productive.

In complete contrast to these situations the complex North Eastern agricultural systems were almost entirely rain-fed, with cropping strategies, land-holding patterns and communal organisations for coping with extremely uncertain environmental conditions and often highly marginal land (Dixon, 1976; Rigg, 1985a, b). Hence the very considerable problems of implementation encountered in the early stages of public irrigation development in the region (see Ng et al., 1978).

During the late 1960s and early 1970s serious problems were encountered in making effective use of irrigation water. These stemmed from technical defects in the design of distribution systems, insufficient capacity (some long-established irrigation reservoirs have never reached full capacity due to shortages of rainfall (*Bangkok Post*, 29 Sept. 1993)), shortages of funds which left a number of distribution systems incomplete, inadequate maintenance arrangements, ineffective organisation of water distribution, lack of coordination between agricultural extension services, credit facilities and the provision of irrigation water and, in many cases, the incompatibility of rain-fed land holding and farming systems with irrigated agriculture (Dixon, 1976; Ng et al., 1976, 1978). Thus the adoption rate of irrigated agriculture proved to be disappointingly low. For many schemes there was little development of dry season cropping, with irrigation only being used to supplement rainfall during the wet season. In addition, the majority of dam sites involved the flooding of substantial areas of agricultural land with consequent problems of resettlement. The resettlement programmes proved both costly and problematic (see e.g. Lightfoot, 1978; Thapa and Weber, 1988). Given that the most suitable irrigation sites were developed first, there has been a steady rise in the cost of proposed schemes – during a period when rice prices have been low and uncertain.

The area classed as irrigated increased from 3.13 million ha in 1980 to 4.51 million in 1993, with very little expansion in the provision of reservoirs and major infrastructure. Similarly, there was an increase in the average dry season crop area from 462,000 ha during the late 1970s to 718,000 ha during the early 1990s. These developments reflect the more effective use of facilities, assisted by the increasing use of water pumps, both by farmers and on a larger scale by the RID. However, by the early 1990s second cropping still only represented 7.3 per cent of the rice area cropped during the wet season. The main constraint on the further expansion of dry season cropping is the limited water supply. This is compounded by the tendency of farmers to over-irrigate and waste water – a consequence of the low level of water control, limited technical knowledge and the fact that water is not charged for. Most facilities were designed for the monoculture of rice; however, in the Central Plain in particular, cultivation has shifted towards other less water demanding crops. Notwithstanding, the limitations of control facilities and organisation waste much water and largely preclude the planning of crops with different water requirements. It is believed that a substantial increase in the cultivation of non-rice crops during the dry season would be possible through the upgrading of existing distribution and control facilities, and improved water and land use management. However, the latter would demand a funda-mental change in the relationship between farmers and the RID, with the latter taking a much clearer managerial role (Ammar Siamwalla et al., 1993: 111). In the absence of this and the increasing pressure that is being placed on water resources by non-agricultural uses, the immediate prospects for any further substantial expansion of the irrigated area appear remote.

The increase in the demands being placed on water storage facilities and the lack of coordinated water planning were sharply highlighted during 1993–4 by the worst drought since the 1950s. The low level of water behind such major Central Plains dams as the Sirikit and Bhumipol meant that once domestic needs had been met water was only available for 'short-term seasonal crops' and the planting of second crop rice was not allowed (*Thailand Development News Letter*, 1993, No. 23: 9). Similarly, for the large multi-purpose dams area under the control of the EGAT, the gener-ation of HEP took precedence over the needs of agriculture. The 1993–4 water crisis exposed the basic contradiction of multi-purpose water resource exploitation.

The 1993–4 situation cannot be attributed merely to one year of excep-tionally low rainfall. It was the result of long-term expansion of demand by farmers, reinforced, particularly in the Central Plain, by increased industrial, domestic and leisure consumption with inadequate investment in water facilities. As is discussed in Chapter 6 (p. 212), the rapid economic growth that had taken place in the BMR and its immediate environs since the mid-1980s placed serious pressure on water resources. There are now major conflicts over supplies, with farmers increasingly losing out to the demands of new housing estates, industrial complexes and leisure facili-ties, notably golf courses (*Thailand Development News Letter*, 1993, No. 23: 5–6).

The RID had long predicted the crisis (*Thailand Development News Letter*, 1993, No. 23: 9). However, that department's solution – the construction of more dams – ignored the problems associated with existing schemes as well as the likely ecological impact and the problems of evacuating whole communities from the flooded areas, particularly given that there are now few areas into which substantial numbers of people could be resettled. In addition, farmers and urban-based middle-class activists have become increasingly vocal and effective in demonstrating against further large-scale dam construction – as witnessed by the shelving in 1988 of the Nam Choan Dam in Kanchanaburi (Hurst, 1990: 235–9). While the Pak Mun Dam in the North East was completed during 1994 it was surrounded by considerable controversy and protest (Rigg, 1995b: 29). Perhaps more significantly, major dam building is unlikely because most of the best sites have already been developed. The remaining possible locations are likely to be costly to develop and are heavily populated. Recently attention has focused on the possibility of exploiting the water resources of neighbouring Myanmar – through the diversion of water from the upper Salween (*Bangkok Post* 'Rejection of charter a setback for dam plan', 1994, 29 March: 6) – and Laos – through the implementation of   part of the long-shelved Pa Mong project.[26] These proposals also reflect renewed interest in the revitalisation of the Mekong Scheme (see Chapter 3, p. 86).

Since the mid-1980s the priority assigned to irrigation has been revised in the light of cost, lack of viable sites, the problems associated with resettling large numbers of households, concern over environmental issues, and the limited success of many existing schemes. Indeed, the productivity of a large proportion of irrigation schemes, particularly the smaller schemes, 'appears at best dubious' (Ammar Siamwalla *et al.*, 1993: 111). Thus under the Seventh Plan (1992–6) while the importance of irrigation was still stressed, it was in terms of making fuller and more effective use of existing provision rather than initiating new schemes or major extensions of existing ones. To this end proposals have been announced to instigate charges for irrigation water in an effort to make its use more effective and provide revenue for organisation, maintenance and improvements in control and distribution systems (NESDB, 1992: 85). It is clear, however, that in the absence of a major increase in the extent and effectiveness of irrigation serious question marks have to be raised over the long-term prospects for the expansion of crop production, raising of farm incomes and the retention of people in the agricultural sector.

Diversification and innovations

Crop production in Thailand since the 1950s has undergone considerable diversification but relatively little technical change. Compared to the majority of other Asian countries there has been little application of what is conventionally regarded as 'modern agricultural technology'. As has already been noted there has been relatively little use of high-yielding varieties and yields and fertiliser application rates remain remarkably low. Only with respect to mechanisation does Thai agriculture appear to be ahead of many other Asian countries (Ammar Siamwalla *et al.*, 1993: 95). However, while the development of the more intensive double-cropped rice areas has been associated with the adoption of rice-tillers, threshing machines and water pumps, the widespread introduction of tractor ploughing reflects the increasingly extensive nature of much cultivation.[27] This is seen in particular with respect to upland crops and the extensive broadcast rice areas of the Central Plain. In addition, the lending policies of the BAAC have greatly encouraged the purchase of machinery.

The low level of adoption of new technology should not be allowed to obscure the considerable dynamism of the agricultural sector, both in terms of the expansion of production and in the adoption of new crops. This, however, has to be seen very much in terms of the responsiveness and adaptability of Thai farmers to opportunities rather than the result of activities of the state.

The government has supported technical change in the agricultural sector through investment, particularly in irrigation, research, credit provision and extension services. However, as has already been stressed, the level of expenditure has been low compared to other Asian economies (Ammar Siamwalla *et al.*, 1993: 96–8).

There is little evidence to suggest that publicly funded research has made a significant contribution to the introduction of new crops. In general research funding has tended to be allocated to new crops once their commercial viability was established. This is not to say that in a number of areas publicly funded research has not made important contributions. Outside the rice sector this has been particularly the case with respect to the development of hybrid maize (Suthad Setboonsarng *et al.*, 1988). Indeed, while the private sector has played a leading role in the introduction of new crops, it has played a very limited role in research and development. Thus to a degree public research activities may be regarded as supporting the spread of innovation led by the private sector.

Overall, some preliminary research by TDRI has concluded that the expenditure on research and irrigation since the early 1960s, and more especially since the late 1970s, has made a relatively small contribution to the growth of agricultural output (Ammar Siamwalla *et al.*, 1993: 98–9).

While the effectiveness of government activity in agriculture may be questioned there is no shortage of programmes and agencies operating in the rural areas. The local activities of the Department of Agricultural Extension (DAE) are accompanied by the various government programmes or programmes of government-backed organisations, notably the Community Development Department (CDD), the Rural Employment Generation Programme, the Land Development Department, Agricultural Land Reform Office (ALRO), farmers' groups and cooperatives. To this great array of official bodies must be added an increasing number of NGOs.

The description of the operation of the main government bodies at village level provided by Hirsch in his study of Ban Rai District in the western province of Uthaithani is probably fairly typical:

> Most of the state developers reside at the district headquarters or at the market of Paak Meuang. ... With few notable exceptions, these officials socialise among themselves, barring special

occasions when a deliberate show of 'mixing' is made as a matter of policy. . . . Publicly, state developers present a show of unity, and in introducing programmes to villagers it is stressed that help is from the state bureaucracy rather than a particular department. . . . On the other hand, individual programmes are carried out independently of each other, and while not normally in open competition, departments tend to avoid treading on each other's toes. For example, the tambon DAE officer stated that she did not bother with Ban Mai since there were already ALRO officials working there, despite the fact the latter had no training, or activities concerning agricultural extension. Meanwhile, duplication arises, for example in the provision of community rice barns by both the DAE and the CDD. The blurring of function is a product of the desire for each department to expand its range of activities. This brings the police, military, and other departments which would not normally be thought of as developers into the rural development field, and such activity also doubles as an image-building tool.

(1990: 81–2)

The large number of agencies providing overlapping and largely uncoordinated programmes results in a far from effective vehicle either to provide for the needs of rural communities or to implement government rural development priorities. The lack of coordination between, for example, the providers of extension advice, rural credit, agricultural inputs and the RID, has in many instances seriously inhibited the development of irrigated agriculture (Ng *et al.*, 1976).

At the level of direct promotion of a crop, probably the only real success has been the introduction of hybrid Guatemalan maize (see p. 71). While this crop was widely adopted by farmers in the Central Plain, North and North East during the 1950s and 1970s, the promotion programme was timely, however, coinciding with the rapid expansion of international demand. In this respect the maize programme differed from the abortive attempt during the late 1950s to introduce kenaf into the North East. The crop was to spread, unaided by any promotional scheme, following the emergence of an international shortage after the failure of the Bengali jute crop in 1958 and a subsequent series of poor harvests (Dixon, 1974: 231). Similarly, the spread of cassava into the North East from the early 1970s reflected the rapid growth of demand in the EU. As a result of its generally higher and more stable price it came to replace kenaf over large areas. The spread of cassava gives an interesting insight into the operation of the MAC. During the initial spread of cassava into the North East Ministry policy discouraged it because of its reputation for exhausting soils. Once the crop began to spread rapidly, however, its expansion became a policy objective.[28]

176

There is considerable evidence to support the view that the complex network of merchants has been more effective in stimulating agricultural innovation than much of the official extension system (see Dixon, 1974: 231–6; Rigg, 1986; Trebuil, 1993a). Merchants have certainly played key roles in the spreading of many upland crops, notably cassava, maize and kenaf in the North East, and in the adoption of a wide range of chemical inputs and new varieties. Middlemen frequently play a multiplicity of roles, acting as technical, commercial and financial advisers to farming communities. It is through these middlemen networks that commercial sales persons find it most effective to reach farmers. Trebuil has stressed how:

> Advice to farmers is now monopolised by myriad technical salesmen trekking through the countryside with their samples to supply their networks of Sino-Thai village middlemen.
>
> (1993a: 14)

The general weakness and ineffectiveness of Thai agricultural programmes have been frequently commented on (e.g. Ammar Siamwalla, 1993). In addition, the MAC has an extremely paternalistic approach which largely precludes farmers from any effective involvement in the planning process (see Chapter 8, p. 243). Similarly, the highly centralised nature of the MAC (like virtually all of the Thai administrative system) excludes local officials from the planning process, largely confining them to the implementation of centrally formulated programmes.

While there have been substantial changes in policy statements concerning approaches to agricultural extension and the involvement of farmers, in practice little has changed for the majority of farmers. The priorities of the MAC remains the efficient diffusion of agricultural information and technology, the distribution of inputs and the administration of farm credit. Despite policy statements in favour of farmer organisations and farmers' participation, in practice the information flow remains firmly 'top-down'. During the late 1970s Thailand like many countries moved towards the 'training and visit' system of agricultural extension. This approach, heavily promoted and funded by the World Bank, centres on visits to 'contact farmers' who are expected to pass information to other members of their communities. However, what information is to be passed on is decided centrally, with little provision for farmer participation or feed back. While the needs for greater flexibility, local responsibility, and responsivness to the requests of farmers have been formally recognised (FAO, 1990; World Bank, 1990), in practice little seems to have changed.

However, as Garforth (1993: 6) has commented, Thailand has a rich history of rural people's organisations. These range from the centuries-old *muang fai* irrigation organisations of the North, to twentieth-century cooperatives; from farmers to land-settlement cooperatives; from political movements to 'housewife groups' sponsored by the MAC. Since the 1960s government policy has generally favoured these varied organisations – other than those perceived as 'political' – such as the Peasant Federation of Thailand. However, rural organisations were seen as means to disseminate information and promote communal linkages – this particularly in areas thought to be susceptible to 'communist subversion' (see pp. 99–100) – they were never seen as vehicles for the rural population to express wishes or views.

In the evaluation of the First National Plan (1961–6) the NEDB (1967a) commented on the weaknesses of agriculture programmes (apart from the physical extension of irrigation), and the general ineffectiveness of planning, research and extension activities. Specific attention was drawn to the low adoption rate of irrigation, the limited progress in rubber research and replanting, ineffective control over forest areas, and the over-exploitation of fisheries. Many of these comments could equally well apply to Thai agricultural programmes in the 1990s. Since the 1960s there has been no shortage of policy statements and programmes directed towards the agricultural sector; however, it is apparent that many government activities in the agricultural sector have produced limited returns, notably irrigation and (since the late 1970s) research into rain-fed cultivation. On the other hand there have been a number of areas of government activity which have been of considerable importance; most significantly – apart from the development of institutional credit – road building, the hybrid maize programme and rubber replanting. Agricultural diversification, into, for example, livestock, upland crops and fruit and vegetables has been very largely the product of private-sector activity. Policies towards these developments have in general been piecemeal and tended to follow developments rather than initiate them. In many ways this mirrors the (Thai) approach to development policy in general (see discussion pp. 241–6).

The closure of the land frontier and the consequences of the long-term expansion of the cultivated area

The long-term consequences of the massive expansion of the cultivated area are far from easy to assess. It is widely asserted that Thailand in the 1990s is experiencing a widespread rural crisis, most serious in the North East and least so in the small plantation dominated South. The crisis manifests itself in land shortage, soil erosion, loss of forest cover, increased incidence of flooding and drought, land passing out of cultivation and poverty. However, there is a serious lack of reliable, comprehensive and recent data on which to base a clear assessment of the national situation.

The vast majority of the expansion has been by forest clearance and settlement.[29] As a result the proportion of the Kingdom under forest declined from an estimated 75 per cent at the beginning of the twentieth century (Feeny, 1984: 53) to an official figure of 26 per cent in 1991. However, the area classed as forest includes large areas of scrub, often the product of commercial cutting or/and abandoned agricultural land, tree crops, open water and some temporary and permanent cultivation of field crops or even rice. Depending on the definition of forest used, a more realistic estimate for the early 1990s would be 10 to 15 per cent (Bryant, 1993: 7–8; Lohmann, 1991: 4).

Since 1964, the attempt to control the removal of forest cover has centred on the establishment of National Forestry Reserves (NFR). The RFD was empowered to designate land that did not have a legal owner as a Reserve. Since 1985 NFRs have covered 21.3 million ha – 40 per cent of the area of the Kingdom.[30] A considerable proportion of this area is not only not forest but, in many instances, was under cultivation long before it was declared part of an NFR. It has been estimated that there are 7–8 million ha of untitled cultivated land within the reserves (Panayotou and Chalongphob Sussangkarn, 1991: 14), occupied by some 1.2–2 million households.[31] It is all too apparent that the designation of these large areas as reserves appears to have done little either to conserve commercial stands of trees or reduce encroachment by farmers. Indeed, Ammar Siamwalla *et al.* have described the National Forest Reserves as:

> grossly unrealistic in administrative and policing terms, and ... hardly justified even from an environmental perspective. The result is that the Department is unable to protect from loggers even those lands that are environmentally fragile (for example, watershed areas), while farmers in perfectly good agricultural lands are prevented from acquiring title to these lands – with adverse economic and social consequences.
>
> (1994: 89)

While current Thai forest laws and land codes define the designated forest areas as state property, their regulation is far from effective.[32] Access to the Kingdom's forests has remained remarkably free amidst confusion over legal and traditional rights (Lohmann, 1991: 335). Existing codes recognise 'squatters' rights' to land, and allow the harvesting of forest products for domestic use. The limited controls and various 'loopholes' in the regulations make the distinction between 'domestic' use and, for example, the cutting of timber and the production of charcoal for sale, a highly problematic one.[33] In addition, apart from the RFD's inability effectively to police the vast areas under its control, a 'blind eye' was turned to much encroachment. This was particularly the case during the 1960s and 1970s when rural insurgency made the whole question of access to land an extremely sensitive issue (Hafner and Yaowalak Apichatvullop, 1990: 336). Indeed, as Lohmann (1991: 4) has noted, in many areas,communities were actively encouraged by the security forces to settle NFR land in order to secure the area against communist subversion. In 1975 a general amnesty was declared for the illegal occupiers of the NFRs. At the same time the national Forest Land Allocation Project (known as the STK Project), and the related Forest Village Programme were implemented, with the intention of regulating and recognising the cultivation of parts of the NFRs. In both cases farmers were to be issued with certificates that granted user rights but not ownership. However, the amnesty merely resulted in new waves of migrants and in the event few certificates were ever issued (Hafner and Yaowalak Apichatvullop, 1990: 337).

Thailand has a history of replanting programmes stretching back to 1906, but only from the mid-1970s were sufficient powers and funds made available for the RFD to implement a major long-term National Plan. Prior to 1979 only 192,000 ha were replanted, the vast majority after 1960. In contrast, between 1980 and 1985 the RFD claimed to have replanted 262,100 ha.[34] However, during this period the official rate of forest loss was some 1.02 million ha.

Until the early 1980s, RFD replanting mainly comprised commercial hardwoods – particularly teak, yang and ironwood – with 40–80 years of growth necessary before they can be cut. Subsequently increasing amounts of fast-maturing softwoods have been planted. These can be cut in 10–15 years and provide rapid growing cover for watershed protection and other environmental rehabilitation projects. Since 1980 the private sector has been encouraged to enter the replanting programmes, to produce softwoods for pulp and woodchips, particularly from fast-maturing eucalyptus.

In 1985 the government announced a major policy change which was aimed at asserting control over the encroaching NFR, and reversing the environmental damage resulting from continued forest loss. The NFR were sub-divided into two categories – 'natural forest' and 'economic forest'. The former was defined purely in environmental terms, comprising fragile areas, including steep slopes and watersheds, and covering 15 per cent of the national area. Where such forest had been denuded it was to be replanted by the RFD. The 'economic forests', covering some 25 per cent of the national area were to be planted to tree crops, including oil palm, rubber and fruit trees as well as commercial timber. Particular emphasis was placed on the planting of fast-growing species, particularly eucalyptus. By the year 2020 it was planned that 61,600 km^2 of degraded NFR,[35] 11.5 per cent of the national area, would be planted to eucalyptus. Some 43,100 km^2 are envisaged to be planted by the private sector. These developments are particularly targeted at the North Eastern region and have become linked to the military dominated 'Green North East' scheme.[36]

Between 1985 and 1991 the area of eucalyptus plantations increased from a variously estimated 100–200 km^2 to 600–1,200 km^2.

Since 1985 the RFD has been prepared to issue farmers in the NFRs with non-transferable title deeds, provided that they use the land in the manner prescribed, that is planting tree crops (Ammar Siamwalla et al., 1993: 110). In addition, the RFD has the power to grant leases to private companies regardless of whether the land is already occupied by farmers. This has engendered a great deal of conflict between villagers, plantation companies and officials (see Lohmann 1991 for a detailed review). Overall, these new policies have raised fears of very large-scale eviction from the NFRs; indeed in 1989 the Director General of the RFD stated publicly that 6 million people would have to be removed (cited in Lohmann, 1991: 4). Not surprisingly the programme has been heavily criticised. For example Ammar Siamwalla et al. (1993: 109–10) have stressed that there appears to be little in the way of environmental motivation behind the decision to demarcate the large areas of 'economic forest'. The blanket reafforestation schemes appear to be more a response to the RFD's desire to reclaim the illegally encroached land (Ammar Siamwalla et al., 1989) and the commercial opportunities for, in particular, pulp and woodchip production, rather than environmental preservation and rehabilitation.

While it is probable that the vast majority of farmers cultivating NFR land have not encroached on environmentally fragile land (Ammar Siamwalla et al., 1994: 94, citing World Bank studies from 1982), there is a serious lack of recent and comprehensive information on the extent and degree of environmental damage resulting from the removal of forest cover and the extension of the cultivated area. Most information is dated and/or fragmented.

Deforestation of upland areas, particularly of the crests of ridges, has led in some areas to the lowering of the water table and increased rates of run-off. Since the mid-1970s the effects of this type of clearance have been apparent in parts of the North East, with farmers reporting increased incidence of drought on upland fields and higher paddy plots and increased 'flash' flooding of lower lying land (Dixon, 1976: 9; Ng et al., 1978). Similarly, Rigg (1995b: 27) has reported that the clearance of upland areas has reduced the water supply for the rice cultivation down-slope. While according to the RID the incidence of flash floods in rain-fed paddies increased from approximately 10 per cent during the late 1960s to 20 per cent in the early 1980s; by the later date this represented some 1 million ha (Paisal Sricharatchanya, 1987: 88). More generally there are reports of more frequent and serious flood damage, reduced rainfall and lengthening dry seasons (Hurst, 1990: 210).

The incidence of soil erosion is a matter of considerable debate, and detailed information is highly fragmented. According to official sources, by the late 1980s 65 per cent of the Kingdom's cultivated area – some

25 million ha, about half the national area – was affected by erosion (Table 5.17). The situation was particularly acute in parts of the North Eastern, Northern and Western regions. In the North East – the region most severely affected – as early as 1982 the Land Development Department reported that 85.4 per cent of farm land was affected by erosion, 53.3 per cent severely so.

Doubts have been expressed over the long-term viability of agricultural practices in many of the more recently cleared areas. Hirsch (1990: 43–4), for example, considers that only a proportion of the area cleared for upland crops is suited to permanent monocropping. There is an increasing tendency for soils to be 'mined' until they are taken over by *Imperata cylindrica*, at which point farmers move on to clear new areas (Hirsch, 1990: 43).

However, in many cases the problems arise from the methods of cultivation as well as from the unsuitability of the land (Ng, 1970). In some cases increased soil erosion has resulted from changed agricultural practices and/or crops. This is particularly striking in the North where opium has been replaced under a variety of projects, and some long-established soil conservation practices abandoned (Forsyth, 1992: 14). While more widely in the North East the planting of cassava, often as a replacement for kenaf or maize, has been widely associated with soil erosion and declining fertility.[37]

Studies of various agricultural systems in Chiang Mai province in the Northern region reported soil loss that ranged from 50 tons/ha for forest and flooded paddy, through 300–400 tons/ha for upland crops (maize, soybean and orchards), to over 1,000 tons/ha for the most erosion prone slopes under maize and upland rice (Wattanachai Damronghanvitaya, 1985: 113). These are exceptionally high levels of loss, which suggest very short effective life-spans for some of the systems involved. However, it is by no means clear how widespread these extreme situations are. Forsyth (1992: 15) reported very much lower levels of soil loss in a detailed study in the Pha Dua district of Chiang Rai. Here the historic pattern of loss ranged from 28 tons/ha on the least eroded slopes (23 per cent of the area) to 70 tons/ha on the most eroded (2 per cent of the area).

Table 5.17 Incidence of soil erosion, 1990

Category	Area (ha)	Percentage of cultivated area
Very severely eroded	4,800,000	20
Severely eroded	6,880,000	28
Moderately eroded	4,160,000	17
Total	15,840,000	65

Source: Department of Land Development.

While the closure of the land frontier is a fact over large parts of the Kingdom, in the North East and the Western regions in particular, clearance is continuing. The rates of clearance since the late 1970s have almost certainly been greater than those indicated in Table 5.13, as the expansion of the cultivated area has been increasingly offset by land passing out of cultivation. Official data on much of this recent clearance is highly suspect. It is unclear how much temporarily cultivated land either fails to be registered at all or, once abandoned, remains recorded as agricultural land. MAC statistics do, however, indicate that the proportion of holdings planted fell from an average of 86.1 per cent in 1982–4 to 81.2 per cent in 1990–2.

On the basis of the 1972 land capability survey, 25.23 million ha were considered suitable for the cultivation of rice and field crops. In 1988 26.94 million ha were classed as suitable for the cultivation of rice, field crops and perennials (Table 5.11, p. 157). In 1991, as may be seen from Table 5.18, according to MAC data 21.38 million ha were classified as farm land. This would suggest that there was still some potential for further expansion. However, it seems very likely that the MAC figure for the cultivated area is an under-estimate (as probably is the FAO figure used in Table 5.12, p. 157). The Department of Land Development (DLD) gives a much higher level of cultivation in 1991 of 28.33 million ha – 53.0 per cent of the surface area. The DLD figure is based on the analysis of land-use maps, and probably contains much land that is either abandoned or cropped very irregularly. In particular the DLD reports a much larger area under rice and a smaller area under field crops than the MAC (Table 5.18). This would suggest that much rice land was unsuited to the crop. As Chumphol Wattanasarn (1993: 217) has stressed, there is a need for a much more detailed study of the extent of such marginal land in Thailand. However, it is difficult to escape the conclusion that by the 1990s there was little scope for the further expansion of the rice area, and much of the potential for the growth of the field and tree crop sectors rests on conversion of land from rice cultivation.

Table 5.18 Land use and land capability (million ha)

	Land capability DLD (1988)	Land use MAC (1991)	Land use DLD (1991)
Paddy	12.93	11.10	15.30
Field crops	11.28	5.36	8.90
Tree crops	2.73	3.24	3.72
Other	–	1.68	0.41
Total	26.94	21.38	28.33

Source: MAC; DLD.

Land holding

The long-term expansion of the cultivated area has been accompanied by an increase in the average size of holdings from 1.7 ha in 1930,[38] to 3.0 ha in 1960 and 4.7 ha in 1990. This reflects the expansion of production, as farmers were able to expanded the size of their holdings in order to produce for the market, diversification, with farmers adding upland plots to their rice holdings, and, as settlement moved into more marginal areas, the clearance of larger holdings to compensate for lower levels of fertility and reliability.

As has been discussed previously, the long-term expansion of the cultivated area has been almost entirely the result of small-scale clearance and the creation of owner-occupied farms. Renting is only significant in the Central Plain and Northern region (Table 5.19). However, there are very considerable variations in the level of renting within these regions, particularly the Central Plain. In general, areas with a high incidence of renting can be traced back to late nineteenth century land reclamation and estate formation (see Chapter 2, pp. 44–5). Subsequently, particularly in the Central Plain, absentee land holding has developed through the acquisition of holdings by, in particular, merchants and rice millers, from indebted farmers. Nationally, only a small number of landlords own more than 150 ha and much renting is from owners of 8 to 25 ha. In addition, much small-scale renting continues to take place within communities and families, sometimes with payment in kind, or even no payment. In the North it is these various petty forms of renting that dominate.

Since the mid-1970s some prominence has been given to land reform in areas with high levels of tenancy. However, progress has been extremely limited (Somchai Jitsuchan, 1989: 49). In part this reflects the very low level of funding allocated to the programme (Panayotou, 1985: 50). As was noted previously, the ALRO has been principally concerned with the resettlement of farmers in frontier areas.

The low level of renting does, however, give a false impression of the security of tenure enjoyed by Thai farmers. While data on tenure are extremely unreliable, it is thought that only about 60 per cent of farmers

Table 5.19 Percentage of land rented

	1983	1988	1991
North East	3.9	4.8	5.2
North	14.7	17.3	17.7
Central	25.3	26.2	25.3
South	4.1	5.4	3.1
Kingdom	11.3	12.7	12.3

Source: MAC.

have title deeds that enable them to use the land as collateral for loans (Ammar Siamwalla *et al.*, 1993: 100; Somchai Jitsuchon, 1989: 47–8). The slow progress of registration has been compounded by the rapid expansion of the cultivated areas, the lack of cadastral surveys in some areas and complex and far from satisfactory procedures. As was discussed previously, large numbers of farmers are effectively precluded from obtaining firm titles because their holdings are in NFRs. For the government the low level of land taxes has been seen as providing little incentive to devote substantial resources to the assigning of property rights (Ammar Siamwalla *et al.*, 1993: 108).

It is frequently argued that the lack of firm title deeds and consequent limited access to institutional credit (and to long-term loans from informal sources who also require some form of collateral) discourages farmers from maintaining their holdings and protecting against erosion and soil exhaustion (Ammar Siamwalla *et al.*, 1993: 75). However, comparatively few farmers have hitherto been evicted from land even in forestry reserves, though the threat is of course always there (Feder *et al.*, 1988). Undoubtedly the lack of title deeds does have an impact on productivity. Active markets have developed in untitled land, but such land may fetch as little as half that of equivalent titled land (Feder *et al.*, 1988: 93).

The consolidation of holdings and the elimination of small farms have as yet made only a limited impact on the Thai agricultural system. However, there are signs that this is now changing very rapidly, with the emergence of land shortages in many areas, the breaking down of traditional inheritance practices[39] and the emergence of active land markets.[40] Although data are limited it appears that the sub-division of holdings, land sales and the renting of holdings (in whole or in part) are all beginning to increase rapidly in many parts of the country (see e.g. Trebuil,

Table 5.20 Distribution of holding size, in rai (0.16 ha)

	Percentage of holdings		Percentage of area	
	1978	1993	1978	1993
Under 2	1.6	2.1	0.2	0.1
2–5	14.4	15.6	2.3	2.7
6–9	12.1	12.9	3.8	4.4
10–19	26.5	28.6	15.5	17.8
20–39	29.3	26.8	34.2	33.1
40–59	9.9	8.7	20.0	18.9
60–139	5.8	4.8	19.8	17.3
Over 140	0.4	0.5	3.8	5.7
Total	100.0	100.0	100.0	100.0

Source: NSO.

1993b; Table 5.19). However, as may be seen from Table 5.20, official data give little indication of any marked change in the overall distribution of the size of holdings. Between the Agricultural Census of 1978 and that of 1980 the percentage of land in holdings of less than 10 rai (1.7 ha.) increased from 6.3 to 7.2, while the percentage in holdings of over 140 rai (23.3 ha) increased from 3.8 to 5.7.

Conclusion

In the mid-1990s the Thai rural sector is at the beginning of what may prove to be a deep and widespread crisis. We are witnessing the tail-end of over a century of rapid expansion in the cultivated area and the closure of the land frontier. Hirsch concluded that the slow process of expansion, supported as it was by 'institutional, economic, and infrastructural measures by government and the agents of capital' (1990: 33), had in the long term brought a disastrous combination of extreme poverty and environmental degradation to large numbers of rural communities. While comprehensive evidence is lacking, there is sufficient information to suggest that land shortage, environmental degradation, limited prospects for the further development of irrigation, and little real effort or success in the development of rain-fed cultivation seriously limit the prospects for continued increase in agricultural production. A combination of land shortage and economic change is making an increasing number of farmers marginal, and pushing households into increased dependence on other activities. For such groups rural opportunities are limited to the increasingly futile search for more land or the development of non-agricultural sources of income. For most, temporary, seasonal, or often permanent migration to the BMR and its immediate environs or the receipt of remittance income from those who have migrated are the only viable options.

As is discussed in Chapter 7, poverty is concentrated in the agricultural sector. It is apparent from the NSO Household Expenditure surveys and the National Rural Development Committee data that with the exception of large-scale rice farming in parts of the Central Plain and the specialist production of certain high-value products, there is a close relationship between low-income households and dependence on agriculture as the sole source of income (see Chapter 7, p. 220). In general the level of income for agricultural households reflects the degree of access to non-agricultural sources of income. According to the National Household Expenditure Surveys in 1991, agricultural households derived 58.3 per cent of their net income from non-agricultural sources.[41] There are, however, considerable regional variations in both the composition and level of incomes of agricultural households. Incomes were highest in the Central Plain and lowest in the North East where households were most dependent on agricultural income sources.[42] It has been estimated that 85 per cent of villagers in the North East and 45 per cent in the North are considered unable to meet their basic needs from agriculture (Sanit Ekachai, 1990: 31–4). However, even in such comparatively favoured agricultural provinces as Ayutthaya in the Central Plain, access to non-farm income was as important as the size and quality of holdings in determining the level of agricultural household income (Wathana Wongsekiarttirat, 1993).

It is projected that by the year 2000 agriculture's share of GDP will have shrunk to 8 per cent, while the sector will still employ 40 per cent of the work force (Dhira Phantumnavit and Theodore Panayotou, 1990: 2). Given that in 1994 55–60 per cent were engaged in agriculture and the absolute numbers were still rising, this level of decline seems unlikely (see Table 1.9, pp. 12 and 19–20). It is also questionable whether the urban sector could absorb the necessary population by the end of the century. However, in the absence of successful and widespread measures to raise incomes in rural areas the continuation into the next century of a situation under which a substantial proportion of the population remains dependent on agriculture is a daunting one. Increased rural–urban income and welfare gaps may well generate serious social tensions.

Hitherto, apart from the early 1970s when the Peasant Federation of Thailand exercised considerable influence (see p. 97), the rural population have had little political influence. In 1986 the *Far Eastern Economic Review* commented:

> The 40 million rice farmers and their dependants project an image of passive acceptance of poverty and government neglect. ... However, any contact with farmers, even in the prosperous areas of the Central Plain, but more particularly in the impoverished areas of the North and North East reveals considerable bitterness over their neglect and their inability to make their protests heard.
>
> (19 June 1986: 48–9)

Despite the accelerated growth that Thailand has experienced since this was written, the situation for the majority of farmers is little different in the mid-1990s.

The limited development of large-scale agricultural estates and plantations has meant that there has not been any appreciable political influence on the part of a rural-based elite, heavily dependent on agricultural income. One notable exception to this are the large-scale sugar producers who have been remarkably successful in lobbying to maintain high levels of protection for the crop. In general however, the political influence of the agricultural sector has been rooted firmly in the domestic trading, exporting, processing, and more recently broader agro-industrial sectors.

During the 1970s, particularly under the civilian governments of the 1973–6 period, there was considerable pro-farmer and pro-agricultural rhetoric in policy statements. While a number of important measures were implemented – notably with respect to price support, rural credit and land reform – their impact was slight. However, since the early 1980s, in the wake of accelerated national economic growth, structural change and general liberalisation, there are again signs that a more positive policy towards agriculture has emerged.

What solutions are proposed? Considerable attention has focused on attempts to 'turn the clock back' by, for example calling for a massive reafforestation programme. This is not only in the realms of idealism, but addresses only one symptom to the detriment of the livelihood of much of the rural population. Too much attention in official and unofficial circles has focused on the question of environmental degradation in general, and forest loss in particular. These are symptoms of the deep-rooted problems discussed in this chapter. Solutions cannot in that sense be 'environmentally driven' – they must be firmly rooted in the agricultural sector of the mid-1990s. The various plans for large-scale reafforestation through the promotion of private-sector eucalyptus planting illustrates the inherent contradictions of this type of policy. Large-scale reafforestation can only be achieved by the eviction of large numbers of agricultural households. Such an action would increase migration from the rural areas and put increased pressure on the remaining forest.

Under the Seventh Plan (1992–6) emphasis was placed on the retention of people in the agricultural sector (NESDB, 1992: 3). Priority was given to diversification, specifically aimed at reducing the number of farmers dependent on single crops, and the development of agricultural systems. The policy objective of reducing out-migration from the rural sector has been underlined in a number of government statements and initiatives. In 1994, for example, US$23.5 million was allocated to a broad-base programme aimed at 'keeping people on the land' (Fairclough, 1994: 26). A number of commentators have suggested that rural industry (e.g. Parnwell, 1992) and tourism (e.g. Forsyth, 1992) offer considerable scope for raising rural incomes and reducing the outflow of people (see also the discussion in Chapter 7, pp. 235–6). However, the prospects for any of these proposals or initiatives providing a substantial brake on out-migration appear remote in the face of the scale of the problem and in the wake of the experience of other countries.

There are those who consider that policies that promote agriculture – notably the price support systems and credit provisions, particularly through the BAAC – are misguided, and merely hinder the transformation of the national economy:

Agriculture can no longer be the dominant sector with 65–70 per cent of the population, in the near future it will have to drop to 30 per cent. There is no future in farming. At least 30 per cent of the population will have to shift in the next five years. It is no good continuing to subsidise farmers, no good continuing to use price controls to raise prices of various agricultural products because we are going to kill ourselves.

If you keep on subsidising then people will think they can keep on farming. No one will change his profession. The subsidies must stop.

(Asavin Chintakanda, 1990: 15–16)

Indeed, during the 1990s the whole question of subsidising rural credit has been questioned by the government. However, given the low labour absorption rate of the urban-industrial sector (Somboon Siriprachai, 1995) and the scale of temporary and permanent migration to the BMR and its immediate environs it is difficult to argue for the removal of any policies which inhibit the transfer of people out of the rural sector. The danger is that the removal of support from the rural sector will result in a massive transfer of poverty into the urban sector, while not significantly reducing the incidence of poverty in rural areas.

6

UNEVEN DEVELOPMENT
Bangkok in the national economy

Introduction

The unevenness of Thailand's development is shown most clearly in the growth of the capital. While the pattern in which one very large city dominates the national economy is common to many Third World economies (London, 1980), and the countries of South East Asia offer classic examples of primacy and uneven development (Hackenberg, 1980; McGee, 1967; Smith and Nemeth, 1986), Thailand demonstrates these features at their most extreme. In terms of measures of urban primacy Bangkok is almost certainly the most primate city in the world, and the national pattern of urbanisation the most uneven. The city dominates the Thai economy and its interaction with the international economy to the extent that it is often asserted that Bangkok *is* Thailand (for a discussion of this view see Krickkiat Phipatseritham, 1983). While this is of course an exaggeration, the unevenness of Thailand's development and the degree of concentration of population, economic activity and political power in Bangkok and its immediate environs is exceptional by any standards. The capital has long been described as the Kingdom's only 'growth centre' (Medhi Krongkaew and Pawadee Tongudai, 1984: 43) and Thailand as 'a Bangkok based state' (Rigg, 1991b: 164).

Bangkok – or, to give it its shortened Thai name *Krungthep*,[1] – can refer to a variety of urban areas (Figure 6.1). From the founding of the city in 1782 until 1971 Bangkok referred only to the settlement on the eastern bank of the Chao Phraya river. There was, however, no administrative definition of the city area until the establishment of municipal authorities in 1933. Expansion on the west bank produced the port-associated settlement of Thonburi, which was merged with Bangkok in 1972 to created the Bangkok Metropolitan Area (BMA); this has provincial status, with a governor being elected every five years. For planning purposes reference is sometimes made to Greater Bangkok (or the Greater Bangkok Metropolitan Area) – this is not a legal administrative unit, it includes the urbanised areas of the adjacent provinces of Nonthaburi and

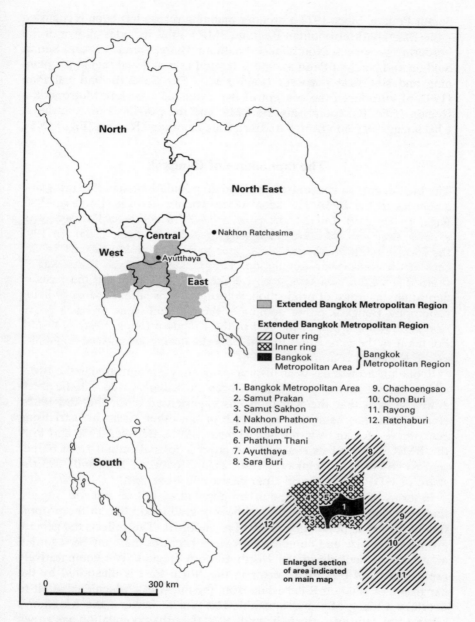

North

North East

Central

West

•Nakhon Ratchasima

•Ayutthaya

East

South

▨ Extended Bangkok Metropolitan Region

Extended Bangkok Metropolitan Region
▨ Outer ring
▨ Inner ring
▨ Bangkok } Bangkok
   Metropolitan   Metropolitan Region
   Area

1. Bangkok Metropolitan Area   9. Chachoengsao
2. Samut Prakan   10. Chon Buri
3. Samut Sakhon   11. Rayong
4. Nakhon Phathom   12. Ratchaburi
5. Nonthaburi
6. Phathum Thani
7. Ayutthaya
8. Sara Buri

Enlarged section of area indicated on main map

0 ———— 300 km

Figure 6.1 The Extended Bangkok Metropolitan Region.
Source: Luxmon Wongsuphasawat, 1997.

Samut Prakan. Since 1977 a broader planning region has been recognised – the Bangkok Metropolitan Region (BMR) – this includes all five of the bordering provinces, Nonthaburi, Phathum Thani, Samut Prakan, Samut Sakhon and Nakhon Pathom, and is treated as a national region for planning and statistical purposes (Figure 6.1). The Seventh National Plan (1992–6) introduced the concept of the Extended Bangkok Metropolitan Region (EBMR), comprising the BMR and the provinces of Ayutthaya, Chachoengsao, Chon Buri, Sara Buri, Ratchaburi and Rayong (Figure 6.1).

The dominance of Bangkok

The high degree of concentration of urban population, manufacturing and amenities in the BMA has been widely commented on (London, 1980; Rigg, 1991b: 139). Indeed, the concentration in every respect equals or exceeds that for any other major city in Asia (Bronger, 1985). In 1993 the BMA contained 10.8 per cent of the national population and 57.6 per cent of the total urban population. The population of the BMA was 30 times that of the next largest city, Nakhon Ratchasima. On the basis of almost any measure of production, consumption, wealth, services or living conditions, Bangkok either dominates the national scene or has a provision several times that of the rest of the Kingdom (Rigg, 1991b: 149–50). For many of these measures the gap between the capital and the remainder of the Kingdom continues to widen.

Economic growth has been disproportionately concentrated in the BMA and its immediate environs. This has been particularly evident in the accelerated growth that the Kingdom has experienced since the mid-1980s. (Indeed, this has been the experience of the other Asian industrialising economies – for an overview see Thomas, 1991). Between 1986 and 1990 the BMR increased its share of the gross industrial output from 62 per cent to 76 per cent (Ichikawa, 1990: 2), and between 1988 and 1993 the share of GDP rose from 50.1 per cent to 55.4 per cent.

In terms of the share of the urban population, official statistics suggest that since the late 1970s there has been a gradual decline in the proportion of the urban population resident in the BMA. This reflects the general growth in the size and number of provincial centres that may be regarded as urban, particularly in the North Eastern Region. The comparatively rapid growth of the urban sector in the North East is illustrated by the expansion of Nakhon Ratchasima from the mid-1980s which enabled it to overtake Chiang Mai and Songkhla-Hat Yai to become the Kingdom's second city. However, since the mid-1980s the urban population has grown fastest in the areas adjacent to the BMA. Thus to a degree the fall in the proportion of the total urban population resident in the BMA reflects the spreading of the urban area into the adjacent provinces (see Figure 6.1 and the discussion on pp. 201–03).

As may be seen from Table 6.1, the level of the BMA'S primacy appears to have declined sharply between 1980 and 1985. However, this is principally the result of boundary changes which recognised the expansion of the urban areas of such major provincial centres as Chiang Mai, Khon Kaen, Hat Yai and Nakhon Ratchasima. In this sense the decline in the primacy of the BMA has been much more gradual than Table 6.1 suggests. However, it is also important to qualify the decline in two ways.

First, in terms of population the significance of the BMA and the BMR is probably greater than the official figures suggest. As was argued in Chapter 1 (p. 20) it is possible that the city's population has long been under-estimated. Particularly since the mid-1980s there has been a very large increase in the number of migrants into Bangkok and its immediate environs, who are either unregistered or remain registered in rural areas. This in addition to the estimated 2 million seasonal migrants (Paritta Chalermpow Koanantakool, 1993). Thus the urban population of Bangkok and its surrounding areas has probably increased very much faster than official statistics suggest.

Second, the dramatic spreading of Bangkok's built-up area suggests that the BMA is no longer the most appropriate unit for measuring the capital's dominance. It may well be that the BMR is a more appropriate measure. The BMA has become the centre of a rapidly growing metropolitan region; in this respect it is perhaps not so much that the capital's domination of the national economy and urban system has diminished, as that the city has spread, incorporating other centres. Indeed, since 1985 official statistics have referred to the 'urban population of the BMA and its vicinity' – that is the five outer provinces which together with in the BMA comprise the BMR (Figure 6.1). If this expanded definition is used the level of primacy increases from 39 in 1985, to 42 in 1990 and 47 in 1993. Thus it could be argued that there has been a rapid spreading of the capital's urban area, rather than a major reduction in Bangkok's dominance of the national and urban economies. However, even the reduced level of primacy based on the BMA and official figures reflects a situation which is extreme in global terms. In 1993 the World Bank reported only four countries with a larger proportion of the urban population resident in the principal city.[2]

The origins of Bangkok's dominance, 1782–1940

The size and growth of Bangkok during the nineteenth century are matters of considerable debate (see Sternstein, 1984). Despite these uncertainties, however, there is little doubt that the city's dominant role as the focus of the national economy and the Kingdom's interface with the international and Asian economy was firmly established during the nineteenth century. Indeed, the growth of the city's unique position may be seen as an integral part of the internationalisation of the economy, particularly after 1855.

193

Given the occasional, partial and uncertain accuracy of data for the pre-1900 period it is difficult to draw any firm conclusions as to Bangkok's level of primacy. Sternstein (1984: 67) concluded from an extensive review of sources from the early nineteenth century onwards until c.1900 that Bangkok was generally some ten times the size of the next largest city, Chiang Mai. The primacy of the capital appears to have increased steadily between 1900 and 1940, rising dramatically thereafter (Table 6.1).

The establishment of the capital at Bangkok in 1782 was followed by a rapid expansion of the Kingdom's overseas trade (see p. 25). Under the 'port polity' of the early nineteenth century the city appears to have developed rapidly as the interface with the expanding and increasingly Western-controlled international and regional trading economies. The economic and political structures of this period tended to concentrate surplus in the capital, creating conditions favourable to international trade but hindering the development of internal trade and provincial centres (Korff, 1986: 26).

Following the signing of the Bowring Treaty in 1855, Bangkok's growth accelerated and generally parallelled that of such colonial centres as Jakarta, Manila, Rangoon and Saigon. Trade, warehousing, processing and related manufacturing concentrated in one major port city, which increasingly overshadowed other, often much longer established, urban centres.

Table 6.1 The primacy of Bangkok, 1782–1992[a]

Time period	Ratio[b]	Second centre
1782–1900[c]	10	Appears to have been Chiang Mai
1990	11	
1910	12	
1920	13	Chiang Mai was the second centre 1900–60
1930	14	
1940	15	
1950	23	
1960	25	
1970	33	Songkhla-Hat Yai[d]
1980	36	Songkhla-Hat Yai
1985	27	Nakhon Ratchasima
1990	28	Nakhon Ratchasima
1993	30	Nakhon Ratchasima

Source: 1900–80 based on Sternstein, 1984: 67; 1985, 1990 and 1993 calculated from NSO data.

Notes:
a Before 1980 this refers to the 'built-up' area of Bangkok. The 1980–93 figures refer to the BMA.
b This is the ratio between the population of Bangkok and the second most populous centre.
c For the period 1782–1900 the ratio is not more than a reasonable supposition.
d These are two separate municipalities, Hat Yai and Songkhla, which may be regarded as comprising a twin city. If Chiang Mai is regarded as the second city during these years then the index of primacy reaches 51 in 1980.

In these respects the growth, form and functions of non-colonial Bangkok differed little from those of the colonial port cities of South East Asia (Smith and Nemeth, 1986: 132–3). However, the concentration of population and function in Bangkok was by the early 1900s (and probably long before) significantly greater than was the case elsewhere in South East Asia (Table 6.2).

From its inception Bangkok may be regarded as the centre of a highly centralised state (Korff, 1986: 25). This situation was greatly reinforced from the late nineteenth century onwards by reforms that substantially increased central control over the provinces (see pp. 37–40). Thus, the monarchy was able effectively to implement decisions which had been nationally made in the capital and with the bureaucracy concentrating power in Bangkok (London, 1980: 50). The centralisation of power was reinforced by the internationalisation of the Thai economy and the spread of the market economy. These developments broke down provincial self-sufficiency and more significantly, bargaining power (Korff, 1986: 26).

In Thailand, like Burma, the focus of the country was on a main river system which canalled produce to one port location. However, the focus was much stronger in the Thai case:

> Bangkok can be compared to a hole at the bottom of a cone where all fluid has to pass through. The Chao Phraya river serves as the prime outlet for many parts of the country. Because Bangkok is situated at the mouth of the river, it plays a leading role in the process of interaction with the international economy.
> (Thai University Research Associates, 1976: 35)

Douglass has stressed that 'Few other cities in Asia so well occupy the centre of gravity of the national economy and its linkages with the outside world' (1990: 24–5). This situation was reinforced with the construction of the railway system and later the modern road system (see Chapters 2 and 3). A glance at the maps of other South East Asian countries does

Table 6.2 Urban primacy in South East Asia, 1900–41[a]

Rangoon		Saigon-Cholon		Manila-Quezon		Singapore		Djakarta	
1911	2.1	1911	1.8	1903	5.7	1911	2.5	1905	2.3
1921	3.3	1918	6.1	1921	2.9				
1931	2.7	1931	2.3	1930	3.9	1931	2.3	1930	1.5
1941	3.9	1939	1.8	1940	4.6				

Source: McGee, 1967: 54.

Note

a The index of primacy used here is the population of the largest city expressed as the ratio of the population of the second largest.

suggest that very simple facets of national geography made for less concentration at the interface of the international and regional economies and of national trade in one major centre.

Given the uncertainty over the growth of Bangkok during the nineteenth century any comments on the source of population growth must be treated with extreme caution. However, it seems highly probable that, certainly before 1850, a major component of Bangkok's growth was Chinese immigration (Korff, 1986: 42–3; Sternstein, 1984: 55–7; see the discussion on pp. 66–7). In 1850 perhaps as much as 50 per cent of the capital's inhabitants were Chinese (Korff, 1986: 35). The comparatively limited migration of the indigenous population into the capital reflected their lack of involvement in commerce and restrictions on their movements, the more attractive and more remunerative nature of agriculture, and the persistence of restrictions on their movements (see discussion on pp. 65–6). Thus even by the late 1930s Bangkok could be described as a Chinese-dominated city (Thompson, 1941: 242) and the central districts remained so at least into the 1950s.[3]

The rapid expansion of the centralised bureaucracy from the later part of the nineteenth century, the removal of restrictions on the movement of individuals, the establishment of educational facilities (Chulalonkorn University was founded in 1916) and the growth of trade, commerce and limited industrial activity, created employment opportunities and attracted migrants from provincial areas (Evers, 1966). As well as facilitating the movement of agricultural labour, the construction of rail links, particularly from the North East to the Central Plain (Sompop Manarungsan, 1989: 17), presumably facilitated migration to Bangkok. However, the scale of seasonal, temporary and permanent migration appears to have remained small until the 1930s (Korf, 1986: 43). The expansion of migration from this period reflected the spreading of the exchange economy and associated 'decomposition' of the rural communities – reinforced by the slowing of the expansion of the rice economy, the loss of income resulting from the international recession, the beginning of a national road building programme, the rise of economic nationalism and the promotion of Bangkok-based industry (see Chapter 2).

While provincial centres grew during the 1900–40 period – responding to the growth of primary production, trade and administration – they served limited hinterlands. Direct linkages between provincial centres remained extremely limited, and they were often principally connected through the capital to which they became increasingly tied. Between 1920 and 1937 Bangkok appears to have grown very rapidly from 345,000 to 681,000 (Sternstein, 1984: 97–109). While Chiang Mai, the second city, also grew substantially over the same period (from 26,500 to 45,400), this was insufficient to prevent the primacy of the capital increasing (Table 6.1). During the period 1900–40 the growth of urban primacy was very much greater in Thailand than elsewhere in South East Asia (Table 6.2).

In the South East Asian colonial states, while urbanisation was dominated by the large multi-functional port towns, there was also a proliferation of smaller provincial centres. These were vital to the effective operation of the colonial economies. As McGee has summarised:

> the railway junction town, the small coastal port, the mining settlement, and the district headquarters enabled the colonial traditional economy and societies of South East Asia. These small centres were the dissemination points of colonial policy, through which the cash economy and the ideas of the West filtered into the countryside. While the 'primate' port cities of the nineteenth century were largely orientated to the West, these smaller urban centres played an intermediary role between the traditional rural society of Southeast Asia and the rapidly urbanising societies of western Europe.
>
> (1967: 53–4)

While Thai provincial centres carried out similar functions to those in the colonial areas, they probably did so far less intensively. This was particularly so with respect to administration and the development of the market economy.

It is tempting to conclude that the forces that gave rise to the pattern of dominance by major port cities during the colonial period operated in Thailand in a situation of already very uneven urban development, and interacted with the Kingdom's non-colonial form of articulation, giving rise to an extreme situation. Whatever the veracity of this view it is apparent that in Thailand there was little to offset the concentration of urban growth in Bangkok, and the seeds of Bangkok's extreme metropolitan dominance had been laid by 1940 (Falkus, 1991: 576).

The dominant role of Bangkok in the national economy was reinforced during the Second World War and its immediate aftermath by the influx of Thai migrants that changed the character of the capital – making it a 'Thai' rather than a 'Chinese' city. (Thompson, 1947: 242). Migration appears to have reflected the war-time disruption of the economy, the virtual cessation of rice exports and the breakdown of administration and control in many outer provinces. In addition, the curtailment of imports stimulated the growth of a variety of small-scale manufacturing concerns (Falkus, 1991: 57) and inflation altered the income distribution in favour of many urban activities (Behrman, 1968: 383).

From the 1940s onwards the growth of Bangkok was closely associated with industrialisation and the internationalisation of the national system (Korff, 1986: 46–7). This was reinforced by the American presence and expenditure which promoted industrial, financial and service sector growth. Despite the growth of manufacturing, between 1964 and 1975 the main growth in employment was in the service and commercial sectors (Kanok Wongtrangan, 1982: 58). In response to increased employment opportunities there was a rapid increase in migration to the capital; by the late 1950s the influx of people from adjacent areas of the Central Plain and the North East accounted for most of the population increase (Thiravet Pramuanratikarn, 1979: 29). Seasonal migration was gradually replaced by permanent migration as the 'decomposition' of rural society accelerated (Textor, 1961).

As was discussed in Chapter 5 (pp. 159–61), it seems likely that work in the rural sector was becoming more arduous and less rewarding for many people. So the dominance of rural–rural migration – in search of new land and employment – was gradually superseded by rural–urban migration, and more significantly rural–Bangkok. In addition, Bangkok was increasingly recognised not only as a source of employment and remittance income, but also as the only place which offered educational facilities and the prospects of social mobility (Evers, 1966).

By 1960 Bangkok contained a far higher percentage of lifetime migrants than the other region's: 22.8 per cent compared to 7.7–10.9 per cent. The proportion of lifetime migrants in the capital increased to 27 per cent in 1970 and 36 per cent in 1980. Throughout the whole period 1955–80 the majority of migrants came from the Central region. However, the percentage share of the Central region fell from 61.8 per cent in the 1955–60 period to 42.4 per cent in 1975–80. Over the same period the share of the North East increased from 20.4 per cent to 35.11 per cent. By 1980 the outer areas of the BMR, notably the provinces of Nonthaburi, Samut Prakarn, Nakhon Pathom and Samut Sakorn, were beginning to grow faster than the BMA – receiving migrants both from other regions and increasingly from the BMA (Askew, 1993: 27; McGee and Greenberg, 1992b: 27).

The rapid population growth in Bangkok during the period from the 1940s until 1980 resulted in a dramatic increase in the level of primacy (Table 6.1). This development cannot be attributed to any one cause. Undoubtedly the capital's growth reflected the position that the city had come to occupy in the national economy – not only the main port and linkage to the international economy, but also the focus of road and rail routes and the seat of a highly centralised administration. However, neither geography nor the way in which Bangkok has evolved as the focus of domestic trade and links with the global economy fully explains the extreme unevenness of urban development. A major factor in the post-1940 period has been government policy which has emphasised the growth of Bangkok to the neglect of the rest of the Kingdom. These policies have included:

- the low priority given to rural development
- the taxation of rice farming
- subsidies to ISI and EOI which were principally located in Bangkok
- emphasis of infrastructure expenditure in Bangkok
- limited, and generally ineffective attention directed at the spatial distribution of development.

Certainly a wide range of 'implicit' policies can be invoked as supporting the case for urban bias in development strategies. However, whatever the strength of government policies, they operated on tendencies towards the concentration of growth in Bangkok that were already very strong and long established. If there had been little such bias in government policies, Egan and Bendick (1984) are probably correct in their conclusion that Thailand would still have come to exhibit a lesser, but still extremely uneven pattern of urban growth. In summary it must be stressed that while none of the policies, historical developments or geographical factors are unique to Thailand it is their strength and combination that gives rise to the extreme spatial imbalance (Douglass, 1990: 25).

The pattern of urban growth

The early spread of the city from the original fortified position in the bend of the Chao Phraya took place north and south along the river or followed the construction of successive lateral and radial canals. These provided transport, water supply and sewerage disposal. The linear settlements that developed along the canals were separated by orchards, gardens and paddy fields (ESCAP, 1986: 30) which were only 'in-filled' at a very much later date. This pattern has continued as the canal links were progressively supplemented and replaced by road construction.

Until the 1940s the urban area expanded gradually; the city retained its essentially compact form, and a high proportion of the increase in population and economic activity was accommodated by increasing density (Korff, 1986: 86). The subsequent acceleration in the growth of the population of Bangkok has been accompanied by a rapid expansion of the built-up area. This has involved the continuation of the established pattern of linear 'sprawl' and the incorporation of large numbers of villages (Thiravet Pramuanratkarn, 1979: 29). From the mid-1960s factory and middle-class housing began to develop at the urban periphery; these had become city-wide trends by the mid-1970s (Thiravet Pramuanratkarn, 1979: 4).

Since the late 1970s rising land prices coupled with traffic congestion and the associated difficulty of commuting between the suburbs and the centre has resulted in the dispersal of CDB functions. In 1978 57 of the top 100 Thai-registered corporations had their headquarters in the city centre. By 1988 12 had relocated either to the city fringe or adjacent areas and in addition seven of the ten companies that entered the top hundred list between 1978 and 1988 were located 5 to 20 km from the city centre (Tetsuo Kidokoro, 1992a: 80–4) – suggesting that new companies were tending to locate further from the centre. This pattern of decentralisation has not been followed by government offices, 90 per cent of which remain in the central area.

The dispersal of corporate headquarters has been accompanied by the development of shopping centres. In 1978 seven of the ten shopping complexes and department stores were located centrally. By 1988 the number of centres had increased to 29, of which 16 were in the outer areas (Tetsuo Kidokoro, 1992a: 80–4). Overall, the dispersal of administrative and retail functions has given rise to a series of commercial sub-centres.

Between the mid-1980s and the early 1990s average land prices in the BMA more than doubled and in some industrial areas increases were as much as five times (Alpha Research, 1992; Luxmon Wongsuphasawat, 1997: 204). The rising cost and increasingly short supply of industrial land has combined with rising relative wage levels (Alpha Research, 1992) and increasing congestion to make the BMA and, increasingly, parts of the outer ring, less attractive to industry (Luxmon Wongsuphasawat, 1997: 205). Additionally, as is discussed more fully in on pp. 226–30, since 1986 the BOI has offered larger tax concessions to locate outside the BMR.

Since the early 1980s large-scale manufacturing has spread rapidly into the five outer provinces of the BMR and, to a lesser extent, the fringes of the ten surrounding provinces (Biggs *et al.*, 1990: 4–5). In 1986 the BMA received 17 per cent of BOI approvals – the inner ring 32 per cent and the outer ring 13 per cent; in 1993 the BMA received 15 per cent, the inner ring 22 per cent and the outer ring 32 per cent (Ichikawa, 1990: 5; Luxmon Wongsuphasawat, 1997: 205–6). These changes were accompanied by an increase in the amount of proposed investment in the inner and outer rings, and a fall in the average size of investments in the BMA. Smaller scale manufacturing activities and service provisions continued to proliferate in the inner-city areas however (Ichikawa, 1990: 5).

To the east of the BMA the above tendencies have been reinforced by the development of infrastructure associated with the exploitation of offshore oil and gas – notably the construction of a new port at Laem Chabang and associated road and rail links to Bangkok. Since 1981 the oil and gas developments have been seen as providing the basis for the development of a major industrial base in the Eastern Seaboard (Figure 6.2). During the early 1980s falling oil prices, recession and a shortage of public and private investment curtailed development. The planned construction of infrastructure and individual private and public projects were repeatedly reduced in scope, postponed or abandoned. However, the acceleration of Thailand's economic growth since the

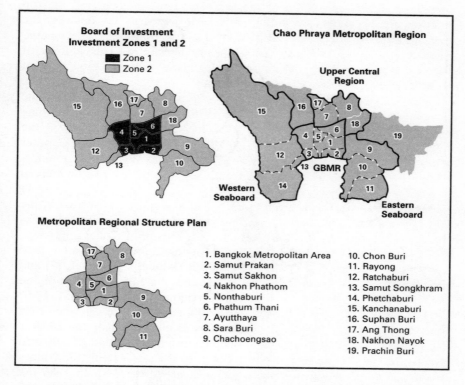

Board of Investment Investment Zones 1 and 2
■ Zone 1
☐ Zone 2

Chao Phraya Metropolitan Region

Upper Central Region

Western Seaboard

GBMR

Eastern Seaboard

Metropolitan Regional Structure Plan

1. Bangkok Metropolitan Area
2. Samut Prakan
3. Samut Sakhon
4. Nakhon Phathom
5. Nonthaburi
6. Phathum Thani
7. Ayutthaya
8. Sara Buri
9. Chachoengsao
10. Chon Buri
11. Rayong
12. Ratchaburi
13. Samut Songkhram
14. Phetchaburi
15. Kanchanaburi
16. Suphan Buri
17. Ang Thong
18. Nakhon Nayok
19. Prachin Buri

Figure 6.2 Variations on the definition of the Extended Bangkok Metropolitan Region.

Source: Luxmon Wongsuphasawat, 1997: 264.

mid-1980s has rejuvenated the Eastern Seaboard developments. Since 1988 the five eastern provinces have been the fastest growing in the Kingdom, with Gross Provincial Product (GPP) growing at an average annual rate of 18.3 per cent between 1989 and 1992, compared to 12.5 per cent for the six provinces to the north and east of the BMA, and 11.9 per cent for the BMA itself.

The spread of the urban-industrial fabric into the outer provinces of the BMR and beyond, particularly to the north and east, has been characterised by extensive, predominantly linear sprawl along the lines of the radiating roads, giving rise to the 'lines and points' development that has come to typify the structure of the EMR (Ginsberg *et al.*, 1991; Luxmon Wongsuphasawat, 1997; McGee and Greenberg, 1992a, b) (Figure 6.3). Growth, particularly in the outer areas, has been almost completely uncontrolled and uncoordinated. Typically, strips some 20 to 40 metres

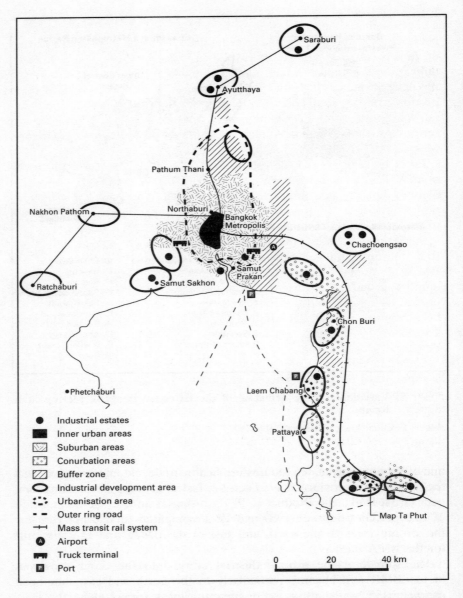

Legend:

- ● Industrial estates
- ■ Inner urban areas
- Suburban areas
- Conurbation areas
- Buffer zone
- ◯ Industrial development area
- ⬭ Urbanisation area
- – – Outer ring road
- ┼┼ Mass transit rail system
- Ⓐ Airport
- 🚛 Truck terminal
- Ⓟ Port

Labels on map:

Saraburi
Ayutthaya
Pathum Thani
Nakhon Pathom
Northaburi
Bangkok Metropolis
Chachoengsao
Ratchaburi
Samut Sakhon
Samut Prakan
Chon Buri
Phetchaburi
Laem Chabang
Pattaya
Map Ta Phut

0   20   40 km

Figure 6.3 A schematic representation of the dots and lines structure of the EBMR.
Source: Luxmon Wongsuphasawat, 1997: 209.

wide have been developed, leaving large areas which are only in-filled at a very much later date (Banasopit Mekvichai *et al.*, 1990: 26). The areas between the main routeways have generally been built up through a pattern of chaotic small *soi* (small side roads). Many of these are dead-ends, linking developments to main roads through a zigzagging route following the ends of intervening plots. Such feeder roads are the product of often protracted negotiations between developers and other owners. The resultant pattern of often extremely poorly surfaced and narrow roads poses serious problems for communications and service provision (Banasopit Mekvichai *et al.*, 1990: 27).

From the early 1980s the established pattern of linear and *soi* development has been increasingly supplemented by a variety of large-scale planned housing and industrial developments. While much better positioned for service and communications, these also tend to be connected to the main routes through dead-end links.

Since the mid-1980s a number of very large-scale 'self-contained' industrial and residential complexes have been established in the fringes of the BMA. Much attention has focused on the 1,667 ha Gateway City development, promoted in terms of easy access to Dong Muang Airport, the port at Klong Toy and the Eastern Seaboard. The industrial element has been almost entirely committed by East Asian firms – Japanese, Taiwanese, Hong Kong and Chinese (Bank of Thailand, *Quarterly Bulletin*, Feb. 1991: 32).

Since the early 1980s the peripheral areas of Bangkok have undergone a rapid transformation. This is apparent in both land use and socioeconomic characteristics. Large tracts of land have passed out of agriculture and into the hands of developers and speculators. Similarly large numbers of people while remaining rural in residence have been absorbed into a variety of urban-industrial activities. In Pathom Thani, for example, in 1991 60 per cent of the population were classified as living in 'rural settlements', while only 24 per cent of employment was in agriculture. To a degree, of course, this reflects the inadequate definition of 'urban' (see pp. 20–1).

Information on land use changes in the BMR is far from satisfactory. According to Department of Land Development data it appears that since the early 1970s on average *c.* 1 per cent of agricultural land was lost every year. However, since the mid-1980s the rate of loss has risen sharply to as much as 7.2 per cent in Nontaburi and 5.9 per cent in Pathum Thani between 1987 and 1989 (cited in Banasopit Mekvichai *et al.*, 1990: 41).

The situation is complicated by data collected by the Ministry of Agriculture which suggest that the agricultural area of the BMR *increased* by 8.8 per cent between 1981 and 1986 and by 16.1 between 1986 and 1988 (cited in Banasopit Mekvichai *et al.*, 1990: 43). However, examination of these data indicate that between 1986 and 1988 the area under paddy, field crops, vegetables and flowers decreased by 6 to 15 per cent, while the areas of grass land, idle land and unclassified land increased substantially (Banasopit Mekvichai *et al.*, 1990).

Thus while continuing to grow ever faster through the concentration of migrants from provincial areas, the capital is now also growing by expansion and incorporation of adjacent, often densely populated areas of the Central Plain. This combination of what McGee and Greenberg (1992a) term urban concentration and regional urbanisation is producing not only very rapid growth but extremely complex patterns of land use, circulation of people and commodities, life styles and economy. These developments have been facilitated by the rapidity of urban-based industrial growth, the proliferation of motor vehicles and the lack of controls over development. In many areas serious conflicts over land use and resources, particularly water, are emerging. Thus the growth of the EBMR is resulting in major problems of planning, regulation, and the supply of services that are posing major new challenges for regional and urban planning.

Transport

The rapid increase in the extent and population of the capital has not been accompanied by significant development of transport facilities. The still heavy concentration of activities in the city centre, together with the unplanned expansion of residential areas – often at a considerable distance from the centre – without the development of the necessary transport facilities, have created major problems of congestion. The rapid spreading of the built-up area has been closely linked to a steep rise in the private ownership of motor vehicles. Since 1980 vehicle registrations in the BMA have increased at an annual average of 25 per cent, reaching 1.23 million in 1991. In the same period motor cycle registrations grew at 44 per cent a year, reaching 1.6 million in 1991. These figures do not include the large numbers of vehicles registered in surrounding provinces and used for commuting into the BMA. However, the vehicle ownership rate in the BMA is the highest for any Asian city outside Japan (Tetsuo Kidokoro, 1992a: 75).

On the basis of estimates of the number of commuters and the capacity of the main radial roads Tetsuo Kidokoro (1992a: 78–80) concluded that transport to the city centre was reaching capacity in 1984. The subsequent period of rapid Bangkok-based economic growth has taken place with little development of transport facilities. While there has been a degree of decentralisation, this has in some respects increased the pressures on transport facilities because of the continuing need for linkages with the central areas. The decentralisation of housing has principally affected the rapidly expanding high and middle income groups, who are predominantly tied to central area employment, services and schooling facilities;

thus these developments have been associated with substantial increases in commuting for work and education amongst these groups (see Sureeporn Punpuing, 1993 for a detailed study of patterns and determinants of commuting).

The congestion and consequent amount of time involved in commuting has resulted in many commuters adopting what appear to be very inconvenient and disruptive life styles. Even for short distances people will leave home one or two hours early in order to reduce the time spent in the traffic, travel on a less crowded bus, or secure a parking space, even if this means arriving at work or school unnecessarily early. Ross has described the situation as one in which:

> Middle-income families try to spend time and conduct essential domestic activities in the car. Meals and preparation for the day are rushed, or carried out on the way to work. Travelling can account for a large proportion of the time couples and children spend together, and it is not unusual for children to be dressed, fed, or even do homework in the car. All of our respondents perceived a strong impact of commuting on family life, and neighbourhood life, since no one had time any more for interaction. Among young people, friendship and recreation activities are more commonly based in the workplace than the neighbourhood.
>
> (1993: 14)

It is all too apparent that the Bangkok road system is inadequate to the level of traffic – this despite efforts since the 1960s to convert the capital into an 'automobile city' (Manop Bongsadadt, 1987: 554). This has involved the filling in of many canals (*klongs*) to facilitate road construction, a process which has interfered with water supply, drainage and flood control. In 1989 there were 2,800 km of roads in the BMA – representing only 12.5 per cent of the area of the city (Country Report, 1989: 4). This compares to the 20 to 25 per cent norm for major western cities (NESDB, 1988: 10).

Congestion is substantially increased by bus services being almost entirely confined to the main road system. The growth of the urban area, particularly in the outer areas, has created an intricate pattern of feeder roads, large numbers of which are dead ends. Thus a large proportion of the population are dependent on either private cars, taxis, minibus services or the varied 'informal' sector either for entire journeys or to and from the bus routes. The informal transport provisions principally comprise *son taw* – a light truck converted to carry 10–15 passengers, often on regular routes – and soi-bikes – motor cycle taxis. For large numbers of new peripheral developments there is little alternative to private vehicles and the informal sector.

Thus Bangkok has an exceptionally high level of traffic volume per unit of road area. The resultant congestion is exacerbated by the incomplete nature of the road network, the very mixed nature of the traffic, inefficient traffic management and, perhaps most critically, the absence of an adequate mass transit system effectively separated from the general traffic.

The Bangkok Metropolitan Transit Authority (BMTA), established in 1975, controls a fleet of some 7,000 buses. These are generally old and their exhaust fumes contribute substantially to the capital's air pollution. The BMTA is under-capitalised, saddled with heavy debts, and faced with government controls which keep fares low. In addition, the route management is considered inefficient. Overall, Bangkok's mass transit system provides a poor and unreliable service.

The planning and design of a separate mass transit system for the city was initiated on the recommendation of the 1971–5 Bangkok Transport Study. The original plan for a 100 km of elevated heavy double track railway was completed in 1981. This was to be entirely state financed; however, the recession of the early 1980s, the lack of development funds and the increasing difficulty the government was experiencing in raising international loans resulted in a decision in 1982 to privatise the scheme. However, the government's proposals, which centred on a 30-year concession with no grant or subsidy, failed to attract private-sector funding. As a result during 1984 the Expressway and Rapid Transit Authority (ERTA) produced a revised proposal. Under this the mass transit system was to be constructed in two stages, with the government holding 25 per cent of the company's concessionary equity. The terms of reference for the first stage were finalised during 1987, subsequently however there was a series of false starts, punctuated by corruption scandals, litigation, and changes of plan. Agreement was reached for three projects, all with start dates early in 1993. Together they were expected to provide 100 km of elevated commuter track capable of moving 3 to 4 million passengers a day by the year 2000. However, the three projects were designed by different government departments. It was reported that there were over 30 places where the systems conflict (Handley, 1992b). Subsequently, after further changes of plan and false starts, the first section was scheduled to open early in 1998, but this has been delayed by threats of litigation by land owners and enterprises along the route, and more significantly the 1997–8 economic crisis.

In the absence of any immediate prospect of the rapid development of a rail system, bus lanes were introduced in 1980 in an attempt to partly separate the only existing element of mass transit from the general traffic. While the operation of bus lanes has reportedly resulted in some improvement in bus and/or car travel time, it is also apparent that drivers widely ignore the regulations and enforcement is almost completely ineffective (Bampen Jatoorapreuk et al., 1992: 96).

The problems that have surrounded the development of the rail mass transit system and the ineffectiveness of traffic controls further underline the inability of either regional or national authorities to control developments effectively or to implement essential infrastructural projects. However, it must be stressed that while there is a chronic need for the establishment of a mass transport system separate from the general traffic, it will not be a panacea. To be effective it will have in the short run to be combined with coordinated transport and traffic management, and in the longer run substantial urban redevelopment and infrastructural programmes.

Housing provision

The growth of housing provision illustrates very clearly the strengths and weaknesses of Bangkok's largely uncontrolled and uncoordinated pattern of growth.

Until the late 1960s housing was constructed on an individual basis either by the occupiers or through the hire of contractors. Sites were either rented or purchased from land sub-dividers (Foo Tuen Seik, 1992: 1138). In the more central areas this involved the sub-division of already small sites. Apart from the limited regulation of the sub-division of plots and building standards there are virtually no controls over land use in Bangkok. During the 1980s regulations governing house building standards, and the sub-division of plots were substantially relaxed. As a result Thailand has the simplest procedures for land sub-division in South East Asia (Tetsuo Kidokoro, 1992: 64, 67). Thus it is asserted that it is possible to build virtually any type of house at any location (Foo Tuen Seik, 1992: 1140). This situation prevails despite attempts by the Municipal Authority since 1937, and the Bangkok Metropolitan Authority since 1972, to control the capital's expansion.

From 1968, with the rapid expansion of the city area and the sub-division of large city fringe plots, private speculative developers began to build mainly detached units for the upper and middle income groups. In 1973 there were 33 firms constructing annually c. 8,000 units on some 800 ha of land (Nathalang, 1974). Between 1974 and 1984 the private sector provided some 90,000 units, principally at the more expensive end of the market. From the mid-1980s the acceleration of Thailand's economic growth was accompanied by a spectacular expansion of private-sector housing output. During the period 1980 to 1986 annual production averaged 15,000 units; in 1987 30,411 units were completed, in 1988 45,192, and in 1989 57,622 (government Housing Bank, 1990). By the later year there were over 1,000 development companies operating (Foo Tuen Seik, 1992: 1138).

Since the early 1980s the production of housing in the BMR has become increasingly associated with private estate development. According to NESDB data the share of estate development in the annual output of housing units increased from 4 per cent in 1974, to 15 per cent in 1984, to 57 per cent in 1989 and 73 per cent in 1990. A high proportion of these developments is occupied by well-educated middle-class, white-collar workers (Watanabe, 1993: 15). However, there is evidence that unintended, and in some cases very unwelcome, small-scale commercial and manufacturing activities are being introduced in the cheaper developments. But, as Watanabe (1993: 14) has suggested, many developments are effectively isolated islands in the suburbs of Bangkok.

The rapid expansion of private-sector housing provision since the mid-1980s, as well as being associated with estate development, has also involved moves towards the provision of lower cost units – including terraced, shophouse, and high-rise housing (made possible by the 1979 Condominium Act). These moves principally reflected the very competitive nature of the higher cost housing markets, rising land prices (reinforced by the rapid expansion of potential home buyers in the wake of the country's accelerated growth), the growth of the housing finance sector (from 1987 insurance and finance companies were allowed to invest in land and the housing market), low interest rates, and the availability of tax relief on housing loans. These developments led Angel and Sureeporn Chuated (1990: 20) to conclude that the private housing and land marketing sectors were moving rapidly towards the mass marketing of low-cost housing. This view is supported by income and housing cost surveys which suggest that the proportion of the BMA's population that could afford to purchase their own home rose from 20 per cent in 1980 to 50 per cent in 1990, but in the light of rising land costs is projected to fall to 40 per cent in 1996 (Bangkok Land Management Study, cited in Sophon Pornchokchai 1992: 48–9).

Until the expansion of low-cost private-sector developments the only provider of mass low cost housing had been the National Housing Authority (NHA). From its establishment in 1973 until 1984 the NHA provided on average some 7,000 low-cost units annually (NHA, *Annual Report*, various years). Between 1984 and 1988 the annual expansion of public housing provision averaged only some 2,000 units, a reflection of budgetary constraints and the limited availability of land for public housing projects (Dowall, 1992: 28). These constraints together with the take off of the mass provision of lower cost housing have caused the NHA to shift its activities from the construction of low-cost housing to the upgrading of slum areas (NHA, *Annual Report*, various years).

In 1990 NHA survey data indicated that there were 946,951 slum dwellers – 16.1 per cent of the BMA's official population – living in 981 slums (these figures were subsequently verified by the Bangkok Metropolitan Authority, cited in Sophon Pornchokchai, 1992: 63). The NHA study was based on a detailed analysis of aerial photographs followed by 'ground truthing'. Studies by Sophon Pornchokchai (1985; 1992) both generally confirmed the NHA findings and suggested that there had been little significant change since the early 1980s. Similarly, Dowall (1992: 280) concluded from an examination of NHA data that between 1984 and 1988 the increase in slum housing was a 'modest' 10,493 units. Such views suggest that slum dwelling had become relatively less important in the BMA (Chantana Chanont, 1990). However, other surveys suggest that large numbers of small clusters of slum dwellings were missed or excluded from the NHA and related surveys, and the density of population and hence numbers of inhabitants have been under-estimated (Setchell, 1991, places the number of slum dwellers as high as 1,495,525 in 1990). In addition, a new type of inner-city slum is emerging: rented 'apartments' generally measuring 4 by 3 metres in sub-divided run-down buildings. Their numbers are unknown but believed to be increasing rapidly (see Nathanon Thavisin and Ksemsan Suwarnarat, 1996: 12). In addition, much construction worker accommodation and other sub-standard accommodation provided by employers should perhaps be added to the slum category (Sophon Pornchokchai, 1992).

The possibly limited increase in the number of slums and slum dwellings in the BMA since the mid-1980s has to be seen in the context of rising land values and the demolition of slum dwellings without their replacement by low-cost housing. In consequence there was considerable expansion of slum accommodation in the five outer provinces of the BMR (Askew, 1993: 31; Dowall, 1992: 28). Thus the 1990 NHA study revealed 529 slum areas in these outer areas, as against the 77 in Sophon Pornchokchai's 1985 study (however this did not cover all of the outer area). While the magnitude of the changes are in doubt, it is apparent that slum dwelling, like other forms of housing and manufacturing activity, has been forced to decentralise since the early 1980s.

During the period 1974 to 1984 51 per cent of the expansion of housing was concentrated in a ring between 11 and 20 km from the city centre. In contrast, between 1984 and 1988 the share of this zone had fallen to 40 per cent (Dowall, 1992: 29). Shortage of land and the limited possibilities for major redevelopment in the central areas under prevailing conditions are pushing developments increasingly to the fringes. Between 1986 and 1990 the average distance of private housing projects from the centre increased from 16.7 km to 20.3 km. In addition, Dowall (1992: 29–30) concluded that between 1986 and 1990 there was a sharp increase in the density of housing projects from 36 to 54 units per ha – a reflection of rising land prices even in the fringe areas. This increase in density is shown most clearly in the development of low-cost high-rise blocks. By 1990 such high-rise developments comprised 43 per cent of project development (Dowall, 1992: 34).

Since the mid-1970s the housing stock in the BMR has grown substantially faster than the population. Between 1974 and 1984 the number of housing units increased by 66 per cent, and between 1984 and 1990 by a further 53 per cent. In the same periods the population increased by 25 per cent and 10 per cent respectively. Given the backlog of housing provision and the poor quality of much of the older stock, serious problems of overcrowding and inadequate housing remain, even for those who can afford the formal sector provision.

Bangkok has been cited as an example of an efficient housing market under which the commercial provision of housing units has substantially exceeded the growth of population and the importance of the informal sector is steadily declining (Dowall, 1989). Such a view fits in well with current World Bank views that the state should only be involved in the housing market (and indeed the economy as a whole) in an 'enabling' role (see Foo Tuen Seik, 1992: 1137). There are very few restrictions on housing construction in Thailand; indeed since the early 1980s these have been simplified and reduced in line with the general deregulation of the economy.

The reality of housing development in the BMR, and indeed urban growth in general, is very different. A number of writers have questioned the wisdom of the continuation of the *laissez faire* approach to the housing market. Indeed, Dowall's 1992 study raises serious concerns over the operation of the land market. Rapid increases in land prices and the continuation of extensive, largely linear sprawl are creating major long-term problems for the management of the housing stock. Dowall concluded that his second study 'has illustrated how rapidly the pattern of land development has shifted in Bangkok and illustrated the critical need for new government initiatives' (1992: 37). In this respect the housing sector is a microcosm of the Thai economy. The euphoria over the post-1986 unregulated economic 'boom' has given way to concern over its sustainability, and calls for government initiatives and controls. In the absence of changes in policies towards land expropriation and infrastructure development, major central area redevelopment projects remain highly unlikely in a city where 80 per cent of the land is privately owned (United Nations, 1987).

The consequences of the concentration of growth in Bangkok

The results of the concentration of growth in Bangkok have been aptly summarised by *Business International*:

> The snarled traffic, filthy air, clogged telephone system and the orgy of building may be the labour pains of a big new business centre in the heart of the dynamic part of the world economy. Or they could be the city's undoing.
>
> (March 1990: 13)

The rapid growth has been concentrated in a metropolitan area with inadequate infrastructure and weak and largely ineffective planning controls and urban management. Environmental degradation in the BMR is not so much a consequence of rapid urban and industrial growth as it is the result of the failure to supply infrastructure and controls consistent with the demands of economic growth. The following factors are particularly significant (Dhira Phantumnavit and Theodore Panayotou, 1990: 21).

- high-density development without adequate provision of mass transit and road networks has led to traffic congestion
- high water demand without adequate municipal water supply has led to excessive ground water pumping and consequent land subsidence
- high density development without adequate drainage and sewerage has led to flooding and water pollution
- industrial development without adequate pollution control investment and enforcement has led to air, water and solid waste pollution.

Quite simply controls were inadequate and infrastructural provision lagged behind economic growth before the boom.

The sharp increases in traffic since 1986 have come to a city already notorious for its congestion. By 1990 the average speed was 7 km per hour (*Business in Thailand*, Feb. 1991: 56).[4] In 1991 the World Bank estimated that the cost of commuting in the BMR was the equivalent of 1.4 per cent of GDP (cited *Far Eastern Economic Review* 1991: 6).[5] In addition, air pollution – 70 per cent of which is derived from motor vehicles – is amongst the worst in Asia (Banasopit Meckvichai *et al.*, 1990; Handley, 1991: 44). In 1989 it was reported that air pollution had become 'critical', with 900,000 people suffering from related respiratory illnesses (*Bangkok Post*, 11 Sept. 1990). As was noted in Chapter 4 (p. 126), the rapid growth of the manufacturing sector has been accompanied by a substantial rise in the number of plants producing hazardous waste. Given the limited enforcement of regulations much of this is discharged directly into the drainage system. In consequence, the lower Chao Phraya is now 'dead' – principally as a result of the large-scale discharge of aniline dyes.

The growth of the urban area has taken place with little regard to the provision of services. Large areas of the city lack any effective drainage or sewerage systems other than the canal system. This has led to the widespread use of septic tanks which in turn has led to pollution of ground-water supplies. The existing water treatment capacity serves only 2 per cent of the BMA's population (Anuchat Poungsomlee and Ross, 1992: 21). The waste-water from most households is discharged directly into canals that drain into the river. While large industrial plants are required to install water treatment facilities in order obtain their annual operating permit from the Ministry of Industry, this is far from rigidly enforced. In addition, large numbers of small and medium sized plants appear to be exempt (Anuchat Poungsomlee and Ross, 1992: 21).

Rapid urban-industrial growth, coupled with limited public water provision has resulted in the excessive extraction of ground-water. In 1990 an estimated 40 per cent of the population was dependent on ground-water from deep wells (den Haan, 1995: 418). This has resulted in salt-water penetration of wells as much as 20 km from the sea (Dhira Phantumnavit and Theodore Panayotou, 1990). In addition, the removal of ground-water and the weight of modern buildings has resulted in widespread subsidence (Yeu-man Yeung, 1988: 170). In areas of eastern Bangkok the annual rate of subsidence exceeds 10 cm per year and in central areas ranges from 5–10 cm per year (Rigg, 1991: 155–6). Subsidence has increased the incidence of flood damage[6] in this already low-lying area, as well as damaging roads, buildings, bridges, drains and water pipes. The continued extraction of ground water reflects the lack of development of public water provision and ineffective controls over urban-industrial growth and water abstraction. The combination of subsidence and inadequate drainage has led to the view that Bangkok is sinking into its own sewerage.

Conclusion

While it is difficult to contradict the view that Bangkok in the 1990s is a 'mess', it must be agreed that it is a dynamic 'mess'. In this respect it is important to see the Thai capital in the context of the historical experience of the presently industrialised nation and in relation to developments elsewhere in Asia. Though not overtly stated the official view appears to be pollute and congest today and clean up later. While this has been the pattern in Taipei, what Bello and Rosenfeld (1990) terms the Taiwanese 'environmental nightmare' was accompanied by very substantial centrally planned and financed infrastructural development. Further, the current 'clean-up stage' involves substantial relocation of predominantly Taiwanese industry to such locations as Bangkok. In this respect the Thai 'clean-up stage' would involve the substantial 're-export' of polluting foreign-owned industry. This raises the wider question of the extent to which Thailand, and the other recently industrialising ASEAN economies, will be able to make the transition to a domestically owned cleaner and higher tech industrial sector, and attract and retain similarly oriented transnational activities.

Bangkok in the mid-1990s lacks any effective comprehensive development plan. Indeed, many believe that it would be politically, as well as practically, impossible to implement one (Anuchat Poungsomlee and Ross, 1992: 14). Attempts to draw up a comprehensive plan date from 1960 when an American consultancy firm drew up *The Greater Bangkok Plan*; this was never adopted (see Romm, 1972: 76–7; Sternstein, 1971: 1; 1973).

In 1971 a revised *Plan for the Metropolitan Area* was published; also not adopted. Though some elements of this Plan were used to provide some partial guidelines for the control of development, these were difficult to implement and largely ineffective. This is illustrated by legislation in 1975 and 1979, providing for the establishment of a 'Green Belt' to control the loss of agricultural land in the BMR. There have been demands by developers, industrialists and government agencies to 're-evaluate' this legislation because it is a major barrier to the city's economic development (Anuchat Poungsomlee and Ross, 1992: 15). In practice, given the rapidity with which agricultural land is being converted to urban-industrial use it is difficult to credit that the Green Belt legislation plays any significant role in controlling development.

In 1992 a *Master Plan for the Metropolitan Area* was finally adopted, drawn up by the Office of Town and Country Planning (OTCP). However, it was subsequently subjected to a protracted process of consultation and modification. The large number of vested interests that are against many of the provisions lead one to question whether the adopted plan will in the event be any more effective than its unadopted predecessors.

The inevitability of the continued development of the EBMR appears to be accepted by planners and politicians – as is reflected in the Metropolitan Regional Planning Study (NESDB, 1993). This study, however, adopts a slightly different and broader definition of the metropolitan region, encompassing the BMR, Eastern Seaboard and the Upper Central Region (Figure 6.2, p. 201). A wide variety of infrastructure projects are envisaged as facilitating the development of these areas. Under the Eighth Plan (1997–2001) an even wider region is proposed, the Chao Phraya Metropolitan Region (NESDB, 1997), which includes the Western Seaboard (Figure 6.2). The promotion of these metropolitan regions is envisaged as resting principally on the development of infrastructure, particularly transport, and the establishment of sub-regional centres: thus the spreading of development from the BMR will be facilitated. However, it does seem to be more a matter of facilitating a process that is already underway, and there is no sign of decentralisation from the BMR to the outer regions of the country (see Chapter 7).

7

INCOME DISTRIBUTION, POVERTY AND SPATIAL INEQUALITY

Introduction

As was discussed in Chapter 3 the developmental role of the Thai state since the 1950s has become increasingly restricted to one of fostering domestic and foreign private enterprise, and creating an environment conducive to rapid economic growth. In this climate distributional issues have received little attention. While commitments to the reduction of personal and regional income disparities and the elimination of poverty are reiterated in government statements and featured in all the National Plans, in practice there have been few effective policy interventions. Thai governments have not found it necessary to devote significant resources to redistributive policies with respect either to personal wealth or the spatial pattern of economic growth (see Christensen, 1993). Thus questions of personal and spatial distributions of income have remained largely peripheral to Thai development policy.

Regional income disparities

The pattern of development in Thailand was already markedly uneven by 1940 (see pp. 194–7 and Chapter 2) – Bangkok and the adjacent areas of the Central Plain being significantly more wealthy and commercialised than the rest of the Kingdom. While this trend appears to have accelerated from the 1940s onwards, data, as in the pre-war period, are sparse. Only with the appearance of regional GDP figures from 1960 onwards could trends in regional income levels begin to be effectively quantified.

The statistics for the 1960s should be treated with some caution. Similarly, even more recent figures are distorted by the under-registration of people in the BMR, over-registration of people in rural areas, under-valuing of the subsistence element that remains in the rural economy, and the under-recording of the flow of remittances from the BMR into the rural areas. To these difficulties must be added changes in the bases of the calculations, the regional definitions used, and some abrupt, and often

214

inexplicable, annual variations. With these qualifications in mind Table
7.1 provides a general indication of the divergence in per capita regional
GDP between 1960 and 1993.

Table 7.1 Regional per capita GDP at constant prices as a percentage of the
national average

	BMR	Centre	East	West	South	North	North East
1960	–	161.3	–	–	125.8	71.0	53.8
1961	–	165.5	–	–	119.2	70.8	53.4
1962	–	165.6	–	–	112.4	72.3	52.9
1963	–	167.8	–	–	110.5	71.2	53.1
1964	–	175.3	–	–	108.4	70.0	48.1
1965	–	175.3	–	–	108.4	69.3	50.0
1966	–	171.8	–	–	96.2	72.7	52.7
1967	–	181.0	–	–	97.1	71.0	46.9
1968	–	178.1	–	–	96.9	68.9	50.1
1969	–	179.0	–	–	98.2	68.9	48.5
1970	–	183.0	–	–	96.2	67.4	45.0
1971	–	182.7	–	–	93.0	68.1	46.4
1972	–	181.5	–	–	92.4	67.8	48.3
1973	–	181.3	–	–	95.7	66.6	53.8
1974	–	184.1	–	–	100.7	63.0	45.0
1975	–	186.1	–	–	100.0	61.1	44.3
1976	–	191.0	–	–	100.3	61.7	44.0
1977	272.7	148.9	190.1	139.2	103.4	66.2	41.6
1978	282.1	105.1	187.9	138.4	90.4	68.7	40.3
1979	297.9	110.6	170.8	123.7	89.7	66.9	41.2
1980	296.4	111.9	175.5	125.1	83.6	65.1	42.4
1981	292.0	86.7	121.1	111.2	82.5	65.8	42.7
1982	289.1	85.9	122.1	116.0	81.7	65.3	45.1
1983	287.2	81.7	116.9	106.2	75.1	62.3	43.4
1984	285.4	87.4	120.1	96.8	74.1	65.4	43.2
1985	283.0	88.2	155.9	98.7	74.9	65.7	44.3
1986	290.0	90.0	158.4	97.7	74.7	63.3	39.2
1987	307.8	86.5	154.4	88.8	71.9	59.9	39.1
1988	315.4	86.0	154.2	84.0	68.9	56.3	38.2
1989	311.4	81.6	151.5	85.3	70.4	55.3	34.9
1990	323.9	77.4	149.1	75.4	67.9	52.1	33.7
1991	323.9	79.3	152.7	75.0	65.6	52.1	33.3
1992	325.1	78.7	144.3	74.9	64.3	51.8	32.0
1993	340.6	78.3	143.3	67.5	60.2	47.9	31.1

Source: NESDB.

Notes
• There have been a number of changes in the basis of these figures.
• Until 1977 the Centre includes Bangkok and the East and West regions.
• From 1977 until 1980 the figures for the BMR excluded Nonthaburi and Pathum Thani
  which were included in the Centre.
• In 1970 nine provinces were removed from the Centre and added to the North.

215

As may be seen from Table 7.1 the disparity between the Central Plain (including Bangkok) and the rest of the Kingdom widened rapidly during the period 1960 to 1976 (see p. 191, Figure 6.1 for a map of the regions). The relative deterioration was greatest and most consistent for the North and North East. The latter region, which represented some 30 per cent of the national area and population, became regarded as *the* problem region – a view reinforced by the level of insurgency activity during the late 1960s and proximity to the former Indo-Chinese states. In the South the pattern was more complex, with a sharp decline phase between 1960 and 1972, followed by a partial recovery, related to the expansion of tin, rubber, oil palm and fishing sectors. From 1977 comparable figures become available for the BMR. These reveal that increasingly the most significant disparity is between the BMR and the rest of the Kingdom. This is even more marked if the analysis is undertaken at the level of the individual provinces (Douglass, 1989: 27). Between the regions outside the BMR there is no clear long-term divergence until the late 1980s. Subsequently, the growth of the Eastern region begins to set it apart – a reflection of the development of the Eastern Seaboard and the emergence of the EBMR.

Poverty and income distribution

Since the early 1960s official data, supported by a large number of empirical studies, suggest that the incidence of poverty has fallen in Thailand, while the distribution of wealth has became more polarised, certainly until the early 1990s (Medhi Krongkaew, 1993; Oey Meestok, 1979; Pranee Tinakorn, 1995; Tables 7.2a and 7.3). These conclusions are almost entirely based on the analysis of the sample[1] socio-economic surveys conducted by the National Statistical Office. While these have been little criticised (see however Booth, 1997), considerable debate has surrounded the poverty lines that have been imposed on the NSO data (Medhi Krongkaew *et al.*, 1992: 206–7). In almost every study these were, until 1994, the 1976 lines computed by the World Bank (see Oey Meestok, 1979), adjusted for price changes. However, the increases in the poverty lines were generally rather less than the increase in the consumer price index.[2] In addition, as Medhi Krongkaew *et al.* (1992: 204) have emphasised, the adjusted poverty lines remained tied to the 1976 consumption basket. Given the time period involved a case can be made for adjustments that take account of changes in population structure, nutritional requirements and consumption patterns. On this basis they suggest that for the 1988 survey a more realistic measure of deprivation would result from increasing the level of both the rural and urban poverty lines by some 65 per cent. This would increase the incidence of poverty to 31.2 per cent in urban areas, 55.7 per cent in rural areas and 48.8 per cent for the Kingdom as a whole – thus

Table 7.2a Incidence of poverty by region and area, old poverty lines

Region	Percentage of total population						
	1975–6	1980–1	1985–6	1988–9	1990	1992	1994
North	33.2	21.5	25.5	23.2	16.6	13.6	8.5
villages	36.4	23.3	27.7	25.1	16.3	14.2	8.2
sanitary districts	19.2	16.2	20.2	18.7	24.6	17.3	13.3
municipal areas	17.8	8.0	6.9	11.3	10.3	3.4	3.6
North East	44.9	35.9	48.2	37.5	28.3	22.3	15.7
villages	48.5	37.9	50.5	39.9	28.3	22.2	15.4
sanitary districts	27.4	20.8	33.3	20.1	35.3	31.5	24.3
municipal areas	20.9	18.0	18.7	19.0	17.6	9.6	5.5
Central	13.0	13.6	15.6	16.0	12.9	6.0	5.2
villages	14.3	14.2	17.4	19.0	12.1	6.2	4.7
sanitary districts	8.0	11.6	11.4	6.4	22.1	8.8	8.3
municipal areas	11.5	11.7	8.9	8.4	6.5	1.0	3.8
South	30.7	20.4	27.2	21.5	17.6	11.8	11.7
villages	33.8	22.2	31.2	24.0	18.0	12.6	12.9
sanitary districts	18.1	6.8	8.1	11.5	28.5	14.7	13.2
municipal areas	21.7	15.2	8.6	11.8	9.6	5.5	3.6
BMR	7.8	3.9	3.5	3.4	2.8	1.3	0.8
city core	6.9	3.7	3.1	3.3	2.0	1.1	0.5
Five Provinces	–	–	–	4.3	–	–	–
villages	–	–	–	3.4	1.7	1.7	0.5
sanitary districts	–	–	–	9.6	4.4	1.8	1.5
municipal areas	6.1	10.8	–	8.4	3.0	0.1	0.0
Whole Kingdom	30.0	23.0	29.5	23.7	18.0	13.1	9.6
villages	36.2	27.3	35.8	29.4	20.5	15.5	11.0
sanitary districts	14.8	13.5	18.6	13.2	25.2	16.8	14.0
municipal areas	12.5	7.5	5.9	6.7	5.3	2.4	1.9

Source: National Statistical Office.

Table 7.2b Incidence of poverty by region and area, new poverty lines

Region	Percentage of total population			
	1988	1990	1992	1994
North	31.6	22.8	24.7	12.6
villages	34.1	25.4	8.5	14.4
sanitary districts	24.6	17.8	23.4	5.5
municipal areas	11.5	7.3	3.6	3.0
North East	42.1	33.5	38.0	22.8
villages	45.0	35.7	40.7	25.1
sanitary districts	24.6	17.8	23.8	15.5
municipal areas	20.9	18.0	18.7	19.0
Central	21.7	17.2	11.7	7.5
villages	25.6	19.2	14.2	8.8
sanitary districts	13.2	16.4	6.4	4.0
municipal areas	5.6	5.6	1.2	3.7
South	35.6	29.5	21.9	19.0
villages	40.9	33.1	25.4	22.3
sanitary districts	21.3	23.8	10.8	10.0
municipal areas	11.3	11.0	6.9	3.9
BMR	7.0	3.0	1.7	1.2
city core	2.7	3.2	1.9	0.6
Five Provinces	–	–	–	–
villages	8.8	2.3	3.0	1.5
sanitary districts	2.6	1.6	1.8	1.5
municipal areas	7.4	3.8	0.7	0.0
Whole Kingdom	29.9	23.5	23.1	14.3
villages	37.4	29.2	29.8	18.7
sanitary districts	19.8	16.0	12.6	8.5
municipal areas	12.5	7.5	5.9	6.7

Source: National Statistical Office.

Table 7.3 Income share by population quintile group (% of total income)

Quintile	1975–6	1980–1	1985–6	1988–9	1990	1992	1994
1st	49.26	51.47	55.63	54.62	57.67	59.04	57.52
2nd	20.96	20.64	19.86	20.42	19.26	18.95	19.60
3rd	14.00	13.38	12.09	12.31	11.50	11.06	11.60
4th	9.73	9.10	7.87	8.07	7.38	7.02	7.29
5th	6.05	5.41	4.55	4.56	4.20	3.94	3.99
Total share	100.00	100.00	100.00	100.00	100.00	100.00	100.00
Gini coefficient	0.426	0.453	0.500	0.489	0.522	0.536	0.525

Source: National Statistical Office.

implying a much less dramatic decline in the incidence of poverty since 1976 than is indicated in Table 7.2a. In marked contrast, the World Bank in 1993 provided a revised estimate of poverty levels which suggested a much earlier and more dramatic decline from an incidence of 26 per cent in 1970 to 17 per cent in 1980 and 16 per cent in 1990 (World Bank, 1993c).[3]

The application of two poverty lines – rural and urban – to the entire country became increasingly unsatisfactory. In particular, application of the rural poverty line to the sanitary districts, an increasing number of which were urban in character, tended to deflate both the rural and national incidence of poverty.[4] This reflects the unsatisfactory definition of 'urban' discussed previously (see pp. 20–1). In addition, the application of uniform national poverty lines ignored regional and sub-regional variations in living costs.

In 1994 the NSO substantially revised the poverty lines. As may be seen from Table 7.4, lines were increased markedly, particularly in rural areas (but not as much as was advocated by Medhi Krongkaew *et al.*, 1992), and a separate line provided for sanitary districts. More significantly, the new NSO methodology took account of age, sex, household composition and size in computing consumption needs, while the cost of the needs was adjusted by region and location. The differing combination of these factors results in the application of a hundred different lines (Nanak Kakwani and Medhi Krongkaew, 1996: 9). There is little doubt that the revised lines are a considerable improvement on the old. As well as applying the new lines to the 1994 survey the NSO reworked the 1988, 1990 and 1992 survey material. As may be seen from Table 7.2b, while the applications of the new lines substantially increased the estimates of poverty, overall the pattern of decline was very similar to that revealed by the use of the old lines.

Table 7.4 New and old poverty lines, 1988–94 (in US$/person/month)

	1988	1990	1992	1994
New poverty lines				
municipal	20.76	24.89	28.46	31.29
sanitary district	17.08	18.29	22.59	22.72
village	16.84	18.01	22.32	22.55
Old poverty lines				
urban	20.44	22.78	25.03	27.48
rural	13.44	14.34	16.29	17.36
Percentage differences				
urban	1.5	9.3	13.7	13.9
rural	27.1	27.5	38.6	30.8

Source: NSO; Nanak Kakwani and Medhi Krongkaew (1996: 7).

Whatever the magnitude of the decline in the incidence of poverty, the decline has been very much sharper in urban areas in general and the BMR in particular, certainly until 1992 (Pranee Tinakorn, 1995; Tables 7.2a, 7.2b). Increasingly poverty became regarded as a rural problem: over 90 per cent of the poor lived in rural areas, were dependent on agricultural production and/or labouring opportunities and were poorly educated (Somchai Jitsuchon, 1989: 16–18). In addition, the incidence of poverty varied according to size of settlement and region, with the highest incidence in centres of less than 20,000 and in the North East region (Medhi Krongkaew et al., 1987). In contrast the lowest incidence of poverty was found in the BMR and the Central Region (Medhi Krongkaew et al., 1987). A similar regional pattern also existed for rural poverty and poverty as a whole, with the highest incidence in the North East, followed by the South, North, Centre and the BMR.

The long-term decline in the incidence of poverty was halted during the first half of the 1980s by the recession and related austerity measures (see pp. 111–16). Between 1981 and 1986 there was a sharp increase in the incidence of poverty, and income distribution became markedly more uneven (see Tables 7.2a, 7.2b and 7.3).

Between 1981 and 1986 the income share of the lowest quintile of the population fell from 5.4 per cent to 4.6 per cent (Table 7.3). The average per capita household income of this group declined by 5.5 per cent (Suganya Hutaserani and Pornchai Tapwong, 1990: 9). Allowing for inflation, their real income declined even more than this. At the same time the income share of the top quintile increased from 51.5 per cent to 55.6 per cent (Table 7.3).

The increase in the incidence of poverty between 1981 and 1986 was almost entirely a feature of rural areas. This was closely related to an average 20 per cent fall in price levels of the main agricultural products (Ikemoto, 1992: 215). This situation was compounded by severe drought in 1982–3 and very serious flooding in 1983–4 and the increasing shortage of uncultivated land. As a result agricultural production virtually stagnated. Between 1975 and 1985 agriculture's share of GDP declined from 31.5 to 16.7 per cent while the sector's share of employment only fell from 73 to 67 per cent. As a result the ratio of per capita income in the non-agricultural sector to that of agriculture almost doubled between 1975 and 1985 (Somchai Jitsuchon, 1989: 9). Further, the National Household Expenditure Surveys revealed that between 1981 and 1986 there was an absolute decline in the mean per capita income of agricultural households of 4.4 per cent.

In contrast to the situation in rural areas the incidence of urban poverty continued to decline during the period 1981–6. This reflects the growth of the urban-based manufacturing and service sectors. The ability of the urban population to maintain or increase income has to be balanced against the unknown numbers of migrants who returned to rural areas. The sharp contraction of the construction sector resulted in increasing numbers of labourers returning to rural areas, particularly in the North East. Thus to a degree, urban poverty migrated back to rural areas.

The 1988 National Household Expenditure Survey revealed a sharp decline in the incidence of poverty since 1986. This decline was greatest in rural areas, particularly the North East. In contrast, there was an increase in the incidence of urban poverty, notably in the BMR (Tables 7.2a, 7.2b and 7.5). The overall decline in the incidence of poverty appears to have been accompanied by a reduction in inequality (see Table 7.3). However, this has engendered considerable debate (see e.g. Ikemoto, 1992; Suganya Hutaserani and Pornchai Tapwong, 1990). Some writers consider the reduction in inequality 'slight', and attribute it to the recovery from a recession rather than indicative of a long-term trend. Since 1987 the rise in international and domestic prices for major crops has played an important role in raising rural incomes. The rise in the price of rice has been particularly significant. Higher international prices have possibly been reinforced by the removal of taxes and controls which had substantially reduced domestic prices (see p. 120, 148). In essence the problem is that 1986 was a very depressed year, particularly for the agricultural sector, while 1988 was a comparatively buoyant one.[5] However, the 1990, 1992 and 1994 surveys suggest a further sharp fall in the incidence of poverty (see Table 7.3). Most striking between 1992 and 1994, was the very much sharper decline in rural poverty, particularly in the North East, compared to urban areas. These findings warrant very careful analysis, for it is difficult to isolate factors to explain this sharp fall. It is tempting to conclude that the sustained growth that the Kingdom experienced from the mid-1980s until the mid-1990s has diffused into rural and low income groups. Nanak Kakwani and Medhi Krongkaew (1996: 12) see a variety of elements, including better targeting of regional and rural expenditure by government agencies, increasing rural industrialisation and stable and even falling prices for basic items.

Table 7.5 Percentage share of registered factories, excluding rice mills, 1986–91

Region	1986	1987	1988	1989	1990	1991	1986–91
BMR	54.3	53.9	51.0	49.0	50.2	49.2	46.3
Centre	16.8	16.4	17.3	16.7	17.3	17.6	17.2
North	9.0	9.3	9.8	10.9	10.3	10.6	13.1
North East	12.7	13.0	14.6	15.6	14.8	15.0	17.4
South	7.2	7.4	7.3	7.8	7.4	7.6	6.0
Sub-total	28.9	29.7	31.7	34.3	32.5	33.2	36.5
Total	100.0	100.0	100.0	100.0	100.0	100.0	100.0

Source: Ministry of Industry.

In marked contrast to the long-term decline in the incidence of poverty, the distribution of income became more uneven until the early 1990s (see Table 7.3). There was a general decline in the income shares of the lowest quintile of the population and an increase in the share of the top 20 per cent. Similarly there was a steady increase in the level of disparity as measured by the gini coefficient. Between 1992 and 1994 there was a slight increase in the income share of the lowest quintile and a rather larger decline in the share of the top quintile. In addition, there was a decline in the level of inequality as measured by the gini coefficient. It may be that these changes are the beginning of a reversal of the long-term trend.

Against the evidence of the NSO data for very sharp declines in the incidence of poverty has to be set the possibility that there is a large and rapidly growing population of unrecorded migrants within the EBMR. As has already been suggested, the population of Bangkok and the incidence of slum dwelling may both have been underestimated (see Banasopit Mekvichai *et al.*, 1990: 16; p. 20, 193, 208–10). It seems highly probable that large numbers of recent migrants have also failed to find regular employment or accommodation. In addition, there has undoubtedly been a substantial rise in the level of informal sector activity.

The extent to which the BMR-based boom has diffused into rural and provincial areas is far from clear. For rural communities the most likely benefit is through remittance income and seasonal migration. A study of rural incomes by Suganya Hutaserani and Somchai Jitsuchon (1988) concluded that a significant distinction could be made between the poor who were dependent on local labouring income, and the less poor who received remittance income. More direct impact on the rural sector is more limited and difficult to assess. Some of the growth in exports involves the use of agricultural products. In addition, contract farming has developed in the North and North East to supply both the export trade and the burgeoning Bangkok 'super markets' with graded, packaged produce to supply the needs of the growing and increasingly Westernised urban middle class. There has been some growth of industrial production in provincial centres.

The long-term expansion of GDP, including the acceleration of growth since the mid-1980s, has delivered social benefits mainly in the form of new employment opportunities rather than in general improvement in the living standards of the bottom 20 per cent of income distribution – certainly until the 1992–4 period. In this respect Thailand's experience does not appear to differ substantially from that of Indonesia, the Philippines and Malaysia (see McFarlane, 1988: 133).

The limited spread of the benefits of growth through the lower income groups in part reflects the weak bargaining position of workers. Except for brief periods, trade unions in Thailand have been weak, fragmented and heavily repressed. The weakness of organised labour has been reinforced by the persistence of high levels of unemployment and under-employment and the still comparatively small and fragmented nature of the working class (Schmidt, 1994: 15).

Regional policy, urban growth and dispersal

Under the Sixth (1987–91) and more especially the Seventh (1992–6) National Plans the issue of widening regional disparity was given considerable prominence. One of the three objectives of the Sixth Plan was to 'Increase the distribution of income and prosperity into provincial and rural areas' (NESDB, 1987: 6). Similarly, a central concern of the Seventh Plan was the 'redistribution of income and the decentralisation of development to the regions and rural areas' (NESDB, 1992: 4–5). However, the Seventh Plan also admits that the dispersal of infrastructural facilities to the regions had to date been 'quite limited' (NESDB, 1992: 121). More significantly, as was noted in Chapter 6 (p. 213), planners and politicians appear to have accepted that the BMR will continue to play the key role in national economic development. The continued rapid growth of the BMR is not seen as a major policy issue (Douglass, 1989: 39). This despite the costs associated with pollution, congestion, population growth and the extension of the urban area outlined in Chapter 6.

Given that the slowing down of the growth of the BMR is not a policy objective *per se*, regional inequalities can only be addressed through the stimulation of provincial growth. This indeed has been the basis of all Thai policy towards the spatial distribution of economic activity and living standards since the early 1960s. However, as Douglass has stressed, given the concentration of growth in the BMR 'the task of creating incentives which will be sufficient to attract new, often foreign-operated, industries to locate away from the national core and in these more distant provinces is a formidable task' (1989: 40).

While all the National Plans have contained a regional element few effective policies have been implemented. Under the First (1962–6) and Second (1967–71) Plans there was little beyond some regional targeting of expenditure, particularly for infrastructure (see pp. 82–3). However, the overall programmes of infrastructural development tended to enhance the primary position of Bangkok (Phisit Pakkesem, 1979: 21).

As was noted in Chapter 3, the need for a fuller regional planning policy was recognised under the Second Plan (1967–72). This stemmed, in particular, from increasing concern over the deteriorating security situation in the North East. Detailed regional plans were commissioned for the North East, North and later, the South, for implementation during the Third Plan (1971–6). In the event these varied considerably in quality, and little that they contained was implemented. However, they did serve to highlight the strengths, weaknesses and possibilities of the outer regions.

In the North East planning on a provincial level was initiated in 1969 under the coordination of the North Eastern Regional Planning Centre (NERPC) located at Khon Kaen. These plans were to be ready for implementation under the Third Plan. They were to coordinate agencies working in the provinces and to identify and implement projects. In the event their value was greatly reduced by the lack of experienced staff and necessary resources at provincial level. This attempt to establish 'people's development ideas . . . and . . . people's wants and needs . . . ' (NERPC, n.d.: 13) proved to be little more than window dressing.

In 1971 the Department of Urban and Regional Planning was set up within NEDB. This department initially developed the use of 'growth centres' or 'growth axes' which had received passing reference in the Second Plan (see Figure 7.1). This approach was built on under the Third Plan (1972–6), which outlined a strategy aimed at encouraging the relocation of industry and a variety of urban-based functions to nine provincial growth centres. It was envisaged that these centres would attract growth which would then disseminate through the surrounding region. Due to budgetary constraints, reduced rural insurgency and the rapidly changing political and policy environments of the Plan period the growth pole strategy was not implemented until the Fourth Plan (1977–81).

The growth of the regional centres was expected to take place through attracting industry as a result of (rather limited) public investment in urban infrastructure, including the construction of industrial estates, the BOI incentives and the lower land and labour costs of the provincial areas. The conspicuous lack of success resulted in a switch under the Fifth Plan (1982–6) to an emphasis on local resource-oriented activities and small enterprises which provided services for agriculture. Under this approach much was made of the comparative advantage of the provincial centres.

Under the Fifth Plan there was also the beginnings of a shift towards the promotion of 'urban industrial regions', starting with the Eastern Seaboard (see Figure 6.2, p. 201). In these the government was assigned the task of creating favourable conditions for private investment in industry and service, by providing the physical infrastructure. However, the economic crisis of the early 1980s and the difficulty of either raising large international loans or attracting substantial private investment severely limited such developments. Despite this, and overall policy changes which from the mid-1980s onwards expected major infrastructural projects to be substantially privately funded (see pp. 117–18), two more urban-industrial regions were demarcated: under the Sixth Plan (1987–91) the Upper South Region (comprising Surat Thani, Phuket, Krabi and Phangnga), and under the Seventh Plan (1992–6) the Upper Central Region (see Figure 6.2, p. 201). The later plan also commented on the need to establish 'other economic zones' (NESDB, 1992: 121).

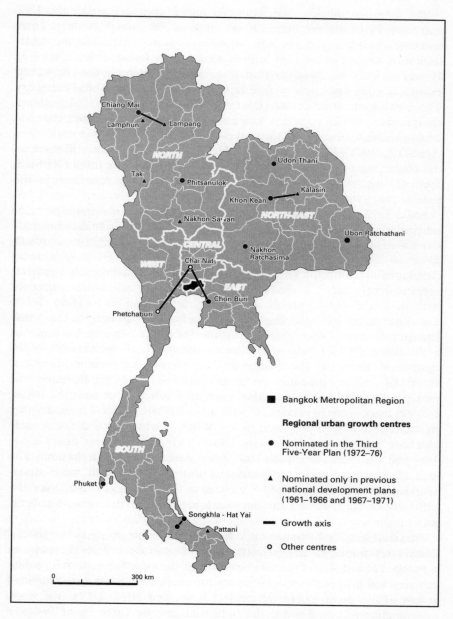

Figure 7.1 Growth centres and axis under the Third National Plan (1972–6).
Source: NESDB.

The adoption of an urban industrial region approach under the Fifth and Sixth Plans did not diminish the emphasis on growth centres. There was considerable expansion in the number of centres, including the delimitation of 'second generation centres' and 'border towns' (see Figure 7.2). However, with the Seventh Plan there was a general retreat from the growth centres approach in favour of a more broadly regional strategy. The division of urban centres used under the Sixth Plan was abandoned; centres were rather regarded as members of a series of 'urban clusters', with emphasis placed on the development of linkages between them (NESDB, 1987: 307–15; Figure 7.3). However, this approach still involved the classifying of centres according to their economic potential (NESDB, 1991: 91), and while more diffuse in its approach than the previous growth pole strategy it remained firmly urban centred.

Since 1972 the BOI has provided extra incentives for firms locating in particular areas outside Bangkok. From the mid-1980s the BOI has divided the Kingdom into three zones, with progressively higher levels of incentives away from the BMR (see Figure 7.4). However, despite these developments, until the late 1980s the location of BOI-promoted projects remained very much a secondary issue. The BOI was more concerned with the scale and nature of investment rather than its location. While the other agencies were charged with industrial promotion, the Small Industry Finance Office (SIFO) and the Industrial Finance Corporation of Thailand (IFCT) have been more concerned with promotion in the peripheral areas of the Kingdom; they have also heavily favoured the BMR and its immediate environs (Parnwell, 1992: 55). Similarly, the majority of industrial estates have been established in or near the BMR. In 1993 there were 54 estates, 44 within the EBMR. While a large number of estates have been proposed in the North, North East and South, only two have become operational – the Lamphun Industrial Estate near Chiang Mai and the Suranaree Industrial Zone near Nakhon Ratchasima. The lack of infrastructure in the provincial area makes it much more expensive to develop estates, and remoteness from Bangkok increases the difficulty of coordinating the necessary activities of the various government agencies.

The failure of industrial estates to develop in the provincial areas is a further illustration of the ineffectiveness of centralised Thai planning. In a number of instances the announcement of the establishment of an estate has resulted in speculators purchasing the available land and pushing land prices to the point where the project is shelved. This reflects the weak coordinating role assigned to the Industrial Estates Authority of Thailand (IEAT), and the continued unsatisfactory nature of the interaction of government agencies with the private sector. In the provincial areas it is extremely difficult to coordinate the establishment of an estate without the involvement of the IEAT, but the standards required by the IEAT

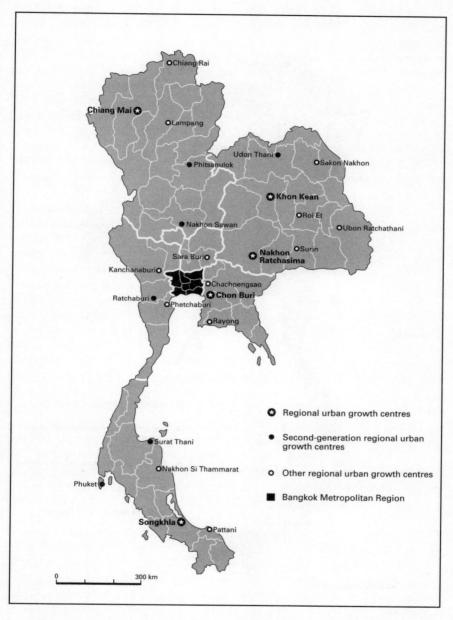

Figure 7.2 Regional urban growth centres under the Sixth National Plan (1986–90).
Source: NESDB.

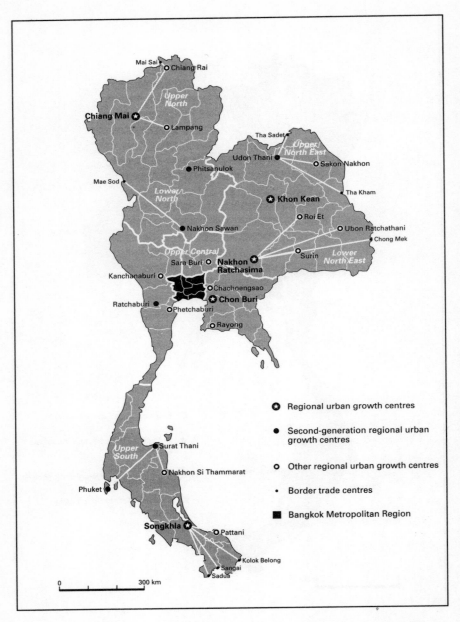

Legend (in map):
- ✪ Regional urban growth centres
- ● Second-generation regional urban growth centres
- ○ Other regional urban growth centres
- · Border trade centres
- ■ Bangkok Metropolitan Region

Figure 7.3 Regional urban clusters and growth centres under the Seventh National
Plan (1992–6).

Source: NESDB.

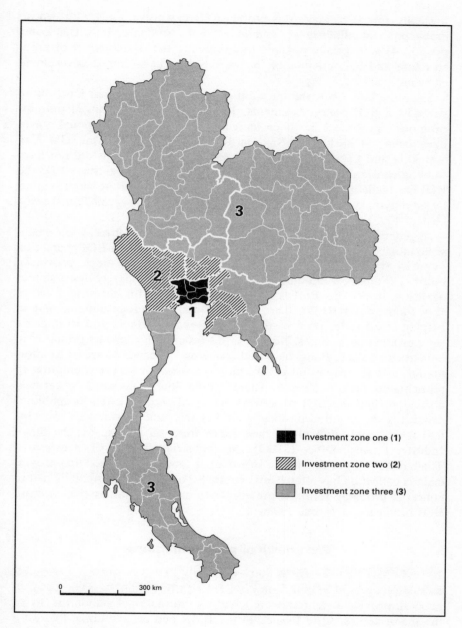

Figure 7.4 Investment zones, 1993.

Source: Board of Investment.

normally appear to make this prohibitively expensive. Only with considerable political influence (see comments on the Surenaree Industrial Zone, pp. 233–4) is it usually possible to coordinate the development of infrastructure and the activities of the various Bangkok-centred government agencies.

Since the late 1980s the question of location has featured much more strongly in BOI policy statements. The number of industries eligible for promotion in Zone 3 has been increased, and since 1988 regional offices have been established at Nakhon Ratchasima, Chiang Mai, Hat Yai/Songkhla and Laem Chabang. As a result, promoted firms did not have to be in constant contact with the BOI offices in Bangkok. Since 1993 the BOI has made greater efforts to attract investment into the outer regions by simplifying procedures and increasing incentives (*Bangkok Post Weekly*, 20 Jan. 1993).

In general the BOI has favoured large-scale modern firms, while small-scale indigenous concerns have found it difficult to obtain BOI promotion (Venzky-Stalling, 1993: 16). Given the structure of much provincial industry (Somsak Tambunlertchai, 1990), this policy clearly discriminates against it. In 1992 the BOI established the BOI Unit for Industrial Linkage Development (BUILD). This was essentially a programme aimed at helping small-scale concerns to find large-scale partners and to upgrade their production facilities. However, this programme appears primarily to benefit small-scale, Bangkok-based concerns – because of access to information and the extension of the three-year corporate tax exemption to participating firms in Zone 1. There is little doubt that small concerns in all regions find the BOI paperwork daunting and are often incapable of producing the required business plan. For the same reason such concerns find it extremely difficult to raise funds from such bodies as the Small Industry Finance Office (SIFO), the Industrial Finance Corporation of Thailand (IFCT) or the banks. However, it should be stressed that provincial tax collection has often been extremely lax. Thus some small industrial concerns probably found it preferable to avoid tax rather than acquire BOI privileges or formal financing.

The growth of provincial centres

In 1991 apart from the BMA there were only 25 urban centres[6] with populations of over 50,000, and only nine with more than 100,000. Thus, in general, provincial centres were small by international standards. Six of the major centres were located in the BMR and an additional five were in the Extended Metropolitan Region (see pp. 200–3). With the exception of some of the centres in the EBMR, provincial growth continues to rest very heavily on collection and processing functions for primary – principally agricultural produce. This pattern of growth has been reinforced by the expansion of tourism, most strikingly in the case of Chiang Mai, and cross-border trade, most significant in the case of the southern centres of Hat Yai and Songkhla. Similarly, the development of trade and communications with Laos and Cambodia is beginning to stimulate the development of such border towns as Arayphatet, Savannakhet and Nong Khai (see pp. 255–8).

As was noted in Chapter 5, the rapid expansion of the industrial sector that has taken place since the early 1980s has been heavily concentrated in the BMR and its immediate environs. In consequence there has been a continued decline in the proportion of gross industrial product originating outside the BMR from 38 per cent in 1986 to 24 per cent in 1990. However, since the mid-1980s there has been a gradual increase in the proportion of industrial establishments locating in the peripheral regions, particularly the North East, and to a lesser extent, the North (see Table 7.5, p. 221). There has also, since 1987, been a general increase in the proportion of BOI-promoted projects located in the outer regions (Table 7.6). These have been predominately Thai-owned concerns, oriented towards primary products and/or the local market.

The increase in the proportion of factories operating in the outer regions of the Kingdom has to be set against the decline of established industry in the wake of improved communications and the integration of the national market (Biggs *et al.*, 1990: 4). Much small-scale, frequently unregistered, manufacturing activity has almost certainly disappeared.

There is no one reason for the increase in the number of provincial industrial plants. It is unlikely, for example, that the BOI incentives in isolation have played a major role (Biggs *et al.*, 1990). Similarly, there is little evidence of genuine relocation of manufacturing from the BMR (Parnwell, 1992: 55). Provincial industrial growth, certainly during the late 1980s, has generally been seen as part of the rapid economic growth that Thailand has experienced since the mid-1980s (Chesada Loha-unchit, 1990; Ichikawa, 1990). It is probable that the BOI incentives have only been effective at the margin, where they might well just 'tip the balance'. Experience elsewhere points to the general ineffectiveness of this type of incentive policy unless it is reinforcing firms' natural inclinations, or the value of the package is extremely high (Biggs *et al.*, 1990: 76).

There is as yet little evidence that new investment is locating in provincial areas because of rising costs and congestion in the BMR, and the emergence of considerable regional differences in land and labour costs. Indeed, it has been asserted that in general the differences in such costs between the outer parts of the BMR and the main provincial centres appear to be insufficient to offset the disadvantages of these locations for anything but primary processing and packaging (Luxmon Wongsuphasawat, 1997: 212–13; Pradit Charsombut, 1990). Given the nature of provincial markets and communications, locations outside the

Table 7.6 Percentage regional distribution of projects approved by the Board of Investment, 1960–91

Region[a]	1960–73	1974–8	1979–83	1984–6	1987	1988	1989	1990	1991
Bangkok and Inner ring	77.4	68.7	62.7	55.7	72.1	44.7	45.7	43.0	31.7
Outer ring	6.9	11.3	9.9	15.2	12.0	24.1	27.7	26.9	25.4
Rest of centre[b]	3.0	2.0	4.9	7.8	5.1	9.5	7.7	8.4	12.1
Total	87.3	72.0	75.5	78.7	89.5	78.2	81.0	78.3	69.2
North	5.3	7.0	5.7	5.3	2.2	3.2	6.2	7.5	9.1
North East	2.5	2.3	3.8	3.6	1.9	2.3	4.8	5.7	10.6
South	4.9	8.7	12.7	11.8	6.2	16.2	7.6	8.5	11.1
Total	12.7	19.0	20.3	19.7	10.3	21.7	18.6	21.7	30.8
Unknown	0.0	0.0	0.2	0.6	0.5	0.1	0.3	0.0	0.0
National total	100.0	100.0	100.0	100.0	100.0	100.0	100.0	100.0	100.0

Source: Board of Investment.
Notes
a see figure 6.1, p. 191
b includes rest of East and West regions

BMR and its immediate environs continues to pose problems for concerns geared to international or extensive domestic markets. The limited size of the secondary cities and the frequently poor inter-provincial transport linkages mean provincial markets remain small in size and frequently better served from the BMR. A study of provincial industry by Somsak Tambunlertchai (1990) revealed that it was overwhelmingly dependent on local markets, with very limited exporting to other provinces.

The many facets of recent provincial industrial expansion are illustrated by the rapid growth of Nakhon Ratchasima, which since the early 1980s has exceeded that of Songkhla-Hat Yai – to make it the Kingdom's second city.

While the rapid growth of Nakhon Ratchasima since the early 1980s can be related to the acceleration of growth nationally, there is little evidence of an influx of investment or enterprise from elsewhere in the Kingdom or from overseas before 1990 (Ueda, 1992: 353). During the late 1980s the national 'boom' conditions stimulated local investment. From 1988 onwards the construction of several high-class hotels, two major department stores and a 23-storey office and shopping complex were initiated. The Suranaree Industrial Zone, completed in 1989, was again locally and privately owned, although it did receive official support through local MPs, including the then Prime Minister, Chatchai Choonhaven. There is little doubt that links to prominent politicians is of great importance in facilitating the development of provincial projects and boosting the confidence of investors (Ueda, 1992: 354–5). This is highlighted by the difficulties generally attendant on the establishment of provincial industrial estates and the general failure of proposals elsewhere in the North East. However, it should be stressed that Nakhon Ratchasima is regarded as the 'gateway' to the North East (and from there into Laos), and is relatively close to Sarburi and comparatively well linked to the BMR and the Eastern Seaboard. Thus it should be seen as a particularly favourable provincial location.

A manufacturing sector has long been established in Nakhon Ratchasima. However, apart from the agricultural processing and silk manufacture this has been small in scale and closely linked to local and regional needs. During the late 1980s the expansion of the manufacturing sector concentrated on the established agricultural processing sector – particularly cassava – motor vehicle assembly and the manufacture of gears and shafts and the production of such items as batteries for local and regional markets. Comparatively high-tech production was confined to one engineering plant which employed c. 300 workers and exported about half its production to the USA, Europe and Singapore (Ueda, 1992: 362).

From 1989 the national export-orientated boom stimulated one investor to develop production facilities on the Suranaree Industrial Estate for the production of parts for construction vehicles, mainly for export to Europe

(Ueda, 1992: 363). This development was followed by an influx of small Japanese and Taiwanese plants. By 1992 there were 25 such plants established on the Suranaree Industrial Estate, assembling a wide range of products, principally for export. In addition, there has been some influx of Thai investment, most notably the 50 per cent partnership between local interests and the Dusit Group (Thailand's largest hotel chain) over the construction of the Royal Hotel.

Behind the twists and turns of Thai regional development policy lies a consistent view, namely that decentralisation and provincial growth will result from a combination of market forces and limited government intervention. Douglass (1989: 41) has argued that under this situation, decentralisation, if it occurs at all, is likely to be in coastal areas where port facilities have already been developed and at international borders where there are substantial cross-border differences in factor prices. Thus he concluded from a comparative study of regional inequality that:

> In the case of Thailand, with the exception of Chon Buri, there are as yet no obvious candidates to become the Pusan, Kaohsiung, or Penang of Thailand: nor are the factor and commodity prices at border markets great enough to suppose that Thailand's border towns will act as significant growth poles on the order of Malaysia's Johore. Such developments can be pursued, however, but with the understanding that the overall approach is one of following a number of avenues rather than resting expectations for decentralisation on one pathway.
>
> (Douglass, 1989: 41)

A major weakness of all the regional policies has been a lack of expenditure and meaningful incentives to counter the 'pull' of the BMR and the disadvantages of provincial locations. Despite this, since the late 1970s a number of provincial centres have generally grown quite impressively, including ones not designated as growth centres. In this it is difficult to attribute more than a marginal role to the various facets of regional policy. In addition, the expansion of such centres as Chiang Mai and Nakhon Ratchasima has since the early 1980s begun to duplicate in miniature the problems that have afflicted Bangkok – a reflection of the fact that Thailand's urban planning mechanisms are, if anything, less effective in provincial centres.

The rural and non-industrial alternatives

The reduction of regional inequalities in Thailand has been principally viewed in terms of the promotion of urban-based industrial development. Similarly, the reduction in the incidence of poverty and the level of

personal income inequalities has been expected to take place almost solely as a result of sustained rapid urban-industrial growth. However, given that over 70 per cent of the Thai population is resident in rural areas, the promotion of agriculture and rural industry would appear to offer considerable potential for the redressing of personal and regional income inequalities. In addition, such developments might slow the rate of migration into the EBMR. While the growth of employment in the predominantly BMR-based industrial sector has been an impressive 3 million between 1980 and 1992, in the same period the labour force increased by 6.9 million. These levels of growth would not provide for the large-scale relocation of people into the urban sector that is expected by the early part of the next century, particularly since the official agricultural labour force is still expanding (see Table 1.9, p. 12; Somboon Siriprachai, 1995).[7] The rapid growth of the BMR is (as outlined on p. 203, 211–12) posing major problems for services, housing and welfare. In addition, as was suggested earlier, it seems likely that large numbers of recent migrants into the EBMR have failed to find anything but irregular and uncertain means of support. Thus there are compelling arguments for programmes that will generate rural employment in order to raise incomes and to slow the outflow of migrants. However, against this has to be set the low level of government support that such programmes have received in Thailand and elsewhere.

Ammar Siamwalla (1989, 1993) stressed that Thai agriculture retains considerable comparative advantage and has the potential to bolster national growth and generate rural incomes. Similarly, Dapice and Flatters (1989) have refuted the view that Thai agriculture can no longer play a leading role in economic growth and poverty reduction. A number of studies have indeed emphasised the way in which rural development by increasing rural incomes raises demand for goods and services and thereby promotes urban-based activities (Grandstaff, 1990; Suganya Hutasarani and Somchai Jitasuchon, 1988). Thus for such writers the development of the rural 'hinterlands' became as important as investment in the urban centres (Douglass, 1989: 42). However, while in no way denying the potential for the agricultural sector making a major contribution to the reduction of regional inequalities, such a development would involve a major reorientation of Thai development policy.

The seasonal nature of much agricultural activity and the continued importance of rural craft activities has been seen by a number of writers to form the basis for a variety of rural industries (Parnwell, 1991, 1992, 1993; Parnwell and Suranart Khamanarong, 1990). Particular attention has focused on the development of traditional craft products for the tourist and export markets. This has been developed most fully in parts of the Chiang Mai Basin, initially to supply the Chiang Mai tourist industry, but increasingly sold in other centres and exported. However, the still strong craft traditions of the North East perhaps have even greater potential (Parnwell, 1992, 1993; Parnwell and Suranart Khamanarong, 1990).

At Ban Chiang, in the North East, where archeological discoveries[8] have attracted tourists, local potters have begun to manufacture pots and ornaments which imitate those exhibited at the excavations for sale to tourists. Similarly, in Nakhon Ratchasima province village potters have expanded and diversified their products, shipping them in particular to Bangkok. In Yasathon province cushion makers have developed new products which are exported to the Middle East. On a larger scale silk production in Chon Na Bot (Khon Kaen province) has expanded, adopting more modern techniques to produce non-traditional designs in small factory units.

There has been some limited development of sub-contracting from provincial-based factories. However, such activities are extremely labour intensive and 'low tech' – for example, fishing net manufacture in Khon Kaen Changwat (cited by Parnwell, 1993). More skill intensive is the sub-contracting of hand-woven silk from the factories in the Paktongchai district of Nakhon Ratchasima.

In a rather different category is the cutting of zirconite for the jewellery trade which has developed in the North East since the early 1980s. This labour-intensive and extremely hazardous activity is a genuine example of an urban-based activity which has located in a rural area. However, gemstone cutting is an atypical activity given the low bulk and high value of both the imported raw material and the final product, the low cost of setting up a cutting workshop and the booming demand for the product.

All of these types of developments have been the product of a small number of entrepreneurs (Parnwell, 1992: 58). Under the Fifth and Sixth Plans there was increased official interest in rural industry, marked by the setting up of the Rural Industry Fund in 1988. This has not been accompanied by any notable state-based programme of rural industrial development.

Since the early 1990s a number of private business programmes aimed at the rural sector have attracted considerable attention. These include an 'adopt a village' scheme, through which a number of companies, such as Bata, have established rural-based production units. Whether the upgrading of the national transport system, continued with rising costs and congestion in the BMR will make these initiatives the norm, remains to be seen. That there is some potential is not in doubt. Indeed, as was noted on p. 226 the BOI believes that the lower cost of some provincial centres could attract activities that would otherwise locate in Vietnam or the PRC.

While none of these developments can be seen as a panacea for the problems of provincial and rural areas, all have some potential. There is a clear need to coordinate these alternative rural strategies with the established urban ones. In Thailand, like most other Asian countries, these activities have been highly separate.

Conclusion

The extremely high level of regional and personal income inequality that prevails in Thailand reflects long-established trends which government policy has done little to halt. In this respect the Thai experience is by no means unique: policies aimed at redressing regional imbalance and income inequalities tend to be implemented in a partial and under-funded manner and run counter to much more vigorous and fully funded policies that promote disparities. However, the current level of disparity must be viewed as a potentially destabilising element in the Kingdom's pattern of growth. The unevenness of development is exacting a high social cost which could easily lead to economic dislocation, social tension and political unrest (for an overview see Rabibhadana, 1993).

Concern over the Kingdom's extremely uneven pattern of development has been expressed by successive governments and National Plans. However, these statements and planning commitments remain essentially rhetoric with little substance behind them. In practice, central government policy remains weak with little concern for distributional issues. Under the Eighth Plan (1997–2001) the emphasis has shifted to the development of 'human resources', with a proviso that this does not mean that the 'development areas', such as the North East, will be neglected (*Australia Thailand Business Council Bulletin*, Dec. 1996: 1).

For the rural poor it is perhaps not too extreme to suggest that government policy comprises little more than limited targeting of the poorest areas and the tolerance of increasing NGO activity. It is little exaggeration to suggest that the only things that the government is offering the rural poor are the receipt of remittance income and relocation to the BMR and adjacent areas.

At the regional level policies not only remain weak, but also highly fragmented. While all the current approaches outlined in this chapter may be expected to have *some* effect on the level of disparities, no one measure is likely to make an overwhelming contribution. Less optimistically, the current set of policies are unlikely to result in any major shift in the spatial patterns of growth or relocation of manufacturing activity under prevailing central government policy towards development and national administration. As with the problems of congestion and inadequate infrastructure in the BMR, discussed in Chapter 6, the solutions rest ultimately on the state becoming much more interventionist and effective (see Chapter 8 for a fuller discussion). In addition to a higher level of state activity there is a need for a much broader and more integrated approach to the promotion of growth in the peripheral areas. While under the Seventh Plan provincial centres were regarded as members of urban clusters rather than individual growth centres, the strategy remains firmly urban orientated. However, as Douglass (1989: 47) has argued, an effective policy towards the peripheral regions necessitates the treatment of urban and rural areas as an integrated whole.[9] Such an approach is entirely contrary to the monolithic and highly centralised Thai administrative structure, under which the activities of the various ministries, departments and agencies are securely compartmentalised and firmly controlled from Bangkok. The statements in the Seventh Plan which suggest that the administrations of provincial centres will have a role in regional planning means little in isolation from reform of the overall national bureaucratic system. To date, despite a variety of official statements and announcements of policy changes which purport to promote local, provincial or regional participation in planning, their effective input has remained extremely limited (Rigg, 1991c; see however, Hewison, 1993a). Many Bangkok-based departments and ministries request annual plans from the provinces, but continue to draw up plans centrally in advance of the receipt of the provincial statements. The centrally produced policies are then disseminated to the provincial areas for implementation.

8

THAILAND IN THE LATE
1990s

Introduction

From the mid-1980s until 1996 Thailand experienced a period of remarkable economic growth and structural change. This final chapter places these developments in the broader historical, national and international context, and reviews the issues and prospects for the sustainability of the present pattern of development. The question of the sustainability of Thailand's economic growth was brought into sharp relief by the 1997 financial crisis.

During 1996 the almost zero growth of export earnings, widening balance of payments deficit, the rapidly mounting private-sector debt, increasing short-term speculative capital movements, and the over-heating of the property and financial sectors were giving particular cause for concern. During the later part of 1996 speculative pressure on the baht began to mount – a reflection of its degree of linkage with the US dollar and the size of the current account deficit – which resulted in a massive intervention by the Bank of Thailand. The attempt to support the currency was doomed to failure and on 2 July the baht was placed on a managed float. This resulted in an almost immediate 20 per cent depreciation and a further 26 per cent by September.

The currency crisis was accompanied by the virtual collapse of the property and stock markets. The depth of the crisis, as in 1980–1, necessitated an approach to the IMF for substantial financial assistance. Agreement on a US$17.7 billion rescue package was reached in July 1997.[1]

The 1997 crisis brought an abrupt halt to Thailand's decade of rapid growth. The problem may be short term, reflecting institutional weaknesses that failed adequately to regulate the financial sector or manage the economy. However, the crisis has thrown into sharp relief a variety of long-term structural problems stemming in the main from the rapid period of growth. Again some commentators have seen these as inevitable side effects of development that will be corrected in the longer term. However, the sharp cuts in government expenditure and public and private

239

investment reduce the possibility of the needed developments in such areas as labour training and infrastructure.

It is against these longer term problems and regional prospects that the 1997 crisis and the tough conditions that the IMF has attached to the funding agreement must be seen. While the Thai economy has long shown remarkable resilience and dynamism, there are signs that many of the targets will be very difficult to meet. On a more optimistic note, the general economic situation during the early 1980s was regarded as grave and the problems deep-seated. Despite a failure to meet many of the IMF targets the Thai economy exhibited a remarkable recovery.

The long-term pattern of growth

From the mid-nineteenth century until the 1930s the integration of Thailand into the global economy and the related development of capitalist relations of production took place very largely as an informal part of the British Imperial structure. During this period Thailand came to exhibit many characteristics common to the neighbouring colonial economies. In general, Western control of the Thai economy appears to have been less complete and less intense than in the colonial possessions. In particular, Western economic activity was not supported by the establishment of a colonial state which promoted infrastructure, access to resources and controls over labour. A considerable measure of indigenous control remained which inhibited Western activity and, to a degree, controlled the nature and speed of economic and social change. Particularly with respect to the form that the non-colonial Thai state took and the developmental and political priorities that it set, the differences between Thailand and the colonial regimes were more than matters of degree.

It has become generally accepted that during the colonial period there was a marked increase in the unevenness of development in South East Asia (Dixon and Drakakis-Smith, 1997; Kirk, 1990). However, in many respects development in Thailand became markedly more uneven than was the case in the neighbouring colonial regimes. It is tempting to make a very direct link between Thailand's unusual 'informal' or 'partial colonial' experience and the extreme form that development took. As has been discussed with respect to such areas as agriculture and the urban sector, there is a wide range of material that is suggestive of linkages. However, as Falkus (1993) has emphasised, the *exact* relationship between Thailand's long-term development, distinctive interaction with the international economy and present patterns of growth and change remain far from fully understood.

Until *c.* 1980, Thailand's economic growth rested very firmly on the extensive exploitation of natural resources, principally land, and to a lesser extent timber, minerals and marine products. Increased agricultural production resulted principally from the extension of the area cultivated. While there was significant diversification into export crops such as maize and cassava there was little intensification of production. This was a reflection of the comparative abundance of uncultivated land, unreliable environmental conditions and limited investment in water control. The availability of land and ease of access to it enabled a much higher proportion of the population to remain in the agricultural sector than would be expected from the rising level of per capita GDP. The sustained growth of the agricultural sector supplied rising export earnings and steady growth of GDP with little direct investment, simply by the application of labour to land. At the same time the state extracted considerable surplus from the agricultural sector in the form of taxation, in particular of rice exports. The agricultural sector was thus the Kingdom's main engine of growth and a major source of government revenue. From the late 1970s the agricultural and fishery sectors entered a new stage of development involving new, more highly processed and higher value products. The resource-based pattern of growth was reinforced from the 1950s onwards by the development of a major import substituting industrial sector and during the 1970s by the growth of tourism and remittance income from overseas workers.

The declining importance of, and increasing problems associated with, the primary sector can be read as indicative of the closing of the intensive resource exploitation phase of Thailand's economic development. However, the primary sector continues to make a major contribution to the domestic and export economies. More significantly, the majority of the population remain directly involved in primary activities.

From the late 1970s the manufacturing sector, particularly textiles, began to turn increasingly towards the export markets. However, the rapid expansion of manufactured exports from the early 1980s onwards has to be seen against changes in the broad Pacific Asian economy and Thailand's position within it. As was suggested in the conclusion to Chapter 4 the continuation of Thailand's pattern of rapid growth appears to be heavily dependent on these broader interactions, the developmental role of the Thai state and the interrelated issue of political stability.

The Thai state and development

During the late nineteenth and early twentieth centuries the Thai state took a lead in promoting reform, establishing a modern legal and bureaucratic system and constructing infrastructure, notably rail and telegraph links. Between 1932 and 1957 the state actively promoted industrialisation through direct participation in production and protectionist policies. Subsequently, however, successive Thai governments have been the least interventionist of any in South East Asia. The developmental role of the

Thai state was increasingly restricted to one of fostering domestic and foreign private enterprise. The government provided infrastructure and attempted to create a secure and attractive environment for investment. The establishment, since the early 1960s, of planning structures at all levels gives the impression that development is highly coordinated and regulated. In practice Thai planning has proved singularly ineffective (see e.g. Ammar Siamwalla, 1993; Demaine, 1986).

Since the late 1950s Thai development policy has relied heavily on conservative monetary and fiscal policies to control inflation and manage the balance of payments (Booth, 1993: 3). Until the late 1970s these policies were comparatively successful in maintaining a stable economic environment. However, the external shocks of the late 1970s and early 1980s revealed significant weaknesses in the macro-control of the economy, particularly with respect to fiscal matters and the control of credit (World Bank, 1980b).

While the level of government expenditure has been substantially lower than that of Malaysia, it has been markedly higher than in Indonesia and the Philippines. However, unlike Malaysia, and to a lesser extent, Indonesia, Thai governments have not found it necessary to devote significant resources to redistributive policies with respect to either personal wealth or the spatial pattern of economic growth.[2] The public sector has remained small in size with limited direct control over production. From the late 1950s onwards a variety of measures were introduced to control prices, minimum wage levels and the marketing of certain commodities. However, these were far from firmly enforced and the controls over the economy remained weak, particularly in comparison to the other ASEAN and East Asian Newly Industrialising economies.

Overall, there have been few signs of any coordinated development strategy (Ammar Siamwalla, 1993). This despite the implementation of National Plans since 1960 under the centralised control of the National Economic and Social Development Board, and the establishment of planning structures and mechanisms at all levels. There has been a general favouring of industrial growth and a neglect of the agricultural sector other than as a source of labour, food, raw materials and revenue. Beyond this there have been few signs of any clear sectoral policies. There has been no question of the state following the Asian NIE pattern of 'picking winners' and actively promoting them. The lack of coordination is rooted in the comparative independence, within the constraints of budgets, of the various government departments, ministries and agencies.

For most of the post-war period successive Thai governments have explicitly promoted industry while implicitly discouraging agriculture. The heavy taxation and general neglect of the agricultural sector contrasts with the promotion of industry, particularly from the 1950s onwards. However, it is important to stress that the discrimination against agriculture was never clearly stated in planning documents. Further, the policies were far from consistent. Certain commodities threatened by imports did receive favourable treatment, notably sugar, oil seeds, cotton and dairy produce. In addition, even within the rice sector, policies were at times contradictory – price support and state purchasing schemes being implemented when low international prices compounded the effect of the export tax on farm incomes.

Overall, the neglect and heavy taxation of the rice sector in particular, reinforced the pattern of extensive cultivation, accelerating the clearance of increasingly marginal and unsuitable land and thereby deforestation, declining yields, soil erosion and the passing of land out of cultivation. However, until c. 1980 the agricultural sector remained the foundation of Thai economic growth. Government policies succeeded in transferring resources from the agricultural sector, but failed to discourage productivity or undermine the sector's international competitiveness.

Within the individual departments, ministries and agencies, policies are not only highly independent but also tend to be centralised and paternalistic. This is particularly apparent in the agricultural sector. The Ministry of Agriculture has long taken a highly paternalistic view of farmers, instructing them in what to plant and what not to – the former usually merely reflecting current trends.[3] There has never been any long-term planning of the sector. The establishment of the National Agricultural Council in 1989 was intended to bring together farmers, agri-business and government to sort out mutually beneficial policies. However, it has proved far from effective and Handley is probably correct in concluding that Ministry policy suggests that 'it will go back to old habits of telling farmers what to do' (1993a: 47). Within the MAC's paternalistic policies and the general neglect of agriculture by the state, government agricultural policies have taken three forms. First, the imposition of various restrictions to prevent shortages of domestic rice (the original reason for the Rice Premium), or restrictions on water buffalo slaughter and export (to prevent a shortage of draught animals). Second, a variety of short-term, often *ad hoc* price support measures aimed at heading off rural distress and protest in years of exceptionally low prices. Third, limited protection for selected sectors threatened by imports, notably sugar, oil seeds and dairying.

As was discussed in Chapter 4, since the early 1980s a degree of liberalisation and reduction of the state's developmental role has occurred. It seems likely that these developments have made successive Thai governments more light-handed and less effective in managing the economy and directing development.

As corollaries of liberalisation, and the reduction of the role of the state, the World Bank (1980b) advocated the development of institutions and government decision making mechanisms. There is little evidence that these aims have been achieved in any way, the Thai government and bureaucracy apparently remaining singularly ineffective at decision making.

While various attempts have been made to improve and streamline decision making processes since the early 1980s, they have met with limited success (Muscat, 1994: 177–9). A series of inter-ministerial committees was set up (or revitalised) to oversee particular aspects of economic policy, for example the Export Development and Debt Committee and the National Economic Steering Committee (this to oversee the structural adjustment programme). With a view to improving relations with the business community the Joint Public Sector Private Sector Consultative Committee was established. In addition, a number of *ad hoc* bodies were set up to deal in the shorter term with a range of priority areas such as tourism. However, while again these developments sent the right general messages to investors the fragile coalition governments of the period were ineffective in making major decisions on such critical issues as major infrastructural projects. This is perhaps most clearly seen in the protracted debate over the development of the Eastern Seaboard and the problems surrounding the Bangkok Mass Transit System.

In terms of economic management, many of the criticisms made by the World Bank during the 1980s were not adequately dealt with and tended to be ignored in the wake of the dramatic period of rapid growth. However, repeated concerns had been expressed over the ineffective regulation of the financial and banking sectors, and the general effectiveness of the Bank of Thailand.

The stock market has been extremely volatile, lacks adequate supervisory mechanisms and appears open to created demand (Kulick and Wilson, 1992: 116). Indeed, it appears to have replaced Hong Kong as the 'casino of the East'. Despite a series of attempts to regulate operations, failures, such as that of First City Investment in 1993, continued to cast doubt over the effectiveness of control exercised by the SET and the Bank of Thailand. Controls over the banking system were also brought into question in May 1996 when the Bank of Thailand was obliged to come to the aid of the massively indebted Bangkok Bank of Commerce. In addition, while the Bangkok Bank is highly regarded,[4] many of the local banks are far from well managed and despite financial liberalisation the banking sector remains highly protected. Overall, between 1983 and 1991 some 30 financial corporations were saved from collapse by government intervention. This despite recommendations from the World Bank (cited in Kulick and Wilson, 1992: 116) that poorly managed banks should be allowed to collapse and the whole financial sector made more competitive.

During the 1990s, in addition to the virtual elimination of foreign exchange controls commented on in Chapter 4, there was substantial liberalisation of the financial sector. Notably the establishment of the Bangkok International Banking Facility (BIBF) in March 1993. This licensed 32 foreign banks to provide offshore facilities. Further liberalisation during 1994 and 1995 allowed foreign firms to own as much as 45 per cent of members of the SET. In 1995 a five-year programme of reforms was announced, aimed at substantially increasing the presence of foreign financial concerns. These reforms, combined with the volatile and poorly regulated nature of the Thai financial sector, facilitated increasingly erratic capital movements, particularly from 1993 onwards. The BIBF gave the private sector access to large amounts of cheap foreign capital. It appears that many loans were not only short term but also far from fully secured. With the benefit of hindsight, from the middle of 1996 an extremely unstable financial situation was emerging. While expressing concern over speculative movements, the Bank of Thailand took no action to regulate the situation.

Doubts over the Thai financial sector came to a head in 1997 with the failure of the Bank of Thailand's costly attempt to support the baht, and the collapse of the property and stock markets. During May and June 58 out of 91 major financial institutions suspended operations, 42 at the behest of the IMF to whom Thailand had appealed for emergency financial aid. Many of those that were allowed to continue operation, as well as 15 of the smaller banks, had serious debt problems. It may well be that there will be further failures and many of the suspended institutions will not trade again in their previous form. This is particularly likely given the IMF's instructions to the Bank of Thailand to cease supporting ailing institutions.

The crisis and its handling led to considerable criticism of the Thai financial sector and its regulation. In particular, the IMF has placed considerable blame on the Bank of Thailand for draining the Kingdom of resources in the attempt to support the overvalued currency, undermining confidence and providing ineffective control. The IMF has suggested that the Bank of Thailand should have recognised during 1996 that many banks and finance companies were over-exposed in the property sector, and that there was an unacceptable escalation of foreign borrowing. Instead of attempting to regulate the situation, additional money was printed and large volumes of funds were spent in abortive attempts to support ailing financial institutions and defend the baht. In addition, the Bank has been criticised for its failure to produce a viable plan to salvage the finance companies. Thus, the IMF's reiteration of criticisms of Thailand's economic management made during the early 1990s reflects the points made in Chapter 4 concerning the limited extent to which many elements of the structural adjustment programme were effectively implemented.

It is perhaps not unfair to characterise Thai development from the late 1950s onwards as the product of limited state intervention, with little overall coordination and direction, and weak and generally ineffective planning mechanisms at all levels. However, there are some paradoxes and uncertainties here. First, as was discussed in Chapter 5, concerning the degree of bias against the agricultural sector, particularly with respect to the balance between the provision of credit and the level of effective taxation. Second, there are a number of key areas in which the action of the state, in the post-war period sometimes supported or even promoted by the USA and or the international agencies, have made vital contributions to the Kingdom's long-term development. Amongst these are the establishment of state corporations during the 1950s and the related protection and promotion of the manufacturing sector; the suppression of malaria and other public health measures; the provision of an effective national family-planning programme; the construction of a substantial infrastructural base, particularly during the 1960s; the establishment of a national primary educational system, and a high level of tertiary educational provision. In addition, the state was also on occasions able to intervene rapidly and effectively, notably in order to mitigate the 1973–4 oil price rise. However effective and vital many of these measures have been they have, despite the establishment of planning structures at all levels since the early 1960s, not been part of any long-term integrated national development plan. In addition, since the early 1980s liberalisation has reduced the role of the state with little indication of increased effectiveness. The latter has undoubtedly been diminished by frequent changes in government and a succession of weak coalitions.

Sustainability of growth

As was noted in Chapters 4, 6 and 7 Thailand is facing serious deficiencies in infrastructure (see Yongyuth Chalamwong, 1995, for a review), which was in many respects grossly inadequate for the Kingdom's economic activity well before the acceleration of economic growth and the expansion of overseas trade that has taken place since the mid-1980s. Thailand's international communications have long been regarded as inadequate, particularly with regard to the Bangkok-Thonburi port facilities. By the late 1980s the congestion at the port was giving rise to considerable concern. The opening of Lam Chabang in 1992, and the completion of the rail link to Bangkok are expected to play a major part in sustaining the Kingdom's export-based growth. However, the use of the port is limited by the lack of dockside facilities. Progress has similarly been slow with respect to the development of deep-water ports at Map Ta Phut, Phuket and Songkhla. In addition, the expansion of cargo facilities at Duang Muang airport during the late 1980s brought considerable relief. However, by the early 1990s the growth of traffic was again causing bottlenecks, necessitating plans for a further expansion which will involve the development of a second airport at Nong Ngu, 30 km east of Bangkok.

The development of the Eastern Seaboard is a further example of Thailand's lack of effective development policy and controls. The failure to form the Eastern Seaboard Development Agency, as originally planned, has resulted in the various government departments and private-sector interests acting in a completely uncoordinated and often conflicting manner. The result is the same linear sprawl of industry and 'shophouses' that has typified the growth of the Metropolitan Region as a whole. Belated attempts by the government to zone land and acquire land for the construction of key infrastructural projects – notably the expansion of the port facilities – have been frustrated by the private sector's purchases and the soaring price of land (Handley, 1992a: 64).

In terms of domestically orientated infrastructure the most glaring deficiencies are apparent in the BMR. It remains, for example, the only Pacific Asian city of comparable size outside the PRC that lacks a mass transit system. In addition, this rapidly growing urban region urgently needs massive investment in roads, water supply, telecommunications and drainage. However, long-term expenditure on infrastructure has been disproportionately concentrated in the BMR. Thus, in many ways the remainder of the Kingdom is even less well provided for. Indeed, the increasing concentration of development in the BMR is to a very considerable extent a result of the inadequacies of the national infrastructure.

The limited progress in upgrading the infrastructure reflects the belated official recognition of the problems, reinforced by vested interests which have to be mollified, frequent changes of government and related delays in the tendering process. The problems attendant on the upgrading of the infrastructure are well illustrated by the protracted saga of the Bangkok mass transit system, outlined in Chapter 6.

During the 1990s the upgrading of the BMR and wider national infrastructure has become increasingly critical to Thailand's continued economic growth. Under the Seventh Plan (1992–6) a number of major projects were outlined including a major highway upgrading programme. Similarly, there is considerable reference to infrastructural development in the Eighth Plan (1997–2001). However, apart from the difficulty of implementing major projects, the critical factor is finance. The government has been unwilling, and given the level of official borrowing, probably unable, to finance the necessary projects. Thus it is the private sector that is expected to provide the majority of the finance. This has been a major consideration in the moves to privatise a wide range of public undertakings and the liberalising of controls to enable the private sector to provide services. This has been most notable, and successful, but by no means unproblematic, in the case of the telephone system (see *Far Eastern Economic Review*, 7 Apr. 1994: 41–4; 16 June 1994: 19; 1 Sept. 1994: 66–7; 20 Apr. 1995: 72).

Since the early 1990s more uncertain economic growth and a reduced inflow of foreign investment have made the private sector reluctant to provide the necessary finance. In 1992 it was estimated that US$275.7

billion needs to be invested in infrastructure and related industrial projects by the year 2000 (Handley, 1992d). Given the level of private-sector debt and the current account deficit it is considered desirable that as much of this amount as possible is raised domestically. However, while the 1992 Securities Exchange Act and the re-writing of the Public Companies Act have laid the basis for the development of a Thai capital market, it remains far from certain that the urgently needed infrastructure can be financed in this way.

In the absence of rapid and major infrastructural developments serious question marks must be raised over the sustainability of Thailand's rapid growth. Undoubtedly, the congestion and pollution in the BMR and its immediate environs has played a part in the sharp falls in foreign investment that have taken place since 1993. However, these have to be seen in a broader domestic and international context.

Domestically, the problems of congestion and pollution and the lack of infrastructure are combining with rising costs of land and labour, and signs of skilled labour shortage are beginning to discourage investment.[5] These factors reflect the lack of long-term investment in infrastructure and training that has characterised the development of the Asian NIEs (McGee and Lim, 1993).

During the late 1980s the reduction and reallocation of government expenditure resulted in a decline in the share of education from 21.1 per cent in 1986 to 16.6 per cent in 1988. While there was a gradual re-expansion of the educational budget in 1989 (17.9 per cent) and in 1990 (20.7 per cent), the cut-back almost certainly exacerbated the shortage of appropriately trained and educated personnel that Thailand is experiencing during the 1990s.[6] Since 1990 a series of private and public educational initiatives have been announced – for example the British University Consortium's major campus facility planned for construction in the North at Phitsanulok. The Eighth Plan (1997–2001) places emphasis on 'people-centred development' and the development of education and training. However, the degree to which these will be able to rapidly fill the skill and training gaps is a matter of some debate.

Faced with the loss of comparative advantage in labour-intensive manufacturing activities, the NIEs were able to move to more skill- and capital-intensive activities. As was suggested in Chapter 4, while there has been some sign of upgrading this has been extremely patchy and limited by the shortages of skilled labour. There has also been some resistance on the part of the labour force to move to upgraded operations because of the resultant contraction of the labour force (*Far Eastern Economic Review*, 15 June 1993: 79).[7] There is here a very disturbing issue, for even if the loss of comparative advantage in labour-intensive activities results in movement to more skill- and capital-intensive activities, this may generate proportionally less manufacturing jobs.

Thailand is now confronting a major contradiction: wage levels are becoming too high for the labour-intensive sector, while the lack of skilled labour is limiting the move into higher labour cost activities. Thus the Kingdom may well not be able to fully benefit from the decanting of more skill-intensive activities from Japan and the NIEs. Indeed, it is Malaysia – with its more costly, but more skilled, labour force – which has overtaken Thailand as ASEAN's most important destination for investment outside Singapore (see Table 4.2, p. 129).

The loss of comparative advantage in labour-intensive manufacturing, pressure on the resource base and the opportunities for lucrative investment elsewhere have, as was noted in Chapter 4, combined to encourage Thai investment to other parts of the region as well as into the USA and EU. While the outflow is increasing rapidly it remains of limited importance and can be taken as indicative of the maturation of the Thai economy. However, when taken with the reduced inflow of long-term capital it could be the beginning of a disturbing trend. It is worth noting that both Taiwan and South Korea went to considerable lengths to prevent the outflow of their domestic capital until the mid-1980s. However, as is discussed on pp. 255–8, the outflow of Thai capital into the neighbouring low-labour-cost, resource-rich states has been seen as laying the basis for the development of a Thai-centred mainland sub-regional division of labour.

Thailand has become heavily dependent on the export of manufactured goods to the EU, USA, and increasingly, to other parts of Pacific Asia. Thus the economy is extremely vulnerable to the loss of markets through increased protectionism or loss of comparative advantage. In addition, the economy has become much more trade dependent than was the case during the 1970s when Thailand's low degree of integration with the global economy provided a degree of insulation from the prevailing unstable trading conditions. While the opening of the Thai economy has been both a contributing factor to, and a consequence of, the reorientating and sustaining of economic growth, it has made the Kingdom far more vulnerable to external 'shocks'. There is no evidence to suggest that the Kingdom has become any more able to deal with such events than it was during the early 1980s – a view confirmed by the handling of the 1997 crisis.

The Thai domestic market has expanded rapidly following the economy's recent rapid growth. However, given the income distribution the prospects for the manufacturing sector basing growth on the internal market are limited. Indeed, since 1992 it has become apparent that many sectors of the domestic market have become saturated (*Far Eastern Economic Review*, 20 Aug. 1992: 38). Since the late 1980s the government has become increasingly interested in the idea of extending the 'local' market into neighbouring Cambodia, Laos, Myanmar and Vietnam (see pp. 255-8).

Thailand's rapid and largely uncontrolled economic growth has been costly in terms of the environment and living conditions for much of the population. This is most apparent in the case of the BMR, but the long-term neglect of the rural sector in favour of urban-industrial development has resulted in a more gradual, but ultimately equally devastating, impact on many rural areas. Concern over environmental damage and the exhaustion of resources has increasingly mobilised rural communities and the concerned urban middle class. However, while government statements and the content of National Plans, particularly the Seventh (1992–6) and Eighth (1997–2001), have increasingly stressed environmental issues, little has been achieved in practice.

Overall, the success of the urban-industrial-based developments have adversely affected other sectors of the economy, notably tourism. The key question is once the labour-intensive and polluting industrial processes that have spear-headed Thailand's recent rapid industrial development move on in search of lower costs, and perhaps less stringent environmental controls, will the capacity for self-sustained growth remain? Additionally, will there be sufficient resources to rehabilitate the environment? Serious doubt has been cast on this (Burnett, 1992: 228).

As was noted in Chapters 3 and 4, from the late 1970s tourism became a major ingredient of Thailand's economic growth. The sector grew dramatically during the late 1980s, but subsequently growth has faltered. The fall in the number of arrivals during 1991 and 1992 can be very largely explained in terms of the uncertainties associated with the Gulf War and the Democracy Movement. However, in the longer run Thailand's image as a tourist centre has been badly tarnished by the AIDS epidemic, the adverse publicity attendant on the drug trade, the sex industry and the associated treatment of women and children, and the increased pollution and congestion of Bangkok. In addition, Thailand is experiencing increased competition from other Pacific Asian tourist centres. Behind the renewed growth in the number of arrivals since 1993 are signs that major tour companies have been avoiding Bangkok or reducing the length of stay because of the level of pollution and congestion. In addition, the increased pollution of the Gulf of Thailand is having an adverse effect on the coastal resorts. Efforts by the Tourist Authority of Thailand (TAT) to rectify this by promoting the 'sanitisation' and refurbishment of such eyesores as Pattaya, in declaring 1992 'Thai Women's Year', and promoting provincial centres, have met with only limited success. It may well be that the tourist industry will become a casualty of Thailand's rapid and largely unplanned and uncontrolled industrial growth.

In gauging the sustainability of Thai growth the HIV issue is a major unknown. The publicity surrounding it has undoubtedly had a serious impact on the tourist trade. However, in the longer term the real concern must be over the proportion of the population who are HIV positive, the degree to which this will increase and the impact on the work force and the levels of medical and welfare expenditure. The more disturbing scenarios are based not so much on the reported HIV positive rate as on the potential for rapid spread given the norms of Thai society. A number of studies point to the high incidence of use of prostitutes by Thai men. Van Landingham et al. (1993) conducted a survey of 20-year-old unmarried men, 87 per cent of whom had had sex with a prostitute. A further study of married men revealed that 85 per cent had visited prostitutes before their marriage, 50 per cent since getting married and 35 per cent continued to do so (Van Landingham et al., 1995). Taweesak Nopkesorn et al. (1991) reported that 73 per cent of 21-year-old men questioned reported that they had their first experience of sex with a prostitute.

In 1991 some 24,000 Thais tested HIV positive and it was officially estimated that there were 75,0000 carriers. Mechai Viravaidya,[8] who has taken a lead in raising public and official awareness of the problem, considered that the actual figures were double these and further suggested that by the end of the decade there would be 20 million people who would be HIV positive and 2 million with full-blown AIDS (Mechai Viravaidya et al., 1992). Given that one-third of those infected were of working age, Mechai further estimated that US$5 billion potential earnings would be lost by the end of the century. In 1993 the number of people testing HIV positive was reported to be 600,000. On the basis of these figures a study conducted by Chulalongkorn University and the Public Health Ministry projected that by the year 2000 there would be 4.3 million testing positive, 500,000 HIV-related deaths and a total financial loss of US$8.5 billion for the period 1991–2000 (cited in Thai Development Newsletter, 1993, 23: 67).

Since 1991 the government has begun to devote attention to the AIDs issue. However, the response has inevitably been determined by the interplay between the bureaucracy, other elite groups and a limited number of organised groups. There has indeed been very considerable controversy over the scale of the problem and the policies that should be implemented. Particularly notable was the very public dispute between the Ministry of Public Health and the Tourist Authority of Thailand, the latter wishing that a much lower key approach should be taken.

Many of the developmental problems facing Thailand in the mid-1990s are closely related to the long-term developmental position adopted by the state. The sustainability of the present pattern of growth is being threatened by the lack of effective planning controls and the lack of long-term investment in infrastructure and training. However, the limited economic role of the Thai state is now presented as a virtue and a major factor in the Kingdom's recent economic success. Indeed, as was noted in Chapter 1, for such agencies as the World Bank and many observers, reduction in the already limited role of the Thai state has been critical for the Kingdom's economic success and attractiveness as a location for investors. Such views appear to ignore the consequences of uncontrolled economic growth with limited central planning of such critical areas as training and infrastructure. Additionally, they overlook the very different pattern of development experienced by the NIEs. For them sustained growth has been a direct product of major state involvement with, and direction of, the economy. The critical difference may be that the NIEs were not only able to sustain growth but also to make the transition to more capital and skill-intensive production.

It is becoming increasingly apparent that the current problems facing the Thai economy can only be dealt with by the state taking a far more overt role in the economy. Indeed, there are signs of increasing political pressure for a much more active interventionist and *competent* state (Booth, 1993: 3). The Seventh Plan (1992–6), Eighth Plan (1997–2001) and associated government policy statements may herald a change. The degree to which a major increase in the role of the state will prove economically or politically expedient remains very much a moot point. This particularly in the light of the 1997 crisis and the IMF requirements.

The international context

The growth of the Thai economy, particularly since the mid-1980s, can only be fully understood in the context of the international and regional economic and political conditions that have prevailed. For Thailand the key question is whether these conditions will continue,

The Pacific Asian region has been characterised by four successive and continuing waves of industrial development: Japan after the Second World War, the NIEs during the 1960s and 1970s – the ASEAN–4, particularly Malaysia and Thailand, since the early 1980s; and from the early 1990s the re-engaging socialist economies of the PRC and Vietnam.

Since the early 1980s the appreciation of currencies, rising production costs, the reduction in the absorption capacity of the USA for the region's exports, and increased reliance on domestic markets have pressurised Japan and the NIEs to relocate – particularly labour-intensive manufacturing activity – into the region's low-cost economies. This process has been facilitated by changes in the methods and organisation of industrial production, and further encouraged by the still comparatively open access that the recipient economies had to developed world markets. The relocation of activities was accelerated by the realignment of currencies following the 1985 Plaza Agreement, and the general liberalisation of trade and investment regimes have facilitated these developments. The relaxation of foreign exchange controls in Taiwan in 1987, for example, was followed by a massive outflow of funds, most significantly into Thailand and Malaysia. Similarly, liberalisation within the ASEAN–4, particularly of controls over imports and investment, initially in Malaysia and Thailand and subsequently Indonesia, encouraged the inflow of investment and manufacturing activity. The result has been a critical interdependence between trade and investment flows which is giving rise to marked regional divisions of labour – most clearly between the ASEAN–4 and the NIEs. In this, as we have seen, Thailand has played a leading role.

Since the early 1980s the USA and the EU have moved to increase restrictions on the importation of Third World products. While initially most interest focused on the exclusion of manufactured goods, principally from the NIEs, barriers were also raised against primary produce. From 1979 onwards, Thailand experienced the adverse effects of the EU restricting the import of cassava and later maize through a variety of non-tariff barriers, including quotas and quality controls. However, initially the manufacturing sectors of such countries as Thailand benefited from the restrictions imposed on the NIEs, for these economies met the moves towards greater levels of protection by relocating production in less developed countries, such as Thailand, whose exports were not yet subject to restriction. These so-called 'third country' arrangements have been increasingly scrutinised and barriers raised or threatened to be raised if the practices continue. In addition, the preferential arrangements under which the produce of low-income economies has entered developed world markets are under increasing threat.[9] Thus the NIEs 'third country' arrangements have to a degree been replaced or supplemented by direct manufacturing investment in the USA and EU in order to produce behind the protective screens. This development may be expected to reduce the intra-regional investment flows in Pacific Asia. However, such an outcome may prove shortlived. There are increasing signs of unease in the USA over the continued influx of Pacific Asian investment. Indeed, Julius (1990) has argued that investment flows will become increasingly restricted, and 'investment wars' will replace trade wars. Thus Pacific Asian investment may either be turned back into the region or elsewhere outside the major trading blocs.

During the 1990s the global economy appears to be moving towards the formation of a series of highly managed trading blocs, a situation predicted by the OECD in 1988. In 1993 the 'single market' was established in the EU and subsequently expanded. In the same year formal agreement was reached between Canada, Mexico and the USA for the establishment of NAFTA (North American Free Trade Area). These developments will produce an environment conducive to the emergence of other blocs. Reduced access to North American and EU markets may be expected to turn the emergent Pacific Asian region in on itself, increasing intra-regional trade flows, accelerating the process of integration and perhaps of a formal regional structure (Asian Development Bank, 1992; Dixon and Drakakis-Smith, 1995; Rowley, 1992b).

There are signs that foreign investment, which has become a major element of Thai growth, is beginning to falter. The out-flow of investment from East Asia has slowed, and there are moves towards automation of labour-intensive processes and the retention of these operations rather than exporting them (*Asian Business*, Dec. 1990: 50–2). This in addition to the diversion of investment into the EU and USA[10] in anticipation of increased protection, and into lower cost locations in the PRC and Vietnam. In these respects, as was noted in Chapter 4, it is not so much that Thai costs have risen as that new locations have become available with much greater comparative advantage in labour-intensive activities.

What are the implications of the above scenarios for the Thai economy? Despite a recent decline Thailand remains heavily dependent on EU and US markets, more so than the other Pacific Asian economies (see Dixon and Drakakis-Smith, 1995). This despite restrictions on the import of such Thai items as textiles and tinned tuna fish. Thailand is thus likely to suffer disproportionately from any further restrictions on trade with the USA. The outlook for cassava exports to the EU, and gem, jewellery and tuna fish exports to the USA look particularly bleak (*Far Eastern Economic Review*, 20 Aug. 1992: 38).

A lead has been taken by the tuna producer Unicord[11] in establishing production facilities in the USA and Europe. In 1990 Unicord purchased the USA's third largest tuna canner, Bumble Bee Sea Foods. Under this deal, frozen Thai-caught tuna fish is shipped to the USA for processing, thus avoiding the higher duties and restrictions on the import of canned goods. Similarly in 1991 Unicord agreed a joint venture with a former East German state-owned herring cannery, thus establishing a beach head into Europe (Kulick and Wilson, 1992: 136).

On the other hand Thailand has significantly increased the proportion of its trade that goes to the NIEs. This can be seen as part of the emergence of an integrated Pacific Asian economy, increasingly independent of growth trends in the USA and Europe. The Pacific Asian region has 'cut its umbilical cord of economic dependence on the USA and Europe' (Nomura Institute Report cited in the *Far Eastern Economic Review*, 31 Dec. 1992: 52–3; see also Kwan, 1994), and is increasingly generating independent growth.

However, the continuation of Thailand's position within this emergent region depends on the continued receipt of labour-intensive manufacturing activity shed by the NIEs and Japan. There are now indications that they are both beginning to retain some of these activities, and to locate others in such markedly lower cost 'fourth generation' locations as the PRC and Vietnam. It is not merely that costs have risen in Thailand, but that Vietnam and the PRC with their substantially lower labour costs[12] have re-engaged with international capital and have become regarded as 'good risks' by investors. Thus, as was noted in Chapter 4, since 1993 the inflow of investment into Thailand has declined sharply. However, it is not merely new increments of investment that are going to locations other than Thailand but some plants established since 1987 have also been relocated.[13] In addition, as was noted in Chapter 4, increasing amounts of Thai capital are flowing out – particularly into Myanmar, Laos, Vietnam and the PRC. These developments are not reflected in the rates of growth of GDP, the manufacturing sector and exports which have only gradually declined since 1991, and remain by regional and global standards, impressive. The critical question is whether, in the longer term, in the absence of high levels of foreign investment and with the loss of comparative advantage in labour-intensive manufacturing, Thailand can maintain its growth rates.

As has been discussed previously there is some doubt over Thailand's ability to follow the NIE path of upgrading manufacturing activities and developing the financial and business service sectors. Since the late 1980s successive Thai governments and the Bank of Thailand have placed considerable emphasis on the development of Bangkok as a major financial service centre. This view is supported by the rapid expansion and internationalisation of the Bangkok Stock Exchange since 1989, aided by the liberalisation of foreign exchange, financial markets and capital markets discussed previously. However, Bangkok's reputation for limited and ineffective financial regulation, the persistence of dubious practices and the recurrence of failures of financial corporations and government rescue operations have tended to undermine the liberalisation measures. The 1997 crisis has been a final blow to the Bank of Thailand's confident expectation that much financial activity would relocate from Hong Kong when the colony was returned to the PRC.

The South East Asian regional context

The rapid internationalisation of the Thai economy since the mid-1980s has been accompanied by a substantial increase in the proportion of trade flowing to the Pacific Asian region (see Chapter 1). However, this increase has principally involved Japan and the Asian NIEs. Within the more restricted South East Asian region the only significant expansion of trade has been with Singapore – a reflection of the wider NIE/ASEAN–4 regional division of labour. There has been little significant growth in the importance of trade with Indonesia, Malaysia and the Philippines, with whom Thailand is essentially increasingly in competition for investment, TNC activity and markets. There is little complementarity between these economies. This indeed has been the principal factor inhibiting the development of any effective South East Asian free trade area. Given the structure of the ASEAN economies, serious doubt has been cast on the prospects of further trade liberalisation resulting in increased intra-regional trade flows (Booth, 1993: 4; Dixon, 1998). However, admission of Vietnam as a full member of ASEAN during 1996 and the prospects of the further opening to trade and investment, and entry of Laos and Myanmar during 1997, may well produce some form of ASEAN regional division of labour. Such a development would result in two groups of economies with high levels of competition within each.

To date overall progress of ASEAN towards economic cooperation has been extremely limited. However, in October 1992 member states decide to adopt a proposal for the formation of the ASEAN Free Trade Area (AFTA). This established a 15-year programme of tariff reduction (Rigoberto, 1992: 50). The prospects of substantial economic gain from AFTA appear limited, for since agreement was reached over AFTA there have been signs that the ASEAN countries are far from committed to free regional trade (Vatikiotis 1993: 48).[14] In Thailand fears have been expressed that freer trade may adversely affect the still poorly developed basic manufacturing sector, and that while this may decrease manufacturing costs it would increase the dependence on imports. However, while the enthusiasm for AFTA has waned, interest in wider Pacific cooperation has increased, particularly under the auspices of the Asia Pacific Economic Conference (APEC).

Malaysia has been a particular advocate of wider economic cooperation between ASEAN and East Asia. More recently Thailand has also appeared to favour this development. For while the prospects for gains from cooperation within ASEAN appear very limited, the ASEAN–4 in particular are becoming increasingly linked to East Asia through trade and investment flows.

At the more local regional level, Thailand took a lead in establishing trade and investment links with the neighbouring 'socialist' states of Cambodia, Laos, Myanmar and Vietnam – reflecting the then Prime Minister Chatichai Choohaven's oft-quoted comments on the need to 'convert Indo-China from a battlefield to a market place' and on the prospect of Thailand becoming 'the Singapore of the mainland' (cited in the *Far Eastern Economic Review*, 19 Dec. 1990: 57).

Thailand's position in Vietnam has been supplanted by Japan and the NIEs, but significant business links remain. In the initial stages of the re-opening of Vietnam to international capital a significant proportion of investment and trade was channelled through Bangkok. Much of this reflected political expediency on the part of investors in view of the continued American embargo on economic links with Vietnam. However, in the longer term, geographical position and the lack of communications dictated that Bangkok was not destined to retain its role as the bridgehead into Vietnam. The 'proximity argument' is largely spurious, particularly in the light of direct communications. Effectively Bangkok is not as close to Hanoi as is Hong Kong, or to Ho Chi Minh as is Singapore.

Thailand, however, has become a major trading partner of Cambodia, Laos, and Myanmar.[15] Since 1990 Thai banks have established operations in Phnom Penh and Vientiane to handle trade finance and remittances. Given that a high proportion of trade is conducted in Thai baht, Thailand has a built-in advantage in local cross-border trade and investment (Handley, 1992c).[16] The sustainability of these developments rests heavily on the continued opening up of the neighbouring countries to international capital and the establishment of transport links. Direct communication between Thailand, Cambodia and Myanmar vary from poor to nearly non-existent. However, the completion of the Friendship Bridge at Nong Khai in 1994 has substantially improved links to Laos, which will be further developed with the construction of a second bridge at Savanakhet.

Despite the ambitious plans of the Bank of Thailand for Bangkok to become an international financial centre – serving in particular the neighbouring states (Handley, 1992c) – Thailand's main interest in these areas remains raw materials and potential markets. The principal Thai imports have been timber and precious stones. There has also been some investment in manufacturing in Laos and in hotel and tourist development. Much trade, particularly with Cambodia and Myanmar remains illegal – this includes timber, gems and cattle.

Since 1989 a number of agreements have been reached with the government of Myanmar. By 1993 there were 47 concessions which allowed Thai companies to cut 50,000 tons of timber a year. However, it is believed that much illegal cutting takes place. It was estimated that during the 1992 dry season 100,000 tons of teak entered Thailand from Myanmar ('Log shifts: timber hitched galore for Thai firms on all borders', *Manager*, March 1992: 68–9). In addition, various agreements have been reached over joint fishing and offshore oil and gas exploration.

Both in Cambodia and Myanmar the operation (legal and illegal) of Thai companies, particularly those engaged in logging, has caused considerable friction with the governments concerned. The Rangoon government has expressed concern over the low level of return on logging, and the degree to which the concessions provide funds for opposition minority groups in the border areas. Similarly, there has been concern over the degree to which Thai activities have been funding the Khmer Rouge. These issues of Thailand's involvement in Myanmar and Cambodia have also resulted in friction with other members of ASEAN and the international community in general (Dixon, 1998).

Various scenarios for the emergence of a 'mainland sub-regional division of labour' have been proposed. These have normally involved a Bangkok 'core' and various parts of the surrounding states. Lee and Chen (1992) advocated a baht economic zone involving North East Thailand, Laos, Vietnam and Yunnan. The Asian Development Bank (1993) has similarly advocated the establishment of a 'subregional cooperation zone' involving Cambodia, Laos, Myanmar, Thailand. Vietnam and Yunnan. There are also proposals to develop a 'Northern Triangle' centring on Penang and incorporating adjacent parts of Indonesia and Southern Thailand (Balakrishnan, 1991).[17]

The degree to which Thailand or, more realistically, Bangkok will develop as a mainland 'core' remains far from clear. The opening up of Myanmar, Cambodia and Laos to international capital may prove for Thailand a 'double edged sword'. The raw materials, low-cost labour and potential markets of these economies may well attract a large volume of NIE, Japanese and domestic investment. This may well not only flow in directly, bypassing Bangkok, but also result in more new investment being diverted away from Thailand.

Civil society and political stability

Since the *coup d'état* which ended the absolute monarchy in 1932, the Thai political system has been characterised by considerable instability. There have been nine successful seizures of power (excluding that of 1932), nine abortive *coups d'état*, 16 constitutions, 30 revisions to the constitution and 87 general elections. These events have been depicted as forming a 'vicious circle' which includes:

> the takeover of power by military force, followed by a new constitution forced on the population by the military junta, a general election which leads to a new government and parliament, and finally, a political crises which leads to another coup, dissolution of parliament, repeal of the constitution, and the outlawing of political parties.
>
> (Tanet Chareonment, 1993: 31)

The constant alternation of parliamentary government and *coup d'état* gives credence to the conclusion that the Thai democratic system is inherently unstable (Chai-Anan Samudavaniji, 1991).

The Thai state is one in which the capitalist class has not been able fully to establish control over the state's apparatus or its cultural and legal hegemony (Hewison, 1993b: 168; Turton, 1984: 29). There have been close links between elements of the military, the bureaucracy, and capital, certainly since the 1950s (Elliott, 1978). Linkages were complicated, particularly during the earlier periods, by the Chinese domination of domestic capital. For capital the route to political influence has been principally through the military and the bureaucracy. Similarly for some elements of the military and bureaucracy, involvement with capital was a source of wealth and thus of political influence.

The officials of the Thai state have tended to define their interests as national interests and have not been willing to accommodate 'democratic interests' (Girling, 1981: 147–8). As Hewison has summarised:

> Concepts such as order, stability, tradition, hierarchy and knowing ones place in it, and unity symbolically entwined in the national shibboleth, 'Nation, Religion, Monarchy', have defined the exercise of legitimate power.
>
> (1993b: 170)

Political activity outside the Parliamentary arena has generally been regarded as something that should take place within carefully prescribed and centrally controlled organisations such as village and *tambon* councils. Indeed, for most of the post-1932 period popular participation in the political process has been regarded with grave suspicion by successive administrations. Trade unions, wider political activity and the media have been heavily controlled; indeed the activities of organised labour have been illegal for most of the modern period, and only in the brief, relatively more 'liberal' interludes (1932–4, 1944–7, 1955–7 and 1972–6), has there been substantial activity (Brown and Frenkel, 1993).

In contrast to the suppression of trade unions, and more especially 'peasant' organisations, many employer and trade associations have been established, for example the Rice Traders' Association and the Sugar Producers' Association. These have proliferated and become increasingly powerful 'lobbies' for their particular interest groups. However, until the early 1980s business interests had acquired remarkably little direct political power (Hewison, 1993b: 177–80).

During the 1980s, however, there were signs that the 'vicious circle' had been broken and the basis of the Thai state was shifting towards a more democratic form. As was discussed in Chapter 4, the 1980s were a period of remarkable political stability and an appearance of increasing democracy. It seemed that the days of direct military intervention in politics were over. The appearance of a developing democracy was furthered by the 1988 elections – Chatchai Choonhaven became the first elected Prime Minister since 1976.

Under the Prem (1980–8) administrations, and more especially that of Chatchai (1988–91), a variety of political organisations and pressure groups became active. From 1982 environmental issues became a focus of activity, bringing together many disparate groups including villagers, students, and members of the urban middle class. Trade union activity remained heavily restricted, though there was an upsurge in union agitation for basic union rights and social security provision. Trade unions were extremely active during the 1988 election and widely courted by political parties. Under Chatchai there was a degree of liberalisation. The right to strike was recognised and a dialogue opened with trade union leaders (Hewison, 1993b: 174).

Business interests came to have considerable direct involvement in government. Anek Laothamatas (1988: 454–6) noted that under the last Prem administration almost half the cabinet were drawn from the business world. The direct input of the interests of capital in government was even more apparent under the Chatchai administration, which indeed was widely accused of being the 'government of big business'. In addition, during the 1990s there was a proliferation of business associations such as chambers of commerce. Between 1979 and 1987 the number of provincial chambers increased from 4 to 72 (Anek Laothamatas, 1988: 456–9). From 1981 business–government relations were formalised through the setting up of the Joint Public–Private Consultative Committee. However, as Hewison (1993b: 178–9) has concluded, informal linkages between legitimate[18] and illegitimate business interests developed at least as significantly. The moves towards 'electoral' politics meant that politicians needed funds, and business was eager to purchase influence.

Overall, between 1980 and 1991 there was considerable development of civil society in Thailand. It became more organised, more complex and more vociferous in its demands. For the rapidly developing middle class the demands made in this period represented the continuation of the student-led struggle for basic democratic rights which precipitated the fall of the military in 1976 and which was brutally halted by the return of military rule in 1976.

As was stressed in Chapter 4, this period of stability and increasing democracy was intimately connected with the Kingdom's rapid economic growth. Political stability was an important ingredient in Thailand's attraction for foreign investors and TNCs. At the same time the sustained growth removed the military's often used excuse for intervening – ineffective development policies and a slowing of growth.

However, in February 1991 the decade of political stability and developing democracy was brought to an abrupt close by a military *coup d'état*. The causes of this move by the military have been the subject of considerable debate (see Hewison, 1993b; McCargo, 1993a, b; for particularly good accounts).

The popularity of the Chatchai government was remarkable shortlived. It was increasingly believed to be corrupt even by Thailand's not very exacting standard. A series of bribery scandals, particularly in connection with major infrastructure projects undermined public and business confidence. In addition, it was widely believed that the financial interests of the cabinet and leaders of many of the coalition parties were the primary interest of the administration. It is pointless to attempt to gauge how the corruption of the Chatchai government ranked relative to its predecessors. However, the proliferation and increasing freedom of the media, combined with increasingly adverse comments by the military and business interests and the increasing political awareness of the Thai population ensured that the government's shortcomings were widely reported and commented on. It was corruption that provided the excuse for military intervention.

The appointment as head of the army of General Suchinda Kraprayoon in 1990 gave a focus for a 'conservative' grouping within the military that subscribed heavily to the view that parliamentary governments were inherently unstable and a threat to national security (Chai-Anan Samudavanija, 1990: 1, 85). The more conservative members of the military and of the bureaucracy appear to have resented attempts to establish cordial relations with the neighbouring 'socialist' states (Surin Maisrikrod and Suparra Limsong, 1991: 3–4). In addition, the conservative military felt that their influence and position had been eroded under Chatchai (Hewison, 1993b: 166–7).

While the 1991 *coup d'état* contains an element of military 'in-fighting', it must primarily be seen as an attempt by the military with some support from the bureaucracy – to preserve the 'traditional' Thai state and their position within it from the social and economic changes which were threatening it. However, unlike previous seizures of power the military was not able to exert complete control over the political agenda. Protest and organised campaigns against the 'junta' continued with the active support of parts of the media. The military were forced to make a variety of concessions, notably with regard to the constitution of the interim Nation Peace Keeping Council, and the setting up of an electoral monitoring panel. Following previous *coups d'état* such activity was effectively stifled.

Following the April 1992 election the military still kept effective control of parliament and nominated General Suchinda as Prime Minister. The escalating protests that followed were brutally suppressed.[19] Following the intervention of the King, Suchinda resigned and Anand Panyarachum was appointed as a caretaker Prime Minister. Elections in 1992 (Chuan Leekpak), 1995 (Banhard Silpa-Archa) and in 1996 (Chavalit Yongchaiyud), indicated a return to the democratic process.

The failure of the military to hold on to power and 'turn the clock back' during 1991 and 1992 suggests that such intervention is increasingly outmoded. However, that does not imply that the interests of business and the middle class will prevail unopposed. It is likely that the military will continue to destabilise the political situation, particularly when the restraining and mediating hand of the present King is removed.[20] Nevertheless, it should also be stressed that the development of democracy and civil society in Thailand, particularly since the 1980s, has been very much greater and more stable than that which prevails in much the remainder of South East Asia.

Conclusion

Whatever reservations there might be concerning the nature, impact and sustainability of economic growth in Thailand, it is important to stress that the economy and the majority of the population have experienced substantial changes over the last 30 years. Since my own first visit to the Kingdom in 1971 much has changed out of all recognition. While the rapid changes that have taken place since the early 1980s can be depicted as a case of 'late and quick industrialisation' or 'a quick industrial miracle' (Amsden, 1989), they have to be seen in the context of the long-term achievement of comparatively high and consistent rates of growth. Since the late 1950s the Kingdom has experienced growth rates that have compared very favourably with those of the present NIEs.

While Thailand has over the last 30 years performed remarkably well with respect to economic growth, serious interlocking imbalances have emerged. Five of these are particularly serious, and if left uncorrected may well have major implications for the continuation of the established pattern of rapid economic growth. First, there is the imbalance between employment and production. The rapid decline in the importance of agricultural production has not yet been matched by a corresponding fall in the sector's share of employment. Thailand remains a country with a remarkably high proportion of its population living in rural areas and dependent on agriculture. In comparing Thailand to the Asian NIEs and in making confident predictions about the Kingdom's rapid transformation to NIE status, the reality of employment and residence patterns is frequently overlooked. The Kingdom has not yet undergone the transformation of the rural sector that Taiwan and South Korea experienced before and during the early stages of their rapid industrial expansion. Indeed, the attempt to bypass (or rather ignore the need for) an agricultural transformation in the drive to NIE status is perhaps the single most important barrier to the Kingdom's chances of sustained economic growth and political and economic stability. In addition, as was discussed in Chapters 1 and 5, Thailand retains a considerable comparative advantage in agriculture which could be much more fully exploited, not only as a source of employment but as a significant component of economic growth and export earnings.

Not only is there considerable scope for the development of higher value agricultural products for domestic and export markets, there is also a pressing need to generate agricultural employment. The urban industrial sector appears incapable of providing gainful employment for the estimated 10 million people who will leave the agricultural sector by early next century (Simon, 1993). In addition, the prospects for the rice sector look increasingly uncertain as the international market contracts. Not only will considerable land and labour become surplus to the rice trade, but given the low prices and productivity of the sector it may become necessary to substantially increase support for, if not subsidise, production in order to maintain domestic supplies. This again underlines the need for a clear pro-active state policy towards the economy in general and the rice sector in particular.

Second, and related to the first point, is the continuing extremely low level of urbanisation. Third, the urban population is heavily concentrated in the BMR. Fourth, the majority of the manufacturing and modern service sector activities are concentrated in the BMR and its immediate environment. This situation has worsened with the acceleration of economic growth since the early 1980s. In consequence the gap between rural and urban incomes and living conditions has widened, and poverty has become predominantly a rural phenomenon. Indeed, the concentration of recent growth and structural change is such that it is little exaggeration to suggest that it is the Extended BMR that is becoming a NIE rather than Thailand. Government attempts to promote a more egalitarian and dispersed pattern of economic growth have been limited and largely ineffective. It may be that growth of personal and regional income disparities, the low income generating capacity of agriculture, the failure of industrial employment to grow fast enough, and serious shortages of housing, services and welfare provisions, may well generate major social tension and political unrest.

Fifth, there is an imbalance in education and training. There is a very low enrolment rate in secondary education, one of the lowest in Pacific Asia. This is resulting in serious shortages of suitably skilled and educated work forces. In addition, secondary enrolments are heavily concentrated in the BMR.

In combination these interlocking imbalances are formidable. As has been discussed the solution to all these issues rests, at least in part, on effective intervention by the government.

Regardless of the outcome of the 1997 crisis, are there any lessons for other Third World countries? While Thailand is at first sight a more 'typical' Third World country than the Asian NIEs its particular non-colonial form of articulation, abundance of land, geopolitical situation and the related involvement of the USA combine to produce a very special background for development.[21] Similarly, the review of development policies suggests little that is transferable. The Thai economy grew consistently and comparatively rapidly until 1979 with a high level of protection and a low level of integration into the world economy. While there was a range of subsidies and market controls, both planning controls and macro-direction of the economy remained weak. Once the boom was well under way there was substantial deregulation of the economy. Indeed in the 1990s Thailand conveys the impression of largely uncontrolled growth. Thus in some ways Thailand is beginning to conform to the model of development that for so long was incorrectly attributed to the Asian NIEs, that is, unfettered *laissez faire* capitalism. However, it is difficult to envisage this as a new 'model of development'; like the Asian NIEs it is the product of a particular set of international conditions and internal economic and political structures. Indeed, the problems that have emerged during the 1990s, and which have been highlighted by the 1997 crisis, might be taken as a warning that neo-liberal development orthodoxy contains serious and perhaps fatal pitfalls.

Thailand in the late 1990s is in a critical period of its development. The problems facing the state and economy are in many ways formidable and much in the regional and international arenas is well beyond the Kingdom's control. The 1997 crisis may be shortlived, or it may herald the end of long-term rapid growth not only for Thailand, but for Pacific Asia as a whole.

NOTES

1 NATIONAL GROWTH AND THE INTERNATIONAL CONTEXT

1 For a discussion of the distinctive background to growth in the old Asian NIEs see Deyo (1987).
2 As with the euphoria that accompanied the emergence of the Asian NIEs, the historical development and the particular national, regional and international circumstances are treated as residual to matters of policy. While this view of the Asian NIEs has been substantially dispelled since the mid-1980s (see Deyo, 1987; White, 1988) it has re-emerged with respect to Thailand, Malaysia and Indonesia (see e.g. World Bank, 1993b). Thus little attention has focused on the antecedents and wider regional and global circumstances of the recent rapid growth of Indonesia, Malaysia and Thailand.
3 Tinned produce and molasses, both classed as manufactured goods, contributed 14.0 per cent of export earnings in 1988 and 9.2 per cent in 1992.
4 In November 1988 the south experienced the most serious floods on record. Some 460 people were killed, hundreds more classed as 'missing' and 70,000 were made homeless. The total damage was estimated at US$40 million (see *Timber Trades Journal*, 'Thailand takes tough line', 14 Jan. 1989; 'Thailand's grief seeks culprit', 21 Jan. 1989; 'Logging ban spreads', 4 Feb. 1989).
5 The depletion of stocks by intensive inshore fishing is compounded by the use of extremely small mesh nets. The large-scale production of fish sauce and paste provides a ready market for fish no matter how small. This situation has been reinforced by the expansion of fish meal production.
6 The North Eastern region has what is believed to be the world's largest deposit of salt. While there have been a number of proposals to exploit these deposits on a large scale for industrial purposes, none have come to fruition. In consequence salt is produced on a declining scale using primitive techniques.
7 The proportion of the population having access to 'safe' drinking water increased from 33 per cent to 71 per cent in 1987 and 81 per cent in 1994 (World Bank, *World development report*, (various years), Oxford University Press).
8 During the 1980s it is believed that the village-based nutrition programmes of the Ministry of Public Health substantially reduced the incidence of pre-school malnutrition (Muscat, 1994: 238).

2 INCORPORATION AND INTERNATIONALISATION: 1850–1957

1 For accounts of the size, products, economy and trade of Ayutthaya see e.g. Dhiravatna Pomlejra (1990), Reid (1988: 19, 21, 31) and Wyatt (1984: 127–42).

2 English traders were calling at Ayutthaya as early as 1611 and trading inland as far as Chiang Mai by the 1613–15 period (Foster, 1933: 211–12).

3 An East Indian Company official.

4 Opium was imported and widely used but was technically illegal.

5 See Ingram (1971: 170–4) for a discussion.

6 From a memorandum sent in 1903 by the Financial Adviser W. J. F. Williams to the Ministry of Finance headed 'Memorandum upon the cash balances of the Government', cited by Ingram (1971: 197).

7 From a memorandum sent during 1908 to the Minister of Finance from the Financial Adviser W. J. F. Williams headed 'Further proposed schemes of the Irrigation Department', cited by Ingram (1971: 198).

8 Itinerant monks, unattached to urban monasteries serving new settlements could, and did, become foci of opposition.

9 For discussion of the impact of peace and stability on the population of South East Asia as a whole see Dixon (1990: 125–9; 1991a: 121–3), Fisher (1964: 172) and Reid (1988: 42–3). Owen (1987: 50) speculates on the possibility of increases in birth rates and some evidence to support this has been provided by Boomgard (1987: 280–1) for Java, and by Smith and Ng (1982: 248–52) for the Philippines.

10 The account of the development of irrigation draws on Brown (1988: 1–59) and Johnston (1955: 51–91).

11 A process which while normally substantially increasing yields also involved three times as much labour as broadcasting.

12 By 1919, of the 66 large steam mills in Bangkok 56 were Chinese owned. In that year all the remaining European mills were either closed down or sold to Chinese firms (Ingram, 1971: 71).

13 In 1905 all males were made liable to military service which may well have created labour shortages in some areas. This was perhaps reinforced by low wages and the availability of construction work, particularly on the railways.

14 From the early 1900s onwards there were reports of shortages of high-quality teak (Sompop Manarungsan, 1989: 137).

15 This is another example of the problems faced by Thailand because of its exclusion from the British Imperial preference system.

16 Some of the Chinese operations employed as many as 1,000 workers (Sompop Manarungsan, 1989: 145).

17 In 1950 the average size of rubber holdings was 3.5 hectares and 96 per cent of holdings were less than 8 hectares.

18 In 1949 Chinese owned 50 per cent of the holdings over 8 hectares but only 7 per cent of the smaller holdings. Ingram suggests that 'about half the total rubber area ... [was] ... owned by persons of Chinese ancestry' (1971: 103).

19 Bowring (1857, vol I: 203–4) was impressed by the Thai sugar industry – predicting that it would become the Kingdom's greatest export.

20 The fall in prices was principally a result of the development of large-scale and often subsidised European beet production.

21 Three key members present were Pibol Songkram, Prayoon Pamornmontri and Pridi Banomyong. The latter, who became the driving force of the group, illustrates both the conspirators' varied and interlocking background which encompasssed Thai and Chinese, bureaucracy, trade and considerable educational achievement (see Stowe, 1991: 10–22, 367–80).

22 In 1935 King Rama 7th abdicated and until the coronation of Rama 9th in 1946 there was no King permanently resident in the country.

23 For a translation of the plan see Landon (1939: 260–93) and Thak Chaloembiarana, 1978: 109–61). For an interesting commentary see Muscat (1994: 31–8).

24 The account of tobacco is based on Tate (1979: 529).

25 In 1954 when most of these concessions expired they were not renewed, effectively ending the dominant Western presence in the teak industry (Suehiro, 1989: 173).

26 The Chinese in Thailand were a far from homogeneous group. In addition the definition of 'Chinese' is often far from clear. Sometimes the term was applied to any person with at least one parent of Chinese blood, or it could be restricted to persons born in China as against Thailand. Thus the estimates of the size of the Chinese population in Thailand at different dates can vary wildly (see e.g. Skinner, 1957).

27 It can be argued that Thailand had little real choice in the matter.

28 The small banks established before the Japanese occupation played a very limited role in the economy and tended to be closely tied to specific areas of Chinese business activity (see e.g. Suehiro, 1989: 155–6). The major Thai Banks and their dates of incorporation are given below:

Siam Commercial Bank	1906
Nakornthon Bank	1933
First City Bank Bangkok	1934
Bank of Asia	1939
Siam City Bank	1941
Bangkok Bank of Commerce	1944
Bangkok Bank	1944
Bank of Ayudhya	1945
Thai Farmers	1945
Laem Thong Bank	1948
Union Bank of Bangkok	1949
Thai Danu Bank	1949
Bangkok Metropolitan Bank	1949
Thai Military Bank	1957
Siam Bank	1965
Krung Thai Bank	1966[a]

Source: Naris Chaiyaasot (1994: 231).

Note:

[a] Established as a result of the merger of the Bank of Agriculture (founded in 1950) and the Providence Bank (founded in 1943).

29 In 1946 Thailand signed a peace treaty with Britain and India. A condition of the treaty was the free delivery of 1.5 million tons of rice to Singapore and an indemnity payment. In the event the rice was never delivered. In 1947 all punitive measures against Thailand were dropped.

30 The death of King Ananda has never been satisfactorily explained. The official statements claimed the death was an accident, but both suicide and murder have also been suggested.

31 Riggs (1966: 251–2) describes the Chinese business community as becoming 'pariah entrepreneurs'.

32 This was the first stage in the development of a comprehensive system of water control for the Chao Phraya basin. A piecemeal version of the plan drawn up by van der Heide in the early 1900s.

33 Riggs (1966: 305–8) refers to 144 'public corporations and organisations'. Muscat (1966: 296–300) refers to 124 organisations. Part of the reason for this discrepancy is definitional, but much of it stems from the varied, complex and often impenetrable holding patterns (see Silcock, 1967b). Indeed, in 1961 J. A. Loftus (an economic adviser to the Ministry of Finance) commented on the difficulty of producing a comprehensive list of state enterprises, particularly given the lack of any agreed definition (cited in Muscat, 1994: 62). See also the discussion by Suehiro (1989: 138–40).

3 THE ESTABLISHMENT OF A DEVELOPMENT FRAMEWORK: 1958–79

1 In terms of the background of the key members of the Sarit regime there was a clear break with its predecessor, whereas Phibun's regime contained many direct links back to the 1932 coup.

2 For a detailed study of the role of the USA in these developments see Muscat (1990).

3 There is a very large literature on the nature and operation of the Thai bureaucracy. See in particular Reeve (1951), Riggs (1966) and Stiffen (1966).

4 This is particularly apparent with respect to agriculture (see Chapter 5) and the conflict between import substitution and export orientated manufacturing promotion (see pp. 88–9).

5 The government's share of investment varied between 30 and 34 per cent, while that of foreign investors ranged from 34 to 36 per cent. The sharp increase in investment was then very much 'across the board'. There was however a marked increase in the share of construction and here the emphasis on this sector under the First Plan is certainly important (Ingram, 1971: 230).

6 The number of American troops stationed in Thailand:

1966	6,500
1967	34,400
1968	44,400
1969	47,600
1970	44,100
1971	36,100
1972	30,200
1973	43,500
1974	35,000

Source: Elliott (1978: 131).

7 The main bases in the North East were Nakhon Ratchasima, Ubon Ratchathani and Udon Thani.

8 Between 1946 and 1978 American economic and military aid to South Korea amounted to US$13 billion (US$600 per capita) and US$5.6 billion (US$425 per capita) to Taiwan (Cummings, 1987: 76).

9 During this period the BOI did not provide effective monitoring of the implementation and performance of promoted firms. In consequence any analysis of the origins of capital and the sectoral distribution of investment has to rely on the less than satisfactory approval data.

10 During the 1940s the Pibul regime had attempted to tax bachelors in order to promote population growth (Kulick and Wilson, 1992: 126).

11 The partial inter-censual survey conducted in 1956 appears to have been seriously distorted by under-registration (Muscat, 1994: 122).

12 A key contribution was made by such effective, flamboyant, uninhibited and dedicated promoters of birth control as Mechai Viravaidya who founded the Community Family Planning Service (renamed the Population and Development Association in 1979, using it to train 12,000 village volunteers. Mechai was prepared to go to almost any lengths to break down inhibitions about sex and contraception – including engaging massage parlour girls to measure customers in order to arrive at the Thai national condom size; persuading Buddhist monks to bless condoms; establishing temporary family planning 'supermarkets' at bus terminals; persuading traffic police to give out condoms to drivers and passengers caught in traffic jams, gaining the interest of school children through the game of 'Cops and Rubbers' and organising national condom-inflating competitions (Kulick and Wilson 1992: 126–7).

13 The opening of the first clinic in Bangkok during 1965 was rapidly followed by a large influx of customers from provincial areas without any national publicity. Buses were chartered in provincial areas by groups anxious to obtain birth control and advice (Kulick and Wilson, 1992: 126).

14 The birth-control propagandist Mechai Viravaidya overcame what objections there were to birth control by citing a Buddhist scripture that stated: 'many births make you poor' and recalling that Buddha only had one child (cited Kulick and Wilson, 1992: 127).

15 Average annual percentage rate of growth of tertiary enrolments in ASEAN:

	Period	Rate	Gross enrolment ratio		
			1970	1975	1985
Indonesia	1970–82	7.9	2.6	2.4	6.5
Malaysia	1970–83	12.1	1.6	2.8	6.0
Philippines	1970–81	6.7	19.8	18.4	38.0
Singapore	1970–83	7.5	6.7	9.0	11.8
Thailand	1970–83	27.9	1.7	3.4	19.6

Source: Sirilaksana Khoman (1994: 331–2).

16 Educational expenditure as a proportion of the government budget:

	1970	1975	1980	1985	1990
Brunei	n.a.	12.2	n.a.	9.6	n.a.
Indonesia	n.a.	13.1	8.9	9.3	9.4
Malaysia	17.7	19.3	14.7	16.3	18.0
Philippines	24.4	11.4	9.1	7.4	10.5
Singapore	11.7	8.6	n.a.	9.6	n.a.
Thailand	17.3	21.0	20.6	21.1	20.7

Source: UNESCO *Statistical Yearbook*, Geneva, various issues.

17 Government expenditure on education as a proportion of GNP

	1970	1975	1980	1985	1990
Brunei	n.a.	2.0	1.2	2.0	3.6
Indonesia	2.8	2.7	2.0	n.a.	1.2
Malaysia	4.4	6.0	6.0	6.6	5.6
Philippines	2.6	1.9	1.7	1.4	2.9
Singapore	3.1	2.9	4.3	n.a.	n.a.
Thailand	3.5	3.6	3.4	3.8	3.6
Vietnam					

Source: UNESCO *Statistical Yearbook*, Geneva, various issues.

18 This, at least in part, was a legacy of the British financial advisers.
19 The oil fund was introduced in 1974 in order to tap the 'windfall' profits made by the sale of old stock at the new price levels. It became a variable levy of subsidy which enabled the government to vary the ex-refinery price without changing the other elements of fuel prices. In order to soften the impact of international price increases the levels of subsidy resulted in the oil fund running a considerable deficit during the period 1975–77 (see Praipol Koomsup, 1993: 309–17 for a fuller discussion). As is discussed in Chapter 4 a similar mechanism was used after the second oil price rise in 1979.
20 The student organisation was one of the few remaining legal bodies that was able to promote opposition to the government. Rapid expansion of university enrolments, particularly in the humanities and social sciences, the limited employment prospects for graduates together with the general opening of the Thai society to international influences all played significant roles in the politising of the student body.
21 The 1973 upheaval, based as it was on a broadly based popular movement, not only differed strikingly from 1932, but was also potentially a much more radical development.
22 A similar scheme was proposed under the Second Plan but was only very partially implemented.
23 Some of these activities were quite bizarre. The author witnessed an intra-village 'boy scout' competition supervised by the local police which involved a number of elderly ladies competing at knot tying.
24 During the 1970s there were violent fluctuations in commodity prices. However, the overall trend was a steep decline. The World Bank's composite index of non-oil commodity prices fell from an average of *c.* 120 in 1968–70 to *c.* 95 in 1978–80 (World Bank, 1983: 11)
25 This account of the Charoen Pokphand is taken from Kulick and Wilson (1992: 137–41).
26 Production of passenger cars, 1984:

Toyota	10,856	34.3
Nissan	5,572	17.6
Mitsubishi	2,975	9.4
Mazda	2,493	7.9
BMW	1,790	5.6
Locally owned	7,924	25.2
Total	31,610	100.0

Source: Bangkok Bank.

270

27 Sidtha International was linked with an Indian-based company but 85 per cent of the shares were held by the World Government of the Age of Concern registered in Switzerland.
28 The trends in trade direction during the 1970s were more complex than this suggests. For example Japan's share rose from 8.9 per cent in 1970 to 23.87 per cent in 1975, before declining to 14.5 per cent in 1979. In contrast the US share fell from 23.7 in 1970 to 8.8 per cent in 1974 recovering to 13.8 per cent by 1979. These changes reflected currency movements as well as the changing composition of exports.
29

Sector	Percentage foreign registered capital 1978–9
Vehicles	55.5
Textiles	54.7
Oil	96.0
Tin	90.0
Soft drinks	65.0
Detergents	60.0
Milk products	70.0
Steel	20.0

Source: Hewison (1985: 274).

It should be stressed that the percentage of registered capital held by foreign concerns does not necessarily reflect the level of actual control.
30 From 1955 until 1978 the baht had a fixed nominal exchange rate with the US dollar. This resulted in long-term over-valuation of the baht which was substantially paid for by the agricultural sector (Somchai Jitsuchon, 1989: 43).
31 Provision was made under the 1963 Industrial Promotion Act to exempt exporters from taxes on imported machinery, raw materials and other intermediate products. In 1972 additional incentives were made available to exporters and the Export Promotion Act gave exporters full tax exemption on imported goods. There were further relaxations of tariffs and increases in incentives in 1974 and 1977.

4 STRUCTURAL ADJUSTMENT AND ACCELERATED GROWTH: 1980–96

1 Special Drawing Rights, the equivalent in the period of US$936 million.
2 These were principally connected to the establishment of private-sector slaughter houses for the export of beef and pork, and the removal of restrictions on rubber exports. None of these measures were of major consequence.
3 In addition to the 8.7 per cent devaluation in 1981, the baht was devalued by a further 14.8 per cent in 1984. More significantly the 1984 devaluation established a managed fixed exchange system which tied the baht to a 'basket' of the currencies of the Kingdom's major trading partners. This not only made Thai exports more competitive but also allowed more flexibility in responding to changes in trade and exchange rates (Somchai Jitsuchon, 1989: 41). The objective was to give maximum flexibility to the Bank of Thailand in using the exchange rate to manage the domestic and external financial situation (see Bangkok Bank, *Monthly Review*, 25 1985: 37–55 for a detailed review).
4 For a detailed review of the implementation of each of the proposed structural adjustment measures see World Bank (1986: Annex 2).

5 Tax yields had in recent years repeatedly fallen below targets – a reflection of cumbersome and inefficient revenue systems. This was an area that the World Bank and IMF had highlighted for reform.

6 The government was reluctant for the break with the IMF to occur, for despite being able to borrow funds on the international market at a lower rate it wanted to have IMF approval for its economic policies (Paisal Sricharatchanya, 1986: 122).

7 For a tabulated comparison with the situation described by the World Bank in 1986 see Chaipat Sahansakul (1992: 20–7).

8 The average level of nominal tariff protection rose during the 1980s at a time when other Asian economies were reducing their levels of protection:

	Percentage	
	1978	1988
Indonesia	33.0	20.1
Malaysia	14.3	13.3
Philippines	44.2	28.3
Singapore	5.6	0.3
Thailand	29.4	40.8

Source: Krause and Lutkenhorst.
(1986: 26–44); UNCTAD (1990).

9 The delay in reducing tariff levels as well as reflecting their importance to government revenue also indicates the continuing importance and political influence of the ISI sector.

10 Since the time of writing it has been suggested to me that for many of the assembly plants the start-up time can be very short indeed. However, this does not detract from the main point that acceleration of the growth of manufactured exports pre-dated the sharp increase in foreign investment.

11 Hourly wage rates in the electronics sector during 1985 (USA = 100):

Hong Kong	16
Indonesia	4
Malaysia	10
Philippines	8
South Korea	14
Singapore	19
Taiwan	16
Thailand	5

Source: Scott, 1987: 145.

The labour costs in the electronic sector were probably rather higher than in other sectors. In general the effective level of labour costs was probably lower than official sources would suggest because of the widespread ignoring and evasion of minimum wage and other regulations – through sub-contracting, outwork, casual forms of employment and the use of child labour and recent female migrants. In addition, large numbers of small firms were not registered and the regulations generally far from stringently enforced. Much anecdotal evidence points to collusion on the part of inspectors and the importance of bribery in avoiding regulations.

12 This needs to be qualified in so far as Prem himself was appointed rather than elected and his cabinets all contained some unelected members.

13 See however the argument in Bell (1995).

5 THE AGRICULTURAL SECTOR

1 However, note the qualification of official figures made on pp. 19–20.

2 The average annual growth of crop GDP at constant 1972 prices:

1961–6	6.6
1967–71	2.7
1972–6	4.8
1977–81	4.1
1982–6	3.3
1987–91	3.0

Source: NESDB.

3 Reparation payments were imposed on Thailand by the allied forces, principally through British pressure because of the formal declaration of war made under pressure from the Japanese occupying forces.

4 The Office licensed private traders to export rice. However, there was widespread evasion of the controls, much rice was smuggled and traded illegally (Muscat, 1994: 75; Silcock, 1967c; Usher, 1967).

5 The official rate was 40 baht to the pound sterling while the free market rate was *c*. 60 baht.

6 This was in effect a variable levy on exports which was originally intended to prevent domestic shortages of rice. Its effectiveness in this respect has been much questioned. In the event the Premium became a major source of government revenue.

7 These included the Ministry of the Interior, the Ministry of Defence, the Army, the Navy and the Air Force.

8 The rate was reduced from 7 per cent to 3 per cent for the first six months and 7.25 per cent thereafter.

9 This was essentially a revised version of the Rediscount Credit Scheme introduced briefly during 1984.

10 A licensing system and export tax were introduced in 1935 but these measures appear to have had little impact on the expansion of the sector.

11 The current scheme, initiated during 1982, is operated by the Thai Cane and Sugar Corporation (TCSC), which combines grower, milling and government interests.

12 The revenue derived from the Premium fell:

	Million US$
1980	73.05
1981	64.83
1982	27.89
1983	27.27
1984	16.69
1985	16.07
1986	0.95

Source: Foreign Trade Department.

13 However, MAC data suggest that between 1988 and 1994 farm-gate prices tended to increase slightly faster than export prices.

14 These were originally introduced to restrict the movements of cattle and water buffalo in order to control the spread of disease and to prevent the slaughter of draft animals creating a shortage and thereby damaging crop production.

15 Charoen Pokphand, Betagro, Centageo, Laem Thong, and Sci Thai.

16 Of these concerns 85 per cent operated pond, 1.5 per cent paddy fields, 1.1 per cent cages. Given the cost of cages the main expansion was expected to continue in the pond and paddy field sectors.

17 In many areas the removal of mangroves has combined with the reduced discharge of rivers resulting from abstraction and diversion of water to increase the landward penetration of salt water. This has adversely affected crop yields, particularly for rice and coconut.

18 These developments include the relocation and internationalisation of agricultural production. For example the 'uprooting' of asparagus production from Taiwan (Trebuil, 1993a: 9). Production, which is primarily for export to Japan, is extremely demanding of labour and other inputs, notably fertiliser.

19 This compares unfavourably with other South East Asia countries. In 1993:

Indonesia	24.3
Laos	16.0
Myanmar	11.5
Philippines	28.6
Vietnam	33.5
Malaysia	32.7

Source: FAO *Production Yearbook* (1996).

20 This is an area that would benefit from some in-depth comparative research. The easier environment argument is less easily sustainable in neighbouring Myanmar and the former Indo-Chinese states. Thus it seems likely that the colonial restrictions and large-scale development of rice cultivation in the delta lands might be the more important factors in distinguishing them from Thailand. It is certainly important to stress that the emergence of colonial Vietnam and Burma as major rice exporters was closely associated with heavy investment in the large-scale schemes in the delta lands of the Mekong and Irrawaddy.

21 It is important to stress that the long-term pattern of clearance has been far from even, with very considerable temporal and spatial variation (Hirsch, 1990: 32–55; Tanabe, 1978: 53–4). In addition, the data, even for most recent years are far from reliable, with considerable under- and mis-recording of land. The rates of change given in Table 5.13 should be taken as indicative only. The very sharp changes in the cultivated area during the 1960s and 1970s are greatly exaggerated by various sudden registration and reclassifications of land. In particular, use of the categories 'other', 'grazing' and 'idle' have varied considerably, even from one year to the next.

22 These were produced by the Rice Department. In general these varieties responded well to small doses of artificial fertiliser. *Sampathong*, a glutinous variety widely adopted in the North and North East, responded particularly well to applications of 60–70 kg/ha; higher rates of application resulted in lodging and lower yields (Mekong Committee, *Bulletin*, Nov. 1979: 47).

23 Government investment in agriculture as a percentage of total government investment:

	1966	1974
South Korea	17.0	28.0
India	15.0	12.0
Malaysia	23.0	20.0
Pakistan	17.0	11.0
Philippines	14.0	36.0
Sri Lanka	16.0	36.0
Taiwan	n.a.	n.a.
Thailand	12.0	10.0

Source: Douglass (1983: 196).

It should be stressed that the basis for these calculations is not given.

24 Many of these areas had been bypassed by settlement despite their agricultural potential because of the presence of malaria, and in some cases their remoteness. As was noted in Chapters 2 and 3 malaria suppression and road building opened up vast new areas to settlement.

25 The percentage coefficient of variability of provincial yields rose from 25.2 in 1968–70, to 27.2 in 1978–80, and 29.3 in 1990–2.

26 This was originally scheduled for implementation during the early 1970s.

27 A considerable proportion of land is ploughed by contractors, some of which are themselves wealthier farmers. Some merchants also supply ploughing, and even additional labour for the preparation of such upland crops as cassava.

28 Based on interviews with district agricultural officers in the North Eastern province of Kalasin during 1972, 1973 and 1976.

29 The only major exception to this was the settlement of the delta grasslands. For a detailed account of this see Takaya (1987).

30 This represents a reduction from the 42.5 per cent classed as NFR during the early 1980s and the 50 per cent of the national area that the RFD was permitted to class as reserves under the 1897 Forestry Law. In addition to the NFR regulations some 5,656 km^2 are classed as Wildlife Sanctuaries, 2,526 km^2 as Non-hunting Areas, and 25,000 km^2 as National Parks.

31 Estimates of the numbers of people living in NFR are variously cited as 1.2–2 million households or 7–10 million people (see eg. Lohmann, 1991: 8; Trebuil, 1993b: 6). In 1988 a study by the Thailand Development Research Institute estimated that 22 per cent of the Kingdom's 56,000 villages held land in NFRs.

32 The first Act aimed at the protection and formation of forest reserves was passed in 1938. Subsequent legislation in 1953, 1954, 1960, 1964 and 1975 eased the formation of reserves and in theory increased controls and penalties.

33 The rising prices of timber, fuel wood and charcoal, coupled with limited controls encouraged farmers to produce for sale. In addition, the law allows the cutting of timber for house construction and the dismantling and sale of lumber after two years. Hafner (1990: 341) reports a case of a North Eastern village with 60 rough part-built houses, four or five of which were sold each year to supplement incomes.

34 This suggests that the annual target set by the RFD of replanting 50,000 ha was met. However, this would be a remarkable achievement given the RFD's previous record.

35 The area of degraded forest within the NFRs was estimated by the RFD as between 48,000 and 71,000 km^2 (Lohmann, 1991: 8).

36 This broad scheme to 'green' the dry North Eastern plateau through reaf-forestation, plantations and water developments was proposed in August 1987 by the then Army Commander-in-Chief General Chaovalit Yongchaiyudh.

37 This is perhaps not so much a reflection of the demanding nature of cassava as the lack of adoption of such soil conserving methods as ridging and the general failure of the crop to have formed an adequate leaf canopy before the main rains start.

38 This is based on Zimmerman (1931), and although widely cited, must be seen very much as an estimate.

39 Traditional inheritance systems which in some cases precluded or severely limited the sub-division of holdings appear to have broken down in the face of land shortage.

40 There has been a substantial increase in land transactions, from 2.3 million in 1988 to 3.6 million in 1989 (Lohmann, 1990: 8).

41 This survey almost certainly under-estimates the importance of the subsistence element of household production.

42

Household incomes	US$
Central Plain	2176
South	1502
North	1176
North East	883

Source: OAE, 1991.

6 UNEVEN DEVELOPMENT: BANGKOK IN THE NATIONAL ECONOMY

1 Krung Thep Maha Nakhon.

2 Percentage of the urban population resident in the largest city:

Congo	68
Burundi	85
Guinea	87
Rwanda	77
Thailand	57

Source: World Bank (1994)
World Development Report.

3 According to Limlingan (1986: 39) in 1952 the percentage distribution of ethnic groups in Bangkok was:

	Chinese	Thai
Central business district	78	22
Surroundings	45	55
Outlying areas	18	82

1952 was the last time in which official data of this type was collected.

4 In 1989 a survey of traffic speeds found average speeds of 7.7 km an hour inside the middle ring road, and as little as 3 to 5 km an hour in the most congested areas (Japan International Cooperation Agency, 1989).

5 This compares with the estimate by Yordpol Tanaboriboon (1990: 57) of an annual opportunity and fuel cost of US$400 million.

6 The deltaic location makes the city and its surroundings vulnerable to flooding – a situation that has been exacerbated by the filling in of canals to facilitate building and road development. As early as 1968 a major programme of dike construction was proposed and a number of major feasibility studies were undertaken, notably during 1983 and 1985. However, despite the increasing frequency and severity of flooding it was not until September 1995 that substantial work was initiated (Nathanon Thavisin and Ksemsan Suwarnarat, 1996: 6).

7 INCOME DISTRIBUTION, POVERTY AND SPATIAL INEQUALITY

1 The 1988–9 sample comprised 11,045 households.
2 Percentage increases in poverty line and consumer prices:

	Change from previous survey		Change in the consumer price index
	Urban	Rural	
1981–2	74.4	74.0	81.0
1985–6	10.7	13.0	22.0
1988–9	8.3	8.4	10.5

Source: Calculated from NSO figures.

3 For a detailed examination of Thai poverty measures and lines in comparison to those used elsewhere in South East Asia see Booth (1997).

4 The 1962–3 survey included sanitary districts in the urban category. In general this would increase the incidence of poverty in urban areas and reduce it in rural areas. For 1975–6 the inclusion of sanitary districts in the urban category would increase the incidence of poverty in urban areas from 14 per cent to 22 per cent, and in rural areas from 35 per cent to 37 per cent, overall increasing the national incidence of poverty from 31 per cent to 33 per cent. Of course the more 'urbanised' the sanitary district, the less its inclusion in the urban category would increase the incidence of poverty and the more its exclusion from the rural area would increase the incidence there.

5 The decline in rural poverty has to be seen in the context of the exceptionally good 1988–9 harvest, particularly in the North East. In addition, particularly for the North Eastern region, the expansion of the Southern fishing industry and the partial recovery of rubber and sugar prices have increased the prospects for migrant labour. In 1991 perhaps half the fishing fleet was manned by North Easterners who also tapped much of the Southern rubber, and in the Central Plain cut sugar cane and provided seasonal labour for rice production (Handley, 1991: 34–5).

6 Of these, eight were centres that were classed as sanitary districts rather than municipal areas.

7 Simon (1993) estimated that 10 million would move.
8 An extremely early agricultural site has been discovered.
9 In its very clear separation of rural and urban development planning, Thailand differs very little from the other Asian economies.

8 THAILAND IN THE LATE 1990s

1 The conditions attached to the July 1997 IMF rescue package include: the enforcement of tight monetary policy; increase in VAT from 7 per cent to 10 per cent; no subsidies to be given to public utilities to prevent price rises; substantial cuts in public expenditure; increased private-sector involvement in infrastructure provision; the current account deficit to be reduced from the 8.2 per cent level to 5 per cent by the end of 1997, and to 3 per cent in 1998; inflation to be reduced from the estimated 9.5 per cent level of 1997 to 5 per cent in 1998; and GDP to grow at 3.4 per cent during 1998.
2 For a discussion of the politics of redistribution in Thailand see Christensen (1993).
3 This is particularly well illustrated with respect to cassava. Until it began to spread rapidly in the North East region during the early 1970s MAC policy was to discourage the crop because of its supposedly adverse effects on the region's fragile soils. Once the crop was spreading rapidly its promotion became favoured and some of the provincial agricultural offices began to set targets for its expansion.
4 The Bangkok Bank is the largest commercial bank in South East Asia.
5 For a survey of the infrastructural problems faced by the Thai manufacturing sector see Yongyuth Chalamwong (1993).
6 Percentage allocation of public expenditure, 1988–91:

	1988–9	1989–90	1990–1
Education	16.6	17.9	20.6
Defence	16.3	16.4	16.3
Economic services	16.2	20.6	22.2
Internal security	4.4	4.4	4.9
Public health and utilities	11.0	12.6	13.5
General administration	2.8	3.2	3.8
Debt service	23.2	20.8	15.1
Others			
Total as a percentage of GNP	16.4	15.6	15.5

Source: NESDB.

7 Attempts to upgrade operation in five Bangkok-based textile plants during 1992–3 were met by strikes and disruption because of the reduction in the work force that would result.
8 Mechai Viravaidya has also been an outspoken and very successful promoter of birth control (see p. 91).
9 In May 1997 the American GPS scheme expired and a range of tariff privileges were withdrawn. The Ministry of Commerce estimated that this would cost Thailand 314,930 jobs.
10 There has indeed been an outflow of Thai investment to the USA. While this has tended to go into property and portfolios there has been some investment in manufacturing, for example the acquisition of Bumble Bee Seafoods in 1990.

11 The largest exporter of tuna fish in Asia, in 1991 commanding one-fifth of the world market.

12 Data on comparative manufacturing labour cost is problematic and fragmented, but point to rates in Vietnam being some 30 per cent of Thai costs. In addition, Vietnam has a more educated work force. However, against these advantages have to be set the shortages and often higher costs of offices and other facilities in Vietnam, and the problems associated with operating in a transitional economy.

13 During 1993 15 Taiwanese textile plants that had been established in Thailand during the late 1980s relocated their operation into the PRC and Vietnam.

14 Indonesia has been less enthusiastic for rapid tariff reduction because of its position as a relative 'late comer' in the manufacturing sphere.

15 Thailand's share of trade value in 1994:

	Exports	Imports
Cambodia	47.1	24.8
Laos	50.1	14.4
Myanmar	6.2	3.1
Vietnam	3.9	2.4

Source: IMF (1996) Direction of Trade Statistics Yearbook.

16 Kulick and Wilson considered that:

Bangkok will, if the domestic banks respond to the opportunity, become a subregional or Indochinese financial centre for neighbouring countries already using the Baht (Vietnam, Burma, Laos, Cambodia) . . .

(1992: 117)

17 For a general review of these and other sub-regional economic zones see Van Grunsven and Verkoren (1993) and Lee and Chen (1992).

18 Turton (1984: 56–9) and Anderson (1990) comment on the increased political significance of those operating illegal or fringe illegal activities.

19 The violent confrontations that swept Bangkok on 17–20 May 1992 officially resulted in 52 deaths and 47 'missing'. However, relatives of those still missing put the number at 167 (Handley, 1993b: 16).

20 The King has played a significant role in maintaining political stability since the fall of the military government in 1974. This role has been particularly evident in periods of crises, most recently in 1992. Considerable doubts have been expressed over his successor being able to play such a role. While the present King commands considerable respect and support, this cannot be said for the Crown Prince.

21 This argument should not be pushed too far, for in some respects every country is unique. It could be argued that Malaysia also has a very unusual colonial and post-colonial experience. Perhaps the point is that all of the very few economies that have experienced rapid and substantial manufacturing development have done so by virtue of a variety of very special internal and external circumstances.

BIBLIOGRAPHY

Aboonyi, G. and Bunyaraks Ninsananda (1989) *Thailand: development planning in turbulent times*, North York, University of Toronto-York University.

Adas, M. (1974) *The Burma delta: economic development and social change on an Asian rice frontier, 1852–1941*, University of Winsconsin Press, Madison.

Aldrich, R. J. (1995) 'Tin, oil and dollars: Western economic policies and Thailand', paper presented at the EUROSEAS Conference, Leiden, 29 June–1 July.

Allen, G. and Donnithorne, A. G. (1954) *Western enterprise in Indonesia and Malaya: a study in economic development*, George Allen and Unwin, London.

Alpha Research (1992) *Pocket Thailand in figures*, Bangkok.

Ammar Siamwalla (1975) 'Stability, growth and distribution in the Thai economy', in Prateep Sondysuvan (ed.), *Finance, trade and economic development in Thailand: essays in honour of Khunying Suparb Ossundara*, Sompong Press, Bangkok: 32–45.

Ammar Siamwalla (1989) *Trade, exchange rate and agricultural pricing policies in Thailand*, World Bank, Washington.

Ammar Siamwalla (1993) 'The institutional and political bases of growth inducing policies in Thailand', paper presented at the Fifth International Thai Studies Conference, London.

Ammar Siamwalla (n.d.) *Labour-abundant agricultural growth and some of its consequences: the case of Thailand*, Thailand Development Research Institute, Bangkok.

Ammar Siamwalla and Suthad Setboonsarng (1986) *The political economy of agricultural pricing policies in Thailand*, World Bank, Washington.

Ammar Siamwalla, Suthad Setboonsarng and Direk Patamasiriwat (1989) *Thai agriculture in the global economy*, Thailand Development Research Institute, Bangkok.

Ammar Siamwalla, Suthad Setboonsarng and Direk Patamasiriwat (1993) 'Agriculture', in Warr, P. G. (ed.), *The Thai economy in transition*, Cambridge University Press, Cambridge: 81–117.

Amranand, P. and Grais, W. (1984) *Macroeconomic and distributional implications of sectoral policy interventions: an application to Thailand*, World Bank Staff Working Paper 627, Washington.

Amsden, A. (1989) *Asia's next giant: South Korea and late industrialisation*, Oxford University Press, New York.

Anat Arbhabhirama, Dhira Phatumvanit, Elkinton, J. and Phaitoon Iingkasuwan (eds) (1988) *Thailand natural resource profile*, Thailand Development Research Institute, Bangkok.

Anderson, B. (1977) 'Withdrawal symptoms', *Bulletin of Concerned Asian Scholars*, 10: 13–30.

Anderson, B. (1990) 'Murder and progress in modern Siam', *New Left Review*, 181: 33–48.

Andrews, J. M. (n.d.) *Siam: second rural economic survey, 1934–35*. Harvard University Press, Cambridge MA.

Anek Laothamatas (1988) 'Business and politics in Thailand: new patterns of influence', *Asian Survey*, 28: 451–70.

Angel, S. and Sureeporn Chuated (1990) 'The down-market trend in housing production in Bangkok, 1980–87', *Third World Planning Review*, 12: 1–20.

Anuchat Poungsomlee and Ross, H. (1992) 'Impacts of modernisation and urbanisation in Bangkok: an integrative ecological and biosocial study', Institute for Population and Social Research, Mahidol University, Thailand.

Apichai Puntasen (1987) 'Internationalization of higher education: a case study of innovative destruction', *Discussion Paper*, No. 94, Faculty of Economics, Thammasat University.

Armanoff, G. (1965) 'State-owned enterprises in Thailand', United States Overseas Mission, Bangkok.

Asavin Chitakanda (1990) 'On our own', *Business Review*, Dec.: 10–16.

Asian Business (various issues), Hong Kong.

Asian Development Bank (1992) *Annual Report*, Manila.

Asian Development Bank (1993) *Subregional economic cooperation*, Manila.

Askew, M. (1993) *The making of modern Bangkok: state, market and people in the shaping of the Thai metropolis*, Thailand Development Research Institute, Bangkok.

Atchada Ruammahasap (1986) 'Effects of deforestation on agricultural productivity', unpublished masters thesis, University of Kasetsart.

Balakrishnan, N. (1991) 'Logical linkage; northern triangle needs support of national leaders', *Far Eastern Economic Review*, 3 Jan.: 38.

Banasopit Mekvichai, Foster, D., Sopon Chomchan and Phanu Kritiporn (1990) *Urbanization and environment: managing the conflict*, Thailand Development Research Institute, Bangkok.

Bangkok Bank, *Monthly Review* (various issues) Bangkok.

Bangkok Post (various issues) Bangkok.

Bangkok World (various issues) Bangkok.

Bank of Thailand, *Annual Economic Report* (various issues) Bangkok.

Bank of Thailand, *Quarterly Bulletin* (various issues) Bangkok.

Bampen Jatoorapreuk, Prapon Wongvichien and Oravit Hemachudha (1992) 'The planning and implementation of mass transist systems in Bangkok', *Regional Development Dialogue*, 13: 93–8.

Bautista, R. M. (1993) 'Development strategies, industrial policies and agricultural incentives in Asia', in Bautista, R. M. and Valdés, A. (eds), *The bias against agriculture: trade and macroeconomic policy in developing countries*, ICS Press, San Francisco: 209–26.

Behrman, J. H. (1968) *Supply response in underdeveloped Thailand: a case study of four major annual crops in Thailand, 1937–1963*, Amsterdam.

Bell, P. F. (1969) 'Thailand's North East: regional under-development, insurgency and official response', *Pacific Affairs*, 42: 47–54.

Bell, P. F. (1978) 'Cycles of class struggle in Thailand', in Turton, A. *et al.* (eds), *Thailand: the roots of conflict*, Spokesman Books, Nottingham: 51–79.

Bell, P. F. (1995) 'Development or mal-development? The contradictions of Thai economic growth', in Parnwell, M. G. (ed.) *Uneven development in Thailand*, Ashgate, Aldershot: 49–62.

Bello, W. and Rosenfeld, S. (1990) *Dragons in distress*, Institute for Food and Development Policy, San Francisco.

Berger, L. Inc. (1972) *North East Thailand: recommended development budget and foreign assistance*, Bangkok.

Bhanupong Nidhiprabha (1993) 'Monetary policy', in P. Warr (ed.), *The Thai economy in transition*, Cambridge University Press, Cambridge: 172–98.

Bhattacharya, Amar and Brimble, P. (1986) *Trade and industrial policies in Thailand during the 1980s: a review and framework for policy reform*, Thailand Development Research Institute, Bangkok.

Biggs, T., Brimble, P., Snodgrass, D. and Murray, M. (1990) *Rural industry and employment study: a synthesis report*, Thailand Development Research Institute, Bangkok.

Board of Investment (n.d.) *The promotion of industrial investment*, Bangkok.

Board of Investment (1994) *Thailand Investment 1994: a directory of BOI promoted companies*, Cosmic Publications, Bangkok.

Boomgard, P. (1987) 'Morbidity and mortality in Java, 1820–1880: changing patterns of disease and death', in Owen, N. G. (ed.), *Death and disease in South East Asia*, Oxford University Press, Singapore: 48–59.

Boonsong Lekakul (1969) 'A campaign to save our national forests from forest bugs', *Conservation News South East Asia*, 8.

Booth, A. (1993) 'Progress and poverty in South East Asia', paper presented to the British Pacific Rim Research Group, Liverpool John Moores University.

Booth, A. (1997) 'Poverty in South East Asia: some comparative estimates', in Dixon, C. J. and Drakakis-Smith, D. W. (eds), *Uneven development in South East Asia*, Ashgate, Aldershot: 45–74.

Borsak, R. (1984) 'Vanishing forests expose the Thai economy', *The Wall Street Journal*, 30 Jan.

Bowring, J. (1857) *The Kingdom and people of Siam, with a narrative of the mission to that country in 1855*, John W. Parker, London.

Bronger, D. (1985) 'Metropolitanization as a development problem of Third World countries: a contribution towards a definition of the concept', *Applied Geography and Development*, 26: 71–97.

Brown, A. and Frenkel, S. (1993) 'Union unevenness and insecurity in Thailand', in Frenkel, S. (ed.), *Organised labor in the Asia-Pacific countries; a comparative study of trade unionism in nine countries*, ILR Press, Ithaca: 82–100.

Brown, I. G. (1975) 'The Ministry of Finance and the early development of modern financial administration in Siam', unpublished PhD dissertation, School of Oriental and African Studies, University of London.

Brown, I. (1978) 'British financial advisers in Siam in the reign of King Chulalongkorn', *Modern Asian Studies*, 12: 193–215.

Brown, I. (1988) *The elite and the economy of Siam*, Oxford University Press, Singapore.

Brown, I. (1993a) 'The Thai economy in the 1930s: some questions and perspectives', paper presented at the Fifth International Conference on Thai Studies, School of Oriental and African Studies, London.

Brown, I. (1993b) 'Imperialism, trade and investment in the late nineteenth and twentieth centuries', in Butcher, J. and Dick, H. (eds), *The rise and fall of revenue farming: business elites and the emergence of the modern state in South East Asia*, St Martins Press, London: 80–8.

Bryant, R. (1993) 'The political ecology of forest change in South East Asia', paper presented at the Franco-British Workshop: Research on Contemporary East and South East Asia, Contemporary China Institute, School of Oriental and African Studies, London.

Bubphanart Suvanmas (1982) 'Bangkok: urban functional structure', *Thammasat Journal*, 11(1): 22–38.

Burnett, A. (1992) *The Western Pacific: challenge of sustainable growth*, Earthscan, London.

Cady, J. F. (1958) *A brief history of modern Burma*, University of California Press, Ithaca.

Calavan, M. M. (1977) *Decisions against nature; an anthropological study of agriculture in Northern Thailand*, Special Report No. 15, Centre for Southeast Asian Studies, Northern Illinois University.

Caldwell, J. C. (1967) 'The demographic structure', in Silcock, T. H. (ed.) *Thailand: social and economic studies in development*, Australian National University Press, Canberra: 27–64.

Caldwell, J. A. (1978) *American economic aid to Thailand*, Heath, Lexington.

Callis, H. G. (1942) *Foreign capital in South East Asia*, Institute of Pacific Relations, New York.

Campbell, B.O., Mason, A. and Pernia, E.M. (eds) (1993) *The economic impact of demographic change in Thailand 1980–2015*, East–West Centre, Honolulu.

Carter, A. C. (1904) *The Kingdom of Siam*, Putnam, New York.

Castells, M. (1991) 'Guest editor's introduction', *Regional Development Dialogue*, 12: iii–vi.

Chai-Anan Samudavanija (1990) 'The military and modern Thai political system', in Pinit Ratanakul and U Kyaw Than (eds), *Development, modernisation and tradition in Southeast Asia; lessons from Thailand*, Mahidol University, Bangkok.

Chai-Anan Samudavaniji (1991) *On the banks of the Chao Phraya*, Phuchatkan, Bangkok (in Thai).

Chaipat Sahansakul (1992) *Lessons from the World Bank, experience of structural adjustment loans: the case of Thailand*, Thailand Development Research Institute, Bangkok.

Chalogphob Sussangkarn, Teera Ashakul and Myers, C. (1988) *Human resource management*, Thailand Development Research Institute, Bangkok.

Chandran Jeshurun (1977) *The contest for Siam 1889–1902: a study in diplomatic rivalry*, Penerbit University, Kebangsaan.

Chantana Chamont (1990) 'A study of slums in Bangkok and its vicinity', paper presented at the First Environment '90 Conference on Environment and Natural Resources, Bangkok, 21–22 Jan. (in Thai).

Chattip Nartsupha and Suthy Prasartset (1978) *The political economy of Siam, 1910–1932*, Social Science Association of Thailand, Bangkok.

Chattip Nartsupha and Suthy Prasartset (1981) *The political economy of Siam, 1851–1910*, Social Science Association of Thailand, Bangkok.

Chesada Loha-unchit (1990) *Policies, measures and institutions for rural industrial development*, Thailand Development Research Institute, Bangkok.

Christensen, S. C. (1993) *Democracy without equity: the institutions and consequences of Bangkok based development*, Thailand Development Research Institute, Bangkok.

Chumphol Wattanasarn (1993) 'Thailand (1)', in *Development of marginal agricultural land in Asia and the Pacific*, Asian Productivity Organisation, Tokyo: 214–22.

Committee for International Coordination of National Research in Demography (1974) *The population of Thailand*, Bangkok.

Coughlin, R. J. (1960) *Double identity: the Chinese in modern Thailand*, Hong Kong University Press, Hong Kong.

Country Report (1989) 'Ecologically sound methods in organising urban transport systems: Thailand country report', International Training Seminar 20–24 Nov., Moscow.

Crawfurd, J. (1830) *Journal of an embassy from the Governor-General of India to the courts of Siam and Co-Chin China*, Burn and Bentley, London.

Cripps, F. (1965) *The far province*, Huchinson, London.

Crouch H. (1984) *Domestic political structures and regional integration*, Institute South East Asian Studies, Singapore.

Cummings, B. (1987) 'The origins and development of Northeast Asian political economy: product cycles, industrial sectors and political consequences' in Deyo, F. C. (ed.), *The political economy of the new Asian industrialisation*, Cornell University Press, Ithaca: 44–83.

Dapice, D. and Flatters, F. (1989) *Thailand: prospects and perils in the global economy*. Thailand Development Research Institute, Bangkok.

Demaine, H. (1976) 'The role of farmers' associations in agricultural development: the case of North East Thailand', Occasional Paper, Department of Geography, School of Oriental and African Studies, London.

Demaine, H. (1977) 'Socio-economic organisation and agricultural development in Northeastern Thailand', unpublished PhD thesis, University of London.

Demaine, H. (1984) 'Self-help land settlement schemes: their contribution to Thai rural development', paper presented at the Fourth International Conference on Thai Studies, 22–4 Aug., Bangkok.

Demaine, H. (1986) 'Kanpatthana: Thai views of development', in Hobart, M. and Taylor, R. (eds), *Context, meaning and power in Southeast Asia*, Cornell University Press, Ithaca: 93–114.

den Haan, R. (1995) 'Influence of infrastructure on spatial development', *Proceedings of the European conference on geographical information systems*, Munich: 418–27.

Department of Mines (1951) *Mining statistics*, Bangkok.

Deyo, F. C. (ed.) (1987) *The political economy of the new Asian industrialisation*, Cornell University Press, Ithaca.

Dhira Phantumnavit and Theodore Panayotou (1990) 'Rural natural resource management: lessons from Thailand', Colombo Plan Consultative Meeting, Bangkok.

Dhiravatna Pomlejra (1990) 'Crown trade and court politics in Ayutthaya during the reign of King Narai (1856–99)', in Kathirithamby-Wells, J. and Villiers, J. (eds), *The Southeast Asian port polity: rise and demise*, Singapore University Press, Singapore: 127–42.

Dixon, C. J. (1974) 'Landuse and marketing in North East Thailand', unpublished PhD thesis, University of London.

Dixon, C. J. (1976) 'Settlement and environment in North East Thailand', *Singapore Journal of Tropical Geography*, 46: 1–10.

Dixon, C. J. (1977) 'Development, regional disparities and planning; the experience of Northeast Thailand', *Journal of Southeast Asian Studies*, 8: 210–23.

Dixon, C. J. (1979) 'Thailand: economic survey', *Far East and Australasia*, Europa, London: 1067–72.

Dixon, C. J. (1981) 'Capitalist penetration, uneven development and government response: the case of Thailand', in Gleave, M. B. (ed.), *Societies in change: studies of capitalist penetration*, Developing Areas Research Group Monograph, University of Salford: 93–128.

Dixon, C. J. (1990) 'Human resources', in Dwyer, D. J. (ed.), *Southeast Asian development*, Longman, Harlow: 149–85.

Dixon, C. J. (1991a) *South East Asia in the world economy*, Cambridge University Press, Cambridge.

Dixon, C. J. (1991b) 'Thailand: economic survey', *Far East and Australasia*, Europa, London: 1030–8.

Dixon, C. J. (1993) 'The impact of structural adjustment on the Thai rural economy', in Dahl, J., Drakakis-Smith, D. W. and Narman, A. (eds), *Land, food and basic needs in developing countries*, University of Goteborg Monograph Series B No. 83: 102–30.

Dixon, C. J. (1995a) 'Structural adjustment in comparative perspective', in Simon, D., Narmen, A. and Dixon, C. J. (eds), *Global change, structural adjustment and the struggle for resources in Sub-Saharan Africa*, Pluto Press, London: 202–28.

Dixon, C. J. (1995b) 'Origins, sustainability and lessons from Thailand's economic growth', *Journal of Contemporary Asia*, 17: 38–52.

Dixon, C. J. (1998) 'Regional integration in South East Asia', in Grugel, J. and Hout, W. (eds) *The new regionalism and the developing world: state strategies in the semi-periphery*, Routledge, London.

Dixon, C. J. and Drakakis-Smith, D. W. (1995) 'The Pacific Asian region: myth or reality?', *Geografiska Annaler*, 77: 75–91.

Dixon, C. J. and Drakakis-Smith, D. W. (1997) 'Contemporary and historical perspectives on uneven devlopment in South East Asia', in *Uneven development in South East Asia*, Ashgate, Aldershot: 1–20.

Dixon, C. J. and Parnwell M. G. (1991) 'Thailand: the legacy of non-colonial rule', in Dixon, C. J. and Heffernan, M. (eds), *Colonialism and development in the contemporary world*, Mansell, London: 204–25.

Dixon, C. J., Simon, D. and Narman, A. (1995) 'The nature of structural adjust-ment', in Simon, D., Narmen, A., Dixon, C. J. (eds), *Global change, structural adjustment and the struggle for resources in Sub-Saharan Africa*, Pluto Press, London: 1–14.

Donner, W. (1978) *Five faces of Thailand: an economic geography*, St Martins Press, New York.

Douglass, M. (1983) 'The Korean *saemaul undong*: accelerated rural development in an open economy', in Lee, D. and Chaudhri, D. P. (eds), *Rural development and the state: contradictions and dilemmas in developing countries*, Methuen, London: 186–211.

Douglass, M. (1989) *Regional inequality and regional policies in Thailand: an inter-national comparative perspective*, Thailand Development Research Institute, Bangkok.

Dowall, D. E. (1989) 'Bangkok: a profile of an efficiently performing housing market', *Urban Studies*, 26: 327–39.

Dowall, D. E. (1992) 'A second look at the Bangkok land and housing market', *Urban Studies*, 29: 25–7.

Egan, M. and Benidick, M. (1984) 'The urban–rural dimension in national devel-opment', *Journal of Developing Areas*, 20: 203–22.

Elliott, D. (1978) *Thailand: the origins of military rule*, Zed, London.

ESCAP (1983) *Foreign investment incentive schemes*, Bangkok.

ESCAP (1986) *Human settlement atlas for Asia and the Pacific: part 3*, United Nations, New York.

Evers, H. D. (1966) 'The formation of a social class structure; urbanization, bureau-cratization and social mobility in Thailand', *American Sociological Review*, 33(4): 323–45.

Evers, H. D. (1987) 'Trade and state formation in the early Bangkok period', *Modern Asian Studies*, 21: 751–71.

Fairclough, G. (1994) 'Off to the city', *Far Eastern Economic Review*, 27 Jan.: 26.

Fairclough, G. (1996) 'Motion sickness', *Far Eastern Economic Review*, 19 Feb. 1996: 115.

Fairclough, G. and Tasker, R. (1994) 'Separate and unequal', *Far Eastern Economic Review*, 14 Apr.: 22–3.

Falkus, M. (1989) 'Early British business in Thailand', in Davenport, R. P. T. and Jones, G. (eds), *British business in Asia since 1960*, Cambridge University Press, Cambridge: 117–55.

Falkus, M. (1991) 'The economic history of Thailand', *Australian Economic History Review*, XXXI: 53–71.

Far Eastern Economic Review, various issues.

FAO *Production yearbook*, Rome, various issues.

FAO (1990) *Report of the global consultation on agricultural extension*, Rome.

Feder, G., Tongroj Onchan, Yongyuth Chalamwong and Chira Hongladarom (1988) *Land policies and farm productivity in Thailand*, Johns Hopkins University Press, Baltimore.

Feeny, D. (1982) *The political economy of agricultural productivity: Thai agricul-ture development*, University of British Columbia Press, Vancouver.

Feeny, D. (1984) *Agricultural expansion and forest depletion in Thailand, 1900–1975*, Economic Growth Centre Discussion Paper No. 458, Yale University.

Feeny, D. (1988) 'Agricultural expansion and forest depletion in Thailand, 1900–1975', in Richards, J. and Tucker, R. (eds), *World deforestation in the twentieth century*, Duke University Press, Darham and London: 112–287.

Fisher, C. A. (1964) *South East Asia: a social, economic and political geography*, Methuen, London.

Foo Tuen Seik (1992) 'The provision of low-cost housing by private developers in Bangkok, 1987–89: the result of an efficient market', *Urban Studies*, 29: 1137–46.

Forsyth, T. (1992) 'Environmental degradation and tourism in a Yao village of north Thailand', unpublished PhD dissertation, School of Oriental and African Studies, London.

Forsyth, T. (1993) 'Non-regulated tourism as a form of environmental management in Northern Thailand: the case of Pha Dua, Chiang Rai', paper presented at the Fifth International Thai Studies Conference, School of Oriental and African Studies, London.

Foster, W. (1933) *England's quest for the Eastern trade*, Black, London.

Friedland, J. (1992) 'Cost of crisis', *Far Eastern Economic Review*, 4 June: 56–8.

Fukuda, S. (1941) *Studies on the economic role of the overseas Chinese*, Ganshodo Shoten, Tokyo (in Japanese).

Garforth, C. (1993) 'Rural people's organisations and agricultural extension in the upper north of Thailand: who benefits?', paper presented at the Fifth International Conference on Thai Studies, School of Oriental and African Studies, London.

Ginsberg, N., Koppel, B. and McGee, T. (1991) *The extended metropolis*, University of Hawaii Press, Honolulu.

Girling, J. L. S. (1981) *Thailand: society and politics*, Cornell University Press, Ithaca.

Gittinger, M. and Lefferts, H. L. (1992) *Textiles and Tai experence in South East Asia*, The Textile Museum, Washington.

Glover, D. and Lim Teck Ghee (eds) (1992) *Contract farming in Southeast Asia*, Institute for Advanced Studies, University of Malaysia, Kuala Lumpur.

Government Housing Bank (1990) *Report of the housing conditions in 1989 by the Housing Policy Subcommittee*, National Economic and Social Development Board, Bangkok (in Thai).

Grabowsky, V. (1995) *Regions and national integration in Thailand: 1892–1992*, Harrassowitz, Wiesbaden.

Grahame, W. A. (1912) *Siam, a handbook of practical, commercial and political information* (two vols), Alexander Moring, London.

Granstaff, S. W. (1990) *The role of demand in provincial industrialisation*, Thailand Development Research Institute, Bangkok.

Gwynne, R. (1992) *Chile to 1994: more growth under democracy*, Economist Intelligence Unit, London.

Hackenburg, R. (1980) 'New patterns of urbanisation in Southeast Asia; an assessment', *Population and Development Review*, 6: 391–419.

Hafner, J. A. and Yaowalak Apichatvullop (1990) 'Farming the forest: managing people and trees in reserved forests in Thailand', *Geoforum*, 21: 331–46.

Hall, D. G. E. (1968) *A history of South East Asia*, Macmillan, London.

Handley, P. (1991) 'Growth without tears', *Far Eastern Economic Review*, 18 Jul.: 34–5.

Handley, P. (1992a) 'Coast of good hope: Thailand's Eastern Seaboard plan yields dividends', *Far Eastern Economic Review*, 19 Nov.: 63–4.

Handley, P. (1992b) 'Twisted tracks', *Far Eastern Economic Review*, 30 Apr.: 50–5.

Handley, P. (1992c) 'Banking on Bangkok', *Far Eastern Economic Review* 16 Jan.: 34–46.

Handley, P. (1992d) 'A bridge too far', *Far Eastern Economic Review*, 9 Jul.: 49.

Handley, P. (1993a) 'Thought for food', *Far Eastern Economic Review*, 29 Apr.: 47.

Handley, P. (1993b) 'Thailand's still missing', *Far Eastern Economic Review*, 27 May: 16.

Harrison, B. (1963) *South East Asia: a short history*, Macmillan, London.

Henderson, J. (1989) *The globalisation of higher-technology production: society, space and semi-conductors in the restructured modern world*, Routledge, London.

Hewison K. J. (1985) 'The state and capitalist development in Thailand', in Higgott, R. and Robison, R. (eds), *South East Asia: essays in political change*, Routledge and Kegan Paul, London: 266–94.

Hewison K. J. (1989) *Bankers and bureaucrats: capital and the role of the state in Thailand*, Yale Centre for International and Area Studies Monograph No. 34, University of Yale, New Haven, Connecticut.

Hewison, K. J. (1993a) 'Non-governmental organisations and the cultural development perspective in Thailand: a comment on Rigg 1991', *World Development*, 21: 1699–1708.

Hewison, K. J. (1993b) 'Of regimes, state and pluralities: Thai politics enters the 1990s', in Hewison, K., Robison, R. and Rodan, G. (eds), *The Southeast Asia in the 1990s: authoritarianism, democracy and capitalism*, Allen and Unwin, St Leonards, NSW: 161–89.

Hirsch, P. (1990) *Development dilemmas in rural Thailand*, Oxford University Press, Singapore.

Hirsch, P. (1993) 'Nam Choan and its aftermath', in Hirsch, P. (ed.), *Political economy of environment in Thailand*, Journal of Contemporary Asia Publishers, Manila: 133–47.

Holm, D. F. (1977) 'The role of the state railways in Thai history', unpublished PhD dissertation, University of Yale.

Holtsberg, C. (1982) 'Rice pricing policy', in Richards, P. (ed.) *Basic needs and government policy in Thailand*, Maruzen Asia, Singapore: 161–81.

Hong Lysa (1984) *Thailand in the nineteenth century*, Institute of South East Asian Studies, Singapore.

Hurst, P. (1990) *Rainforest politics: ecological destruction in South-East Asia*, Zed, London.

Ichikawa, N. (1990) *Foreign investment in Thai development – special focus on Japan*, Thailand Development Research Institute, Bangkok.

Ikemoto, Y. (1992) 'Income inequality in Thailand in the 1980s', *Southeast Asian Studies*, 30: 213–35

Ingram, J. C. (1971) *Economic change in Thailand: 1950–1970*, Stanford University Press, Stanford.

International Labour Office *World labour report*, Geneva, various issues.

Jacobs, J. W. (1995) 'Mekong Committee; history and lessons for river basin development', *Geographical Journal*, 161: 135–48.

Jacoby, H. E. (1961) *Agrarian unrest in South East Asia*, Asia Publishing House, Bombay.

Japan International Cooperation Agency (1989) *Medium to long-term road improvement/management of roads and road transport in Bangkok*, JICA, Bangkok.

Johnston, D. B. (1975) 'Rural society and the rice economy in Thailand: 1880–1930', unpublished PhD dissertation, University of Yale.

Julius, de Anne (1990) *Global companies and public policy: the growing challenge of foreign direct investment*, Pinter, London.

Kanok Wongtrangan (1982) 'The growth of Bangkok community', *Thammasat University Journal*, 11(1): 39–62.

Kathirithamby-Wells, J. (1990) 'Introduction and overview', in Kathirithamby-Wells, J. and Villiers, J. (eds), *The Southeast Asian port polity: rise and demise*, Singapore University Press, Singapore: 1–16.

Kemp, J. (1989) 'Peasants and cities: the cultural and social image of the Thai peasant village community', *Sojourn*, 4: 6–19.

Kemp, J. (1991) 'Dialectics of village and state in modern Thailand', *Journal of Southeast Asian Studies*, 22: 312–26.

Keyes, C. F. (1967) *Isan in a Thai state*, University of Cornell Press, Ithaca.

Keyes, C. F. (1987) *Thailand: Buddhist Kingdom and modern nation state*, Westview Press, Boulder.

Kirk, W. (1990) 'Southeast Asia during the colonial period', in Dwyer, D. J. (ed.), *Southeast Asian development*, Longman, Harlow: 14–47.

Knodel, J., Aphchat Chamratritirong and Nighon Debaralya (1987) *Thailand's reproductive revolution*, University of Wisconsin, Madison.

Korff, R. (1986) *Bangkok: urban system and everyday life*, Breitenbach, Saarbruken.

Krause, P.H. and Lutkenhorst, W. (1986) *The economic development of the Pacific Basin: growth dynamics, trade relations and emergent cooperation*, C. Hurst and Company, London.

Krickkiat Phipatseritham (1983) 'Thailand is not Bangkok', paper presented at the symposium 'Thailand is Bangkok?', Thammasat University, 17–18 Feb.

Kruger, A. O., Schiff, M. and Vadés, H. A. (1988) 'Agricultural incentives in developing countries: measuring the effect of sectoral and economy wide policies', *World Bank Economic Review*, 2: 255–71.

Kulick, E. and Wilson, D. (1992) *Thailand's turn: profile of a new dragon*, Macmillan, London.

Kwan, C. H. (1994) *Economic interdependence in the Asia-Pacific Region*. London, Routledge.

Landon, K. P. (1939) *Siam in transition*, Oxford University Press, London.

Lee, T. Y. and Chen, S. Y. (1992) 'Subregional economic zones: a new motive force in Asian Pacific development', paper presented at the Twentieth Pacific Trade Development Conference, Washington, 10–12 Sept.

Lefferts, H. L. (1992) 'An examination of Tai textile forms', in Gittinger, M. and Lefferts, H. L. (eds) *Textiles and Tai experience in South East Asia*, The Textile Museum, Washington.

Lightfoot, R. P. (1978) 'The cost of resettling reservoir evacuees in Northeastern Thailand', *Journal of Tropical Geography*, 47: 63–74.

Likhit Dhiravegin (1977) *Siam and colonialism (1855–1909): an analysis of diplomatic relations*, Thai Watana Panich, Bangkok.

Limlingan, V. S. (1986) *The overseas Chinese in ASEAN: business strategies and management practices*, Vta Development Corporation, Manila.

Lindblad, J. T. (1995) 'Western business strategy in Southeast Asia during the late colonial period', paper presented at the EUROSEAS Conference, Leiden, 29 June–1 July.

Lipton, M. (1977) *Why poor people stay poor: a study of urban bias in world development*, Temple Smith, London.

Lohmann, L. (1991) 'Peasants, plantations and pulp: the politics of eucalyptus in Thailand', *Bulletin of Concerned Asian Scholars*, 23: 3–17.

London, B. (1980) *Metropolis and nation in Thailand: the political economy of uneven development*, Westview, Boulder.

Luxmon Wongsuphasawat (1997) 'The extended Bangkok metropolitan region and uneven development in Thailand', in Dixon, C. J. and Drakakis-Smith, D. W. (eds), *Uneven development in South East Asia*, Avebury, Aldershot: 198–222.

MAC *Agricultural statistics of Thailand* (various issues), Bangkok.

MAC *Agricultural statistics in brief* (various issues), Bangkok.

Makoto Nambara (1993) 'Phra Sarasasna: economic plans in Thailand in the 1930s', paper presented at the Fifth International Thai Studies Conference, School of Oriental and African Studies, London.

Malloch, D. E. (1852) *Siam, some general remarks on its production*, Baptist Mission Press, Calcutta.

Manager, various issues.

Manop Bongsadadt (1987) 'Reflections on city planning development of Bangkok: the past, the present and the possible future', paper presented at the International Thai studies Conference, Australian National University, Canberra.

Marzouk, G. A. (1972) *Economic development and policies: case study of Thailand*, Rotterdam University Press, Rotterdam.

McCargo, D. (1993a) 'The three paths of Major-General Chamlong Srimuang', *South East Asian Research*, 1: 25–67.

McCargo, D. (1993b) 'Towards Chamlong Srimuang's political philosophy', *Asian Review*, 7: 54–78.

McDowell, R. (1990) 'The development of the environment in ASEAN', *Pacific Affairs*, 64: 307–29.

McFarlane, B. (1988) 'Growth and cycles in Southeast Asian development', *Journal of Contemporary Asia*, 18: 119–38.

McGee, T. (1967) *The Southeast Asian city*, Praeger, New York.

McGee, T. and Greenberg, C. (1992a) 'The emergence of extended metropolitan regions in ASEAN 1969–1980: an exploratory outline', in Amara Pongsapich, Howard, M. C. and Amyot, J. (eds), *Regional development and change in Southeast Asia in the 1990s*, Chulalongkorn University Social Research Institute, Bangkok.

McGee, T. and Greenberg, C. (1992b) 'The emergence of Extended Metropolitan Regions in ASEAN: towards the year 2000', *ASEAN Economic Bulletin*, 9: 22–9.

McGee, T. G. and Lim, G. C. S. (1993) 'Footprints in space: spatial restructuring in the East Asian NICs 1950–90', in Dixon, C. and Drakakis-Smith, D. (eds), *Economic and social development in Pacific Asia*, Routledge, London: 128–51.

McGee, T. and Robinson, I. M. (eds) (1995) *The mega-urban regions of South East Asia*, UBC Press, Vancouver.

McVey, R. (1987) 'Thailand: history', in *The Far East and Australasia*, Europa, London.

Mechai Viravaidya, Obremskey, S. A. and Meyers, C. (1992) 'The economic impact of AIDS in Thailand', Working Paper No. 4, Department Population and International Health at the Harvard School of Health.

Medhi Krongkaew (1993) 'Poverty and income distribution in Thailand', in Warr, P. (ed.), *The Thai economy in transition*, Cambridge University Press, Cambridge: 401–37.

Medhi Krongkaew, Pranee Tinakorn and Suphat Supachalasai (1992) 'Rural poverty in Thailand; policy issues and responses', *Asian Development Review*, 10: 199–225.

Medhi Krongkaew, Hirunrak, V. and Ary-Aum, O. (1987) *A study on the urban poor in Thailand: phase II*, Thai Khadi Suksa Research Institute, Bangkok.

Medhi Krongkaew and Pawadee Tongudai (1984) 'The growth of Bangkok: the economics of unbalanced urbanisation and development', Thammasat University Faculty of Economic Discussion Paper, No. 90, Bangkok.

Mekong Committee (1974) *Bulletin*, November.

Ministry of Commerce (1922) *Monograph on sugar in Siam*, Board of Commercial Development, No. 3.

Ministry of Health (1984) *Public Health Statistics*, Bangkok.

Moerman, M. (1968) *Agricultural change and peasant choice in a Thai village*, University of California Press, Berkeley.

Moffat, A. L. (1961) *Mongkut, King of Siam*, Cornell University Press, Ithaca.

Morrell, D. and Chai-Anan Samudavanija (1981) *Political conflict in Thailand*, Ogelgeschlager, Gun and Hain, Cambridge.

Mounge, C. (1982) 'The social and economic correlates of demographic change in a Northern Thai community', unpublished PhD thesis, University of London.

Muscat, R. J. (1966) *Development strategy in Thailand*, Praeger, New York.

Muscat, R. J. (1990) *Thailand and the United States: development, security and foreign aid*, Columbia University Press, New York.

Muscat, R. J. (1994) *The fifth tiger: a study of Thai development policy*, United Nations University Press, Tokyo.

Nakahara, J. and Witton, R. A. (1971) *Development and conflict in Thailand*, University of Cornell Press, Ithaca.

Nakarin Mektrairat (1992) *The 1932 revolution in Siam*, Sangsoan, Bangkok (in Thai).

Nanak Kakwani and Medhi Krongkaew (1996) 'Big reduction in poverty in Thailand', *Poverty Alleviation Initiatives*, 6: 7–12.

Naris Chaiyaasot (1993) 'Commercial banking', in Warr, P. G. (ed.) *The Thai economy in transition*, Cambridge University Press, pp. 226–64.

Narongchai Akrasanee (1973) 'The manufacturing sector in Thailand: a study in growth, import substitution, and effective protection', unpublished PhD dissertation, Johns Hopkins University.

Narongchai Akrasanee (1975) 'Import substitution', in Prateep Sondysuvan (ed.), *Finance, trade and economic development in Thailand: essays in honour of Khunying Suparb Ossundara*, Sompong Press, Bangkok: 265–82.

Narongchai Akrasanee (1983) *Rural off-farm employment in Thailand: summary and synthesis of the rural off-farm assessment project*, Industrial Management Consultants, Bangkok.

Narongchai Akrasanee, Daprice, D. and Flatters, F. (1991) *Thailand's export-led growth: retrospect and prospects*, Thailand Development Research Institute Foundation, Bangkok.

Nathalang, W. (1974) *Housing in Thailand*, National Housing Authority, Bangkok.

Nathanon Thavisin and Ksemsan Suwarnarat (1996) 'City study of Bangkok', in Stubbs, J. and Clarke, G. (eds), *Megacity management in the Asian and Pacific Region*, vol. II, ADB, Manila: 2–25.

Nation (various issues), Bangkok.

National Housing Authority *Annual Report* (various years), Bangkok.

NEDB (1961) *National Economic Development Plan, 1961–66*, Bangkok.

NEDB (1967a) *Evaluation of the First Six Year Plan, 1961–66*, Bangkok.

NEDB (1967b) *National Social and Economic Development Plan, 1967–1971*, Bangkok.

NEDB (1971) *The Third National Social and Economic Development Plan, 1972–76*, Bangkok.

Neher, C. D. (1988) 'Thailand in 1987: semi-successful democracy', *Asian Survey*, 28: 192–201.

NERPC (n.d.) *Changwat development planning in the North East*, Khon Kaen.

NESDB (1974) *The population of Thailand*, Bangkok.

NESDB (1977) *The Fourth National Economic and Social Development Plan (1977–81)*, Bangkok.

NESDB (1981) *The Fifth National Economic and Social Development Plan (1982–86)*, Bangkok.

NESDB (1987) *The Sixth National Economic and Social Development Plan (1987–91)*, Bangkok.

NESDB (1988) *Economic report*, July (in Thai).

NESDB (1991) *National urban development policy framework, final report, vol. II*, Bangkok.

NESDB (1992) *The Seventh National Economic and Social Development Plan (1992–96)*, Bangkok.

NESDB (1993) *Metropolitan Regional Structure Planning Study*, Bangkok.

NESDB (1997) *The Eighth National Economic and Social Development Plan (1992–96)*, Bangkok.

Ng, R. C. Y. (1968) 'Rice cultivation and rural settlement density in North East Thailand', *Tijdschrift voor Economische Socale Geographie*, 19: 200–10.

Ng, R. C. Y. (1970) 'Some landuse problems of North East Thailand', *Modern Asian Studies*, 4: 23–42.

Ng, R. C. Y. (1978) 'Man and land in Northeast Thailand', in Stott, P. A. (ed.), *Nature and man in Southeast Asia*, School of Oriental and African Studies, London: 54–76.

Ng, R. C., Demaine, H. and Dixon, C. J. (1976) *The development of second cropping in the Lam Pra Pleurng irrigation scheme*, School of Oriental and

African Studies, London.

Ng, R. C., Demaine, H. and Dixon, C. J. (1978) *Land-use and socio-economic change under the impact of irrigation in the Lam Pao Project Area in Thailand*, School of Oriental and African Studies, London.

Nidhi Aeusrivongse (1982) *Bourgeoisie culture and literature of the early Bangkok period*, Thaikhadi Research Institute, Thammasat University, Bangkok (in Thai).

Norman, M. J. T. (1973) 'The potential and limitations of Thailand's environment for agriculture', in Chapman, E. C. and Ho, R. (eds), *Studies of contemporary Thailand*, Australian National University, Canberra: 111–36.

North East Regional Planning Centre (n.d.) 'Changwat development planning in the North East', Khon Kaen.

NSO (1990) *Labour force survey*, Bangkok.

NSO *Key statistics of Thailand* (various issues), Bangkok.

Oey Meestok (1979) 'Income, consumption and poverty on Thailand, 1962/63 to 1957/6', World Bank Staff Working Paper No. 364, Washington.

Owen, N. G. (1987) 'The paradox of nineteenth century population growth in South East Asia; evidence from Java and the Philippines', *Journal of South East Asian Studies*, 18: 45–57.

Paisal Sricharatchanya (1986) 'A burgeoning problem', *Far Eastern Economic Review*, 20 Mar.: 122–4.

Paisal Sricharatchanya (1987) 'Jungle warfare; Thailand mounts campaign to save its trees, *Far Eastern Economic Review*, 17 Sept.: 86–8.

Panayotou, T. (1985) *Food policy analysis in Thailand*, Agricultural Development Council, Bangkok.

Panayotou, T. and Chalongphob Sussangkarn (1991) *The debt crisis, structural adjustment and the environment; the case of Thailand*, Thailand Development Research Institute, Bangkok.

Paritta Chalermpow Koanantakool (1993) *Urban life and urban people in transition*, Thailand Development Research Institute, Bangkok.

Parnwell M. G. (1991) 'Confronting uneven development in Thailand: the promotion of rural industry', *Malaysian Journal of Tropical Geography*, 22: 51–62.

Parnwell, M. G. (1992) 'Confronting uneven development in Thailand; the potential role of rural industries', *Malaysian Journal of Tropical Geography*, 21: 51–63.

Parnwell, M. G. (1993) 'Tourism, handicrafts and development in North East Thailand', paper presented at the Fifth International Thai Studies Conference, School of Oriental and African Studies, London.

Parnwell, M. G. and Rigg, J. (1996) 'The people of Isan: missing out on the economic boom', in Drakakis-Smith, D. W. and Dwyer, D. J. (eds) *Enthnicity and development*, Longman, London: 215–48.

Parnwell, M. G. and Suranart Khamanarong (1990) 'Rural industrialisation and development planning in Thailand', *Southeast Asian Journal of Social Science*, 18: 1–28.

Pasuk Phongpaichit and Baker, C. (1995) *Thailand: economy and politics*, Oxford University Press, Kuala Lumpur.

Pasuk Phongpaichit and Baker, C. (1996) *The Thai boom*, Silkworm Books, Bangkok.

Pasuk Phongpaichit and Samart Chiasakul (1993) 'Services', in P. Warr (ed.), *The Thai economy in transition*, Cambridge University Press, Cambridge: 151–71.

Patanapongsa, N. (1990) 'Private forestry development in Thailand: a survey of tree growers in the Northeast Region', *Commonwealth Forestry Review*, 69: 63–8.

Pelzer, K. (1945) *Pioneer land settlement on the Asiatic tropics*, American Geographical Society, New York.

Pendleton, R. L. (1962) *Thailand; aspects of landscape and life*, Duell, Sloan and Pearce, New York.

Pendleton, R. L. and Sarot Montrakun (n.d.) *The soils of Thailand*, Ministry of Agriculture, Bangkok.

Phisit Pakkasem (1973) *Thailand's North East development planning: a case study in regional planning*, NESDB, Bangkok.

Phisit Pakkasem (1975) 'Development planning and implementation in Thailand', in Baldwin, W. L. and Maxwell, W. D. (eds), *The role of foreign financial assistance to Thailand in the 1980s*, Lexington Books, Lexington: 6–19.

Phisit Pakkasem (ed.) (1979) *Rural–urban relations in the Bangkok Metropolitan Dominance Subregion*, United Nations Centre for Regional Development, Nagoya.

Phitsane Jessadachatr (1977) 'A history of sugar policies in Thailand', unpublished MA dissertation, Thammasat University, Bangkok.

Piker, S. (1976) 'The closing frontier', *Contributions to Asian Studies*, 9: 7–26.

Pradit Charsombut (1990) *Labour market in rural industries*, Thailand Development Research Institute, Bangkok.

Praipol Koomsup (1993) 'Energy policy', in Warr, P. (ed.), *The Thai economy in transition*, Cambridge University Press, Cambridge: 296–324.

Prakarn Virakul (1992) 'Thailand', in *Mechanisms and practices of agricultural price policy in Asia and the Pacific*, Asian Productivity Organisation, Tokyo: 390–420.

Pranee Tinakorn (1995) 'Industrialisation and welfare: how poverty and income distribution are affected', in Medhi Krongkaew (ed.), *Thailand's industrialisation and its consequences*, Macmillan, London: 218–31.

Prayod Buranasiri and Snoh Unakol (1965) 'Obstacles to effective planning encountered in the Thai planning experience', *Philippine Economic Journal*, 4: 327–40.

Puey Ungphakorn (1965) 'Thailand', in Onslow, C. (ed.), *Asian economic development*, Ebenezer Baylis, London: 151–74.

Purcell, V. (1951) *The Chinese in Southeast Asia*, Oxford University Press, Oxford.

Rabibhadana, A. (1993) *Social inequality: a source of conflict in the future*, Thailand Development Research Institute, Bangkok.

Ray, J.K. (1972) *Portraits of Thai politics*, Orient Longman, Delhi.

Reeve, W. D. (1951) *Public administration in Thailand*, Royal Institute of International Affairs, London.

Reid, A. (1988) *Southeast Asia in the age of commerce, 1450–1680*, Yale University Press, New Haven.

Resnik, S. A. (1970) 'The decline of rural industry under export expansion: a comparison among Burma, Philippines and Thailand, 1870–1938', *Journal of Economic History*, 39: 51–73.

Rigg, J. (1985a) 'The problem of agricultural intensification in a marginal rain-fed environment: a case study of farmers' practices and government policies in two villages of North East Thailand', unpublished PhD thesis, University of London.

Rigg, J. (1985b) 'The role of the environment in limiting the adoption of new rice technology in Northeastern Thailand', *Transactions of the Institute of British Geographers*, 10: 481–94.

Rigg, J. (1986) 'The Chinese middlemen in Thailand: efficient or exploitative?', *Singapore Journal of Tropical Geography*, 7: 68–97.

Rigg, J. (1991a) 'Homogeneity and heterogeneity: an analysis of the nature of variation in Northeastern Thailand', *Malaysian Journal of Tropical Geography*, 22: 63–77.

Rigg, J. (1991b) *Southeast Asia; a region in transition*, London, Unwin Hyman.

Rigg, J. (1991c) 'Grass roots development: a Thai lost cause?', *World Development*, 19: 199–211.

Rigg, J. (1994) 'Redefining the village and rural life; lessons from Southeast Asia', *Geographical Journal*, 160: 123–35.

Rigg, J. (1995a) 'Errors in the making: rice knowledge, technical change and applied research in Northeast Thailand', *Malaysian Journal of Tropical Geography*, 26: 19–33.

Rigg, J. (1995b) 'In the fields there is dust: Thailand's water crisis', *Geography*, 80: 23–32.

Riggs, F. W. (1966) *Thailand; the modernization of a bureaucratic polity*, East-West Press, Honolulu.

Rigoberto, T. (1992) 'On the launching pad: ASEAN ministers set for countdown to freer trade', *Far Eastern Economic Review*, 5 Nov.: 50.

Robison, R., Higgott, R. and Hewison, K. (1987) 'Crisis in economic strategy in the 1980s: the factors at work', in *South East Asia in the 1980s: the Politics of Economic Crisis*, Sydney, Unwin: 1–15.

Romm, J. (1972) *Urbanisation in Thailand*, The Ford Foundation, New York.

Ross, H. (1993) 'Environmental and social impacts of urbanisation in Bangkok', paper presented at the Fifth International Conference on Thai Studies, School of Oriental and African Studies, University of London.

Rowley, A. (1992a) 'Coming together', *Far Eastern Economic Review*, 17 Dec.: 64.

Rowley, A. (1992b) 'Growth turns inwards', *Far Eastern Economic Review*, 23 Apr.: 66.

Rubber Research Centre (1971) *Annual Report*, Hatyai.

Rubber Research Centre (1994) *Annual Report*, Hatyai.

Saneh Chamarik (1983) *Problems of development in Thai political setting*, Thai Khadi Research Institute, Thammasat University, Bangkok.

Sanit Ekachai (1990) *Behind the smile: voices from Thailand*, Thailand Support Committee, Bangkok.

Sarasin Viraphol (1977) *Tribute and profit: Sino-Siamese trade, 1652–1853*, Harvard University Press, Cambridge MA.

Sar Desai, D. R. (1977) *British trade and expansion in South East Asia*, Allied Publishers, New Delhi.

Schmidt, J. D. (1994) 'State capacities in Southeast Asia: creating growth without welfare', paper presented at the Conference on Emerging Classes and Growing Inequalities in Southeast Asia, Gl. Vraa Slot, Denmark, 23–25 Sept.

Scott, A. J. (1987) 'The semi-conductor industry in South East Asia: organisation, location and international division of labour', *Regional Studies*, 21: 143–60.

Scott, J. C. (1976) *The moral economy of the peasant*, Yale University Press, New Haven.

Setchell, C. (1991) *The emerging crisis in Bangkok: Thailand's next boom?*, Thailand Development Research Institute, Bangkok.

Silcock, T. H. (1967a) 'Outline of economic development', in *Thailand: social and economic studies in development*, Australian National University, Canberra: 1–26.

Silcock, T. H. (1967b) 'The promotion of industry and the planning process', in *Thailand: social and economic studies in development*, Australian National University, Canberra: 258–88.

Silcock, T. H. (1967c) 'The rice premium and agricultural diversification', in *Thailand: social and economic studies in development*, Australian National University, Canberra: 231–57.

Simon, J.C. (1993) 'The expansion of the manufacturing sector: an economic New Deal and social revolution. Who benefits from industrial development in Thailand', paper presented at the Fifth International Thai Studies Conference, School of Oriental and African Studies, London.

Sirilaksana Khoman (1993) 'Education policy', in Warr, P. (ed.), *The Thai economy in transition*, Cambridge University Press, Cambridge: 325–54.

Sitiporn Kridakara (1969) *Rice farming in Siam*, Siam Society, Bangkok.

Skinner, T. H. (1957) *Chinese society in Thailand: an analytical approach*, Cornell University Press, Ithaca.

Skinner, T. H. (1958) *Leadership and power in a Chinese community in Thailand*, Cornell University Press, Ithaca.

Small, L. E. (1973) 'Historical development of the Greater Chao Phraya Water Control Project: an economic perspective', *Journal of the Siam Society*, 61: 1–24.

Smith, D. A. and Nemeth, R. J. (1986) 'Urban development in Southeast Asia: an historical, structural analysis', in Drakakis-Smith, D. W. (ed.), *Urbanisation in the developing world*, Croom Helm, London: 121–39.

Smith, P. C. and Ng, S. M. (1982) 'The components of population growth in nine-teenth-century South East Asia: village data from the Philippines', *Population Studies*, 36: 253–5.

Somboon Siriprachai (1994) 'Problems of industrialisation process in Thailand, 1932–1993', paper presented at the Conference on Emerging Classes and Growing Inequalities in Southeast Asia, Gl. Vraa Slot, Tylstrup, Denmark, 23–25 Sept.

Somboon Siriprachai (1995) 'Export-orientated industrialisation strategy with land-abundance: some of Thailand's shortcomings', Research Paper, Department of Economic History, University of Lund.

Somchai Jitsuchon (1989) *Alleviation of rural poverty in Thailand*, Thailand Development Research Institute, Bangkok.

Somchai Ratanakomut, Chruma Ashakul and Thienchay Kirananda (1994) 'Urban poverty in Thailand: critical issues and policy measures', *Asian Development Review*, 12: 204–24.

Sompop Manarungsan (1989) *Economic development of Thailand, 1859–1950: response to the challenge of the world economy*, Institute of Asian Studies Chulalongkorn University, Monograph No. 42, Bangkok.

Sompop Manarungsan and Suebskun Suwanjindar (1992) 'Contract and outgrower schemes in Thailand', in Glover, D. and Lim Teck Ghee (eds), *Contract farming in Southeast Asia*, Institute for Advanced Studies, Kuala Lumpur: 10–70.

Somsak Tambunlertchai (1977) *Japanese and American investment in Thailand's manufacturing industries*, Institute of Developing Economies, Tokyo.

Somsak Tambunlertchai (1990) *A profile of regional industry*, Thailand Development Research Institute, Bangkok.

Somsak Tambunlertchai (1993) 'Manufacturing', in Warr, P. G. (ed.), *The Thai economy in transition*, Cambridge University Press, Cambridge: 118–50.

Somsak Tambunlertchai and McGovern, I. (1984) 'An overview of the role of multinational corporations in the development of Thailand', in Nongyao Chaiseri and Chira Hongladarom (eds), *The role of multinational corporations in Thailand*, Thammasat University Press, Bangkok: 71–108.

Sophon Pornchokchai (1985) *1020 slums: evidence, analysis and critics*, School of Urban Community Research and Actions, Agency for Real Estate, Bangkok.

Sophon Pornchokchai (1992) *Bangkok slums: review and recommendations*, School of Urban Community Research and Actions, Agency for Real Estate, Bangkok.

Sternstein, L. (1965) 'A critique of Thai population data', *Pacific View Point*, 6: 16–38.

Sternstein, L. (1971) 'Planning the developing primate city', Department of Geography Occasional Paper No. 9, Australian National University, Canberra.

Sternstein, L. (1973) 'Bangkok 2000', in Chapman, E. C. and Ho, R. (eds), *Studies of contemporary Thailand*, Australian National University, Canberra: 345–66.

Sternstein, L. (1984) 'The growth of population of the world's pre-eminent "primate city": Bangkok at its bicentenary', *Journal of Southeast Asian Studies*, 15: 43–68.

Sternstein, L. (1993) 'Population of Siam on the eve of the European colonisation of mainland Southeast Asia', paper presented at the Fifth International Conference on Thai Studies, School of Oriental and African Studies, London.

Stiffen, W. J. (1966) *The Thai bureaucracy: institutional change and development*, East-West Centre Press, Honolulu.

Stowe, J. A. (1991) *Siam becomes Thailand: a story of intrigue*, University of Hawaii Press, Honolulu.

Suehiro, Akira (1989) *Capital accumulation in Thailand: 1855–1985*, Centre for East Asian Cultural Studies, Tokyo.

Suganya Hutaserani and Somchai Jitsuchon (1988) 'Thailand's income distribution and poverty profile and their present situations', paper presented at the Thailand Development Research Institute Year-end Conference, Bangkok, Dec. 17–18.

Suganya Hutaserani and Pornchai Tapwong (1990) *Urban poor upgrading: analyses of poverty trend and profile of the urban poor in Thailand*, Thailand Development Research Institute, Bangkok.

Sungsidh Piriyarangsan (1983) *Thai bureaucratic capitalism 1932–60*, Chulalongkorn University Social Research Institute, Bangkok.

Sungsidh Piriyarangsan and Kitti Limsakai (1994) *Minimum wage*, Chualongkorn University, Bangkok (in Thai).

Suranart Khamanarong (1993) 'Village base industries: an alternative basis for rural development in North–East Thailand', paper presented at the Fifth International Thai Studies Conference, School of Oriental and African studies, London.

Sureeporn Punpuing (1993) 'Correlates of commuting patterns: a case study of Bangkok, Thailand', *Urban Studies*, 30: 527–46.

Surin Maisrikrod and Suparra Limsong (1991) 'Thailand: deconstructing the coup', *Pacific Research*, 4: 3–4.

Suthad Setboonsarng, Boonjit Titapiwatanakun and Somnuk Tubpun (1989) *Competitiveness of animal feed and livestock production in Thailand*, Thailand Development Research Institute, Bangkok.

Suthad Setboonsarng, Sarun Wattanutchariya and Banlu Puthigom (1988) *Seed industry in Thailand: structure conduct and performance*, Research Report No. 32, Tilburg University Development Research Institute, the Netherlands.

Tachai Wonaporn (1991) 'Consequences of using pesticides to control crop pests', *Khao Kasettakorn*, 41: 7–14 (in Thai).

Takaya, Y. (1987) *Agricultural development of a tropical delta: a study of the Chao Phraya*, University Press of Hawaii, Honolulu.

Tanabe, S. (1977) 'Historical geography of the canal system in the Chao Phraya Delta from the Ayutthaya period to the fourth reign of the Ratanakosin dynasty', *Journal of the Siam Society*, 65: 23–73.

Tanabe, S. (1978) 'Land reclamation in the Chao Phraya Delta', in Ishii, Y. (ed.), *Thailand: a rice growing society*, University Press of Hawaii, Honolulu: 125–89.

Tanabe, S. (1994) *Ecology and practical technology: peasant farming systems in Thailand*, White Lotus, Bangkok.

Tanet Chareonment (1993) 'Decentralisation stuck in a vicious circle', *Thailand Development Newsletter*, 22: 31.

Tasker, R. (1990) 'Bangkok on the brink', *Far Eastern Economic Review*, 29 Nov.: 52–3.

Tasker, R. (1991) 'Wedded to success', *Far Eastern Economic Review*, 3 May: 49–50.

Tate, D. J. M. (1971) *The making of modern South East Asia, vol. I, the European conquest*, Oxford University Press, Kuala Lumpur.

Tate, D. J. M. (1979) *The making of modern South East Asia, vol. II, the Western impact*, Oxford University Press, Kuala Lumpur.

Taweesak Nopkesorn, Sunkorom, S. and Dornlum, R. (1991) *HIV prevalence and sexual behaviour among Thai men aged 21 in Northern Thailand*, Thai Red Cross Society, Bangkok.

TDRI (1995) *Thai Economy*, Bangkok.

Tej Bunnag, T. (1977) *The provincial administration of Siam 1892–1915*, Oxford University Press, Kuala Lumpur.

Tetsuo Kidokoro (1992a) 'Strategies for urban development and transport systems in Asia metropolises, focusing on Bangkok Metropolitan Area', *Regional Development Dialogue*, 13: 74–87.

Tetsuo Kidokoro (1992b) 'Development control systems for housing development in Southeast Asia', *Regional Development Dialogue*, 13: 64–73.

Textor, R. B. (1961) *From peasant to pedicab driver*, Southeast Asian Studies Cultural Report No. 9, Yale University, New Haven.

Thailand Development Research Institute (1992) *Managing the urban informal sector in Thailand: a search for practical policies based on the basic minimum needs approach*, Bangkok.

Thailand Development Research Institute (1996) *Thai economy*, Bangkok.

Thai Farmers' Bank (1985) *Multipurpose woods*, Technical Paper No. 1, Bangkok.

Thai University Research Associates (1976) *Urbanisation in the Bangkok Central Region*, Kurusapha Ladprao Press, Bangkok.

Thak Chaloemtiarana (1978) *Thai politics, 1932–57*, vol. I, Thammasat University Press, Bangkok.

Thak Chaloemtiarana (1979) *Thailand: the politics of despotic paternalism*, Thai Kahadi Research Institute, Bangkok.

Thapa, G. B. and Weber, E. (1988) 'Resettlement experiences and alternatives in Thailand', *Singapore Journal of Tropical Geography*, 9: 141–50.

Thomas, M. L. (1991) 'Social changes and problems emanating from industrialisation in the ASEAN region' *Regional Development Dialogue*, 12: 1–20.

Thiravet Pramuanratkarn (1979) 'Impact of urbanization on peripheral areas of Bangkok', unpublished MSc dissertation, Thammasat University, Bangkok.

Thompson, V. (1941) *Thailand the new Siam*, Macmillan, New York.

Thompson, V. (1947) *Labour problems in Southeast Asia*, New Haven, New York.

Timber Trades Journal (various issues) Tonbridge.

Tirasawat Penporn (1990) *Patterns and trends of urbanization*, Thailand Development Research Institute, Bangkok.

Trebuil, T. (1990) 'Croissance agricole et transformation economiques et sociales en Thailande', SOLAGRAL colloquium on 'How to feed the world', Paris: 203–311.

Trebuil, T. (1993a) 'Pioneer agriculture, green revolution and environmental degradation in Thailand', paper presented at the Fifth International Conference on Thai Studies, School of Oriental and African Studies, London.

Trebuil, T. (1993b) 'Farmer differentiation in Southern and Central Thai agricultural systems: who benefits from agricultural growth?', paper presented at the Fifth International Conference on Thai studies, School of Oriental and African Studies, London.

Tubpun Tachai Wonaphorn (1991) 'Consequences of using pesticides to control pests', *Chao Kasettakorn*, 41: 7–14 (published in Thai by the Office of Agricultural Economics, MAC).

Turton, A. (1984) 'Limits of ideological domination and the formation of social consciousness', in Turton, A. and Tanabe, S. (eds) (1984) *History and peasant consciousness in Southeast Asia*, Senri Ethnological Studies No. 13, National Museum of Ethnography, Osaka: 19–74.

Turton, A., Fast, J. and Caldwell, M. (1978) *Thailand: the roots of conflict*, Spokesman Books, Nottingham.

Turton, A. and Tanabe, S. (eds) (1984) *History and peasant consciousness in Southeast Asia*, Senri Ethnological Studies No. 13, National Museum of Ethnography, Osaka.

Ueda, Y. (1992) 'Characteristics of local entrepreneurs in Nakhon Ratchasima city', *Southeast Asian Studies*, 30: 331–72.

UNCTAD (1990) *Trade and development*, New York.

UNDP (1991) *Human development report*, Oxford University Press, New York.

UNESCO *Statistical Yearbook* (various issues) Geneva.

United Nations (1987) *Population growth and policies in mega-cities: Bangkok*, Population Policy Paper No. 10, New York.

United Nations (1991) *Integrating development and population planning in Thailand*, New York.

United States Overseas Mission (1967) *Kenaf in Thailand*, Bangkok.

Usher, D. (1967) 'The Thai rice trade', in Silcock, T. H. (ed.), *Thailand: social and economic development*, Australian National University, Canberra: 209–30.

Utis Kaothien (1995) 'The BMR: policies and issues in the Seventh Plan', in McGee, T. G. and Robison, I. M. (eds), *The mega-urban regions of South East Asia*, UBC Press, Vancover: 328–42.

Van der Heide, J. H. (1903) *General report on irrigation and drainage in the lower Menem valley*, Ministry of Agriculture, Bangkok.

Van der Heide, J. H. (1906) 'The economic development of Siam during the last half century', *Journal of the Siam Society*, 3: 74–101.

Van Grunsven, L. and Verkoren, O. (1993) 'Adjustment and industrial change in South East Asia', paper presented at the Trilateral Conference on Global Change and Structural Adjustment, University of Amsterdam.

Van Landingham, M., Somboom Suprasert, Werasit Sittitrai, Chayan Vaddhanaphuti and Grandjean, N. (1993) 'Sexual activity among never-married men in Northern Thailand', *Demography*, 30: 297–313.

Van Landingham, M., Knodel, J., Chanpen Saengtienchai and Anthony Pramualratana (1995) *Friends, wives and extramarital sex in Thailand*, Institute of Population Studies, Chulalongkorn University.

Van Roy, E. (1971) *Economic systems of Northern Thailand*, Cornell University Press, Ithaca.

Vatikiotis, M. (1993) 'Market or mirage', *Far Eastern Economic Review*, 15 Apr.: 48–50.

Vella, W. F. (1955) *The impact of the West on government in Thailand*, University of California Press, Berkeley.

Vella, W. F. (1978) *Chaiyo! King Vajiravudh and the development of Thai nationalism*, University Press of Hawaii, Honolulu.

Venzky-Stalling, M. (1993) 'Industrial estates and regional industrialisation in Thailand', unpublished BA dissertation, School of Oriental and African Studies, London.

Vickery, M. (1970) 'Thai regional elites and the reforms of King Chulalongkorn', *Journal of Asian Studies*, 29, 4: 863–81.

Volden, M. (1995) 'Contract farming of maize in Northeast Thailand', in Hesselberg, J. (ed.), *Development in the South: issues and debates*, Department of Human Geography, University of Oslo: 123–35.

Waranya Patarasuk (1991) 'The role of transnational corporations in Thailand's manufacturing industries', *Regional Development Dialogue*, 12: 92–134.

Warr, P. (1993) 'The Thai economy', in *The Thai economy in transition*, Cambridge University Press, Cambridge: 1–80.

Warrington-Smyth, H. (1898) *Five years in Siam* (two vols), John Murray, London.

Watanabe, S. (1993) 'Who benefits from the urbanisation of Thailand in the late 1980s?', paper presented at the Fifth International Conference on Thai Studies, School of Oriental and African Studies, London.

Wathana Wongsekiarttirat (1993) 'Socio-economic benefits of rural development in Central Thailand: a case study of land and labour utilization in Ayutthaya', paper presented at the Fifth International Conference on Thai Studies, School of Oriental and African Studies, London.

Wattanachai Damronghanvitaya (1985) 'Estimation of soil erosion in Chiang Mai province by using the general soil loss equation', unpublished MA thesis, University of Kasetsart.

White, G. (1988) 'Developmental states in East Asia: an introduction', in *The developmental state in East Asia*, London, Macmillan: 1–29.

Wilson, C. M. (1989) 'Bangkok in 1883: economic and social profile', *Journal of the Siam Society*, 17(2): 49–58.

Wilson, D. A. (1962) *Politics in Thailand*, Ithaca, New York.

Wong Lin Ken (1965) *The Malaysian tin industry to 1914*, University of Arizona Press, Tucson.

Wong Lin Ken (1978) 'Singapore: its growth as an entrepot, 1819–41', *Journal of South East Asian Studies*, 9: 50–84.

World Bank *World development report* (various issues) Oxford University Press, New York.

World Bank *Tables* (various issues) Washington.

World Bank (1959) *A public development programme for Thailand*, Johns Hopkins Press, Baltimore.

World Bank (1969) *Current economic position and prospects of Thailand, 1969*, Washington.

World Bank (1970) *Current economic position and prospects of Thailand*, vol. I, Washington.

World Bank (1978) *Thailand: review of the need for deep-water port at Laem Chabang*, Washington.

World Bank (1980a) *An industrial development strategy for Thailand*, Washington.

World Bank (1980b) *Thailand: coping with structural adjustment*, Washington.

World Bank (1980c) *Thailand: towards a development strategy of full participation*, Washington.

World Bank (1983a) *Managing public resources for structural adjustment*, Washington.

World Bank (1983b) *Thailand: rural growth and employment*, Washington.

World Bank (1983c) *World development report*, Oxford University Press, New York.

World Bank (1984) *Thailand: managing public resources for structural adjustment*, Washington.

World Bank (1986) *Program performance audit report Thailand: first and second structural adjustment loans*, Washington.

World Bank (1988a) *Adjustment lending: and evaluation of ten years experience*, Washington.

World Bank (1988b) *World development report*, Oxford University Press, New York.

World Bank (1990) *Agricultural extension: the next step*, Policy and Research Series, No. 13, Agricultural and Rural Development Department, Washington.

World Bank (1991) *World development report*, Oxford University Press, New York.

World Bank (1992) *World development report*, Oxford University Press, New York.

World Bank (1993a) *The East Asian miracle economies*, Washington.

World Bank (1993b) *World development report*, Oxford University Press, New York.

World Bank (1993c) *Sustaining rapid development*, Washington.

World Bank (1997) *World development report*, Oxford University Press, New York.

Wyatt, D. K. (1984a) *The politics of reform in the reign of King Chulalongkorn*, Yale University Press, New Haven.

Wyatt, D. K. (1984b) *Thailand: a short history*, Yale University Press, New Haven.

Yeu-man Yeung (1988) 'Great cities of Eastern Asia', in Dogan, M. and Kasarda, J. D. (eds), *The metropolis era volume 1: a world of giants*, Sage, Newbury Park: 154–86.

Yip Yat Hoong (1969) *The development of the Malaysian tin industry*, University of Malaya Press, Kuala Lumpur.

Yongyuth Chalamwong (1993) *A study of infrastructural problems experienced by Thai manufacturing industries*, Thailand Development Research Institute and the World Bank, Bangkok.

Yongyuth Chalamwong (1995) 'Brakes on growth: infrastructure bottlenecks and Thai industry', *TDRI Quarterly Review*, 10(2): 20–25.

Yordpol Tanaboriboon (1990) 'Recommendations for relieving traffic problems in Bangkok', *Proceedings of the first conference on environment and natural resources conservation in Thailand*, 20–1 Jan.: 57–76.

Zimmerman, C. C. (1931) *Siam: rural economic survey, 1930–1*, Times Press, Bangkok.

Zimmerman, C. C. (1936) 'Some phases of land utilization in Siam', *Geographical Review*, 27: 373–93.

INDEX

Aboonyi, G. 109
Accelerated Rural Development (ARD)
  programme 85, 99
'adopt a village' scheme 236
Adrich, R.J. 56, 60, 65
advisors, foreign 32–3, 35, 61
advisory services for farmers 177
afforestation 188, 276
Agency for International Development
  (AID) 85
agri-business sector 9, 102, 107, 135, 138,
  151
Agricultural Land Reform Office
  (ALRO) 158, 175, 184
agricultural sector 80–2, 140–89; credit
  for see credit; depression of prices in
  142–5, 220–1; discrimination against 87,
  140, 148, 242–3, 246, see also urban
  bias; diversification and innovations in
  174–8, 188; employment in 19–20, 220,
  235, 262; future role of 235;
  government investment in 175, 275;
  government policy for 70–1, 86, 110,
  140–8, 175, 178; growth and
  importance of 89, 93, 101, 156–61, 220,
  241; income levels in 186–7, 220;
  intensification of production in 161–70;
  land available for 13–14, 83; structure
  of 149–52
agro-processing plants 101–2
aid programmes 78–9, 83, 90
AIDS 250–1
airport facilities 71, 84, 246
Alpha Research 200
Ammar Siamwalla 19, 88, 120, 129,
  140–1, 145–8, 177, 235, 242, 273;
  et al. 14, 20, 150, 162, 170, 173–5, 179,
  181, 185
Amranand, P. 148
Amsden, A. 127, 262
Anand Panyarachum 261
Ananda, King 69, 267

Anat Arbhabhirama et al. 14
Anderson, B. 97, 279
Anek Laothamatas 260
Angel, S. 208
Anglo-Thai relations see Britain
animal feed stuff 151
animal rearing see livestock sector
annual operations plans 83
Anuchat Poungsomlee 211–13
Aphchat Chamratritirong see Knodel, J.
  et al.
Apichai Puntasen 91
aquaculture 151–2
arable farming see crop production
Arbor Acres (company) 102
Armanoff, G. 73
Ary-Aum, O. see Medhi Krongkaew
  et al. (1987)
Asavin Chintakanda 189
Asia Pacific Economic Conference
  (APEC) 256
Asian Business 254
Asian Development Bank 2, 253, 257
Askew, M. 198, 209
assimilation into market economy 57, 59,
  66
Association of South East Asian Nations
  (ASEAN) 11, 92, 124–5, 129, 252–3,
  255, 257; ASEAN Free Trade Area
  (AFTA) 256
Atchada Ruammahasap 169
austerity measures 112, 115, 220
Australia-Thailand Business Council
  Bulletin 237
autocratic rule 93
Automobile Development Committee 103
Ayutthaya 23–5, 43, 187, 192, 266

baht, the 33, 94, 239, 245, 257, 271, 273;
  devaluation of 116, 123, 125, 141, 148,
  271; time-series of exchange rate
  against US$ 113

303

government role in development 2, 72–5,
78, 93, 115, 139, 237, 241–6, 252, 263;
see also agricultural sector; public
expenditure; rice cultivation
Grabowsky, V. 39
Grahame, W.A. 39, 44
Grais, W. 148
Grandjean, N. *see* Van Landingham, M.
et al.
Grandstaff, S.W. 235
Greater Bangkok 190
Greater Bangkok Plan 212
Greater Chao Phraya irrigation scheme
171
'green belt' land 213
'Green North East' scheme 180
Greenberg, C. 198, 201, 204
gross domestic product (GDP): per
capita 16–17, 19, 21, 127, 241;
projections of 187; regional
estimates of 215; sectoral distribution
of 10; time-series of growth in 113
'ground truthing' 208
growth, economic xvii–xviii, 1–3, 7, 75–6,
81, 83, 90, 93–4, 101, 107–9, 120, 214,
222, 262; industrial analysis of 74; long-
term pattern of 240–1;
see also sustainability
growth axes 224–5
growth centres 225–8
Gunny Bag Factory 121

Hackenberg, R. 190
Hafner, J.A. 180, 275
Hall, D.G.E. 25
Handley, P. 2, 206, 211, 243, 247–8, 257,
277, 279
Harrison, B. 31, 51
Hat Yai 193, 231
hazardous wastes 126, 211
health services 71, 101, 246
herbicides 169
Hewison, K.J. 84, 107, 238, 258–61, 271;
see also Robison, R. *et al.*
Higgott, R. *see* Robison, R. *et al.*
high-rise housing developments 209
high-tech and low-tech production 134–5,
137–8, 236
'Highly Performing Asian Economies'
group 1
hinterlands, rural 235
Hirsch, P. 35, 59, 82, 87, 100, 156, 158,
175, 182, 186, 274

Hirunrak, V. *see* Medhi Krongkaew
et al. (1987)
HIV 250–1
Holm, D.F. 36, 55
Holtsberg, C. 141
Hong Kong 106, 255
Hong Lysa 25–6, 29, 43
hotels 138, 233–4
'housewife groups' 178
housing provision 207–10
Hurst, P. 14, 16, 173, 181
hydro-electric power (HEP) 16, 173

IBM 131
Ichikawa, N. 126, 192, 200, 231
Ikemoto, Y. 220–1
illegal trade 257
immigration *see* Chinese immigrants
import substituting industrialisation (ISI)
73, 86–9, 93, 103–4, 109, 117, 122, 199,
241, 268
imports 9, 11; dependence on 138, 256;
restrictions on 121, 146; time-series of
6–7
income distribution 21–2, 117, 142, 186–7,
214–23, 234–7, 249; regional disparities
214–16
independence, political 31–3, 35, 56–7
industrial estates 203, 224, 226, 233
Industrial Estates Authority of Thailand
(IEAT) 226
Industrial Finance Corporation of
Thailand (IFCT) 226, 230
industrial policy 88
Industrial Promotion Act 88, 271
industrialisation 197
inequalities of income, measurement of
222
inflation 69, 112, 242; time-series of 113
informal sector of the economy 222
infrastructure, investment in 100, 117–18,
121, 143, 148, 156, 199–200, 207,
210–13, 223–4, 226, 230, 237, 240, 242,
246–8, 251, 278
Ingram, J.C. 27–36 *passim*, 40–52 *passim*,
58–67 *passim*, 72–5, 77–80, 88, 266, 268
inheritance systems and practices 185, 276
insurgency, outbreaks of 78, 81–4, 95, 98,
180, 216, 224
integrated circuits, export of 131, 133
intensification of production 241
international communications,
inadequacy of 246